# The Psychoanalysis of Suffering

*The Psychoanalysis of Overcoming Suffering: Flourishing Despite Pain* offers a guide to understanding and working with a range of everyday causes of suffering from a psychoanalytic perspective.

The book delineates some of the underappreciated, everyday facets of the troubling and challenging psychological experiences associated with love, work, faith, mental anguish, old age, and psychotherapeutic caregiving. Examining both the suffering of the patient and therapist, Paul Marcus provides pragmatic insights for changing one's way of being to make suffering sufferable.

Written in a rich but accessible style, one that draws from ancient wisdom and spirituality, *The Psychoanalysis of Overcoming Suffering* provides an essential guide for psychoanalysts and psychotherapists and their clients, and will also appeal to anyone who is interested in understanding how we suffer, why we suffer and what we can do about it.

**Paul Marcus** is a training and supervisory analyst at the National Psychological Association for Psychoanalysis in New York City and the author/editor of nineteen books.

Recently published titles by Paul Marcus

*The Psychoanalysis of Career Choice, Job Performance, and Satisfaction: How to Flourish in the Workplace* (Routledge, 2017)

*Sports as Soul-Craft: How Playing and Watching Sports Enhances Life* (Marquette University Press, 2015)

*Creating Heaven on Earth: The Psychology of Experiencing Immortality in Everyday Life* (Karnac, 2015)

*They Shall Beat Their Swords into Plowshares: Military Strategy, Psychoanalysis and the Art of Living* (Marquette University Press, 2014)

*How to Laugh Your Way Through Life: A Psychoanalyst's Advice* (Karnac, 2013)

*In Search of the Spiritual: Gabriel Marcel, Psychoanalysis and the Sacred* (Karnac, 2013)

*Theater as Life: Practical Wisdom Drawn from Great Acting Teachers, Actors and Actresses* (Marquette University Press, 2011, with Gabriela Marcus)

*In Search of the Good Life: Emmanuel Levinas, Psychoanalysis and the Art of Living* (Karnac, 2010)

# The Psychoanalysis of Overcoming Suffering

## Flourishing Despite Pain

Paul Marcus

Routledge
Taylor & Francis Group

LONDON AND NEW YORK

First published 2019
by Routledge
2 Park Square, Milton Park, Abingdon, Oxon OX14 4RN

and by Routledge
711 Third Avenue, New York, NY 10017

*Routledge is an imprint of the Taylor & Francis Group, an informa business*

© 2019 Paul Marcus

*British Library Cataloguing in Publication Data*
A catalogue record for this book is available from the British Library

*Library of Congress Cataloging in Publication Data*
Names: Marcus, Paul, 1953- author.
Title: The psychoanalysis of overcoming suffering : flourishing despite pain / Paul
Marcus.
Description: Abingdon, Oxon ; New York, NY : Routledge, 2018. | Includes
bibliographical references.
Identifiers: LCCN 2018005808| ISBN 9781138482159 (hardback) | ISBN
9781138482166 (pbk.) | ISBN 9781351058896 (epub) | ISBN 9781351058889
(mobipocket)
Subjects: LCSH: Suffering. | Psychoanalysis.
Classification: LCC BF789.S8 M37 2018 | DDC 150.19/5--dc23
LC record available at https://lccn.loc.gov/2018005808


ISBN: 978-1-138-48215-9 (hbk)
ISBN: 978-1-138-48216-6 (pbk)
ISBN: 978-1-351-05891-9 (ebk)

Typeset in Times New Roman
by Taylor & Francis Books

[God says out of the whirlwind] "Where were you when I founded the world. Tell, if you have the understanding."

[Job responds] "Behold, I am of little worth, what can I answer you? I have put my hand over my mouth."

(Job 38:4; 40:4, Helaine Helmreich's translation)

To my first grandchild, Talia Pearl, may the Almighty "cause His Presence to shine upon you."

# Contents

# Chapter 1

# Introduction

## Making suffering sufferable

The purpose of psychoanalysis, said a gloomy Freud, "is to convert hysterical [neurotic] misery into common [normal] unhappiness" (1893, p. 305). Indeed, like so many profound thinkers who have written before him, Freud recognized that to live is to suffer. "For the individual," he said, "life is hard to bear, just as it is for mankind in general" (1927, p. 16). According to Freud, profound suffering takes place within the everyday contexts of love or work, what he believed were the twin pillars for a sound mind and for living the "good life." Moreover, Freud insisted in a letter to his friend Wilhelm Fliess, whose daughter had overcome a serious illness, that one should be grateful for any reprieve from suffering: "One has to assume happiness when fate does not carry out all its threats simultaneously" (Freud, 1985, p. 440). Not only is suffering an unavoidable constituent aspect of being-in-the-world, but it is also a central potentiating factor to living the "good life." Without synthesizing or coming to grips with the emotionally painful existential challenges that beset the human condition – like despair, loss, tragedy, anxiety and conflict – it is nearly impossible to grow and develop into an autonomous, integrated and humane person.

For Freud, psychic pain was the necessary precondition for differentiation and individuation and the ability to experience the object as separate and independent. As Aeschylus noted in *Agamemnon*, "Wisdom comes alone through suffering" (p. 178).[1] In a sense, Aeschylus's insight speaks to the heart of my study, namely, that suffering is not only the mother of all wisdom, but it is also the mother of all flourishing, if only one knows how to make suffering sufferable. Flourishing is a key "positive psychology" term that means living "within an optimal range of human functioning, one that connotes goodness, generativity, growth, and resilience" (Fredrickson & Losada, 2005, p. 678).

My book is a contribution to a rather large gap in psychoanalytic thinking and practice, namely, developing the rudiments of a psychoanalytically infused psychology of flourishing. As I will elaborate shortly, such a psychoanalytic psychology is rooted in the ancient religious "spirituality" and "wisdom" that flowered during the Axial Age, that "pivotal age" from 800 to 200 BCE when the spiritual foundations of our current society were established

(Jaspers, 2011, pp. 51–60). As sociologist Anthony Giddens pointed out in his discussion of structuration theory, such a psychoanalytically infused Axial vision is always mindful of the "duality of structure" of important existential experiences – their "constraining and enabling," or painful and enhancing, aspects that must be creatively integrated to potentiate the will and ability to press on, especially when the going gets tough (1984, p. 25).

For many years now, I have been publishing books that deal with what is most important to the average person in terms of everyday existence: in other words, how to live the "good life."[2] By "good life" I mean a life that is characterized by deep and wide love and creative and productive work, one that is also guided by reason and ethics and is aesthetically pleasing. This book further delineates what constitutes the "nuts and bolts" of living a flourishing life, a way of being that blends practicality and passion as it attempts to illuminate some of the underexplored and often deeply distressing aspects of love, work, faith, mental anguish, old age and psychotherapeutic caregiving. Each chapter of this book will delineate some of the underappreciated, everyday facets of these very troubling, or at least challenging, psychological experiences, as well as offer utilitarian, pragmatic insights for changing one's way of thinking, feeling and acting to make suffering sufferable.

Suffering can be psychologically metabolized to become an opportunity for personal growth, development and flourishing. Indeed, the art of living the "good life" requires that one be willing and able to metamorphose one's suffering into "something more," "something higher" and "something better" – a psychic achievement that is easier said than done.[3] As philosopher Bertrand Russell famously quipped about a universe that he regarded as ethically indifferent and unjust, "The secret of happiness is to face the fact that the world is horrible, horrible, horrible – you must feel it deeply, and not brush it aside. You must feel it right here" – thumping his chest – "and then you can start being happy again" (Mailer, 1998, p. 157). Metamorphosing one's suffering can involve a wide range of conscious and unconscious relations to the world and strategies, including those of transcendence, resignation and transformation (Erikson, 2006, p. 48).

In simplified ideological terms, a person lodged in a Christian way of being-in-the-world, for example, could draw from his belief in a comforting kingdom not of this world, but of heaven, to help transcend earthly suffering; one who is lodged in a Stoic outlook can regard his "inner world," his character/virtue building, as what really matters in life, and thus resignation without despair is the best strategy to manage the suffering inflicted on him by what he views as impersonal forces. A person who views suffering from a Marxist angle would be inclined to accept the facticity of his suffering, and would focus on transforming the outside world, such as changing the oppressive class differences, forms of socioeconomic conflict or the stronger overpowering the weaker. From a Freudian perspective, suffering is best dealt with through astute personal compromises between drive satisfaction and reality considerations, always with an eye toward "higher" forms of sublimation (Erikson, 2006, pp. 48, 72).

In real life, most people engage with suffering in love, work or faith by using a wide range of interdependent, interrelated and interactive psychological resources. Regardless of one's frame of reference, all agree that while life is steeped in suffering, the "royal road" to making suffering sufferable – to coming out of it enhanced, if not wiser – involves being able to face the tough truths about one's personal limitations, vulnerabilities and character flaws with an eye to transforming them into their opposite. Using one's sufferings as a base for life-affirming action requires considerable critical self-understanding (i.e., owning up to one's contribution to one's problems in living) and expanded and deepened self-awareness, which almost always feels distressing. As Carl Jung aptly put it, individuals are extremely pain avoidant: "People will do anything, no matter how absurd, in order to avoid facing their own souls. One does not become enlightened by imagining figures of light, but by making the darkness conscious" (1969, p. 99). Playing off of Jung's metaphor, my study assumes that sunlight illuminates the outside world, and darkness the inner one.

## Situating psychoanalysis in the Axial Age

To better contextualize my study, I must discuss how I situate and define psychoanalysis, my angle of vision, as it differs somewhat from how most analysts conceive of it. My view of psychoanalysis is as a contemporary offshoot of the ancient religious "spirituality" and "wisdom" tradition that emerged during the Axial Age, the socially tumultuous period when there was an explosion of spiritual creativity in four regions of the world, each having different socio-intellectual realities and traditions. As German philosopher and psychiatrist Karl Jaspers first pointed out in his original formulation of the concept, the Axial Age was a "spiritual process" in which "extraordinary events" took place:

> In China lived Confucius and Lao Tse, all the trends in Chinese philosophy arose ... In India it was the age of the Upanishads and of Buddha; as in China, all philosophical trends, including skepticism and materialism, sophistry and nihilism, were developed. In Iran Zarathustra put forward his challenging conception of the cosmic process as a struggle between good and evil; in Palestine prophets arose: Elijah, Isaiah, Jeremiah, Deutero-Isaiah; Greece produced Homer, the philosophers Parmenides, Heraclitus, Plato, the tragic poets, Thucydides and Archimedes. All the vast development of which these names are a mere intimation took place in those few centuries, independently and almost simultaneously in China, India and the West.
>
> (Jaspers, 2003, p. 99)

Most importantly, says Jaspers, these philosophers and religious leaders gave birth to our conception of what it meant to be human,[4] both at its best and worst, a vision of humanity that still has a strong interpretive grip on human consciousness, on what Pierre Bourdieu called our "symbolic field" (Lambert, 1999, p. 304). As the eminent sociologist Robert N. Bellah noted, "Neither the Enlightenment nor any of the great ideological movements of the twentieth century have supplanted the axial heritage; often they have enacted it out in parody even as they imagined themselves rejecting it" (2002, p. 273). Even more significantly for this book, not only is "the spiritual life of men … still oriented towards the axial age," but throughout the world there have been "conscious attempts to restore it, renaissances" (Jaspers, 2003, p. 102). These "great new" Axial-inspired "spiritual creations" are a testament to its formidable influence in today's world (ibid.). Psychoanalysis, with its emphasis on helping analysands transcend suffering in their lives, can be viewed as just such a "new spiritual creation" that is lodged in the Axial vision.[5]

As comparative religion scholar Karen Armstrong noted, all the traditions that evolved during the Axial Age expanded and deepened "the frontiers of human consciousness and discovered a transcendent dimension in the core of their being" (2006, p. xvii). However, and this is most important when we consider psychoanalysis as a modern expression of the Axial vision, these traditions "did not necessarily regard" the transcendent dimension "as supernatural, and most of them refused to discuss it" (ibid., p. 393).[6] This was mainly because the experience of what was felt as "ineffable, indescribable, and incomprehensible"[7] evoked only reverential silence (ibid.),[8] a response that calls to mind philosopher Ludwig Wittgenstein's famous statement in the *Tractatus*: "What we cannot speak about we must pass over in silence" (1961, p. 3).

This being said, in the Axial Age there was a sharp differentiation between the world as it is typically experienced and a world beyond this world, in whatever way that otherworldliness was imagined. As the well-known sociologist S.N. Eisendstadt noted, it is precisely "the emergence, conceptualization, and institutionalization of a basic tension between the transcendental and mundane orders" that distinguish the Axial Age (1986, p. 1). Out of this differentiation, the notion emerged that while "we are *in* this world, we are not *of* this world" (Erikson, 2006, p. 5; italics original). Such an orientation, in which one is in and yet not in the world, both inside and outside, affirmed the profound paradoxical thought that authentic inner independence is always entwined with a type of dependence on the world (Jaspers, 2003, p. 116). In this Axial model, human existence can be construed "as a journey," one "that leads from appearance to reality, bondage to liberation, confusion to insight, and darkness to light" (Erikson, 2006, p. 5). For example, Buddha taught that it is possible to find and create an inner center of gravity, an internal "place apart, separate from the world, and yet wondrously within it" – one "that is impartial, utterly fair, calm, and that fills us with a confidence that, against all odds, there is value in our lives" (Armstrong, 2006, p. 342). Buddha called this spiritual place *nibbana*, the Hebrews called it God, and the Hindus called it *brahman* (ibid.). When recast in psychological terms, existential themes that point to an ultimate reality (e.g., the mind is fundamentally spiritually cast to strive for "something more," "something higher" and "something better") resonate with a psychoanalytic outlook as they pertain to the evocative notion of transcendence that is central to the Axial vision.

A psychoanalytically glossed view of transcendence could refer to the sudden intrusion of the unconscious, of otherness in rational thought. Through the analytic dialogue, transcendent truths in the form of life-altering self-understanding and self-knowledge are derived.[9] Put differently, the greater the inner freedom from unconscious bondage and neurosis (the more one becomes an authentic self who is radically open to existence) the greater the potential for helpful transcendence (Jaspers, 2003). Most importantly, as ethical philosopher Emmanuel Levinas describes it, such transcendence involves "the movement of the self (or 'same') toward the outside (the 'other,' or alterity)" (Smith, 2005, p. 1), always with the awareness that it is never possible to fully comprehend the irreducible particularity, the alterity of the self and other. Transcendence is achieved through the inter-human encounter and expanded and deepened sociality, especially through embracing an other-directed, other-regarding, other-serving way of being-in-the-world. Says Levinas, "The subject who says [like the biblical Abraham] 'Here I am' testifies to the Infinite" (1985, p. 106), and, "Through the relations with the Other, I am in touch with God" (1989, p. 17).

Similar to psychoanalysis, what mattered most in Axial traditions was not what you consciously believed and verbalized, including with regard to the ineffable transcendent dimension, but rather "how you behaved" (Armstrong, 2006, p. xviii). As psychoanalyst Wilhelm Reich pithily noted, "Words can lie. The mode of expression never lies" (1961, p. 145). That is, in the Axial tradition what mattered most was whether your actions in the real world were in accordance with ethical conduct, with "goodness," the ultimate transformational force (ibid.). For example, "charity and benevolence," expressions of deep and wide empathy, were highly valued (ibid., p. xix). In addition, one is not able to be happy if one is only self-serving in outlook and behavior (Hadot, 2009).

Such empathic capacity is central not only to psychoanalytic technique but also to its ethos, for in everyday life the capacity for wholesome intimacy requires accurate empathic immersion in the inner world of one's partner. Freud, too, believed that "goodness," what can be called love without lust, was the lynchpin to the art of living the "good life" (Marcus, 2008, p. 219). As Wallwork (2005, p. 287) noted, Freud quietly encouraged people to live according to the love commandment. "I myself have always advocated the love of mankind," he wrote to the Nobel Prize-winning French dramatist Romain Rolland (Freud, 1975, Letter 218, p. 374). In his essay "Why War"

Freud also noted that the commandment to love was the best cure for the human proclivity to violence, hatred and war: "There is no need for psychoanalysis to be ashamed to speak of love in this connection, for religion itself uses the same words: Thou shalt love thy neighbor as thyself" (Freud, 1933, p. 212).

In light of the above, Freud can be plausibly regarded as a modern exemplar of the Axial model,[10] excluding the explicitly otherworldly transcendent dimension – unless you regard, as I do, psychologically engaging the otherworldliness of the unconscious, especially its infantile aspects, as the master key to transcending the neurotic self, with its inordinate egoism and narcissism. By this I mean that if the Axial tradition is right that the greatest impediment to so-called "enlightenment" is excessive egoism and narcissism, then it is through other-directed, other-regarding and other-serving love and work that a new and better self and interiority can flourish.

Jaspers, too, believed that there was a transcendent aspect in man, a kind of earthly self-spirituality, "to be found within oneself and especially through the value of life and the need for achievement" (Lambert, 1999, pp. 308, 322, 323). This is particularly true in the existentially significant realms of love, work, faith and art: "Only transcendence can make this questionable life good, the world beautiful, and existence itself a fulfillment" (Jaspers, 2003, p. 126).[11] Armstrong also claims that "the transcendent experience that humans seem to require" centrally involves reclaiming the "compassionate vision [to] find a way of expressing it in an innovative, inspiring way – just as the Axial sages did" (2006, pp. xvi, 472). It is precisely this process of "ethicization," as it has been called, "the interpretation of events or practices in ethical terms," that is a main feature of Axial Age religions that has positive implications for our era (Muesse, 2007, p. 130).

The claim that Freud can be reasonably conceived as lodged in the Axial tradition becomes more plausible when we note that while not a religious or Zionistic Jew, he was strongly identified with Jewish ethics, history and group destiny, once explaining in a speech to his B'nai B'rith Society in Vienna in honor of his seventieth birthday:

> There remained enough other things to make the attraction of Judaism and Jews irresistible – many dark emotional forces, all the more potent for being so hard to grasp in words, as well as the clear consciousness of an inner identity, the intimacy that comes from the same psychic structure.
>
> (Bakan, 1958, p. 305)[12]

Thus, my claim is that Freud (and his followers) calls to mind one of those Hebrew "wisdom" writers of the Axial Age, those ancient professional teacher-sages depicted in the books of Proverbs, Job and Ecclesiastes, who were committed "to developing a realistic approach to the problems of life, including the practical skills and the technical arts of civilization" (Gordis, 1951, pp. 16–17). Like the ancient teacher-sages, Freud and his followers are mainly concerned with issues of "ultimate concern" – as Paul Tillich used the term – to describe the summoning nature of faith and religion (1957, p. 10). While human beings have many types of concerns, their "ultimate concerns," such as the meaning of life, suffering and death, have an irrepressible quality of urgency and ultimacy. That is, whether such issues are cast in cognitive, aesthetic, moral or political terms, they have a distinctly "spiritual" or "religious" feel to them, for they demand committing oneself with the fullness of one's whole being to bringing about the fulfillments that it promises (ibid., pp. 11, 1). Psychoanalysis summons the analysand to wholeheartedly engage his life, especially in the realms of love and work, with just such existential seriousness as he tries to transform his suffering into "something more," "something higher" and "something better," that is, to a practical wisdom that can be artfully used to live the "good life."

## Defining psychoanalysis

In light of the above placement of Freud and his followers in the Axial model, psychoanalysis as I conceive it is a form of life, a resource for individuals who can appropriate the life- and identity-defining narrative of psychoanalysis when they seek to understand, endure and possibly conquer the problems that affect, if not assault, the human experiences of love, faith, mental anguish, old age, work and caregiving. Psychoanalysis can be viewed as what Michel Foucault called a "technology of the self": "an exercise of the self, by which one attempts to develop and transform oneself, and to attain a certain mode of being" (1989, p. 433). As philosopher Pierre Hadot notes about ancient Greek philosophy, psychoanalysis can be understood as a "spiritual exercise," a tool for living life skillfully, more fully and wisely (1997, p. 83). Erikson may have had this in mind when he wrote that "free association" was a "western form of meditation" (Hoare, 2001, p. 88), while Symington explicitly states that "psychoanalysis has a spiritual function," such that "purifying motivation" becomes "the organizing center of his activities" (1993, p. 47).

The aim of a spiritual exercise is to foster a deep modification of an individual's way of "seeing and being," a decisive change in how one lives one's practical, everyday life. Most importantly, the objective of a spiritual exercise is "a total transformation of one's vision, life-style, and behavior" in the service of increased personal freedom and peace of mind (Hadot, 1997, pp. 83, 103, 14), and, I would add, a less self-centric outlook and behavior. According to this view, as Levinas described "Jewish Humanism" at its best, psychoanalysis is "a difficult wisdom concerned with truths that correlate to virtues" (1989, p. 275). While psychoanalysis shuns moralizing, as Nina Coltart noted, it "may be defined as a moral activity," one in which symptoms are "disabling painful moral puzzles" (Phillips, 1994, pp. 138, 139).

Psychoanalysis is a harrowing, deconstructive, demythologizing and defamiliarizing process for acquiring greater self-awareness and self-understanding, especially of one's destructive unconscious emotional activity, one that transforms moral consciousness by expanding and deepening one's capacity to love. As Axial sages viewed it, self-understanding leads to self-mastery, which leads to self-transcendence. In fact, Freud described psychoanalytic treatment as the "scientific cure by love" (McGuire, 1974, pp. 12–13). In this sense, psychoanalysis is animated by both the "love of wisdom" and the "wisdom of love," by Greek and Hebrew values, and is a powerful tool for the art of living a "good life," as one construes and fashions it.[13]

## Why another book on suffering?

There have been hundreds of books written on the subject of suffering from a wide range of perspectives. Some are lodged in lofty philosophical or religious points of view, while others are more "up front and personal," like "survival" accounts or grief memoirs. There are also many psychologically based self-help books that are geared toward helping people "cope" with their painful circumstances (Rice, 2014, p. 14). All of these books, and the points of view they represent, have some value to the average person amidst very trying times in their lives when they feel "a sense of forsakenness" (Jaspers, 2003, p. 20).[14] My book draws from all of these perspectives as it mines some of the best insights that those before me have graced us with about both the nature of suffering and how best to respond to it. However, what is novel about this study is that I use a psychoanalytic angle to unravel some of the forms of suffering associated with common human experiences.

Psychoanalysis is particularly adept at conceptualizing and working with an individual's painful emotions, for they are regarded as both the enabling and constraining forces that potentiate and impede positive change. Moreover, I focus on suffering that is mainly self-inflicted and neurotic, the bailiwick of psychoanalytic theory and treatment, as opposed to psychologically coping with a natural disaster or a genocidal attack (these forms of "externally" imposed suffering are also "internally" filtered and responded to in better and worse ways). As Carl Jung noted in his essay "Psychotherapists or the Clergy," "Psychoneurosis must be understood, ultimately, as the suffering of a soul which has not discovered its meaning" (1932, p. 497).

As an analyst embedded in a Freudian outlook – man as pleasure seeking in an erotically tinged universe; the self fashioned by its defenses against instincts; treatment as "the taming of the beast within" through reason and love – my focus is on the role of sexuality and aggression in problems in living (Roth, 1998, p. 327).[15] It is well known that the particular manner in which we interpret our painful circumstances will greatly influence not only how we experience our ordeal but also how we respond to it as we lean into the future. Needless to say, this is a deeply personalized matter that includes the role of unacknowledged sexual and aggressive wishes and the conflicts they generate. Indeed, what Harold Bloom said about literature and understanding suffering also applies to psychoanalytic thinking: "What matters in literature in the end is surely the idiosyncratic, the individual, the flavor or the color of a particular human suffering" (Bloom, 1986, p. 138).

Having been practicing psychoanalysis and psychotherapy for over thirty years, as well as having been a court-appointed forensic evaluator in Family and Supreme Courts, I have been privileged to helpfully engage with a wide range of people who were intensely struggling with problems in living. Most importantly, I have noticed that there are people who are more and less skillful at facing their suffering and transforming the brute psychic pain into "something more," "something higher" and "something better," a basis for practical wisdom in the service of living the "good life."

## Forms of suffering

While I will not engage in any detail with the philosophically and psychologically murky issue of defining the difference between pain and suffering, given that my book is mainly about suffering and not pain, I will provide what I regard as a rudimentary and serviceable way of thinking about what distinguishes one from the other. Indian American author Deepak Chopra has succinctly described a central difference between pain and suffering:

> Pain is not the same as suffering. Left to itself, the body discharges pain spontaneously, letting go of it the moment that the underlying cause is healed. Suffering is pain that we hold on to. It comes from the mind's mysterious instinct to believe that pain is good, or that it cannot be escaped, or that the person deserves it.
>
> (2004, pp. 65–66)

Another related way of distinguishing pain from suffering is to view it as the average person literally speaks about it in everyday life: pain tends to be described as a physical happening, like toothache or backache, while suffering tends to be situated in the emotional realm, like when a love relationship abruptly ends or one gets fired and can't find another job. It is worth noting that pain can morph into suffering, such as when debilitating chronic physical pain becomes the basis for feeling hopeless; and suffering can morph into pain, like when one has successfully mourned a loved one and then their birthday is remembered, which leads to an upsurge of searing feelings. While all of these distinctions are debatable, the reader understands that I am mainly interested in the suffering associated with some existentially compelling aspects of life that are not easily remedied by traditional "pain management," such as via prescription medication, physical rehabilitation or going to a medical doctor.

As noted earlier, I have chosen to explore the suffering in love, work, faith, mental anguish and old age. In the last chapter, I take up the suffering of the psychoanalyst as he practices the "impossible profession," as Freud called it. Analysts have to suffer with their own compassion overload, frustration and sense of radical ineffectiveness as they attempt to help their suffering patients get their lives "on track." As Erikson said, "people and peoples would rather die than change ... they would rather murder than take chances with their identity" (Hoare, 2001, p. 69). While there are many compelling topics to write about that involve suffering, the ones I have chosen include what, in my experience, really matters to most people. For example, adult love relations are a fabulously fertile breeding ground for the later development of a wide range of forms of suffering. As Freud wrote in *Civilization and its Discontents*, "We are never so defenseless against suffering as when we love, never as helplessly unhappy as when we have lost our loved object or its love" (1930, p. 82).

To loathe one's work, or to experience it as barely tolerable, is a kind of personal horror that calls to mind a bad marriage or failed relationship with a significant other in which one feels utterly trapped. Camus recognized this when he noted that if work does not have soul, life can be stifled and deadened. To feel the agony of being abandoned or rejected by God, especially in one's hour of need, has been immortalized in the pained words of Jesus on the Cross: "My God, my God, why hast thou forsaken me?" (Matthew 27:46). To experience extreme mental anguish, like ongoing anxiety or depression, is to feel a form of mental unhinging that is aptly described as the horror of existence. Who can't relate to some degree to the pained words of Canadian singer and songwriter Leonard Cohen, who said in an interview, "I speak of a clinical depression that is the background of your entire life, a background of anguish and anxiety, a sense that nothing goes well, that pleasure is unavailable and all your strategies collapse" (Lynskey, 2012)?

The process of getting older, especially when one reaches so-called old age, is notoriously challenging for most people, for it can be mainly experienced as disintegration, disillusionment, and a variety of other assaults on one's narcissism, such as the sharp awareness of one's finitude and mortality. Typically in old age there is also suffering related to the death of a loved one, such as a significant other, combined with the sense that the loss is irreplaceable, leaving one feeling utterly adrift and forlorn.

What I hope to make clear throughout this book is that all of these forms of suffering should not be lumped together, for they have their unique phenomenologies and psychodynamics, and are to a large extent context-dependent and setting-specific. Moreover, when taken as a totality of circumstances, these forms of suffering also provide the psychological context and conditions of possibilities for individuals to transform their suffering into "something more," "something higher" and "something better." What British psychiatrist R.D. Laing said about insanity, about feeling like one is "going crazy," also applies to the other forms of suffering I will discuss: "Madness need not be all break-down. It may also be break-through. It is potential liberation and renewal as well as enslavement and existential death" (1967, p. 133).

## Notes

1  The Axial Greeks were often focused on the notion of tragic circumstances, that is, circumstances in which there appear to be no reasonable and acceptable way of resolving the serious problem in living. In fact, one of the main Axial Greek insights into tragedy, says Martha Nussbaum, was "there is a kind of knowing that works by suffering because suffering is the appropriate acknowledgment of the way human life ... is" (Zaretsky, 2013, pp. 115–116).

2  See Marcus (2003), Marcus (2010), Marcus (2013a), Marcus (2013b), Marcus (2014), Marcus (2017) and Marcus, with Marcus (2011).

3  Philosopher Roberto Mangabeira Unger has argued that limit breaking is the most powerful motive in human existence: "Only the beyond ultimately concerns us. The sense of a permanent power of transcendence over all limits – of openness to the infinite – is inseparable from the experience of consciousness" (2007, p. 13). This being said, as the Axial sages have noted, what matters most is whether the limit breaking takes a life-affirming or life-denying form, that is, whether it is animated by ethical considerations. Of course, what is judged as "ethical" is perspectival – and therein lies the rub.

4  As Muesse points out, the notion of "selfhood" first appeared during the Axial Age: the "self" was regarded "as a separate individual with agency and moral responsibility," engaged in the project of "personal transformation," including thinking differently about "ultimate reality" (2007, pp. 118, 119).

5  Scholars have noted other aspects of Axial vision that I believe are in sync with psychoanalysis as a disruptive discourse and self-fashioning resource. The Axial Age has been described as "an age of criticism," "second order thinking," a period of increased "reflexivity," "historicity" and "agentiality" (Casanova, 2012, pp. 209, 203). Neville Symington, an ex-Catholic priest and member of the Middle Group of British Psychoanalysis, describes psychoanalysis as "a mature natural religion" (accessible to reason without drawing from revelation) and "a spiritual method relevant to the modern world," one that he claims calls to mind aspects of the Axial Age (1993, pp. 137, 192; 2012, p. 408).

6  According to Symington, the collective message of the Axial masters was: "cultivate the good, attend to what is inner, and have compassion for your fellow man and woman" (1993, p. 105). A lot easier said than done, as the Axial masters emphasized.

7  For example, it says in the *Upanishads*, "the Spirit supreme is immeasurable, inapprehensible, beyond conception, never born, beyond reasoning, beyond thought. His vastness is the vastness of space" (Mascaro, 1965, p. 101).

8  The notion of the "transcendent" is much debated and hard to pin down. For example, the Christian "believer" Gabriel Marcel was committed to what he called the "authentic, vertical transcendent," that is, "the transcendence, holiness, and sanctity of Christ and the martyrs." The "non-believer" Albert Camus was committed to what has been called "horizontal transcendence" as manifested by charity, humanity and solidarity (these valuative attachments were of great concern to Marcel and most "believers"). Thus, for Marcel, transcendence is rooted in divinity, while for Camus it is rooted in history (Heffernan, 2017, pp. 17, 20, 16).

9  http://plato.stanford.edu/entries/jaspers, retrieved 7/12/16.

10  Armstrong situates Freud (and Newton and Einstein) in what she calls the "second Axial Age." Taking her lead from Jaspers, who referred to "our age of science and technology...a kind of second beginning" (2003, p. 103), Armstrong describes the Western genius for science, which radically changed the world, beginning in the sixteenth century when its scientific revolution initiated a new Axial Age (2006, p. 424). This being said, I maintain that the Freudian version of the human condition, its view of psychopathology or problems in living, and its treatment modality are all in sync with the Axial vision.

11  For a clarifying discussion of the ambiguous notion of transcendence in the Axial Age, see Dalferth (2012).

12  Freud appears to be alluding to what feels "unsayable" to him, "hard to grasp in words" as he puts it. Wittgenstein notes a connection between the "unspeakable and mystical": "There are, indeed," says Wittgenstein, "things that cannot be put into words. They make themselves manifest. They are what is mystical" (Hadot, 2009, p. 81).

13  The "art of living" is a phrase that deserves some clarification. Foucault aptly defines the term as "those intentional and voluntary actions by which men not only set themselves rules of conduct but also seek to transform themselves ... and to make their life into an *oeuvre* that carries aesthetic values and meets certain stylistic criteria" (1990, pp. 10–11). Foucault may well have been influenced by Epictetus, who viewed philosophy as the Stoic "art of life." In Epictetus's view (though not Foucault's), philosophy is what a person requires "to become properly themselves [as they are lovers of truth], to fulfill their natures, to achieve the happiness that is everyone's natural goal" (Long, 2002, pp. 97, 111). Epictetus was following the lead of Socrates, who viewed philosophy a "whole way of life," one that is lived "correctly and well," not as an intellectual, theoretical pursuit. In this view, philosophy was a "guide, and unifying component of a good life" lived "on the basis of philosophical reasoning," and characterized by the pursuit of virtue, wisdom and happiness (Cooper, 2012, pp. 24, 33, 31, 36). Finally, for the Axial-inspired spiritual aspirant, the "art of living" was a high religious art that was characterized by "doing God's work" (however the divine/transcendent was conceptualized), such that the "good life" was one that was infused with inner beauty, truth and goodness.

14  As the Axial-inspired analyst Michael Eigen points out, "Texts can be like living organisms, at times, more real than life ... [a] book takes you to places you value, opens possibilities, and supports the unfolding of your own sensibility" (2012, p. xii).

15  As French phenomenological philosopher Maurice Merleau-Ponty noted, as we are fundamentally bodily beings (i.e., embodied), sexuality is an intrinsic dimension of human existence: "it is always present like an atmosphere" and "spreads forth like an odour or like a sound" (Cooper, 2015, p. 124).

## References

Aeschylus. (2007). *The Oresteia*. I. Johnston (Trans.). Arlington, VA: Richter Resources.

Armstrong, K. (2006). *The Great Transformation: The Beginning of our Religious Traditions*. New York: Knopf.

Bakan, D. (1958). *Sigmund Freud and the Jewish Mystical Tradition*. Princeton, NJ: Van Nostrand.

Bellah, R.N. (2002). Epilogue. Meaning and Modernity: America and the World. In R. Madsen, W.M. Sullivan, A. Swindler, & S.M. Tipton (Eds.), *Meaning and*

*Modernity: Religion, Polity and Self* (pp. 255–276). Berkeley: University of California Press.

Bloom, H. (1986). *Newsweek*. Volume 108.

Casanova, J. (2012). Religion, the Axial Age, and Secular Modernity in Bellah's Theory of Religious Evolution. In R.N. Bellah & H. Joas (Eds.), *The Axial Age and Its Consequences* (pp. 192–223). Cambridge, MA: Harvard University Press.

Chopra, D. (2004). *The Book of Secrets: Unlocking the Hidden Dimensions of Your Life*. New York: Three Rivers.

Cooper, J.M. (2012). *Pursuit of Wisdom: Six Ways of Life in Ancient Philosophy from Socrates to Plotinus*. Princeton, NJ: Princeton University Press.

Cooper, M. (2015). *Existential Psychotherapy and Counselling: Contribution to a Pluralistic Practice*. Los Angeles: Sage.

Dalferth, I.U. (2012). The Ideal of Transcendence. In R.N. Bellah & H. Joas (Eds.), *The Axial Age and Its Consequences* (pp. 146–190). Cambridge, MA: Harvard University Press.

Eigen, M. (2012). *Kabbalah and Psychoanalysis*. London: Karnac.

Eisenstadt, S.N. (1986). The Axial Age Breakthroughs: Their Characteristics and Origins. In S.N. Eisenstadt (Ed.), *The Origins & Diversity of Axial Age Civilizations* (pp. 1–25). Albany: State University of New York Press.

Erikson, S.A. (2006). *Philosophy as a Guide to Living* (Course Guidebook). Chantilly, VA: The Teaching Company.

Foucault, M. (1989). The Ethics of the Concern for Self as a Practice of Freedom. In S. Lotringer (Ed.), *Foucault Live: Collected Interviews, 1961–1984* (pp. 432–449). New York: Semiotexte.

Foucault, M. (1990). *The Use of Pleasure*. New York: Vintage.

Fredrickson, B.L., & Losada, M.F. (2005). Positive Affect and Complex Dynamics of Human Flourishing. *American Psychologist*, 60, 678–686.

Freud, E.L. (1975). *The Letters of Sigmund Freud*. New York: Basic Books.

Freud, S. (1893). The Psychotherapy of Hysteria from Studies on Hysteria. In J. Strachey (Ed. & Trans.), *Standard Edition of the Complete Psychological Works of Sigmund Freud* (Vol. 2, pp. 253–305). London: Hogarth Press.

Freud, S. (1927). The Future of Illusion. In J. Strachey (Ed. & Trans.), *Standard Edition of the Complete Psychological Works of Sigmund Freud* (Vol. 21, pp. 1–56). London: Hogarth Press.

Freud, S. (1930). Civilization and Its Discontents. In J. Strachey (Ed. & Trans.), *Standard Edition of the Complete Psychological Works of Sigmund Freud* (Vol. 21, pp. 57–146). London: Hogarth Press.

Freud, S. (1933). Why War? In J. Strachey (Ed. & Trans.), *Standard Edition of the Complete Psychological Works of Sigmund Freud* (Vol. 22, pp. 203–215). London: Hogarth Press.

Freud, S. (1985). *The Complete Letters of Sigmund Freud to Wilhelm Fliess 1887–1904*. J.M. Masson (Trans.). Cambridge, MA: Belknap Press.

Giddens, A. (1984). *The Constitution of Society*. Berkeley: University of California Press.

Gordis, R. (Trans.). (1951). *Koheleth: The Man and His World*. New York: Jewish Theological Seminary of America.

Hadot, P. (1997). *Philosophy As a Way of Life*. Oxford, UK: Blackwell.

Hadot, P. (2009). *The Present Alone Is Our Happiness: Conversations with Jeannie Carlier and Arnold I. Davidson.* M. Djaballah (Trans.). Stanford, CA: Stanford University Press.

Heffernan, G. (2017). The Meaningless Life is Not Worth Living: Critical Reflections on Marcel's Critique of Camus. *Marcel Studies,* 2, 1–22.

Hoare, C.H. (2001). *Erikson on Development in Adulthood: New Insights from the Unpublished Papers.* Oxford, UK: Oxford University Press.

Jaspers, K. (2003). *Way to Wisdom: An Introduction to Philosophy.* New Haven, CT: Yale University Press. (Original work published 1951)

Jaspers, K. (2011). *The Origins and Goal of History.* London: Routledge. (Original work published 1953)

Jung, C. (1932). *Psychotherapists or the Clergy. C.W., 11,* 327–347. London: Routledge & Kegan Paul.

Jung, C. (1969). *Psychology and Alchemy* (2nd ed.). R.F.C. Hull (Trans.). New York: Routledge.

Laing, R.D. (1967). *Politics of Experience.* New York: Pantheon.

Lambert, Y. (1999). Religion in Modernity as a New Axial Age: Secularization of New Religious Forms. *Sociology of Religion,* 60(3), 303–333.

Levinas, E. (1985). *Ethics and Infinity: Conversations with Philippe Nemo.* R.A. Cohen (Trans.). Pittsburgh, PA: Duquesne University Press.

Levinas, E. (1989). *Difficult Freedom: Essays on Judaism.* S. Hand (Ed.). Baltimore, MD: Johns Hopkins University Press.

Long, A.A. (2002.). *Epictetus: A Stoic and Socratic Guide to Life.* Oxford, UK: Oxford University Press.

Lynskey, D. (2012). Leonard Cohen: "All I've Got to Put in a Song Is My Own Experience." www.theguardian.com/music/2012/jan/19/leonard-cohen, retrieved 7/26/16.

Mailer, N. (1998). Reading Camelot. In J. Updike (Ed.), *A Century of Arts and Letters* (pp. 156–197). New York: Columbia University Press.

Marcus, P. (2003). *Ancient Religious Wisdom, Spirituality, and Psychoanalysis.* Westport, CT: Praeger.

Marcus, P. (2008). *Being for the Other: Emmanuel Levinas, Ethical Living and Psychoanalysis.* Milwaukee, WI: Marquette University Press.

Marcus, P. (2010). *In Search of the Good Life: Emmanuel Levinas, Psychoanalysis and the Art of Living.* London: Karnac.

Marcus, P. (2013a). *How to Laugh Your Way Through Life: A Psychoanalyst's Advice.* London: Karnac.

Marcus, P. (2013b). *In Search of the Spiritual: Gabriel Marcel, Psychoanalysis, and the Sacred.* London: Karnac.

Marcus, P. (2014). *They Shall Beat Their Swords into Plowshares: Military Strategy, Psychoanalysis and the Art of Living.* Milwaukee, WI: Marquette University Press.

Marcus, P. (2017). *The Psychoanalysis of Career Choice, Job Performance, and Satisfaction: Flourishing in the Workplace.* New York: Routledge.

Marcus, P., with Marcus, G. (2011). *Theater as Life: Practical Wisdom from Great Acting Teachers, Actors and Actresses.* Milwaukee, WI: Marquette University Press.

Mascaro, J. (Trans.). (1965). *The Upanishads.* London: Penguin.

Mason, J. M. (Ed. & Trans.). (1985). *The Complete Letters of Sigmund Freud to Wilhelm Fliess 1887–1904.* Boston, MA: Harvard University Press.

McGuire, W. (Ed.). (1974). *The Freud/Jung Letters*. Princeton: Princeton University Press.

Muesse, M.W. (2007). *Religions in the Axial Age: An Approach to the World's Religions* (Course Guidebook). Chantilly, VA: The Teaching Company.

Phillips, A. (1994). *On Flirtation*. Cambridge, MA: Harvard University Press.

Reich, W. (1961). *The Function of the Orgasm: Sex-Economic Problems of Biological Energy*. New York: Farrer, Straus, Giroux. (Original work published 1942)

Rice, R. (2014). *Suffering and the Search for Meaning: Contemporary Responses to the Problem of Pain*. Downers Grove, IL: IVP Academic Press.

Roth, P.A. (1998). The Cure of Stores, Self-Deception, Danger Situations, and the Clinical Role of Narratives in Roy Schafer's Psychoanalytic Theory. In P. Marcus & A. Rosenberg (Eds.), *Psychoanalytic Versions of the Human Condition* (pp. 306–331). New York: New York University Press.

Smith, M.B. (2005). *Toward the Outside: Concepts and Themes in Emmanuel Levinas*. Pittsburgh, PA: Duquesne University Press.

Symington, N. (1993). *Emotion and Spirit: Questioning the Claims of Psychoanalysis and Religion*. New York: St. Martin's Press.

Symington, N. (2012). The Essence of Psycho-Analysis as Opposed to What Is Secondary. *Psychoanalytic Dialogues*, 22, 395–409.

Tillich, P. (1957). *Dynamics of Faith*. New York: Harper & Row.

Unger, R.M. (2007). *The Self Awakened: Pragmatism Unbound*. Cambridge, MA: Harvard University Press.

Wallwork, E. (2005). Ethics in Psychoanalysis. In E.S. Person, A.M. Cooper, & G.O. Gabbard (Eds.), *Textbook of Psychoanalysis* (pp. 281–300). Washington, DC: American Psychiatric Publishing.

Wittgenstein, L. (1961). *Tractatus Logico-Philosophicus*. D.F. Pears & B.F. McGuinness (Trans.). New York: Humanities Press.

Zaretsky, R. (2013). *A Life Worth Living: Albert Camus and the Quest for Meaning*. Cambridge, MA: Harvard University Press.

# Chapter 2

# The suffering of love

In Woody Allen's film *Love and Death* (1975), a spoof of nineteenth-century Russian philosophical novels like *War and Peace* and the Soviet-style epic films that were made from them, Boris Grushenko is passionately in love with his pseudo-intellectual cousin, Sonja. While Sonja loves Boris because he also is a pseudo-intellectual, she is not *in love* with him. Amidst the social upheaval caused by Napoleon invading Austria during the Napoleonic Wars, a pining Boris and sophist Sonja enter into an amusing pretentious philosophical debate in which Sonja argues that one's love life and suffering life are equivalent: "To love is to suffer. To avoid suffering one must not love. But then one suffers from not loving. Therefore, to love is to suffer; not to love is to suffer; to suffer is to suffer" (Grunwald & Adler, 2015, p. 291). Allen is making fun of the neurotic intellectual (and pseudo-intellectual) who is "bound, tied and gagged" by his inability to both find a suitable and reciprocating love partner and sustain an intimate relationship without it imploding, usually due to heightened ambivalence and other neurotic considerations. Indeed, there are many reasons why adult romantic love relationships (henceforth, love relationships) that begin with so much hope, enthusiasm and passion morph into hopelessness, apathy or hatred. For, as Freud taught us, the fault line between relational bliss and suffering is remarkably thin and permeable.

In this chapter I describe some of the practical forms of suffering that occur in love relationships, including those in which the parties remain together, often feeling psychologically tormented or estranged, and those that result in breakup or divorce.[1] I will also suggest what can be done internally (i.e., thinking and feeling) and externally (i.e., behaviorally) to stop a love relationship from turning into its opposite. Centrally, this means asking the pertinent questions about one's contribution to the troubling and painful downhill spiral and implementing self-correcting behavior. A desire to fashion the "good life," to adequately metabolize the inevitably distressing aspects of love, is of no benefit unless you come to know what you are up against in yourself.

Before I get into the heart of this chapter, it will be helpful to contextualize our discussion by familiarizing ourselves with some of the characteristics of individuals who avoid sustained love relationships because they are unwilling and/or unable to engage in such a relation. By way of a placeholder, recall the book/film character Mr. James Stevens (played by Anthony Hopkins), the butler of Darlington Hall from Kazuo Ishiguro's award-winning novel set in post-war Britain, *Remains of the Day* (1989). If such people do attempt to engage in a love relationship, it usually implodes or falls apart soon after the courtship phase. Alternatively, the love relationship operates strictly instrumentally and functionally, with no symbolic revelation of the self, associated with the deeper realms of intimacy.

## Living in a "loveless hell"

"Father and teachers, I ponder, 'What is hell?' I maintain that it is the suffering of being unable to love," wrote Dostoevsky in *The Brothers Karamazov* (1922, p. 343), a book that Freud called "the most magnificent novel ever written" (1961, p. 177). In his essay, "Dostoevsky and Parricide," Freud describes Dostoevsky's character flaws that inevitably tainted his ability to wholesomely give and receive love, such as his masochism, his proclivity to guilt, his psychologically motivated epileptic attacks, his ambivalence regarding his Oedipus Complex, and his passion for gambling and its origins in intense masturbatory wishes. However, what is most important in terms of this chapter is Freud's remark that Dostoevsky had an "astonishing helplessness in face of the phenomena of love" (ibid.). By this Freud meant that "all he really knew were crude, instinctual desire, masochistic subjection and loving out of pity" (ibid., p. 196).

As we shall see, while there are countless conscious and unconscious ways to botch a love relationship, each generating its own form of suffering, they all involve a radical sense of conscious and unconscious helplessness, hopelessness and haplessness, especially in the frustrating bewilderment and lack of skillfulness at not being able to put things "right." Indeed, one might say that the tragic endpoint of such troubled attempts to give and receive love, the culminating point of personal defeat, is to give up trying to find, create and maintain a love relationship, and instead live out one's days often painfully alone and self-occupied. If, as Axial philosopher Confucius claimed in his discussion of *ren* (the highest Confucian ethical value, benevolence/compassion), transcendence is not something that we "get" but something that we "give," then such people remain trapped in the magnetic field of their self-oriented outlook, a mode of being that blocks their access to a "higher" and "better" transcendent reality (Armstrong, 2006, p. 251).[2] In this view, transcendence is not about going "beyond" this world; it is about "crossing" worlds, living in the "real" world in a different way. Indeed, from my clinical experience, these forlorn people often exude a kind of small-minded and unforgiving quality in their overall comportment. Such individuals epitomize British playwright W. Somerset Maugham's perceptive statement from his novel *The Moon and Sixpence*: "It is not true that suffering ennobles the character; happiness does that sometimes, but suffering for the most part, makes men petty and vindictive" (1919, Ch. XVII).

### The self in exile

In psychoanalytic theory, the concept of "schizoid" is used both as a description (of signs and features) and as severe psychopathology (causes, psychodynamics and differential diagnoses) covering a broad array of over-lapping and hard to adequately distinguish clinical "overt" and "covert" conditions (Rycroft, 1995, p. 162; Akhtar, 1992, pp. 139–142). The diagnostic category "schizoid personality" or character has somewhat more clarity in terms of there being a consensus among theorists of what the concept clinically refers to, at least elementally speaking (Abraham & Torok, 1994; Akhtar, 1992; Doidge, 2001; Fairbairn, 1952a, Fairbairn 1952b; Guntrip, 1969; Klein, 1952; Winnicott, 1960).

Schizoid individuals typically fashion a life that avoids significant affiliation in both love and work, for they find anything but the most superficial and functional social contact to be tremendously threatening, even annihilating. They greatly fear emotional intimacy and self-disclosure, including on the rigorously sexual level, often preferring voyeuristic and pornographic activities and/or compulsive masturbation to romantic attachments with a significant other (Akhtar, 1995, p. 9). They come across as detached and withdrawn, and their emotional and intellectual faculties appear disconnected. The "self in exile," as schizoid personality disorder has been called by Ralph Klein, has a number of typical characteristics that are worth reviewing.[3]

By situating the world of love relationships against the backdrop of the radically different world of the schizoid, we are more likely to illuminate what might or ought to be otherwise – how our world could be modified to become the world we want it to be, or to show why it is so difficult to change it in a particular way (Dalferth, 2012, p. 154). Thus, while the schizoid personality disorder is an extreme diagnosis, being familiar with some of these typical characteristics provides a rich context for understanding a wide range of less extreme, but toxic, difficulties associated with what Saint Augustine called "disordered love." In the case of the schizoid personality, what is "disordered" about their love is that they regard their own self as their supreme and main love object, calling to mind Aristotle's notion of God as the Unmoved Mover, utterly self-absorbed and self-sufficient. "Disordered love," wanting the right things in the wrong order, is a useful trope for further illuminating the phenomenologies and dynamics of these problematic aspects of love relationships, especially when compared with "rightly ordered love," which Augustine equates with virtue. In his *On Christian Doctrine* (I.27–28), Augustine succinctly defines "rightly ordered love":

But living a just and holy life [a "mature" or "healthy" one, in psychoanalytic lingo] requires one to be capable of an objective and impartial evaluation of things: to love things, that is to say, in the right order, so that you do not love what is not to be loved, or fail to love what is to be loved, or have a greater love for what should be loved less, or an equal love for things that should be loved less or more, or a lesser or greater love for things that should be loved equally.

(quoted in Pasquarello, 2011, p. 55)

Augustine believes there is an ideal order to love. We should love God (the transcendent reality), others and ourselves. The trouble, however, is "when a good thing becomes a God thing." Psychologically recasting Augustine's notion of "rightly ordered love" means finding and creating the ideal psychological fit between various human needs and wishes and the objects that can gratify them (Marcus, 2003, p. 143). Disordered love is expecting more from an object of love than it is capable of giving. The schizoid person makes a huge category mistake; by putting all of his "psychic eggs" in one basket, a kind of self-deification, he overlooks what all of the Axial thinkers emphasized: surpassing and letting go of the self-absorbed and self-sufficient ego, in love and responsibility for the other, is the way to transcendence. Freud, too, believed that only when one has thrown off the unconscious bondage of the neurotic self, of the narcissistic, inordinate worry and easy upset, of depression and irritability, and the over reactivity to stress that is so typical of neurotics, is it possible to be capable of deep and wide love and creative and productive work.

### Disconnection vs. connection

The typical schizoid person has a duality of structure to his mode of being-in-the-world. On the one hand, he is very comfortable spending vast amounts of time alone. For example, the four schizoid patients I currently work with spend most weekends by themselves, running errands, going for walks, reading and going to the movies, hardly ever meeting up with friends or local family members. This "lone wolf" behavior is of a much greater magnitude and frequency than the common statement of love partners: "I need some space for myself." The main impediment of the schizoid personality to generating and sustaining a love relationship is that they are too comfortable being alone for long stretches of time. A schizoid person does not sharply experience what is often an omnipresent conscious and/or unconscious anxiety among most people, namely, as they age they become more and more aware of their finitude and mortality, and they do not want to grow old and die alone. Ironically, the schizoid person feels most safe and secure separated from others than with them, including in the later phases of the life cycle when the elderly long for a feeling of being venerated and remembered by those whose lives they have touched. If the schizoid person reaches out to others, particularly in the latter years, it is typically to promote mere physical and psychological survival, rather than from a wish to flourish, to seek out something spiritually "more," "higher" and "better" with a significant other. Even worse, the schizoid person is largely incapable of implementing what Axial thinkers regarded as the ideal way of relating to others, namely, being for the other before oneself, or at least as much as oneself. Rather, the schizoid person is self-occupied with their creature comforts and has little or no time for generative ways of being that centrally include enhancement of the best interests of others.

On the other hand, while a schizoid individual also feels considerable loneliness and consciously and/or unconsciously yearns for connection with others, he acutely feels that he does not fit in with those around him, whether in social or work settings. Such a paradoxical sense of longing and estrangement is rooted in intense fear of rejection and betrayal, something that his detachment and withdrawal actually tends to induce in others. Most people find this disengagement to be unappealing and not worth the effort to try to break through. Likewise, others in a social or work setting can regard a schizoid person as an "easy target" to be self-servingly "played" or in other ways mistreated. This schizoid person experiences this as "betrayal," which often generates intense retaliatory fantasies that can "leak" into everyday behavior with co-workers and cause havoc.

The schizoid person's drastic problems around disconnection put into sharp focus the enormous challenges for the average person to have effective "distance regulation" in a love relationship. Distance regulation means control over personal space and intimacy levels. A couple has to be willing and able to consciously negotiate and unconsciously intuit how much autonomy and togetherness is necessary to keep their relationship flourishing. There is an ideal zone that couples need to co-produce to engage happily in their "closeness-distance dance" so that it does not turn into a "dance of death." For example, too much togetherness and closeness can stir up engulfment anxiety, while too much autonomy and distance can cause abandonment anxiety. There are no hard and fast rules for getting this closeness-distance dance right, as every couple has to find their own equilibrium. However, what is clear is that both parties have to be willing and able to engage in thoughtful and empathic dialogue when they get derailed so that their "love train" does not crash and burn.

### Fantasy vs. reality-consciousness

A schizoid person typically has a very active fantasy life, so much so that his fantasized relationships and wishes are more summoning than his real-life ones. In many instances, while more or less functional and superficially adapted in his everyday life, his fantasy life tends to subsume reality rather than improve it. While it is true, as Carl Jung said, that "[t]he debt we owe to the play of the imagination is incalculable" (Art Direction, 1992, p. 86), it is also true that if the average person's fantasy life is more summoning than engaging reality, he will run into serious trouble in his love relationship. Think of young social media/internet-obsessed millennial men who have permitted themselves to be "virtually emasculated by porn and video games." These men, researchers found, are playing video games for nearly thirty hours a week, including watching omnipresent pornography that has probably reconfigured their brain wiring so that they are only reactive to kinky images that they muster at will, leaving them either daunted or bored by real-life women.[4] One can say that emotional suffering is generated when a person does not recognize and admit to their reality. This lack of reality testing and adaptation causes suffering in a love relationship because it tends to land the ignorant and/or denying person in a self-centric mode of being. Such a regressive comportment, especially with its inordinate need for affirmation, makes it near impossible to accurately perceive, let alone reasonably respond to, the needs and desires of a significant other. As a result, the couple is caught in a seemingly endless thicket of disconnection that usually morphs into a downward spiral of emotional violence.

### Right vs. wrong

Schizoid people can also have a strong sense of right and wrong, calling to mind the severe super-ego of the typical latency child, combined with an intuitive awareness and sensitivity to the needs and desires of others. This is especially the case when it comes to discerning concealed self-serving motives and agendas that others have, such as in the workplace where they are forced to interact and mingle with people, at least superficially. In some sense, this commitment to fairness and justice can be a positive feature of their way of being-in-the-world, for they notice everyday "cruelties" that most other people appear to be blind to or simply do not care about. While this moral perceptiveness can lead to trying to put things right, their lack of interpersonal skillfulness can lead to overreaction of moral indignation that is hardly containable and sometimes provokes inept interventions that make things worse. Alternatively, such moral upset can lead to shutting down, a way of avoiding righteous indignation and other painful feelings, such as resentment toward enforced passivity. To the outsider, sometimes such schizoid behavior comes across as lonely rootlessness or sullenness that can be very off-putting.

For the average person, a set of strongly held moral values and beliefs that point toward transcendence are crucial to one's inner center of gravity, including when a love relationship gets difficult. These moral values and beliefs need to be maintained in a flexible, reality-based manner and be continually open to critical self-reflection and, when necessary, creative revision and adaptation. Indeed, as Primo Levi noted about survival in the Nazi death camps, one has to reside in the "gray zone," a "zone of ambiguity," and somehow do the best one can in trying to make wise life-affirming decisions about what is true, right and good (1986, p. 58). Unlike the schizoid individual, who tends to be "black and white," "all or nothing" and "good or bad" in his moral life, for a love relationship to survive, let alone flourish, requires that both parties recognize the radically perspectival, context-dependent and setting-specific nature of all relational mishaps. This requires empathic, compromising and skillfully crafted dialogue to "put things right."

### Inauthentic vs. authentic self

The schizoid person also has a very hard time effectively managing face-to-face confrontation. This deficit is not only with those acquaintances or colleagues who they feel have treated them or others cruelly. It also can include people they say they love, like a family member, or someone they like, such as a longstanding friend, from whom they need or want something but feel an internal limitation, as if something is "broken" inside them. This impedes, if not incapacitates, their ability to shield themselves from others' aggression and protect their anchor in integrity, leading to a profound sense of inauthenticity. They feel estranged from their "real self" and experience the unnerving sense that "the person I appear to be" and "the person I am" are not the same. Such a discrepancy between appearance and reality is something we can all feel in common social situations.

When it comes to love relationships, what Polonius famously recommends in *Hamlet* (1.3) should be embraced without reserve by the average person: "This above all: to thine own self be true." In a love relationship, the need for authenticity is paramount. Authentic and inauthentic acts refer "to those acts which are done in good and bad faith, which are true and false to the self" (Rycroft, 1995, p. 10). While there is no tried and true way of deciding which behaviors are authentic and sincere, the fact is that to the extent that one is authentic, at least to the best of one's knowledge and belief, the more a love relationship is likely to flourish. Do not attempt to be someone you believe your partner wants you to be at the expense of your own integrity. Instead, have the will and ability to have your significant other feel confident that there is congruence between appearance and reality, and that you are unswervingly committed to doing what is in the best interests of the relationship.

### Trust vs. mistrust

The issue of trust is especially problematic for the schizoid personality, and this has at least three variations to it. First, they have such strong fears of rejection and betrayal, unconsciously experienced as unbearable abandonment, that they cannot trust another human being in any kind of existentially serious manner. Second, they have fears of engulfment that if they do trust someone, they will be completely enveloped and controlled, even cannibalized, with no escape possible. Third, usually in less intimate social contexts, the schizoid person appears to be naïve and socially unintelligent, and trusts others too easily and gets hurt in the process. What is common to these variations is that the schizoid person has tremendous trouble trusting themself; the schizoid individual does not believe in the efficacy of his own vital powers. This is mainly because they do not have access to their own authentic voice. Since they do not know or feel what really matters to them, they have no access to an inner center of gravity as an animating force in their lives; thus, they are left feeling and acting chameleon-like. As a result of vigorous and exhausting impression management (changing opinions, behavior or appearance according to the circumstances to win others over), they miss the opportunity to enjoy the benefits of authentic intimacy and love or meaningful forms of connection to others.

A high degree of "basic trust," as Erikson called the first stage of psychosocial development that is correlated with Freud's oral stage, is necessary for the average person to sustain a satisfying love relationship. Basic trust is continuous optimism, hope and goodness as it relates to oneself and one's partner (and the world in general) rooted in attuned and trustworthy early parenting. Without basic trust it is unlikely that the average person will be able to function effectively in a love relationship, especially over extended periods and/or when the going gets tough, which it inevitably does. Rather, similar to a child who has had unreliable and often frustrating early parenting, he is prone to "basic mistrust," an outlook that is characterized by marked pessimism, a tendency to disengage or withdraw, a lack of faith and openness, and a generalized suspiciousness. Such negativity undermines one of the most important foundational aspects of any love relationship, the trust in the co-created dream of being able to fashion a flourishing future together. Indeed, as the Axial religiously minded sages tell us, this dream is based not so much on "having" a significant other, but on being grateful for this "gift" that has fallen from Heaven, as it were, and the opportunity to joyfully co-create a blessed life.

### Prone to abusive relationships

The schizoid person has a tendency to have abusive relationships in which dominance and submission is a key dynamic. Sometimes this becomes highly erotically charged and turns into a full-blown, alternating, sadomasochistic relationship in which the schizoid individual fluctuates in assuming both poles of this mode of relation (including in their relationship to themselves). The gist of this power dynamic is that the schizoid person attempts to project onto, and into, his profound hurt and boundless anger, and then attempts to fight, repair or resolve his difficulties with the other. This approach usually fails because the schizoid person is unconscious of his projections and projective identifications, and is therefore bent on repeating his abusive relationships rather than using his increased self-understanding and self-awareness in the service of putting things "right," both in terms of his self and other relation. Sadomasochistic or "master–slave" relationships, as they have been popularly called, characterize a spectrum of exploitive, imprisoning, devouring and manipulating childhood experiences that the schizoid individual has often had to submit to or fantasized submitting to in his childhood. In their adult lives they tend to repeat these self-destructive forms of relating and are prone to "flight" or ill-fated "fight" responses, not realizing that, unlike when they were vulnerable, helpless children, they now have the autonomy and strength to defend themselves in a reasonable and effective manner.

While there is a huge professional and lay literature on the psychology of abusive relationships (including to oneself), for the average person what is most important to know is how to avoid them from the get go. One should be ever mindful of the fact that there are often troubling signs that a potential partner is prone to be abusive, such as their tendency to be extremely controlling, jealous, to blame others, set impossible standards and to be isolationist as a couple. In short, if there are any signs that one's autonomy, integration and humanity are not passionately respected by a potential partner, leave the relationship. Feeling dehumanized, or fearing dehumanization, is one of the worst feelings, whether this takes place in love or work contexts. The gist of such everyday dehumanization is that the person feels objectified. That is, he is treated by others (and/or himself) as less than human and, therefore, he is not entitled to be morally acknowledged or embraced. It is as if he is not a constituent part of the shared human community. Thus, protecting one's autonomy, integration and humanity in the face of dehumanizing assaults should be a central animating value in love and work. This requires that one has lodged their sense of self in moral values and beliefs that one regards as transcendent, as reflecting something "more," "higher" and "better" (Marcus, 1999).

### Feeling undeserving

In contrast to the narcissistic personality, who feels mainly entitled, the schizoid personality feels mainly unentitled. This sense of unworthiness is lodged in the feeling that before he can have access to what he believes everyone has or expects to have, like a loving spouse or significant other, he has to do or be something extra before he feels entitled to what others more comfortably and contentedly achieve or expect to have. This feeling of being unentitled is often reinforced by intrusive fantasized conversations in which the schizoid person tries to fathom what the extra or special thing is he needs to do or be before he can have his "place in the sun," to obtain a position of favor or advantage.

The capacity for the average person to behave in a loving, responsible and competent manner in a love relationship depends on having a reasonable sense of self-esteem and self-worth. Self-esteem, how one views oneself, whether high, low or somewhere in the middle, can negatively impact the infrastructure of a love relationship. For example, low self-esteem is usually correlated with being in a lousy mood, such as feeling down, angry, ashamed and anxious; low self-esteem impacts one's ability to motivate oneself to try and make things better since such a person assumes failure. A person with low self-esteem often feels that he does not merit a good love relationship, often leading to unconscious sabotage as part of a self-fulfilling prophecy. He is unlikely to try new things or venture out of his comfort zone, believing that it is not worth the effort because he will not be successful in the activity. Likewise, such a person is not very resilient, so that when the going gets tough, his pessimism makes effectively reckoning with a challenge unlikely. Finally, low self-esteem is correlated with poor self-care – whether in terms of a poor diet, lack of exercise or sleep deprivation – which reflects a person's lack of self-regard and makes a significant other feel that they are with a person who is giving up on himself and the relationship.[5]

## Some common forms of suffering in love relationships

While psychoanalysts have been masterful in describing many of the problems of giving and receiving love in those individuals with severe character disorders – such as the narcissist, borderline, schizoid, paranoid, antisocial and schizotypal personalities – they have written much less about some of the less clinically extreme, though very distressing, aspects of typical love relationships that cause considerable individual suffering and eventually erode the wholesome relational foundations between ordinary couples, unless, of course corrective actions are taken.

### Asymmetrical and symmetrical relationships

French actress Catherine Deneuve has said that love can frequently be unbalanced, with one person loving more than the other person.[6] Indeed, Deneuve is putting her finger on a common form of distress that people in love relationships have: most of the time they are doing more giving than receiving. Eventually this lack of symmetry erodes their will and ability to comfortably and happily reside in the relationship. The primary difficulty with putting one's emotional needs and desires constantly before one's partner's and responding differently only when it involves little effort is that one's partner feels uncherished. Usually such selfishness is not acknowledged as hurtful or aggressive to their partner; or, worse, they don't care that their behavior is disrespectful and unloving as long as their needs and desires are satisfied. For example, when one spouse is financially reckless, it can undermine the present stability and future security of the marital unit. If a couple with children has agreed on a fair division of labor in parenting and domestic responsibilities, and this working principle is not honored, it often leads to the unsticking of the emotional glue that keeps the couple happily together.

Many individuals complain, including in psychotherapy, that their relationship with their significant other is markedly unbalanced, causing much heartache – even if they have "gotten used to it," as one of my patients told me, and have decided to remain in the relationship for the time being. Enjoyment is replaced by endurance. To understand asymmetry is to understand how power is wielded by one partner over the other. In these asymmetrical contexts there is no "level playing field," that is, the totality of circumstances do not allow for a fair and equal chance of prevailing. As is well known, those on the weaker side of the power dynamic find ways to resist the asymmetry and to "put it right," as they construe such recalibration. Such tactics do not necessarily involve drawing from those wholesome values associated with reinstating symmetry through reciprocity, empathy and apology. Rather, the goal in such negatively based tactics is to reverse the power balance to their advantage, including inflicting punishment on the offending partner as a form of retaliation for perceived subjugation. This is often because their reactions are emanating from a sense of violent and uncontrolled anger. As psychoanalyst Henry Krystal noted, "rage" is "love outraged," that is, when one expects to be cherished but is instead violated (1988, p. 82).

Such rage responses are often connected to feelings of having been humiliated, though they can be linked to other asymmetrical emotions such as envy (e.g., feeling inferior to one's partner), jealousy (e.g., not feeling special enough to one's partner), unrequited affection (e.g., feeling your partner does not love you as much as you love them) and hypocrisy (e.g., treating your partner as you refuse to be treated). There are, of course, a wide range of emotional contexts in which individuals in a love relationship can feel narcissistic rage, a severe wounding to self-esteem and self-worth. This is especially the case for those at the lower registers of personality and relational functioning.

What makes asymmetrical relationships, especially longstanding ones, toxic for a couple is that they tend to generate intense hatred in the person who feels mistreated or victimized by the other's abuse of power. The intermittent rage morphs into perpetual hatred. Trust, the firm belief in the reliability, truth, ability or strength of your partner, has been decisively, if not irreparably, ruptured. In the mind of the weaker partner, the stronger partner uses his power to "force" the other to submit to his will; not because it is reasonably claimed that it would be best for the couple, as can be the case, but because it will advance the interests of the more powerful at the other's expense. Using one's physical superiority, as in classic physical abuse, is an extreme example of this destructive dynamic. However, more typically, the tools of such power-wielding are psychological, such as the threat of abandonment or unrequited love; sexual, such as withholding sex or threatening to have an affair; or material, such as refusing financial support or manipulating monies/property to shortchange the partner. Such power-wielding is often played out within the broader psychological context of an alternating, see-saw, sadomasochistic dynamic, one that becomes the leitmotif of such relationships. One thinks of August Strindberg's 1900 masterpiece, *Dance of Death* (I and II), in which battling spouses can't live with or without each other, perpetually locked into a diabolical marriage. Indeed, there have been hundreds of books written describing such toxic asymmetrical dynamics, emphasizing that there are a multitude of overt and covert, harsh and subtle ways that lovers mistreat, neglect and/or abuse their spouse or partner, often leading to breakup, divorce or perpetual misery.

Most individuals are raised to feel, think and act as if the ideal love relationship is one that is symmetrical. As Darvas (2016) notes, the appeal of relational symmetry is often connected to the Axial notions of beauty, truth and the good that signify affirmative values and praiseworthy beliefs in the arts, sciences and ethics correspondingly. Most importantly, when the relational symmetry is seriously disrupted, especially over an extended period, there are many kinds of emotionally driven actions that are implemented to reinstate relational symmetry. If such tactics are not successful it can lead to intolerable asymmetrical dynamics mentioned above, signaling the beginning of the demise of the relationship. These destructive power dynamics are to be distinguished from "asymmetrical balance," the kind of equilibrium that permits an apology to be judged as fair exchange for a palpable loss.

Symmetrical interactions are based on the conscious and/or unconscious assumption that both partners are equal. In fact, German philosopher/sociologist Theodor Adorno indicated that being able to embrace such an assumption and act accordingly gets to the heart of what love is: "Love is the power to see similarity in the dissimilar" (1951, p. 191). While people are objectively and subjectively different, it is our common humanity (though always respectful of alterity) that is the modulating bridge from one person to another that ultimately makes love between two people possible and enduring. In light of this observation, most people in a love relationship believe in the Axial insight that their relationship should be based on a governing principle of cooperative interchange, the practice of exchanging psychic gains and enhancements, with their partner for mutual benefit. As recorded in the *Analects* (15:24), when Confucius was asked, "Is there a single word such that one can practice it throughout one's life? The Master said: Reciprocity perhaps? Do not inflict on others what you yourself would not wish done to you" (2000, p. 62).

This is probably the first time the Golden Rule, generally regarded as the foundation for empathy in all major religions and many moral systems, was stated in its negative form. The "norm of reciprocity" is a sociological concept that alleges that people should assist those who have assisted them, and they should not assist those who have denied them assistance for no sound reason. In other words, if your partner does something for you, you then feel obligated to return the favor. By reciprocating we safeguard that our partner receives help when they require it and that we receive it when we require it. This is a morality based on a "win-win" outcome, one that ends well for both parties just as it promotes societal stability (Gouldner, 1960). Without a high degree of reciprocity in a love relationship, it is doubtful that a relationship will flourish or even subsist. Pointing out to one's wayward partner how his behavior departs from the norm of reciprocity may be enough to get the disconnect reconnected.

In addition to the value of behaving according to the norm of reciprocity (and encouraging one's partner to do so), what are some of the corrective, emotionally driven actions that occur in a love relationship when it becomes asymmetrical and a partner attempts to reinstate a symmetry, usually psychologically conceived in terms of creating a workable balance, proportion and harmony?

Accurate empathic immersion is a vital process for discerning what is perceived as the same in the self and the other, and thus is necessary to create the sense of mutuality that is so important in love relationships. Empathy, a major concept in psychoanalytic theory and technique, has been defined in two major clinical texts as "the imagining of another's subjective experience through the use of one's own subjective experience" and "the ego's capacity to transiently identify with someone else in order to grasp his or her subjective experience" (Person et al., 2005, p. 551; Akhtar, 2009, p. 93). This being said, while empathy as psychoanalytically defined has its usefulness in terms of reinstating symmetry and mutuality between two lovers, it is a concept that those who are informed by the Axial spirit have enlarged and deepened, which suggests why empathy as defined above may not be enough to "put things right." Something "more," "higher" and "better" is required.

Let's use an evocative example in which a man is caressing a woman he is making love with and his singular goal is not to satiate his lustful sexual urge. Rather, it takes on a very different meaning in which he makes giving the woman pleasure, satisfaction and comfort his priority before he seeks and concentrates on his own. In this context the goal is to bring about the living presence of the one to the other, as a constant responsibility for the other's soul. I am here interested in mapping the subtle co-creative interplay of two subjectivities (Wyschogrod, 2000, p. 131), the sharing of worlds of subjective experience. Martin Buber beautifully captures this form of caress:

> A man caresses a woman, who lets herself be caressed. Then let us assume that he feels the contact from two sides – with the palm of his hand still, and also with the woman's skin. The twofold nature of the

gesture, as one that takes place between two persons, thrills through the depth of enjoyment in his heart and stirs it. If he does not deafen his heart he will have – not to renounce the enjoyment but – to love.

(1965, p. 96)

Buber is here making a crucial point that psychoanalysis misses in its understanding of empathy, or at least underplays the ethically transformative potential of the erotic encounter: the need for a person to be able to "experience the other side" (1965, p. 96).

"Experiencing the other side," says Maurice S. Friedman, Buber's preeminent interpreter, "means to feel an event from the side of the person one meets as well as from one's own side" (2002, p. 102). Most importantly, it involves what Buber calls "inclusiveness," which realizes the other person in the actuality and presentness of his being (Buber, 1965, p. 97). For Buber, inclusiveness should not be confused with the psychoanalytic notion of "empathy," the defining means by which the data of psychoanalysis is collected according to self-psychologists. Empathy, say Buber and Friedman, implies the capacity to "transpose oneself over there and in there," into the dynamic structure of an object, to "the exclusion of one's own concreteness, the extinguishing of the actual situation of life, the absorption in pure aestheticism of the reality in which one participates" (Buber, 1965, p. 97; Friedman, 2002, p. 102). Inclusion, says Buber, is the opposite of this: "It is the extension of one's own concreteness, the fulfillment of the actual situation in life, the complete presence of the reality in which one participates" (1965, p. 97).

Put in more conventional psychological language, following the Axial vision, we can roughly say that such a recast notion of empathy involves both being able to put your self inside the other, without losing your self, while at the same time being able to put the other in yourself without eradicating the other's difference and otherness. How a self's ego is supple enough to incorporate or, more aptly, embrace the other into its experience without having to project anything upon or into the other is not clear; nor is it agreed upon by most psychoanalytic and social psychological theoreticians on empathy.

Another common way that relational symmetry can be reinstated is through a heartfelt apology. An apology is a regretful affirmation of an offense or failure in which what was palpably lost to the aggrieved partner cannot be replaced or restored. In this psychological context, symmetricality is reinstated because the regret of the offender is judged as a counterbalance to the loss inflicted on the hurt partner. Frequently, some form of material compensation (e.g., stereotypically, a bouquet of flowers) and/or emotional reparation (e.g., a hug and kiss) is necessary to facilitate a closer symmetry. Winch (2013) has described five aspects of a sincere apology that clearly convey why an apology can offset the palpable loss and hurt that the aggrieved partner feels. An effective apology involves:

1   a strong "I am sorry" affirmation;
2   a genuine expression of remorse for what one has done wrong;
3   recognition that what is generally regarded as normatively "right" and "expected" behavior has been violated;
4   an empathic expression that clearly indicates that one understands in a detailed manner the negative emotional impact of one's actions on the other person;
5   an appeal for forgiveness.[7]

I would add to Winch's list a "promise" that, to the best of one's ability, what was hurtful to the partner will not happen again. It is through an apology, one in which the aggrieved partner feels that the apology is aimed at making the other feel better and not oneself (though it often does reduce guilt), that what has been psychologically "broken" and/or made "bad" between the persons as a result of one's actions of commission or omission can be made "whole" and "good" again. Through this heartfelt effort at reparation, the relational symmetrical balance, proportion and harmony can be happily reestablished.

It is important to be mindful of the fact that the three ways of effectively reinstating relational symmetry that I have touched upon – reciprocity, empathy and apology – all presuppose three operational assumptions:

1   An individual's dedication and skillfulness in engaging in reasonable and respectful dialogue is guided by a sense of justice, usually referred to as fairness in the intimate context.
2   In relationships that have become asymmetrical, there has been a history of a symmetry of respect and power, as well as a joint wish to remain emotionally linked and attached. This is in contrast to other types of communication that are not symmetrical and tend to be destructive – like those animated by anger, revenge, humiliation or unfairness – and are geared to get the other to submit to one's will or other self-serving motivations. Indeed, the Axial sages were well aware of these radically different forms of communication, and, even more importantly to them, the contrasting ways of being-in-the-world that these divergent communicative practices were lodged in and emanated from.
3   Axial sages have always emphasized the transcendent significance of other-directed, other-regarding and other-serving communication as the way to "put things right," to restore "wholeness" and "goodness" between lovers and, for that matter, in all communications with others. Such creative and healing ways of communicating point to transcendence because they suggest a different and ethically enhanced way of viewing reality.

## Asymmetrical relationships revisited

As I have said, following the Axial model, symmetrical relationships are built on the love commandment, the Golden Rule: "Thou shalt love thy neighbor as thyself." While Freud and most other psychoanalytic theorists embrace the love commandment as one of the important guiding metaphors of the ideal love relationship, such a view may not go far enough, at least in terms of what the Axial vision suggests is the "royal road" to "something more," "something higher" and "something better" between two people in a love relationship. That is, while reciprocity is a praiseworthy guiding ethic in relationships, there are some Axial thinkers, particularly those lodged in the Hebrew wisdom/spiritual tradition, who have taken this guiding ethic further that informs the potentially transcendent dimension of asymmetrical relationships. In this view, asymmetrical relationships are not morally degrading "power plays" or other attempts to dominate, but life-affirming instantiations of what is most morally praiseworthy about emotionally attached human beings. As Levinas pointed out, the love commandment "still assumes the prototype of love to be love of oneself," that is, "self-love is accepted as the very definition of a person." Rather, Levinas's conception of the ethical subject asserts, "be responsible for the other as you are responsible for yourself" (Levinas, 1987, p. 225). Levinas thus invites us to consider the cultivation of "goodness" as our guiding metaphor. Drawing from biblical thought and its rabbinical commentaries, he asserts that "[g]oodness consists in taking up a position such that the Other counts more than myself" (Levinas, 1969, p. 247).[8] Such an ethical ideal that emphasizes "taking upon oneself of the fate of the other" (Robbins, 2001, p. 165) goes beyond the commandment to love in that it demands an even greater transformation of one's narcissism toward a responsibility for the other calculus. "I suffer, therefore you are," said Elie Wiesel in his depiction of this ethical outlook (Berenbaum, 1994, p. 139). This way of conceptualizing love and personhood has practical ramifications for relationships that I will discuss shortly.

The typical psychoanalyst might claim that Levinas's notion of love as roughly equated to the cultivation of goodness is a viewpoint that smacks of masochism, or at least inordinate self-denial and self-sacrifice. This form of self-negation is precisely what Freud was criticizing in *Civilization and its Discontents* in his discussion of the love commandment, especially its Christian interpretation.

As Wyschogrod has pointed out, such a charge does not adequately appreciate to what extent Levinas is advocating a "remarkable transvaluation of values" (2000, p. xvi). Like Nietzsche and Foucault, Levinas is proposing revolutionizing the dominating tendencies and sentiments, the ways of thinking and being of our age. Levinas, says Wyschogrod, is not advocating submissiveness as analysts usually construe the term, as merely giving in to the demands or the authority of the other. Rather, for Levinas "submissiveness is

reinstated as self-donation" (ibid.). With Levinas we are dealing with a radically different notion of the self, of the I, one that I think needs to be included
in any psychoanalytic version of the human condition (and embraced by
others as well), for it locates the person first and foremost, as an ethical subject seeking out the "Good." The ethical subject is struggling to transform the
very conditions, the form of his life, such that his capacity to love the other is
deepened, expanded and, finally, is his ultimate concern: "the self is a *sub-
jectum*; it is under the weight of the universe, responsible for everything"
(Levinas, 1998, p. 116). Moreover, says Levinas, "Perhaps the possibility of a
point of the universe where such an overflow of responsibility is produced
ultimately defines the I" (1969, p. 244).

As I have argued elsewhere (Marcus, 2008), the Levinasian view of love
challenges the psychoanalytic theorizing of Freud, Klein, Erikson, Kohut and
Lacan, as well as most relational thinkers who have written on the subject. It
does so in two ways. First, a Levinasian outlook challenges the notion of
selfhood that underlies these theories, man as first and foremost egocentric
and self-centric in outlook and behavior.[9] Instead, as Atterton and Calarco
point out, Levinas claims that "the relationship of responsibility for the Other
is just as early, if not earlier than egoism" (2005, p. 72). Levinas's main
objective has been to create "a metaphysics upon ethical foundations by
showing man's being in the world to be moral being," a "moral self"
(Wyschogrod, 2000, pp. 228, 229). Second, in part as a consequence of this
ego-centered version of self, love relations tend to be viewed in terms of two
related forms of questionable approaches toward the other.

First, love relations are conceptualized essentially as hedonistic and utilitarian, with the other viewed as a need-satisfying object: how can the other
pleasure me; what can the other do for me? Freud's view of love tended to
embrace such an outlook. Second, in an improved variation on this conceptualization, in the work of Rubin (1996, p. 49) and Benjamin (1995, p. 29),
love relations are viewed largely in terms of a mutual instrumental calculus of
two equal subjects who appreciate the uniqueness of each other, and give each
other satisfaction. This surely goes further than the strict hedonistic-utilitarian
view in that it acknowledges the other as unique in terms of desires, goals,
values and needs, and it makes satisfying those needs as important: "I am for
you, you are for me" (Robbins, 2001, p. 193). This is the love relation as
symmetrically conceived. For Levinas, such a relational ethic is serviceable
but does not go far enough, for it mistakenly treats entering the ethical realm
(i.e., of moral principles) with becoming "good" (i.e., responsibility for the
other); the latter way of being-in-the-world points to transcendence.

For Levinas, while such a reciprocal approach moves in the direction of
relating to the other as other, this view still subtly retains the wish to make
the other the same, to totalize the other, and thus to open him or her up to
disrespect, disregard, de-individuation and other forms of intersubjective violence. Such an ontologically based approach seeks to comprehend the

otherness of the other by including him under a notion "that is thought within *me*, and thus is in some sense *the same* as me" (Atterton & Calarco, 2005, p. 10). To the extent that the other is construed in terms of his or her Being and is comprehended and thematized on the basis of what he or she has in common with other beings, the other becomes conceptually the same as others, and therefore loses his uniqueness and individuality.[10] According to Levinas, to comprehend the other in this way is roughly equivalent "to predicting, manipulating, controlling, even dominating the Other" (ibid., pp. 15, 16).

Instead of approaching the other in terms of ontology, of knowing and comprehension, Levinas offers an ethical approach that always strives to respect the radical alterity of the other: "The relation with the other is a relation with Mystery" (1987, p. 75). The consequences of this viewpoint are profound for understanding the limitations of the psychoanalytic theories of love. They point us in the direction in which I think psychoanalytic theory, as well as people who have knowingly or unknowingly embraced such an outlook in their practical lives, should go.

Psychoanalytic theory tends to assume that from birth the self is concerned only, and later, mainly, with itself. This is the form of self-love that Freud called "primary narcissism." Given this assumption about the human condition, one would therefore require a rationale, a compelling reason to be moral. That is, to love as responsibility for the other. This is precisely the assumption and formulation that Levinas rejects. Instead, he vigorously claims that the question, "Am I first and foremost responsible for the Other?" is a question that makes sense only within a version of the human condition that is lodged in a philosophy of ontology and human reason. In contrast, for Levinas, the self has no such freedom to choose with regard to responsibility for the other. The Levinasian self does not need a rationale to be moral: "Responsibility is what is incumbent on me exclusively, and what *humanly*, I cannot refuse" (Levinas, 1985, p. 101; Atterton & Calarco, 2005, p. 71).

Perhaps most importantly, at least as it relates to the reciprocity–mutuality assumption lodged in certain symmetrical relational views of love, I am responsible for the other without the other being responsible for me in return. It may well be reasonable to assume that the other has responsibilities toward me, but I can never discern this for sure: "Reciprocity is *his* affair" (Levinas, 1985, p. 98; Atterton & Calarco, 2005, p. 30). Thus, the other's actions toward you must not be the criterion of your conduct toward him. I am obligated to tend to the other's needs without expecting emotional or other forms of payback. This is asymmetrical love. Says Levinas, "We are all guilty of all and for all men before all, and I more than the others" (1985, p. 98).

## The "antidote" to the suffering of love[11]

Lodged in the Axial Jewish tradition of the Bible and the Talmud, Levinas, more than most modern philosophers, has written perceptively about love, conceived as responsibility for the other before oneself. While his altruistic descriptions are inspiring, they do not adequately address the problems that such "for the other" loving entails on an everyday, real-life basis. For most of us, it is hard enough to live according to the Golden Rule, a moral conception that has been challenged as deeply flawed by Kant, Nietzsche and, most recently, by British writer Iain King (2008). To love our significant other more than we love ourselves, to put her needs and desires before our own, especially in a sustained manner, seems like an impossible challenge. In fact, the philosopher John D. Caputo claims Levinas "weaves a fabulous, poetic story about absolute alterity," which ultimately is not credible (Poole, 1998, p. 71). Certainly, most of us can remember times when we acted altruistically, but such moments tend to be the exception rather than the rule. That every major Axial-based religious tradition makes selfless love its ideal, the personification of what is best, most divine, speaks to the difficulties of achieving such a mode of relatedness.

To be capable of sustained selfless love requires not just the willingness to give, nurture and comfort; it also requires the capacity to contain, if not sublimate, the opposite wishes, the "dark side" of oneself, the selfishness and the hostility that is the basis for so much relational suffering. This is one of Freud's great insights, that the love relation is fundamentally an ambivalent one, reflecting the metaphorical struggle between Eros and Thanatos. Levinas was aware of this when he wrote about "the ambiguity of love," the fact that love simultaneously involves need and desire, physicality and spirituality, immanence and transcendence, ontology and ethics. Love is impossible to pin down; to abide forever, it "ceaselessly escapes" the solicitor, it "slips away" (Levinas, 1969, pp. 254–255, 257).

While Levinas is aware of the fragility of the love relation, his observations and descriptions are sanitized, at least to this psychoanalyst. In contrast, Germaine Greer, in *The Female Eunuch*, has superbly, though harshly, captured the essence of what both Freud and, to a lesser extent, Levinas were getting at – the difficulties, if not the impossibility, of sustaining a love relationship in real life:

> Love, love, love – all the wretched cant of it, masking egotism, lust, masochism, fantasy under a mythology of sentimental postures, a welter of self induced miseries and joys, blinding and masking the essential personalities in the frozen gestures of courtship, in the kissing and the dating and the desire, the compliments and the quarrels which vivify its barrenness.
>
> (Greer, 1970, p. 72)

Greer is overstating the matter, as most people do not experience their beloved spouse or significant other with such negativity. That being said, what are some of the psychological hindrances to achieving a more selfless mode of relatedness with one's significant other? What forms of self-inflicted suffering stand in the way of a more bountiful and generous expression of love and goodness, enacted as being responsible for the other before oneself?

### Levinasian love

In a number of revealing and thoughtful interviews (Robbins, 2001), Levinas tells us what he thinks the nature of love is, including its "essence" and its "perfection." To Levinas, love is not merely a strong feeling, it is an obligation; authentic love does not mainly strive after union and fusion; it always respects the other's radical otherness and cherishes the other as unique. Love is not primarily characterized by mere mutual pleasure giving and reciprocal affirmation; rather, it is expressed as acts of goodness for the sake of the other's best interests, often requiring self-sacrifice.

For Levinas then, love is conceived as responsibility for the other, such that the other's being and death are more important than one's own. This, he suggests, may be "the human vocation in being" (Robbins, 2001, p. 250). Such responsibility for the other, says Levinas, is a kind of "madness"; it is "an absurd thesis" (ibid., p. 108). I do not know if Levinas's claim is mad or absurd, but it does seem far-fetched both historically and at present. After all, in a certain sense, as with Adam and Eve, the story of love is often a "tale of a fall from harmony into chaos and disorder" (Spiegelman, 2002, Part 1, p. 26).

How does Levinas's heady notion of love as entailing a fundamental responsibility for the other play out in everyday relations between adults? To briefly answer this important question I ask the reader to keep in mind the above list of Levinas's key terms that describe his notion of love. Following Levinas, there are two figures in the real world who perhaps best depict the inner attitude and outer behavior of persons capable of living their love as responsibility for the other: first, the devoted mother, or caregiver; second, the master teacher. The devoted mother is known through her boundless self-sacrifice, compassion and forgiveness for her children, while the master teacher facilitates in his students the birth of a new self, a better self, a self that is capable of actualizing the best of its intellectual, emotional and moral capacity. What both of these authentic figures of responsibility ideally express is that they are devoted to the other's best interests before their own.

### Two primary hindrances to love: narcissism and aggression

Somewhat like the great English romantic poet Percy Bysshe Shelley, Freud depended on the notion "of Eros as the impelling spirit that rolls through all things and all human consciousness" (Spiegelman, 2002, Part 2, p. 15). Indeed, for Freud, the drive theorist, man is fundamentally pleasure-seeking and lives in an erotically tinged universe. That being said, Freud and all of his subsequent followers were mainly concerned with what gets in the way of the wide and deep expression of Eros and causes relational suffering. Eros is defined more broadly than as the sexual instincts, but rather as a poetic metaphor for the affirming life force. While this subject could be the basis of another twenty-four volumes of Freud's *Standard Edition*, I wish to focus on two key hindrances to the proper expression of Eros – namely, inordinate narcissism (selfishness) and aggression (hostility). Indeed, Melanie Klein, one of Freud's great disciples, the originator of object-relations theory, noted that the main human struggle is "between love and hate, between care and concern for others and their malicious destruction" (Alford, 1998, p. 120). Let us take a closer look at these two interconnected hindrances to Eros.

### Inordinate narcissism

Levinas, like Freud, assumed that man is fundamentally egotistical. Man takes his own needs and desires as most important, and in most instances he thinks about the other second. In many cultures, human beings seem to be mainly for themselves. Altruistic behavior, even everyday kindness like someone holding the door open for you, is so striking because it is rare. In a simple gesture of courtesy, the other's respect and dignity is affirmed.

Why are people typically so self-centered and selfish? Following Buddha, it is due to the "three poisons": greed, hatred and delusion. In psychoanalytic terminology, greed mainly refers to the wish to aggressively possess all the goodness of the other; hatred refers to the persistent wish to injure or destroy the despised other; and delusion refers to holding to a false or unchallengeable conviction about the other and/or about the workings of the world. To the extent that these "poisons" are not modulated, one is likely to be self-centered and hostile in outlook and behavior. As I have suggested earlier, beyond the basic human inclination to be absorbed in the three poisons is early inadequate parenting and other harmful childhood experiences. Such experiences force the person to circle the wagons, as it were, and to assume an inordinate self-protective and self-referential mode of being in the world. Within the context of an intimate relation, often this mode of being has a psychologically "violent" feel to it, both in its active mode of aggressive and mean-spirited expression and in its passive mode of emotional withdrawal and passive-aggression.

For example, in greed, as Greenberg and Mitchell point out (1983, pp. 128–129), the needy and dependent person wants to obtain all the contents, the love and nurturance, of the good other, regardless of its impact on the other. Like the farmer in Aesop's famous fable of "The Goose with the Golden Eggs," it is irrelevant what terrible harm can befall the other as a result of his greed. Upon killing and opening the golden goose, the farmer found nothing, hoping to find gold. Most often, the greedy person experiences the other's nurturance and goodness as inadequate and begrudges, if not greatly resents, his control over it. For instance, the husband who wants his wife to tend to him and becomes furious if she does not is reacting like an entitled infant who expects his mother to nurture him on demand, to be perfect. In the mind of the regressed husband, his wife is withholding and selfish, and thus becomes all "bad," which is the basis for his fury.

In hatred, as Rycroft has pointed out (1968, p. 61), the person has a sustained wish to harm or kill the hated other (in contrast to anger, which is a passing feeling). Whether the wish to harm is directed at a hated or loved other, whether it is a sustained or transient wish, according to Freud, hate is most often a response to threats to the ego's stability and integrity, though in his later writings he viewed it as an expression of the Death Instinct. In other words, in general, most forms of hatred as they play out in ordinary love relations are a response to frustration and conflict pertaining to one's narcissistic need to be respected, valued and loved. Most often, however, these needs are inordinate and produce hatred in the aggrieved person who experiences his significant other as unreasonably, if not arbitrarily, depriving. So, for example, a needy and dependent woman who experiences her husband as distracted and fundamentally ungratifying of her need to be cherished may develop a deep sense of resentment of him, leading to endless skirmishes and more serious relationship problems.

Finally, we come to delusion, a persistent false belief held in the face of strong contradictory evidence. Delusion is a more subtle poison in intimate relationships. There are many common delusions that people hold in their love relationships. For example, the man who believes that his wife should be all things to him all the time, that she should always be perky and happy, his antidepressant, as it were, has unrealistic expectations. As I have noted earlier, according to St. Augustine it is a mistake to expect more from a particular object of love than its unique nature can provide. Such "disordered love" is usually anxiety-ridden, frightened, greedy and clinging. In contrast, "rightly ordered love" allows us to evaluate things according to their proper value and priority; it helps us to generate reasonable and appropriate goals, desires, and actions for the pursuit of what we love.

Quite simply, the goal of psychoanalysis is to view things in terms of their "true" nature: to transform greed into generosity, hatred into loving-kindness and delusion into realistic thinking. To accomplish this is no easy task, for it requires the transformation of the substructure that supports this self- and other-destructive mode of being in the world – the prison-house of the selfish self. It requires the subversion of one's narcissistic identification with one's unreasonable desires; the irrational, often child-based feelings and thoughts that we are utterly bound to, that constitute the "I," that tend to subvert proper ego functioning and pollute the very core of the person. Only when one has modulated one's selfish cravings, or what is referred to as "infantile narcissism" in psychoanalytic parlance, by reconfiguring one's subjectivity along less self-centered lines, can the main hindrances to love, at least as Levinas conceives of it, be overcome.

*Inadequately modulated aggression*

One of the main difficulties of accomplishing a reconfiguring of one's sub-jectivity from self-centric to other-directed is due to the second great hin-drance to love – aggression, the irrational, self-subverting human propensity to hurt those we love. As one gets older, it becomes increasingly apparent just how limited, flawed and downright deficient one's behavior is in one's love relation, a self-awareness that is the basis for much suffering. Following Freud, we can say that many people "are born with limited capacities to pursue the good, and left to our own devices all of us will betray ourselves and our fellow man" (Pattison, 1988, p. 89). Nietzsche, a predecessor to Freud in many ways, and someone whom the young Freud greatly admired, put the matter more severely by describing man as "the cruelest of animals" (Assoun, 2000, p. 151). Thus, it is not altogether surprising that human rela-tionships are often infiltrated by man's "dark side," by the "three poisons" and other forms of destructive emotions, thoughts and, most importantly, behavior. Put straightforwardly, we are all fundamentally flawed beings, often inclined toward selfishness, impatience, dishonesty, envy and cruelty in our relationships, including love relationships.

The one aspect of human aggression expressed within love relations that I want to elaborate further is the fact that almost always the aggression direc-ted at one's significant other reflects the perpetrator's wish that the other person be what he wants her to be. We all suffer, at least to some extent, from what in the surgeon's world of elective plastic surgery is called the Pygmalion Complex – the zealous, if not obsessive, wish to make beautiful and perfect people, according to what we think they should be. This belief or wish, or arguably a demand, is rooted in an inflated infantile narcissism, a kind of hypertrophied pride, that unashamedly asserts that the universe, which includes one's significant other, is not fashioned as it "should" be – that is, as one wants it to be; therefore, the significant other must be reconfigured, with oneself as God, the Creator. In this view, deployment of aggression in the most rudimentary sense boldly expresses the narcissistic claim that one is essentially self-sufficient, self-sustaining and self-dependent, and that one does not need anyone or anything, except to the extent that one can use the other to feed one's infantile, pleasure-seeking, self-aggrandizing desires. Put simply, within the context of intimate relationships, aggression is almost always a way of "strong-arming" the other, the satellite in one's orbit, to affirm the perpe-trator's narcissistic grandiose self as the Creator. Aggression is thus a form of self-valorization and glorification; it is an aggressive selfishness (Assoun, 2000, pp. xxxiv, 61).

Thus, we can say that one of the goals of analysis is a re-education of moral identity (Assoun, 2000, p. xxxviii). By this I mean transforming the moral being, sublimating one's primitive, destructive narcissism/aggression into more "for the other" ways of being in the world. In this view, following

Levinas, sublimation – one of the hallmarks of any "successful" analysis – is conceived as a fundamentally ethical process, the channeling of selfish and hostile impulses and energies into activities regarded as more socially acceptable. This is the main ingredient that constitutes the antidote to much relational suffering.

### Levinas vs. Freud on love

As the reader must sense by now, my two intellectual lights, Freud and Levinas, have rather different views about what constitutes adult love and what is possible to sustain between two people who reside in what they call a love relation. Let's attempt to bridge their seemingly divergent views for a workable formulation that can help *real* people in *real* love relationships reduce their relational suffering. Such a view reflects Freud's "paradoxical proposition," as he called it, "that the normal man is not only far more immoral than he believes but also far more moral than he knows" (Freud, 1923, p. 52).

Levinas's conception of love rests on an assumption about the human condition that is at odds with Freud. He says, "I speak of responsibility as the essential, primary and fundamental structure of subjectivity" (Levinas, 1985, p. 95). In other words, we are "hardwired" to be responsible for the other. As I have pointed out elsewhere, for the psychoanalyst such a view sounds implausible (Marcus, 2008). Indeed, Levinas does not really tell us that he knows with certainty how to effectively substantiate his bold claim. This lack of adequate substantiation, or at least clarification, is noteworthy, especially when we appreciate a crucial feature of language: meaning is not fixed, but is emergent, tied to specific situations and constantly changing. Thus, the concept of responsibility, like any concept or term, cannot itself convey to us how it is to be properly used. There is no set of rules or instructions that intrinsically come with the concept; it is open-ended and revisable. Therefore, if the proper usage of a term or concept like responsibility is simply the usage communally judged to be proper, and is no more predetermined than idiosyncratic individual usage, then the "essential, primary and fundamental" nature of responsibility is questionable and ethically troubling. Put more starkly, if the meaning of language is really no more stable than the particular situations it may be used to describe, then one could conceivably claim that the Nazis were acting in a manner that reflected "responsibility for the other" in killing the Jews who were "destroying" the Aryan nation. That the concept of responsibility for the other is radically philosophical, without a fixed ethical meaning, and, as such, open to abuse, is not, to my knowledge, addressed by Levinas.

A second psychoanalytically oriented criticism of Levinas's claim that "responsibility for the Other is an essential, primary and fundamental structure of subjectivity" is that the notion of the other is not something we come into the world with (Marcus, 2008). So far as we know, the infant only apprehends or "knows" that there is an "other" well after birth, about five to nine months if you accept Margaret Mahler's separation and individuation theory (Mahler et al., 1973).[12] Therefore, to speak of "responsibility for the Other" as "hardwired" does not take into consideration that the infant's sense of the "other" is a later developmental acquisition. Even more troubling is the fact that an infant's notion of "responsibility" as conventionally understood, and certainly in a Levinasian ethical sense, is an even later developmental acquisition. This raises the question of whether it is reasonable to claim that "responsibility for the Other" is an essential, primary and fundamental structure of subjectivity.

Though such criticisms of Levinas are not easily or convincingly answered, the fact is that Levinas is correctly capturing a dimension of the adult-to-adult love experience, at least in its ideal form: "responsibility for the other is the grounding moment of love" (Levinas in Robbins, 2001, p. 133); but only its grounding moment, not its sum and substance in everyday reality. There is a real–ideal dichotomy that Levinas's description of love does not adequately address or resolve. Most people do not seem to relate to their significant other, at least in a sustained way, the way Levinas describes love. The "I" of the mature person will recognize such a conception as a valid ideal but not an easily reachable goal, to put it mildly. As Jean-Paul Sartre said, every book is an attempt to improve one's biography, and one wonders if Levinas's idealistic descriptions of love reflect the way he would wish love relationships to be, rather than the way they most often play out in real life. Love relations, like all human relationships, are messy and complicated, laced with contradictory feeling and attitudes, as Freud has noted and as most honest and self-aware people will tell you.

In contrast to Levinas, Freud's view of love is driven, if not limited, by his guiding assumption that man is fundamentally egotistical and pleasure-seeking. For Freud, all forms of love are seen as derivatives of instinct, and their function is to give instinctual gratification. In a sense, all love is love of a need-satisfying object. Mature object love – in contrast to infantile, dependent, need-satisfying love – is love that recognizes the reality of the other, his otherness, and that he is a separate person with needs and wishes requiring and deserving gratification. Perhaps most importantly, for Freud the capacity for mature love requires object constancy, the capability to maintain an enduring relationship with a specific, single, separate other. This, in turn, presupposes the development of both a stable, structurally sound, coherent self and secure internalized object relations. Normal love, says Freud, thus results from the blending of caring, affectionate and sexual feelings toward a person of the opposite sex. Its accomplishment is characterized by genital primacy in sexuality and by object love in relationships with others. (Freud's heterosexual bias is exemplified. The term "significant other" could be used as a replacement for "opposite sex.")

For Freud, however, to accomplish this is not simple, for it requires resolving at a higher level of personality integration at least three aspects of love:

"narcissistic versus object love, infantile versus mature love, and love versus hate" (Moore & Fine, 1990, p. 113). To the extent that love is dominated by inordinate, unhealthy and pathological narcissism (e.g., self-centeredness and selfishness), infantile and dependent wishes and behavior (e.g., the other exists mainly to gratify one's needs and wishes on demand) and hate (e.g., heightened ambivalence), one's love relation is doomed to failure, or at least much suffering. To the extent that it is animated by altruistic concerns (e.g., enhancing the other), is mature (e.g., recognizes that the separate other has needs and wishes worthy of gratifying) and is mainly affectionate (e.g., not corrupted by aggression), it is likely to succeed. For Freud, while all relationships are ambivalent, the ultimate precondition for maintaining a stable, healthy, mature love relation is that affectionate sentiments toward one's significant other be much stronger and more pervasive than the aggressive ones.

Thus, we have two formulations of the nature of love: for Levinas, love is responsibility for the other before oneself, whereas for Freud, love is the love of a need-satisfying object (i.e., significant other). Is there a way to converge these two valid but incomplete views of love to reduce relational suffering? How can Freud's more realistic description of love as essentially ambivalent be joined with Levinas's ideal, "for the other" formulation?[13]

### "Moment love" – love viewed as a dialectical tension

The capacity for a sustained love relation depends on a number of factors as described above, perhaps the most important being the ability to "manage" one's ambivalence. Love requires the mingling or balancing of opposites: for example, closeness versus distance, dependence versus independence and, of course, affection versus hostility. The latter opposites are the sharpest expression of ambivalence, a derivative of the love–death (Eros–Thanatos) struggle that underlies all the love relations. Exactly how most people accomplish the reasonable balancing of such opposites, of which these are only a few, is not exactly clear, though no progression in a love relation is likely to occur without doing so. Put simply, unless one can live within the dialectical tension between Eros and Thanatos, with a tilt toward the positive side of the ambivalence, toward Eros, one is not going to be able to adequately sustain a love relation with a significant other.

If love is potentially redeeming, if it is so utterly self-, other- and life-affirming, why then must love be a "moment love," when love and the redemptive vision of love are present, though interspersed with times when the difficult, if not hellish, aspects of the love relation dominate (Greenberg, 1977, pp. 33, 27)? How does one keep the redemptive vision of love alive and present in the face of its death-tinged opposite?

The answer is that one must to learn to reside in what William Wordsworth called the "border states," the space between love and death. This imaginary place, the boundary between two people, which I call "moment love/moment death," is best known by its experienced paradoxes (Carnes, 1989, p. 245). For example, "fidelity to oneself" leads to being faithful to the other; recognizing and admitting personal limitations and faults creates a deeper understanding and acceptance of the other's limits and inadequacies; honesty with oneself fosters greater realism with the other; to be reasonably loving of oneself liberates new caring capacities that can be utilized for the best interests of the other; to nurture oneself creates new resources of support for the other. And, of course, to do all of these things encourages the significant other to be "forgiving, realistic, honest, loving and nurturing" in return. While for Levinas, being for the other should not be based on the expectation of reciprocity, as then it is fundamentally self-love, the fact is that most love relations in the practical realm operate according to the norm of reciprocity – "I do for you, you do for me" – and are not asymmetrical or selfless, as Levinas wants.

This is where Levinas and Freud disagree. From my clinical and life experience, Freud, sadly, seems to be more accurate than Levinas, at least pertaining to our current era. Most of us are not saints, not even nearly so, as our love is fundamentally selfish. This is not as bad as it sounds, because the "right" behavior – acting lovingly though for the "wrong" reason, narcissistic gratification – is better than acting unlovingly. Indeed, from a psychoanalytic point of view, all selfless acts have some kind of narcissistic "payoff," though the predominant motivation – being for oneself versus being for the other – is an important difference in terms of individual psychology. In a certain sense, in a love relation what most counts is behavior, not motivation.

There are three essential elements in a high-functioning adult love relation, elements that must animate the imaginary border space of "moment love/ moment death" such that the death-tinged forces do not overwhelm and destroy workable love: hope, faith and forgiveness. A brief elaboration of these three key interrelated elements that have been under-researched in the psychological literature is a fitting way to conclude this chapter.

## The redemptive triad to love's suffering: hope, faith and forgiveness

Levinas's claim that "responsibility for the other is the grounding moment of love" is certainly plausible; but for responsibility to survive and flourish, it needs to be grounded in or fueled by something equally if not more personally summoning. Perhaps the best defense against ambivalence in a love relation – the ever-present shadow of Thanatos – is a mindfully held counter-vision, a new way of thinking, imagining and valuing of the other. This counter-vision is, in part, characterized by infinite hope, "a passion for what is possible," as Søren Kierkegaard described it (Barth, 1995, p. 63), faith, an attitude of openness, especially to the truth, fused with absolute trust and, finally, perhaps the ultimate expression of love and reparation, forgiveness, the capacity for pardoning the significant other for a mistake or wrongdoing directed toward oneself.

As Levinas noted, "[t]he other is ... the first rational teaching, the condition of all teaching" (1969, pp. 171, 203). Elie Wiesel has aptly rendered one of the important meanings of Levinas's hard-to-understand claim that the other is the teacher, as it relates to the psychology of hope within a love relationship: "just as despair can come to one only from other human beings, hope, too, can be given only by other human beings" (quoted in Edgoose, 2008, p. 110). Hope, that necessary sense of destination to somewhere better, the space between dreams and reality, that imaginative victory over experience, is an unrefusable obligation if a love relationship is to endure. Moreover, paradoxically, hope is also the reward for one's faith in the other, in the other's infinite goodness.

Erik Erikson has aptly made a similar point in describing hope as the essential "ego virtue" that emerges after a successful negotiation of the psychosocial stage of infancy he calls "basic trust versus basic mistrust." Says Erikson, hope "is the enduring belief in the attainability of fervent wishes, in spite of the dark urges and rages which mark the beginning of existence" (1964, p. 118). Moreover, as hope is cultivated by the parents' deep and abiding faith that what the child does has significance and is "good," the child's overall feeling of hopefulness will eventually be transformed into adult faith, a self-assurance that does not require either evidence or reason that the universe is essentially trustworthy and benign (ibid., p. 153).

In other words, within a love relation, the lover ideally has a deeply internalized sense of hope and its mature derivative faith that helps animate, if not sustain, the relationship, especially during hard times. Moreover, as Erich Fromm has noted, while hope means to be prepared at every moment for that which is not yet born, it also means not becoming frantic if there is no birth during the course of one's love relation. To love, says Fromm (1956), requires dedication without ultimate assurance, to give of oneself wholeheartedly in the deep and abiding hope that one's love will evoke love in the loved other. Such love is a faith affirmation, and without such faith, there is very little love.

Faith, like its cousin hope, pertains to things not actually seen between two people, "a passionate intuition," as Wordsworth described it. Similar to hope, faith often tends to originate or, at least is most sharply perceived, in the darkness. It is often a response to difficulties in a relationship. Indeed, as Abraham Joshua Heschel noted, the essence of faith is faithfulness to a moment, fidelity to a self- and other-consecrating event, to a transforming response between two people that reveals the awesome, mysterious, ineffable goodness of the other, the basis for trust in the future (1955, pp. 132, 155). This faith gives one the strength of waiting, the patient acceptance of the other's concealment of his goodness during hard times in a relationship. Faith, in other words, evokes a sense of daring confidence that love is stronger than death, what in religious circles is called God's grace. As religious scholar Huston Smith wrote (1979), faith reflects the human tendency "to see, to feel, to act in terms of a transcendent dimension," to sense meaning and significance that is more than ordinary and commonplace. Faith is vital to maintaining a love relationship and living, for it provides it with "coherence and direction," it connects one to "shared trusts and loyalties," it existentially "grounds" one's "personal stances and loyalties in a sense of relatedness to a larger frame of reference," and it helps people to cope adequately with the "limit conditions" and inevitable suffering of existence, all by using compelling psychological resources that have a sense of "ultimacy" and transcendence (Shafranske, 1996, p. 168).

Finally, we come to forgiveness, the pardoning of the other's misdeeds when one feels mistreated. Indeed, as the well-known saying goes, "there is no love without forgiveness and no forgiveness without love." Forgiveness expresses the renewal of hope that is essential to any workable love relation. Indeed, in a love relation we all periodically feel hard done by, that is, narcissistically assaulted, or at least disrespected in terms of what we think we should be getting from our significant other – greater care, more accurate empathy, willingness to sacrifice and the like. Such narcissistic assaults tend to foster resentment, anger, revenge and other forms of aggression that are common in intimate relationships in some form. However, the capacity to forgive, the compassionate reconfiguration of thought and feeling about the other that forgiveness requires, generates a new moral context for the interpretation of the other's hurtful behavior. When the aggrieved person chooses to give up *his* resentment, even hatred of the perpetrator for his misdeed, it signifies that he is, in effect, willing to deal with the pain that underlies the narcissistic rage evoked by his significant other's misdeed. Forgiveness increases one's range of alternatives just as it enhances one's freedom to grow and develop. It is the basis for the healing process that needs to occur to keep a love relation from disintegrating as a result of our all too human capacity to be destructive to our loved other. As Voltaire said, "every man is guilty of all the good he didn't do" (Klosterman, 2006, p. 263).

Sustaining a love relation, let alone one that is "for the other," as Levinas has in mind, is no easy accomplishment. For living and loving according to a regulative principle of "responsibility for the other," of being for the other before oneself, requires considerable modulation and sublimation of the human tendency to be inordinately narcissistic and aggressive, that is aggressively selfish. Moreover, love requires the development of the mature capacity for hope, faith and forgiveness, these being necessary to support the love relation, a relation that is always fragile given the ubiquity of ambivalence. For love to flourish one must adequately negotiate the dialectical tension of "love-death," to give up the controlling fantasy/demand that there is anything more than "moment love/moment death." One must be willing and able to go through a lot of suffering to love well.

This vision of love relations may strike the reader as excessively gloomy, but one should take some comfort in the words of the great American

Protestant theologian Reinhold Niebuhr, words that hearken back to the Axial Age and remind us that while sustaining a love relation has its enormous difficulties, it is also the answer to our ultimate questions, especially those involving personal transformation. Even better, it is an eternally renewable resource for those who have the necessary self-understanding and self-mastery to cultivate other-directed, other-regarding and other-serving love:

> Nothing worth doing is completed in our lifetime.
> Therefore, we are saved by hope.
> Nothing true or beautiful or good makes complete sense in any immediate context of history. Therefore, we are saved by faith.
> Nothing we do, however virtuous, can be accomplished alone. Therefore, we are saved by love.
> No virtuous act is quite as virtuous from the standpoint of our friend or foe as from our own. Therefore, we are saved by the final form of love which is forgiveness.
>
> (Niebuhr, 1952, p. 63)

## Notes

1 The concept of love (and love relationships) is radically philosophical; what constitutes love depends on one's theoretical frame of reference. Moreover, what one takes to be instantiations of love will differ depending on one's philosophical and psychological assumptions and overall narrational perspective. Unraveling this is beyond the scope of this book. My notion of love is situated in the Axial vision, namely, that the "highest" form of love is being for the other before, or at least as much as, oneself. In contemporary philosophy, the work of French/Jewish ethical philosopher Emmanuel Levinas best depicts this outlook, one that is in sync with psychoanalysis as I understand it (Marcus, 2008). This being said, as Karl Jaspers notes, any form of psychoanalysis and psychotherapy has to be regarded as "a philosophical effort and must be examined from the point of view of ethics and metaphysics" (2003, p. 129).

2 There are non-romantic adult love relationships that involve compassion, such as between two friends, a parent and an adult son or daughter, or a teacher and his college students, that point to a transcendent reality and/or dimension of being.

3 www.selfinexile.com/Characteristics_2.html, retrieved 8/9/16. I have liberally drawn from this website in this section as it provides a fairly comprehensive rendering of typical schizoid characteristics with little psychological jargon, as it appears to be written by intelligent laypeople diagnosed as schizoid.

4 *The Week*, August 11, 2016, p. 16.

5 www.au.reachout.com/the-effects-of-low-self-esteem, retrieved 9/27/16.

6 www.azquotes.com, Authors: Catherine Deneuve, retrieved 8/31/16.

7 www.psychologytoday.com/blog/the-squeaky-wheel/201311/the-five-ingredients-effective-apology, retrieved 9/6/16.

8 Goodness, for Levinas, is the central moral value associated with "Biblical wisdom," his only "Absolute value." Compare this highest good with those

conceptions rooted in Axial "Greek wisdom": happiness (Aristotle); pleasure (Epicurus); resignation without despair (Aurelius); and quasi-mystical apprehension of the forms, that is, knowledge (Plato).

9  Lacan vigorously rejected ego psychology. However, his view of the "I" as a distorting, alienating screen, a mirage, that conceals the divided, conflicted and fractured nature of unconscious desire still retains a self-centric bias. For example, Lacan insinuates that all desire is doomed to be a desire to consume the other, to make the other the same. Lacan, a man "in constant need of admiration and power," as he has been described, seems unable or unwilling to consider a more selfless "for-the-other" mode of being in the world as an authentic non-neurotic human striving (Scarfone, 2005, p. 425).

10  In a certain sense, social psychological findings do not support such a sweeping conclusion. For example, in newly married couples it was reported that partners were strongly motivated to monitor each other closely and to attempt to attain a "shared cognitive focus" (Ickes & Simpson, 1997). That is, more generally, "the self is expanded through including the other in the self, a process which in a close relationship becomes so mutual that each person is including the other in his or her self" (Aron & Aron, 2001, p. 484). Aron and Aron cite Schutz, who describes this intersubjective process as "living in each other's subjective context of meaning" (ibid., p. 485). They also note that Neuberg, an evolutionary theorist, suggests "that interpersonal closeness, experienced as including" the other in the self, may be the method we use to "recognize those with whom we share genes...in the interest of knowing with whom one should share resources" to increase "collective fitness."

11  An earlier version of some of the material in this section is found in Marcus (2010).

12  The notion of the "other" and "otherness" is hardly a straightforward one in psychoanalytic theory. How one defines and instantiates the "other" depends on one's theoretical outlook, which includes judging when an infant "knows" there is an "other," developmentally speaking.

13  Such a view of love and the version of the human condition that Levinas puts forth has been a marginal and inadequately formulated theme for psychoanalysts. The exception is Erich Fromm, an enormously under-appreciated psychoanalytic codifier and theoretician on love since Freud. In his gem, *The Art of Loving: An Enquiry into the Nature of Love,* he challenges Freud's physiological instinct-dominated view that human capabilities and inclinations for love and aggression are merely biological potentials. Rather, Fromm reconceptualizes all interpersonal relationships in terms of specific kinds of "being-with," modes of relatedness. In this context, love is one of the key characteristics of the "productive type." The productive person has achieved a high level of autonomy and personality integration: he is capable of being spontaneous, creative, positively related to others, transcendent, and grounded. He has a developed sense of personal identity and a stable though flexible frame of orientation toward living. Most importantly, following Freud, the productive person can love and work. "Mature love," says Fromm, "is union under the condition of preserving one's integrity; one's individuality." That is, "love is an active power in man; a power which breaks through the walls which separate man from his fellow men, which unites him with others; love makes him overcome the sense of isolation and separateness, yet it permits him to be himself, to retain his integrity." For Fromm, similar to Levinas, the active character of love can be described as "primarily giving, not receiving." Love is characterized by "care, responsibility, respect and knowledge." In essence, "to love means to commit oneself without guarantee, to give oneself completely in the

hope that our love will produce love in the loved person. Love is an act of faith" (Fromm, 1956, pp. 20–21, 22, 26, 128).

## References

Abraham, N., & Torok, M. (Eds.). (1994). *The Shell and the Kernel: Renewals of Psychoanalysis*. Chicago: University of Chicago Press.

Adorno, T. (1951). [2005]. *Minima Moralia: Reflections on a Damaged Life*. E.F.N. Jephcott (Trans.). New York: Versos.

Akhtar, S. (1992). *Broken Structures: Severe Personality Disorders and Their Treatment*. Northvale, NJ: Jason Aronson.

Akhtar, S. (1995). *Quest for Answers*. Northvale, NJ: Jason Aronson.

Akhtar, S. (2009). *Comprehensive Dictionary of Psychoanalysis*. London: Karnac.

Alford, C.F. (1998). Melanie Klein and the Nature of Good and Evil. In P. Marcus & A. Rosenberg (Eds.), *Psychoanalytic Versions of the Human Condition: Philosophies of Life and the Impact on Practice* (pp. 117–139). New York: New York University Press.

Armstrong, K. (2006). *The Great Transformation: The Beginning of our Religious Traditions*. New York: Knopf.

Aron, A., & Aron, E.N. (2001). The Self-Expansion Model of Motivation and Cognition in Close Relationships and Beyond. In M. Hewstone & M. Brewer (Eds.), *Blackwell Handbook of Social Psychology: Interpersonal Processes* (Vol. 2, pp. 478–501). Oxford, UK: Blackwell.

*Art Direction*. (1992). Advertising Trade Publications (Vol. 44). (Original from the University of Michigan). Digitalized 2008.

Assoun, P.-L. (2000). *Freud and Nietzsche*. R.L. Collier (Trans.). London: Continuum.

Atterton, P., & Calarco, M. (2005). *On Levinas*. Belmont, CA: Wadsworth.

Barth, K. (1995). *A Map of Twentieth Century Theology: Readings from Karl Barth to Racial Pluralism*. C.E. Braten and R.W. Jenson (Eds.). Minneapolis, MN: Fortress.

Benjamin, J. (1995). *Like Subjects, Love Objects: Essays on Recognition and Sexual Difference*. New Haven, CT: Yale University Press.

Berenbaum, M. (1994). *Elie Wiesel: God, the Holocaust and the Children of Israel*. New York: Behrman.

Buber, M. (1965). *Between Man and Man*. M.S. Friedman (Trans.). New York: Macmillan.

Carnes, P. (1989). *Contrary to Love: Helping the Sexual Addict*. Center City, MN: Hazelden.

Confucius. (2000). *The Analects*. R. Dawson (Trans.). Oxford, UK: Oxford University Press.

Dalferth, I.U. (2012). The Idea of Transcendence. In R.N. Bellah & H. Joas (Eds.), *The Axial Age and Its Consequences* (pp. 146–188). Boston, MA: Harvard University Press.

Darvas, G. (2016). "Symmetry." Retrieved 9/1/16 from www.emotionalcompetency.com/symmetry.htm.

Doidge, N. (2001). Diagnosing "The English Patient': Schizoid Fantasies of Being Skinless and Being Buried Alive. *Journal of the American Psychoanalytic Association*, 49, 279–309.

Dostoevsky, F. (1922). [1880]. *The Brothers Karamazov.* C. Garnett (Trans.). New York: Macmillan.

Edgoose, J.M. (2008). Teaching Our Way Out When Nobody Knows the Way: A Levinasian Response to Modern Hope. In D. Egéa-Kuehne (Ed.), *Levinas and Education: At the Intersection of Faith and Reason* (pp. 100–114). London: Routledge.

Erikson, E.H. (1964). *Insight and Responsibility: Lecture on the Ethical Implications of Psychoanalytic Insight.* New York: Norton.

Fairbairn, W.R.D. (1952a). *An Object Relations Theory of the Personality.* New York: Basic Books.

Fairbairn, W.R.D. (1952b). Schizoid Factors in the Personality. In W.R.D. Fairbairn, *Psychoanalytic Studies of the Personality* (pp. 3–27). London: Routledge & Kegan Paul.

Freud, S. (1961) [1927–1928]. Dostoevsky and Parricide. In J. Strachey (Ed. & Trans.), *Standard Edition of the Complete Psychological Works of Sigmund Freud* (Vol. 21, pp. 177–194). London: Hogarth Press.

Freud, S. (1923). The Ego and the Id. In J. Strachey (Ed. & Trans.), *Standard Edition of the Complete Psychological Works of Sigmund Freud* (Vol. 19, pp. 3–66). London: Hogarth Press.

Friedman, M.S. (2002). *Martin Buber: The Life of Dialogue* (4th ed.). London: Routledge.

Fromm, E. (1956). *The Art of Loving: An Enquiry into the Nature of Love.* New York: Harper Colophon.

Gouldner, A. (1960). The Norm of Reciprocity: A Preliminary Statement. *American Sociological Review*, 25, 161–178.

Greenberg, I. (1977). Cloud of Smoke, Pillar of Fire: Judaism, Christianity, and Modernity after the Holocaust. In E. Fleischner (Ed.), *Auschwitz: Beginning of a New Era? Reflections on the Holocaust* (pp. 7–56). New York: KTAV.

Greenberg, J.R., & Mitchell, S.A. (1983). *Object Relations in Psychoanalytic Theory.* Cambridge, MA: Harvard University Press.

Greer, G. (1970). *The Female Eunuch.* London: HarperCollins.

Grunwald, L., & Adler, S. (Eds.). (2015). *The Marriage Book.* New York: Simon & Schuster.

Guntrip, H. (1969). *Schizoid Phenomena: Object Relations and the Self.* New York: International Universities Press.

Heschel, A.J. (1955). *God in Search of Man: A Philosophy of Judaism.* New York: Farrar, Straus, and Giroux.

Ickes, W., & Simpson, J.A. (1997). Empathic Accuracy in Close Relationships. In W. Ickes (Ed.), *Empathic Accuracy* (pp. 194–217). New York: Guilford Press.

Jaspers, K. (2003). *Way to Wisdom: An Introduction to Philosophy.* New Haven, CT: Yale University Press. (Original work published 1951)

King, I. (2008). *How to Make Good Decisions and Be Right All the Time.* London: Continuum.

Klein, M. (1952). Notes on Some Schizoid Mechanisms. In J. Riviere (Ed.), *Developments in Psycho-Analysis* (pp. 292–320). London: Hogarth Press.

Klosterman, C. (2006). *A Decade of Curious People and Dangerous Ideas.* New York: Scribner.

Krystal, H. (1988). *Integration and Self Healing: Affect, Healing and Alexithymia*. London: Routledge.

Levi, P. (1986). *The Drowned and the Saved*. New York: Summit Books.

Levinas, E. (1969). *Totality and Infinity: An Essay on Exteriority*. A. Lingis (Trans.). Pittsburgh, PA: Duquesne University Press.

Levinas, E. (1985). *Ethics and Infinity: Conversations with Philippe Nemo*. R.A. Cohen (Trans.). Pittsburgh, PA: Duquesne University Press.

Levinas, E. (1987). *Time and the Other (and Additional Essays)*. R.A. Cohen (Trans.). Pittsburgh, PA: Duquesne University Press.

Levinas, E. (1998). *Otherwise than Being: Or Beyond Essence*. A. Lingis (Trans.). Pittsburgh, PA: Duquesne University Press.

Mahler, M.S., Pine, F., & Bergman, A. (1973). *The Psychological Birth of the Human Infant*. New York: Basic Books.

Marcus, P. (1999). *Autonomy in the Extreme Situation: Bruno Bettelheim, the Nazi Concentration Camps and the Mass Society*. Westport, CT: Praeger.

Marcus, P. (2003). *Ancient Religious Wisdom, Spirituality and Psychoanalysis*. Westport, CT: Praeger.

Marcus, P. (2008). *Being for the Other: Emmanuel Levinas, Ethical Living and Psychoanalysis*. Milwaukee, WI: Marquette University Press.

Marcus, P. (2010). *In Search of the Good Life: Emmanuel Levinas, Psychoanalysis and the Art of Living*. London: Karnac.

Maugham, W.S. (1919). *The Moon and Sixpence*. Retrieved from www.gutenberg.org/cache/epub/222/pg222.txt.

Moore, B.E., & Fine, B.D. (Eds.). (1990). *Psychoanalytic Terms and Concepts*. New Haven, CT: American Psychoanalytic Association and Yale University Press.

Niebuhr, R. (1952). *The Irony of American History*. New York: Charles Scribner's Sons.

Pasquarello, M. (2011). *Christian Preaching: A Trinitarian Theology of Proclamation*. Eugene, OR: Wipf and Stock.

Pattison, E.M. (1988). The Holocaust as Sin: Requirements in Psychoanalytic Theory for Human Evil and Mature Morality. In S.S. Luel & P. Marcus (Eds.), *Psychoanalytic Reflections on the Holocaust: Selected Essays* (pp. 71–94). New York: University of Denver and KTAV.

Person, E.S., Cooper, A.M., & Gabbard, G.O. (Eds.). (2005). *Textbook of Psychoanalysis*. Washington, DC: American Psychiatric Publishing.

Poole, R. (1998). The Unknown Kierkegaard: Twentieth-Century Receptions. In A. Hannay & C.D. Marino (Eds.), *The Cambridge Companion to Kierkegaard* (pp. 48–75). Cambridge, UK: Cambridge University Press.

Robbins, J. (Ed.). (2001). *Is It Righteous to Be? Interviews with Emmanuel Levinas*. Stanford, CA: Stanford University Press.

Rubin, J.B. (1996). *Psychotherapy and Buddhism: Toward an Integration*. New York: Plenum Press.

Rycroft, C. (1968). *A Critical Dictionary of Psychoanalysis*. Harmondsworth, UK: Penguin.

Rycroft, C. (1995). *A Critical Dictionary of Psychoanalysis* (2nd ed.). London: Penguin.

Scarfone, D. (2005). Psychoanalysis in the French Community. In E.S. Person, A.M. Cooper, & G.O. Gabbard (Eds.), *The American Psychiatric Publishing Textbook of Psychoanalysis* (pp. 423–435). Washington, DC: American Psychiatric Publishing.

Shafranske, E.P. (Ed.). (1996). *Religion and the Clinical Practice of Psychology.* Washington, DC: American Psychological Association.

Smith, H. (1979). *Forgotten Truth: The Primordial Tradition.* New York: Harper & Row.

Spiegelman, W. (2002). *The Lives and Works of the English Romantic Poets* (Course Guidebook, Parts 1 and 2). Chantilly, VA: The Teaching Company.

*The Week* (2016, September 19). Sex: Why Millennials Are Having Less.

Winch, G. (2013). *Emotional First Aid: Healing Rejection, Guilt, Failure, and Other Everyday Hurts.* New York: Penguin.

Winnicott, D.W. (1960). Ego Distortion in Terms of True and False Self. In D.W. Winnicott (Ed.), *The Maturational Processes and the Facilitating Environment* (pp. 140–152). New York: International Universities Press.

Wyschogrod, E. (2000). *Emmanuel Levinas: The Problem of Ethical Metaphysics* (2nd ed.). New York: Fordham University Press.

# Chapter 3

# The suffering of faith

In *The Future of Illusion*, Freud indicates that theistic religion has three major psychologically protective tasks for the individual: "the gods ... must exorcise the terrors of nature, they must reconcile man to the cruelty of Fate, particularly as it is shown in death, and they must compensate them for the sufferings and privations which a civilized life in common has imposed on them" (Freud, 1927 [1961], p. 18). For Freud, God (and the devil) emanates from an infantile fairytale world of universal unconscious fantasies focusing on "good" and "bad" omnipotent, primal parenting figures (Shengold, 1999, p. 142). Moreover, Freud notes that religion is "the universal obsessional neurosis of humanity," calling to mind the obsessional neurosis of children, a condition that emanates from the Oedipus complex in connection to the father (Freud, 1927, p. 43). In Freud's view, the conscious and unconscious God image is equated with the law-giving, guilt-inducing and conquering father.[1] It is an illusion to embrace such unverifiable beliefs about the "gods" and to engage in the obsessive behaviors that support them, says Freud. This wish fulfillment obliterates reality; and, like any radical denial of reality, it ultimately leads to unhappiness and worse. Most importantly for this chapter, Freud claims that because the individual embraces without reserve these illusions, one would think that "devout believers are safeguarded in a high degree against the risk of certain neurotic illnesses." In other words, by embracing the "universal neurosis," they are spared "the task of constructing a personal one" (ibid., p. 44). While Freud was putting forth a credible if not intriguing view of the psychological appeal and function of religion, he was limited in his understanding of religious ways of being-in-the-world by his obsolete, late nineteenth-century outlook that was steeped in rationalism and scientific materialism. Freud's personal atheism and complex, if not ambivalent, Jewish identity probably also played a role in his lack of deep and nuanced understanding of the ways the *homo religious* thinks, feels and acts in "real life."[2]

In contemporary psychoanalytic theory, Freud's "classical" view of God (and religion and spirituality) – which alleges that a person's conscious and unconscious images of God emanates from emotionally infused parental caregivers as they are filtered and metabolized through unconscious fantasy – has been expanded to include approaches that are rooted in ego psychology, object relations, self-psychology and attachment theory (Rizzuto & Shafranske, 2013, p. 133). As I have discussed elsewhere, each psychoanalytic approach reflects its own "version of the human condition" and "philosophy of life." These theoretical assumptions play a pivotal role in guiding and delimiting the investigation and practice of the clinician, though they often go unacknowledged (Marcus & Rosenberg, 1998). Thus, how each theory views God, religion and spirituality will be animated by their controlling explicit and implicit philosophical assumptions, by their "master narrative."

In modern ego psychology, for example, God images are conceived as dynamically fashioned from "real-life" emotionally infused parental caregivers and childhood experiences and resources. God images play a contributory part in inner conflict as well as serviceable compromise formations. That is, God is involved in complicated psychological cognitive and affective functions which can promote adaptation or express neurotic conflict; in object relational theory, a person's conscious and unconscious God image is the consequence of the internalization of relational happenings between the person and emotionally significant others, usually the parental caregivers, always under the animating influence of phantasy (for Melanie Klein, phantasy with a *ph* and not *f*antasy, emphasizes its strictly unconscious nature). In this view, God images act like a psychic "container," as Bion (1963) called it, of diverse kinds of unconscious projections that are typically re-introjected and enhance individual functioning. A container, like an empathic and attuned mother or other caregiver, ideally serves as a source of practical emotional sustenance and helps the person process and "manage" disagreeable feelings. God images thus mainly reflect unconscious projections whereby God symbolizes "good" and sometimes "bad" psychological experiences. Likewise, religious practices and involvement in a faith community act as something of a "holding" environment, a "total environmental provision," as Winnicott (1965) described it, that, like a "good enough" mother, facilitates a sense of trust, acceptance, and safety of emotions and promotes growth and development.

For the self-psychologist, one's experiential relationship to God is lodged in specific kinds of selfobject functioning, modes of relating to emotionally significant others, originally one's emotionally infused parental caregivers, that promote self-esteem, self-continuity and self-cohesion. However, God images can act otherwise; they can facilitate dread and annihilation anxiety, especially when they morph into attacking "bad objects," such as upsurges of guilt and anxiety about divine punishment. In attachment theory, a person's relationship with God reflects internal working models of relationships (i.e., childhood-based templates of psychological connectedness to others) that provide other compensatory experiences of relationships. God conceived as a relational partner, a symbolic attachment figure, ideally facilitates secure attachments; but sometimes this conception creates insecure attachments that are characterized by avoidance, disorganization or ambivalence.

All of these psychoanalytic approaches have expanded and deepened Freud's original insights, and they clearly have their usefulness in terms of understanding a particular "believer's" way of experiencing God and the sacred in both good and bad times. Indeed, in our era the everyday life of many individual "believers" is more phenomenologically complex, multifaceted and profound than Freud first thought, both in terms of what is life affirming and life denying about God images, religion and spirituality. This is especially true as it pertains to those I would call "enlightened believers" (henceforth, "believers") – those persons of theistic faith who are devoted to rigorous critical reflection, self-examination and truth-seeking.

Freud's pejorative views on adult religious consciousness and behavior are tainted by his acceptance of the "genetic fallacy," a line of reasoning that involves "basing the truth claim of an argument on the origin of its claims or premises."[3] He mistakenly argues that there is a neurotic origin to adult religious consciousness and behavior, and therefore it is logical to conclude that adult manifestations of the same must also be neurotic. In terms of this chapter, what Freud did not adequately reckon with is that believers have modes of suffering that are not animated by the alleged neurotic origins of their religious faith (though they are shaped by their real and imagined childhood experiences). Rather, they are mainly lodged in what are painful, "authentic," "mature" and "healthy" struggles that animate the religious consciousness of a person of faith as he searches for something "more," some form of transcendence. For example, Elie Wiesel struggled with his religious faith after the Holocaust in ways that were agonizingly ambivalent and ambiguous:

> I was very, very religious. And of course I wrote about it in *Night*. I questioned God's silence … I don't have an answer for that. Does it mean that I stopped having faith? No. I have faith, but I question it … I have moments of anger and protest. Sometimes I've been closer to him for that reason.[4]

Fathoming and contending with God's inscrutability, mysteriousness and unknowability is a form of suffering that nearly every person of faith has experienced in one form or another in his lifetime.

In this chapter I investigate underexplored areas of suffering for the believer. The notion of faith is a complex one both philosophically and psychologically. The great German American Protestant existentialist philosopher Paul Tillich called faith "an act of a finite being who is grasped by, and turned to, the infinite" (1958, p. 18). For the purposes of this chapter, I refer to faith similarly. Moreover, says Tillich, "Faith consists in being vitally concerned with that ultimate reality to which I give the symbolic name of God.

Whoever reflects earnestly on the meaning of life is on the verge of an act of faith" (1968, p. 387). Faith, as I use the term, is psychologically suggested by a person's openness and trust, especially in relation to what Axial philosophers have called Beauty, Truth and Goodness, those primary transcendental values that are perhaps the most powerful points of entry to sensing the infinite, or God's presence, as a believer would describe it.

This chapter is organized in terms of three real-life struggles that "enlightened believers" contend with in the context of their theistic faith, including some suggestions on how to more artfully respond to these existential challenges. Believers are faced with having to psychologically metabolize and reconcile, or at least learn to creatively live with, the following existential tensions:

1   When the conscious and unconscious belief in the existence of an all-powerful, all-good, loving and just God is contradicted by the prevalence of evil in the world. This is the problem of "when bad things happen to good people" (i.e., theodicy) and, most importantly, this includes "to me."
2   When God does not appear to "hear" our prayers. This is the problem of reconciling one's finite efforts to passionately connect with an allegedly infinitely compassionate, moral and personal God who seems to be unresponsive (or worse – indifferent) to our overtures and heart-felt pleadings.
3   When, despite the believer's best efforts, their theistic outlook and religious lifestyle is rejected by his offspring, such as when a believer's child repudiates God and a religious lifestyle, thus evoking a feeling of abandonment or betrayal that can feel divinely punitive.

As is plainly obvious, for the person of serious faith, these three problematics are usually experienced as painful moments, if not spiritual crises, in their full devotion to their living God.

## The dark night of the soul

Before I systematically discuss these three existential tensions, I want to contextualize them in terms of what the great Roman Catholic saint and mystic, St. John of the Cross, evocatively called *la noche oscura*, the "dark night" of the soul or spirit. I describe in general terms the more important aspects of the painful experiences that believers sustain as they strive to grow in spiritual depth and maturity, and develop a joyful union or identification with God. For while the typical believer is hardly perfect, issues raised by St. John of the Cross in his spiritual masterpiece *Dark Night of the Soul* (1619 [2003]) and by Mother Teresa, or Saint Teresa of Calcutta, in her somewhat tortured correspondences (2007) resonates with all believers. For what believer has not become aware of how deeply flawed an aspirant "partner" he is in his relationship with God, the One with whom he wishes to lovingly unite, a condition of acutely felt imperfection in need of radical transformation, what St. John of the Cross calls, "purification"? What brutally honest soul-searching believer does not episodically lose or seriously question his faith in God, or feel utterly estranged from Him, as did Mother Teresa for many years? And yet, extraordinarily, for reasons that are largely unintelligible to the person of faith and to onlookers, they still feel compelled to strive for something "more" – whether it is called God, the infinite, transcendence, immortality or some other equivalently evocative word that points to the "otherworldly" and a radically different dimension of being.

The great sociologist of religion, Max Weber, made this point just right when he observed that all religions require a surrendering of the intellect (Joas, 2012, p. 20) to the nonrational (not the irrational), for there is something more primordially summoning that animates the believer than the play of mere reason. "It is the heart," a person's sense of identity and self-worth, said the Axial-inspired mathematician and Catholic theologian Blaise Pascal, "[t]hat is what faith is: God perceived by the heart, not by the reason" (McGregor, 2016, p. 285).

In the *Dark Night of the Soul*, St. John of the Cross described the believer's painful "purifications" of pride, avarice and envy that are necessary before attaining loving union with God. The "dark night" metaphor refers to the believer's internal world, those extreme feelings of emptiness, desolation and despair that are associated with the experience of God's distance or absence in everyday life. "Hell," for the believer, is this absence of God. In our time, the believer can experience the "dark night" in a variety of ways that, while not narrated in the evocative language of the Christian mystic, are nevertheless compelling sufferings.

For example, consider St. Augustine's concept of "original sin," the claim that there is an innate evil in humans. While the concept of "original sin" is not usually considered to have a pertinent role in the modern psychoanalytic project, a less literal formulation of this concept suggests it is not nearly as far-fetched a notion when it is applied to the internal sufferings, the "dark night" of the "enlightened believer." The concept of original sin can be illuminating if we consider that all people come into this world with truncated capacities and abilities to seek and attain the "good," and, left to our own contrivances, all of us will deceive ourselves and our fellow humans (Pattison, 1988, p. 89). As psychoanalyst Leonard Shengold noted, "With our human weaknesses and failures, and because of the conditions of our existence, we are all condemned, at least to some extent, to be victims and perpetrators of soul murder" (purposefully destroying or seriously undermining a person's separate identity) (1999, p. 163). Moreover, all of us are prone to "distort the reality" of our fellow humans and have major empathic failures; we "choose or fail to choose" important matters in ill-conceived ways; and we are acutely aware that we do not fulfill our potentialities.

All of these seemingly "built-in" human limitations are the basis for what existential psychologists have called "ontological guilt" (May, 1958, p. 55). Analysands and analysts would benefit from the almost inevitable reduction in their narcissism that comes about through a greater mindfulness of the fact that we are all fundamentally flawed creatures. We are selfish, impatient, dishonest, envious, mean-spirited and sometimes downright cruel. We are limited and flawed in our capacity to love and in our relations with others, the main area of focus in psychoanalysis. In other words, the concept of original sin teaches us that unless checked by moral force, by our conscience, we are all prone to the everyday "inhumanity" toward others, especially to those dear to us, which is often the basis of our own subversion in terms of guilt and other forms of unhappiness.

Freud memorialized a similar insight in his concept of the death instinct, that innate instinct to destroy or dissolve oneself, a view that Melanie Klein more fully developed in her claim that aggression was a projection of the individual's inherent self-destructive drive. Later analysts have mostly preferred to speak about the general innate tendency of aggression toward others. Both formulations, however, speak to Freud's awareness of our flawed nature, to our inherent "sinfulness," as Augustine and St. John of the Cross described it.

What is most pertinent to our discussion of the "dark night" is how this recast notion of "original sin" is experienced in the everyday life of the believer (and, for that matter, all of us), a mode of self-awareness that is infused with suffering, and at its best leads to self-correcting internal and external actions. While Augustine may be wrong about "original sin," and perhaps it makes more sense to believe that we are born innocent or a *tabula rasa*, to most people it *feels* the other way, as if for as long as one can remember one has been sinning and impure. Moreover, from a psychological perspective, it seems wise to take account of that feeling.[5] Is there a single critically reflective person who, when retiring to sleep at night, can honestly say that during the past day they could not have been a better parent, significant other, friend, colleague or psychotherapist? For the person of faith, this sense of sinning and impurity is taken particularly seriously and is often the basis for genuine and neurotic guilt, a distinction that I want to briefly comment on, as it speaks to the heart of the "dark night" of the soul in our modern era, at least as I conceive of it.

According to Freud, the neurotic sense of guilt emanates from an unconscious, intra-psychic conflict between the super-ego (roughly, the conscience) and the id (representing aggressive and sexual wishes that are the touchstones of clinical psychoanalysis). The conflict is an internalized representation and continuation of early, so-called "primitive" conflicts between the child and parents or caregiver. As Rycroft further points out, this internalized scenario is made more complex by the fact that the super-ego is conceptualized as getting its motivational energy from the child's own aggressive wishes. As a consequence of this, guilt is affected directly by the extent to which the person expresses, via conscious and unconscious self-narrative, aggressive wishes and feelings by turning them on oneself in the form of severe moral judgment and censure (1995, pp. 66–67). This moral censure can be manifested in the believer's unreasonable blame, disapproval, criticism and the other forms of extreme self-punishment and retribution meant, in part, to assuage the sense of guilt.[6]

In contrast to neurotic guilt that is the result of internalized conflict, genuine guilt is the consequence of injured or spoiled relations between people, of whom the perpetrator is consciously or unconsciously aware and about which they feel deeply regretful. As Martin Buber points out, "existential guilt" occurs "when someone injures an order of the human world whose foundations he knows and recognizes as those of his own existence and of all common existence" (1965, p. 127).

Psychoanalysis, as I construe and practice it, attempts to show the analysand (believer or not) the variety of ways in which he tries to avoid the meaningful awareness of his genuine guilt, often preferring to get bogged down in the endless emotional thicket of neurotic guilt, especially its guilt/punishment cycle. The libidinal, aggressive and archetypal interpretations of Freud, Klein and Jung the believer may know by heart and use as an avenue of flight from himself, not as a vehicle for moral insight and changed behavior. Such an escape from the awareness of being genuinely guilty is based on having failed to comprehend and empathically meet the other's needs before one's own. In this sense, unaccepted, disavowed or repressed genuine guilt can morph into neurotic guilt (May, 1958, pp. 52–55). In a manner of speaking, the "believing" analysand says to oneself, "Better such [neurotic] guilt and punishment than facing the awful burden of freedom and responsibility for, and to the other" (Becker, 1973, p. 213).[7]

As I have said, neurotic guilt can be psychoanalytically understood as a defense for avoiding confrontation with genuine guilt. It is a centripetal psychic process in that it gets one more deeply enmeshed in oneself, mainly through the self-accusations of worthlessness and the guilt/punishment self-narrative. In other words, neurotic guilt is highly narcissistic: it is self-obsessing as it keeps the self utterly focused on its own center isolated from the real other, a reflection of the self's tendency to isolation and self-sufficiency. Neurotic guilt also retards any real self-illumination, personal growth and development. By definition, it always has a moribund trajectory, that is, it always leads to clinical symptoms. Neurotic guilt is most evident in the clinical context in that the "believing" analysand has both a vague fear of retribution and the need to expiate punishment in some form. Moreover, the internal dialogue that the analysand has with oneself is experienced by the analyst as a narcissistic monologue (Silberstein, 1989, pp. 143–145). This mode of relation to oneself reflects the overall conceptual and behavioral impoverishment, a bogging down of the forward movement of life that characterizes the neurotically guilty "believing" analysand. As we shall see, where neurotic guilt always wounds and cripples the human animal, genuine guilt heals and sets him free.

In contrast to neurotic guilt, genuine guilt is characterized by authentic self-confrontation and self-understanding. Paradoxically, rather than being centripetal in character, genuine guilt is centrifugal and this is a positive and hopeful development. Genuine guilt is a psychic process that moves one away from the interiority of egoistic psychism, away from the ego with its egological accusations of worthlessness and failed conquests. In other words, genuine guilt steers one away from one's inordinate self-centricism and narcissism toward an other-directed, other-regarding and other-serving mode of being in the world. Clinically, this manifests itself in the "believing" analysand's lessened presentation of self-obsession; rather, he is more for the other. His dialogue with himself is not a largely narcissistic form of monologue, but reflects the "believing" analysand's willingness to struggle to find the apt words through which to articulate his profoundest fears, wishes and misgivings. Most importantly, the genuinely guilty person seeks out the injured, aggrieved other in order to make reparations, real and symbolic, to put things right, to restore the damaged other to his or her original whole, uncompromised state. Unlike neurotic guilt, genuine guilt that is honestly faced is asymptomatic and leads to greater freedom and expansiveness. Most importantly, it leads to efforts that reflect the perpetrator's willingness to assume greater responsibility, not only toward the damaged particular other, but also, by extension, all others, everywhere.

Finally, genuine guilt that is confronted leads to other positive developments in the personality, including one's evolving "for the other" mode of being-in-the-world. These developments, to some extent nurtured by the psychoanalytic process, include the "believing" analysand's greater sense of humility and forgiveness of himself and others. Such a consciousness is, in part, rooted in the awareness that it is an aspect of our existential make-up that we hurt others, especially those we love. As the Axial-inspired Kant noted, there is at least a smudge of "radical evil" in human being, in that we all at times subordinate the moral law to our own selfishness (Card, 2002). For the believer who is amidst the "dark night," coming to terms with his genuine guilt is precisely the "purification" process that St. John of the Cross was getting at, whether one uses religious or secular language to describe the amelioration of his painful sufferings about his flawed and sorrowful state of being.

Mother Teresa's correspondence puts into sharp focus another aspect of the believer's sufferings, "the darkness – the loneliness & pain – the loss & the emptiness – of faith – love – trust," the latter three feeling states being the psychological basis of a believer's life-affirming existential odyssey:

> Lord, my God, who am I that You should forsake me? The child of your love – and now become as the most hated one – the one You have thrown

away as unwanted – unloved. I call, I cling, I want – and there is no One to answer – no One on Whom I can cling – no, No One. – Alone. The darkness is so dark – and I am alone. – Unwanted, forsaken. – The loneliness of the heart that wants love is unbearable. – Where is my faith? – Even deep down, right in, there is nothing but emptiness & darkness. – My God – how painful is this unknown pain. In pains without ceasing. – I have no faith. – I dare not utter the words & thoughts that crowd in my heart – & make me suffer untold agony. So many unanswered questions live within me – I am afraid to uncover them – because of the blasphemy. – If there be God, please forgive me.

(Teresa & Kolodiejchuk, 2007, p. 187)

These are powerful, poignant words coming from a woman whose alienation from God in 1959 was extreme, and extremely painful to her, for it "rocked" her universe of ultimate concerns for nearly fifty years, though she astonishingly always pressed on with her ministry of service to the poor (ibid., p. 337). Perhaps this is because Mother Teresa did not view her suffering in terms of the internal "purification" depicted in St. John of the Cross's "dark night." Rather, she had the inkling that though her sufferings were somewhat alike, their purpose and function was dissimilar. As Father Brian Kolodiejchuk, the editor of Mother Teresa's private writings, noted, "her darkness was an identification with those she served: she was drawn mystically into the deep pain they experienced as a result of feeling unwanted and rejected, and above all, by living without faith in God" (ibid., p. 216). Moreover, while earlier in her career of service to the poor she had been willing and able to offer herself as victim for even a single soul, "she was now united in the pain, not only with one soul, but with the multitude of souls that suffered in this terrible darkness" (ibid.).

In other words, Mother Teresa had found a way to creatively metabolize her suffering as a mysterious connection that joined her to Jesus, an expression of intimate longing for God that emanated uniquely through God's own hidden presence. Once she viewed her agony as a reflection of God's agony, her darkness and pain was His darkness and pain, lodged in a deep trust in divine providence. She was content with taking her suffering upon herself as her personal cross to bear (ibid., pp. 216, 224, 217). "Sorrow, suffering," wrote Mother Teresa, "is but a kiss of Jesus – a sign that you have come so close to Jesus that He can kiss you. – I think this is the most beautiful definition of suffering" (ibid., p. 281). What made Mother Teresa saintly was not the terrible internal suffering she bore but, rather, the love that infused her everyday life in her service to the poor *through* all of her suffering.

Psychologically speaking, we can say that while St. John of the Cross stressed the painful purifications necessary to lovingly unite with God (Mother Teresa also felt this to a lesser extent), Mother Teresa's psychic pain can be regarded as more reparative than purgative (ibid., pp. 337, 255).

Indeed, Mother Teresa's two favorite exhortations – "Take whatever He gives and give whatever He takes with a big smile" and "Give Jesus a free hand and let Him use you without consulting you" – both express the near complete surrender, loving trust and joyfulness that ultimately characterized her way of embracing her darkness without reserve. All this, remarkably, occurred without her wavering from her enormously demanding service to the poor (ibid., p. 225).

It is not an understatement to claim that the pained and complex internal world of a saint/mystic like Mother Teresa or St. John of the Cross is not typical to the "enlightened believer" of our era, the main focus of this chapter. However, I highlight the fact that for any person of theistic faith who is engaged in a serious spiritual journey and regards oneself as what Gabriel Marcel called a *homo viator*, a spiritual pilgrim geared to glimpsing God, this journey does not necessarily involve decades of the extreme despair of Mother Teresa; it quite likely will require metabolizing a fair amount of unavoidable sufferings that, to some extent, call to mind Mother Teresa's lifelong spiritual and psychological struggles. It is to these subjects that I now turn.

## Innocent suffering

"Wherefore doth the way of the wicked prosper?" asked the Axial prophet Jeremiah to God (12:1). This is the issue of theodicy, attempting to rationally reconcile divine goodness and providence in the face of the existence of evil, suffering and death. For the contemporary believer this is usually experienced as a demanding intellectual conundrum, the domain of the speculative. "Why hast Thou set me as a mark for Thee?" asked Job (7:20), an emotional challenge of making undeserved suffering sufferable, which is the domain of the existential (Holy Scriptures, 1964, pp. 580, 930). While these two problematics are intellectually and emotionally mingled, I focus on how the typical person of faith who has, by his estimation, been unintelligibly struck down by undeserved and disproportionate suffering, assimilates his distressing personal experience with his belief in an all-powerful, all-good and just personal God. While there have been hundreds of books written about the first problematic of theodicy, there have been far fewer written about the internal world of the typical innocent sufferer who navigates through this ordeal, a subject that psychoanalysis can help illuminate as a resource for artfully living the "good life." There have been at least two types of response to innocent suffering, though they are rarely so clearly delineated in real life: an abandonment of faith, and a re-affirmation of faith, usually with some modification. As we shall see, both of these responses are distressing in different ways. Most important, we must never forget that the likely conscious and unconscious cognitive and emotional factors that may be at play always reflect the person's idiosyncratic trajectory about which we are, at best, making only an educated guess.

### Abandonment of faith

The loss of faith can be usefully understood as a "climate change" of the mind or, more accurately, the "loss of a world," sometimes referred to as a "home world" or "symbolic world," though these terms are a bit different in emphasis. By a "home world" I mean, following sociologist Erving Goffman, "a way of life and a round of activities taken for granted" (1961, p. 12). A "home world" gives the individual direction to his life and a sense of safety and ontological security, as sociologist Anthony Giddens called it. Ontological security is a deep and abiding feeling of order and continuity in one's life that is rooted in the individual's "confidence and trust that the natural and social worlds are as they appear to be, including the basic existential parameters of self and social identity" (Giddens, 1984, p. 376). Ontological security, in other words, is what generates a stable and positive experience of the self, world and future. However, if one's world is radically disrupted or assaulted, such as when one is incarcerated in a "total institution" like a mental hospital, prison or concentration camp, then one's personal moral identity is attacked, and it is traumatically invalidated, subverted or obliterated (Goffman, 1961).

Thus, a person needs to have a rich, involving personal and social existence, a meaningful "world" to reasonably sustain himself throughout adult life, especially during the more challenging times. As Bettelheim pointed out, while Freud believed that a person's life is mainly governed by the battle between the life and the death drives, it is perhaps more precise to say that a person's life is governed by a "struggle of the life drives against being overwhelmed by death anxiety" (Bettelheim, 1979, p. 8). That is, "there is an omnipresent fear of extinction which threatens to run destructively rampant when not successfully kept under the safe control by our conviction of the positive value of life" (ibid.). The sociologist Peter L. Berger, too, notes that the "confrontation with death," of others or imagining one's own in fantasy, constitutes what is likely the most important marginal situation that subverts our socially constructed, taken-for-granted definitions of the world, of others and of the self (1967, p. 43). To make matters even more internally challenging, Freud and others have noted that mindfulness of death can also be potentiating of life-affirmation: "Death is the shadow that gives shape to existence, urgency to love, brilliance to life," especially when one realizes that eternal life would morph into boredom without resolution (Cohen, 2016, p. A23). For Freud, it was the everyday life of deep and wide love and creative and productive work, those personal domains that were infused with self-affirming meanings, that are the best defense against death anxiety.

For the person of faith, his religious world of meanings is what matters most; it is the most self-authenticating and self-protective. Such a mode of being is based on the core conviction that there is an all-powerful, all-good and just personal God who cares about him and is willing and able to intervene in his life, often in ways that are not easily discernible but still reflec-tive of His love. Such people find self-unifying strength and self-transcending inspiration in the revealed world of an absolute, objective and omnipotent creator, as they see it, not in personal values meaningful only to themselves. It is such a conviction, the lynchpin of Berger's "sacred canopy," the over-arching and extremely practical, supportive and transforming connection to a meaning-giving, affect-integrating and action-guiding universal matrix (Jones, 1991), that allows a believer to press on in a life-affirming manner, despite the many distressing challenges of everyday life. As I will suggest in the next section, this includes experiences of profound suffering that are effectively psychologically "managed" by the conscious and unconscious implementa-tion of various self-protective strategies and tactics, such as justifying one's suffering through theodicy, including, at its worst, blaming oneself for one's dire fate – "because of our sins we have been punished" (*mipenei hata'einu*) as it is articulated in Judaism.[8]

Recasting this point in psychoanalytic language can be illuminating when we remember that for the typical devout believer, God is conceived and experienced as being analogous to a good "psychological parent," that is, one who most symbolizes nurturance, stability and protectiveness. As Rabbi Jonathan Sacks recently wrote, "The God of Israel is the God who loves and cares for us as a parent loves for and cares for a child" (2016b, p. 2). For example, in some instances God is referred to in the Hebrew Bible as "our father": in the prophetic book of Malachi (2:10) it reads, "Have we not all one Father? Has not one God created us?" In other instances, such as in the prophetic book of Isaiah, God is denoted as mother: "Like one who his mother comforts, so shall I comfort you" (66:13); "Can a woman forget her nursing child and have no compassion on the son of the womb? Even these may forget, but I will not forget you" (49:15). Moreover, says Sacks, the main characteristic of God, specifically when the four-letter name of *Hashem* is used, is compassion (*rachamim*), originating from the Hebrew word for "a womb" (*rechem*). Thus, "our relationship with God is deeply connected with our relationship with our parents," and our comprehension of God is poten-tially made more profound if we have had the "blessing of children" (Sacks, 2016a, pp. 1–2) if we have engaged in the huge loving and sacrificial effort to raise them to be autonomous, integrated and humane adults.

Sacks is confirming what Freud claimed was the main motivation behind theistic religion, namely that God functions in the everyday life of a believer in a manner that calls to mind the best qualities of a "psychological parent": loving, trustworthy and, most importantly for Freud, protective of His "chil-dren." In the case of the Jews whose group identity is lodged in biblical wisdom, God is especially guarding and watchful of His "chosen" children. The question that is of interest to us is this: What happens in the mind and heart of the "child"/believer when, in his view, his "psychological parent" inexplicitly becomes neglectful, to the point that it morphs into a feeling of abuse by the "Parent"/God? Such an "extreme situation," as Bruno Bettelheim evocatively called it, sometimes leads the abused "child"/believer to utterly reject his once beloved and trusted "psychological" "Parent"/God, creating havoc in his world of everyday meanings that had been taken for granted.

While there are many less "extreme" psychodynamic and other reasons why an adult can lose his faith and devotion to his tradition and community – such as rejecting a harsh, overbearing or hypocritical religious upbringing, or regarding God/tradition as less summoning than other outlooks/practices in the marketplace of ideas – I focus on the adult believer who is steeped in faith/tradition/community, but renounces it following a sudden (though it need not be) massive and decisive blow to his religiously infused "symbolic world." While Goffman's "home world" emphasizes the essential role of taken-for-granted activities and routines to sustain an individual narrative of self-identity, a "symbolic world" emphasizes the individual's outlook, his "particular manner of construing the world" (Geertz, 1973, p. 110).

Religion, politics and psychoanalysis can operate as symbolic worlds. As Wuthnow et al. point out, a symbolic world is a total system of beliefs, values, morals and knowledge, which for the believer are usually extremely abstract and appear far above ordinary life, yet palpably intrude themselves on every-day life in their ability to inspire or to infuse meaning to individual or collective activity, to de-legitimate other activity and to wield social control (1984, pp. 37, 75). Symbolic worlds provide a significant ordering impulse to social affairs and to collective outlooks of the world.

Most importantly for our discussion, for the believer these socially structured, taken-for-granted meanings have a stability originating from more powerful, otherworldly sources, usually called "God," than the historical labors of human beings, and contribute therefore to the creation of ultimately powerful and meaningful notions of reality ("sacred cosmoi"). A symbolic world thus provides a framework of ultimate meaning and concern (Berger, 1967, pp. 35, 36). While the study of the symbolic world is essentially focused on what constitutes such a world as real and how it both forms and penetrates ordinary life, which is our characterization of the believer's world, the believer might simply regard his world as the "real" world,[9] and this may be why the breakdown of his world is so traumatic.

For the person who ultimately abandons his faith, who loses his "home"/symbolic world of religious meanings, he often has first experienced the terrible ordeal of being "thrown" into a radical life- and identity-altering "extreme situation." For example, having been a practicing psychoanalyst for more than thirty years in Queens, the most ethnically diverse borough in New York City, I have counseled formerly devout Jews, Christians and Muslims (and others steeped in eastern religious traditions) who have survived Nazi death camps (or other genocidal universes). They have lost family members and communities; have been sexually abused by clergy as children, teenagers and young adults; have lost young children to drunk drivers and cancer, and lost teenage and young adult offspring to drug addiction and mental illness; they have been physically tortured in prisons in foreign countries; and have survived terrorist attacks and natural disasters.

While each of these traumatic losses and their psychological after-effects are phenomenologically unique and do not allow for easy generalizations, what is common to each is that in all such horrid experiences, these adult survivors could not reasonably assimilate their experiences into their religiously animated "symbolic world," especially their deep and abiding belief in an all-powerful, just personal God, which led to a partial or complete loss of faith. By "partial loss" I mean their faith structure's plausibility or subjective reality was seriously compromised and degraded; while they may still go through the motions of religious observance and lifestyle, for them "God is dead," or "nearly dead," the latter of which can be experienced as a type of "ambiguous loss." By this I mean "incomplete or uncertain loss," such as when a daughter or son has been designated by the military as "MIA," which lands a parent in an unresolved state of "waiting and wondering," of "frozen grief" (Boss, 1999, pp. 3, 5). While Bettelheim described such "extreme" situations in terms of the onset of schizophrenia or being imprisoned in a concentration camp, much of what he writes is applicable to the person who loses his faith and world of religious meanings following an assault on his "symbolic world":

> Characterizing this situation were its shattering impact on the individual, for which he was totally unprepared; its inescapability; the expectation that the situation would last for an undetermined period, potentially for a lifetime; the fact that, throughout its entirety, one's very life would be in jeopardy at every moment; and the fact that one was powerless to protect oneself.
>
> (Bettelheim, p. 115)

As Giddens wrote, such an extreme or "critical situation," as he calls it, fundamentally involves "circumstances of radical disjuncture of an unpredictable kind ... that threaten or destroys the certitudes of institutionalized routines" (1984, p. 60). What this means for the person of faith is that his ordeal of suffering, such as surviving a genocidal universe or the loss of his young child, has so robbed him of his religiously suffused ways of thinking, feeling, acting and coping, his "symbolic world," that he feels inundated by disorganizing affects, including death anxiety, making it near impossible to maintain his autonomy, integration and humanity or coherent narrative of self-identity. Without his viable faith structure and the world of meanings that support it, he feels trapped in a maze of grotesque happenings. Such a Kafkaesque situation makes options seem severely limited, causing feelings of helplessness, hopelessness and haplessness. Terrence Des Pres, for example, notes that the deepest cause of early death in the Nazi death camps among inmates was:

the horror and irreparable hurt felt by the prisoners when he or she first encounter[ed] the spectacle of atrocity. Moral disgust, if it arises too abruptly or becomes too intense, expresses itself in the desire to die, to have done with such a world ... No feeling remains except absolute refusal to go on existing when existence itself seems vile beyond redemption.

(Des Pres, 1977, p. 89)

While mercifully not imprisoned in a concentration or death camp, the person of deep and abiding faith who experiences, in somewhat analogous contexts, an irreparable assault on his religious world of meaning is left feeling bereft of the all-good and just God in his everyday life. He feels betrayed and abandoned by God, as if something has been utterly "broken" inside him, a feeling of lack of integration and wholeness that prevents him from ever again emotionally reconnecting with his once strongly believed in, omnibenevolent God. Thus, the only compelling response to this crisis, to what he feels is an unhealable wounding, a "soul murder," is to reject and abandon such an abusive God. "Extreme" situations often evoke an extreme response in the victim. Such a person is typically left feeling consciously and/or unconsciously depressed and anxious, rooted in a kind of "incomplete" mourning; though if he is willing and able, and also lucky, he can gradually find and create a "replacement world" that allows him to carry on with a modicum of love of life.

It is important to note that the loss of a "world," as described above, in particular the decision to reject and abandon God, is not a one-off decision as much as a gradual realization that one no longer *feels* God's presence except as an object of one's rage. As Berger noted, "The subjective reality of the world hinges on the thin thread of conversation" (1967, p. 17) – that is, of maintaining an ongoing dialogue with a loving God and active involvement with the religious tradition and community that supports it. While, paradoxically speaking, rage and hatred intensely tie you to the offending other (recall Elie Wiesel's anger and protest at God), they are hardly a way of being that one can endure without becoming utterly corrupted by all-consuming toxic emotions as bitterness, cynicism and fury. As I have noted in a previous chapter, rage can be best psychoanalytically understood as "love outraged" (Krystal, 1988, p. 82). It is felt when one's reasonable and heart-felt expectation to be loved is not only not gratified, which is bad enough, but in addition, one is aggressively assaulted and despoiled by the offending other. This outraged/enraged dynamic is often experienced as a radical betrayal that demands a powerful if not punitive response similar to a deserted lover, who cries out in distress, "I don't love you anymore; for me you no longer exist." Indeed, as the Marquis de Sade noted in another context, "No lover [believer], if he be of good faith, and sincere, will deny he would prefer to see his mistress [God] dead than unfaithful" (Thiessen, 1998, p. 50). Thus, the perceived betrayal and abandonment by God is experienced by the former believer as a terrible narcissistic wounding, one that can never be fully healed. Sometimes, however, being unloved – betrayed and abandoned by God – induces a strong need not uncommon in romantic relationships that binds the lover to the beloved in a condition of tormented longing, as it renews the idealization of the beloved God who is regarded as salvation (Shengold, 1999, p. 117).

The rejection and abandonment of God/tradition/community following a traumatic assault on the believer's religiously animated "symbolic world," one that he was securely and happily enmeshed in, can probably be best psychoanalytically conceptualized as being equivalent in its main negative psychological effects to what an abused/neglected child typically feels toward his offending parents: that he has been unintelligibly the victim of "soul murder." "Soul murder," as Shengold points out, is a term most likely first used by the Scandinavian master playwrights who laid the foundations of modern drama, Henrik Ibsen and August Strindberg. Ibsen described "soul murder" as "the destruction of the love of life in another human being" (Shengold, 1999, p. 1). In the child psychoanalytic context, says Shengold, "soul murder" is "the apparently willful abuse and neglect of children by adults that are of sufficient intensity and frequency to be traumatic" (ibid.). Moreover, such children's ensuing emotional development is deeply and negatively impacted; what has happened to them has markedly affected their motivating unconscious fantasies that animate their outlook and capacity to flourish in love and work, and they have become self-subjugated by "the compulsion to repeat the cruelty, violence, neglect, hatred, seduction, and rape of their injurious past." This is, in part, because unconscious identifications with parents are the touchstones of our identities, self-concept and self-esteem (ibid., p. 7).

Indeed, with some recasting, much of what Shengold describes can be analogously applied to understanding the main thrust of what those once devout believers who have traumatically lost their religious symbolic world have experienced, their sufferings and the challenges that lay ahead for them in terms of finding and creating a "replacement world." For example, "soul murder" brings about the loss of the love of life that the believer once felt when he was happily ensconced in his religious symbolic world. In his "God is dead" (or "almost dead") world, he feels the loss of the main basis of his life and identity-defining narrative, his dialogue with a loving God who cares about him. Shengold says that it is precisely the obliteration of an individual's identity by one's sadistic parents that characterizes "soul murder." In the case of the believer, God is consciously and/or unconsciously experienced as a "cosmic sadist," as the Holocaust theologian Richard Rubenstein (1966) provocatively put it. Such a God should not be honored, obeyed or loved. To do so, as happens to so many victims of child abuse, is to get into a sado-masochistic relationship – we love someone whom we fear – that is self-injurious and altogether self-undermining, and therefore can never be the basis for crafting the "good life."

Likewise, the former believer is not capable of effectively and comfortably applying rational thought to his "extreme" circumstances and his subsequent loss of faith, a second aspect of "soul murder." That is, the believer is no longer willing and able to experience his "extreme" situation and its negative spiritual sequelae as having an acceptable degree of "interpretability" (Geertz, 1973, p. 100). Such a person feels overwhelmed by the situation that is "at the limits of their analytic capacities, at the limits of their powers of endurance, and at the limits of their moral insight" (ibid.). Indeed, when such situations of "bafflement, suffering, and a sense of intractable ethical paradox" become intense enough, or are endured long enough, they radically challenge a person's ability to orient themselves effectively. Such situations are so mind-splitting they threaten "to unhinge" one's mind (ibid.).

Finally, says Shengold, like in "soul murder," a common effect is "brain-washing – the cultivation of denial of what has occurred and the suppression of what was experienced – in the mind of the child victims" (1999, p. 6). This is rooted in "the universal stake in needing good parenting. 'This didn't happen' is often explicitly said or in some way forcibly implied to the child by the abuser" (ibid.). Such an abuser may be driven by an internal need for denial and/or the wish to avoid discovery and punishment. This invalidating parental order from without reinforces the abused child's "own internal need to feel that 'this couldn't have happened'" (ibid.). Such a person is forever in an unusually torturous "knowing/not knowing" and "remembering/not remembering" state of mind that is typical of survivors of extreme trauma.

Variations of this process of "self-brainwashing" occur in former believers too, such as when they generate far-fetched rationalizations for God's discernible lack of protectiveness and love, including blaming oneself ("because of our sins we were punished"), rationalizations that they may unconsciously regard as implausible, if not outrageously wrong, but still put forth to themselves. Such defensive rationalizations are consciously embraced in order to satisfy their need/desire to maintain their comforting security-generating connection to their "all good" "parent"/God, similar to the abused child who is forever hopeful that his abusive parent will act otherwise or find out that his father or mother "didn't really mean it." When in the face of radical evil, the sufferer's ability to make moral judgments is seriously challenged. When one's "resources to provide a workable set of ethical criteria, normative guides to govern" are utterly subverted (Geertz, 1973, p. 106), a feeling of absurdity takes hold of one's mind and heart, in that one's suffering is experienced as "useless: 'for nothing,'" as Levinas evocatively puts it. Indeed, Geertz notes, if one's religiously animated "symbolic world" no longer provides "a cosmic guarantee not only for their ability to comprehend the world, but also, comprehending it, to give a precision to their feeling, a definition to their emotions" (ibid., p. 104), then they are left feeling robbed of their will and ability to press on amidst and after their "extreme situation." In other words, when intense, relentless brute pain cannot be metabolized "by placing it in a meaningful context, providing a mode of action through which it can be expressed, being expressed understood, and being understood, endured" (ibid., p. 105), then a believer's faith/tradition/community structures give way to pronounced anomie (feeling socially cut off, disoriented, worldless). This ultimately lands them in an existential abyss characterized by despair and high anxiety. Psychologically speaking, they experience a near-lethal degree of "analytic, emotional and moral impotence" in the face of their experienced evil and suffering (ibid., p. 108). However, some believers who find themselves amidst the "extreme situation" of what I call innocent suffering are willing and able to sustain aspects of the integrity of their "symbolic world" through creatively drawing on their religious resources. Indeed, such efforts are experienced as "soul-saving," the opposite of "soul murder." It is to this subject that I now turn.

## Reaffirmation of faith

"A casual stroll through the lunatic asylum," said Nietzsche, "shows that faith does not prove anything" (Donaldson, 2015, p. 18). Some believers who experience an extreme situation are remarkably able to generate a set of responses to their suffering that maintains the grounding existential coordinates of their religious lives, allowing them to live in a life-affirming manner. Still, they almost always have some "stress fractures" or periodic upsurges of ambivalence and doubt which blunt their ability to devote themselves with the fullness of their being to their God. However, for the most part, to paraphrase the great Axial philosopher Plato, we are twice armed if we fight with faith (Durant, 1933, p. 35).

## Theodicy

An essential part of a religious "symbolic world" is its capacity to generate a compelling degree of understanding, predictability, safety and satisfaction in everyday life, and this includes when the going gets tough, when faced with evil, suffering and, especially, death. That is, even amidst an ordeal of extreme suffering, a religious "symbolic world," at least in principle, allows the believer to develop and maintain a credible and viable sense of self-esteem, the reflective and intuitive feeling that one is engaged in a vitally significant role in a meaningful cosmic drama (Becker, 1964, p. 44). Put differently, it is through a theodicy, a way of vindicating the all-powerful, all-good, and – most importantly – just personal God in the face of *my* suffering, that mercifully takes hold of the believer's heart and mind and helps him endure if not prevail. In general, a theodicy helps a person recreate their "symbolic world" to preserve their sense of being part of a meaningful order, with the consequent feeling of having a serviceable sense of self-esteem, self-continuity and self-cohesion, the bedrocks of a viable narrative of self-identity. As Berger indicates, a theodicy legitimates the marginal and alienating experiences that constantly threaten a person's existence. Sickness, injury and death are interpreted and experienced as events in a larger cosmic history, and as such are given an ultimate significance. So, for example, in the course of everyday life theodicy allows a person to carry on living after the death of a significant other, and to anticipate their own demise without being paralyzed by terror or death anxiety. Thus, to the extent that a person is able to make sense of the pain and suffering of life, so is he able to feel that he is securely moored in the world, with a past worth remembering, a present worth living and a future worth facing.

It is by maintaining this lynchpin of his religious "symbolic world," his faith in a just personal God, that allows the believer to integrate his ordeal of suffering into a framework that fosters the feeling that his suffering makes credible sense: "It is not happiness the theodicy primarily proves, but meaning" (Berger, 1967, pp. 54, 58). In situations of extreme suffering, the need for meaning is greater than the need for happiness, at least in terms of "symbolic world" maintenance, and, as Freud pointed out, this can include meanings that are lodged in neurotic guilt and punishment. As Nietzsche perceptively said, "any meaning is better than none at all" (Welshon, 2004, p. 33), which can include a sadomasochistic relationship to God in which one loves the God one fears. As Berger notes, some theodicies constitute "an essentially sado-masochistic collusion, on the level of meaning, between oppressors and victims" (1967, p. 59). One only has to think of various forms of apocalyptic religion in which the God image is intimately linked to the belief in the destruction of the world and the salvation/redemption of the righteous; or when violence is perpetrated in the name of the Messiah; or simply when one's God image is characterized by "fire and brimstone," requiring submission in thought, feeling and, most importantly, in action, or else face God's wrath. Similar to the abused child, to embrace such a vengeful, angry, judgmental and altogether severe God (to "suffer" him) is to stay intimately linked with the "parent" God, without whom the "child"/believer feels that life is not possible (Shengold, 1999, p. 163).

There are many different theodicies that are available to the believer amidst innocent suffering, especially when it is inflicted by other humans as opposed to a natural disaster, and survivors of such an ordeal often consciously and unconsciously use these well-tried traditional theodicies to make their suffering sufferable, that is, to maintain the integrity of their "symbolic world." For example, one Holocaust survivor I treated interpreted his personal tragedy in terms of other tragedies that have befallen the Jewish people over centuries. For him, the murder of his family was yet another example of the problem of evil, specifically of extreme anti-Semitism, that the Jewish people have endured and survived for time immemorial. This survivor put his personal tragedy into an interpretive framework in which it was viewed as a worst case example of the perennial problem of evil with which Jews have always struggled, but without traumatic discomfort to his faith structure. As a result, he was able to maintain a modicum of self-esteem, self-continuity and self-cohesion, the psychological basis for his willingness and ability to press forward in a life-affirming and Jewish manner. In another instance, a religious survivor of political torture interpreted his ordeal in terms of human evil, the price humankind has to pay for God-given human freedom. In this survivor's mind, innocent suffering reflects shamefully on humans but does not taint God's existence or perfection.

In both of these examples the distressing conundrum of theodicy becomes the conundrum of anthropodicy, an effort to justify the existence of humanity as good (Berger, 1967, p. 74). The question of God's injustice and perceived unfairness becomes a question of man's cruelty and sinfulness. There is a submission to God's omnipotence – a submission to the totally, exalted other who can neither be seriously questioned nor challenged, and who, by his very nature, is sovereignly above any human ethical standards. These religious survivors, like all of us, fight against being uprooted and disorganized; they tenaciously cling to the cosmic perspective and unified vision which assures them a secure place in a universe of known dimensions and definite purposes. To refrain from aggressively challenging God's inaction during an ordeal of innocent suffering, focusing on human depravity and cruelty becomes a way to maintain the self-transcending meanings for which he and all humans hunger.

Another response to the ordeal of innocent suffering is to view it as an unfathomable mystery, a test of one's deep and abiding faith. In this view, similar to all of God's ways, innocent suffering transcends human comprehension and requires faith and silence. In other words, God tests His "believers"; and while it is unclear that one is being challenged or why (think of the book of Job), it is one's obligation to rise to the challenge in faith and devotion. While such a view may seem dogmatic, it actually can reflect a philosophical acceptance of the lack of explanatory certainty one has in the face of God's enigmatic behavior. Indeed, it is the awareness that, for a believer, the heart of the matter is always mystery, especially the riddles of innocent suffering in an assumed ethically caring universe. As the Axial-inspired Spinoza noted, "simple obedience [faith] is the path of salvation" (Elwes, 1891, p. 276).

Believers amidst innocent suffering can also draw from a theodicy that has been described by Buber as a temporary "eclipse of God." That is, there are times when God is inexplicably absent from history or unaccountably chooses to turn His face away. In the biblical context this was due to God punishing his disobedient "children." The antidote to this painful "eclipse of God" is to be absorbed by one's love and trust of God rather than attempt to rationalize His absence. From my clinical experience, there are at least two ways this theodicy manifests itself: either the believer is nearly always in a debate/dialogue with God – "it is all I think about" – or the opposite, "I never think about it." Regardless of which orientation the survivor of innocent suffering takes, he still feels rooted in a secure self-transcending "symbolic world," feeling God's presence and safely lodged in his sheltering "sacred canopy," which, as I have repeatedly stressed, is what really matters in terms of maintaining the will and ability to press on in a life-affirming manner.

Another theodicy that religious Jews and Christians may draw from is one called "vicarious atonement." For example, a believing Jew may reason that the Jewish people are the "suffering servant" of Isaiah – Israel suffers and atones for the sins of others. Some Jews die so that the Gentiles might be purified and live; or, in another variation, the "good" Jews suffered to save the sinful ones, as one devout Holocaust survivor told me. The view that suffering is redemptive is personified in the biblical notion of "sanctification of the Name" (*kiddush-hashem*). As Saint Augustine noted, for the believing Christian, suffering only becomes sustainable and ultimately transfigured when one's life imitates and is fused with Christ, especially in his crucifixion that powerfully shows not only the transient nature of earthly existence, but also the magnificent love that God has for His human creation. It is this passionate internal connection with Christ that constitutes grace, that transformational indwelling of the Holy Spirit, the gift of divine love that for the believing Christian ultimately makes one's suffering sufferable.

A belief in messianism is also drawn from in the face of innocent suffering, including the notion that there will be a resurrection for the dead upon the arrival of the Messiah. It follows, therefore, that martyrs and innocent sufferers who survive honorably will be reborn and enjoy eternal bliss with the Messiah within God's kingdom. As Berger points out, the belief in messianism permits one to relativize and rationalize the suffering of the present in terms of ultimately being overcome in a glorious future. Berger states: "The anomic phenomena are legitimated by reference to a future nomization, thus reintegrating them within an over-all meaningful order" (1967, p. 69). By articulating such a theodicy, the survivor feels the comfort of knowing that in the final analysis the sufferer will be comforted, the good rewarded and the evil punished. This "not yet" perspective permits the survivor to maintain messianic hopes amidst innocent suffering, but at the same time, says Berger, transposes such beliefs to a mysterious, empirically inaccessible sphere that is safe from the vicissitude and challenges of history (ibid., p. 71).

I have described a few of the more common theodicies that survivors of innocent suffering consciously and unconsciously draw from, at least in the Judeo-Christian tradition. All religions and "symbolic worlds" have their theodicies, for all people have a tremendous need to consciously and unconsciously maintain the credibility and viability of their "symbolic world" in the face of overwhelming suffering, especially when it is innocent suffering. The reason for this, says Hannah Arendt, is that when one loses one's "sacred canopy" – that all-embracing system of meaning and metaphor that allows a believer to effectively organize their individual experience into a coherent and patterned whole – one finds oneself without a guide in the wilderness of bare facts, "for when man is robbed of all means of interpreting events he is left with no sense whatsoever of reality" (Arendt, 1978, p. 24).

Psychoanalytically speaking, what is most important in maintaining faith in an omnibenevolent God during and after an experience of innocent suffering is the quality of the mental representation of God (i.e., the God image) that was developed during one's formative years. This mental representation becomes the core of one's life and identity-defining faith structure and sense of residing underneath a protective sacred canopy. A mental representation has been defined as "a relatively permanent image of anything that has been previously perceived, or alternatively, the process by which such images are constructed (acquired)" (Rycroft, 1995, p. 157). This definition underscores the difference between "external reality" and "psychic reality." The latter is shaped by the sexual and aggressive drives, the degree of ego integration and maturity at the time the representation was developed, the existing sociocultural context, and the so-called objective characteristics of the object that is being represented. The object refers to that upon which action and desire are focused, what a person needs to gratify his instinctual wishes (Akhtar, 2009, pp. 169, 170; Rycroft, 1995, p. 113). Psychoanalytic insight is thus in sync with the findings of many empirical studies on object relations and the God image, namely, that research "consistently indicates that those who have loving and nurturing parental images generally develop loving and nurturing images of God" (Hall & Fujikawa, 2013, p. 281).

Moreover, there is a positive relationship between an individual's God image and his self-esteem, as "self esteem was positively correlated with loving and accepting God images and negatively correlated with rejecting ones" (ibid., p. 284). Most importantly, these positive images act as emotional "shock absorbers" during innocent suffering. In a variety of ways, one's personal conception of God (conscious and unconscious, explicit and implicit, cognitive and affective), conceived as a secure and positive attachment figure, helps the innocent sufferer in engaging the manifold levels of emotional processing that are necessary during a nightmarish ordeal. In short, faith in God can sustain the integrity of one's sanity and "symbolic world" because faith is meaning-giving, affect-integrating and action-guiding, even if there are painful and disorganizing moments when God is experienced as punitive and critical or, worse, remote and absent. Such troubling doubt and related disquieting thoughts and feelings, said Tillich, "is not the opposite of faith; it is one element of faith. Therefore, there is no faith without risk" (1991, p. 220). Indeed, as Freud noted, it is precisely having the will and ability to creatively and reasonably manage the ambivalence that characterizes all intimate relationships, such as those wishes to love/idealize and hate/devalue the other – including the Absolute Other – that is the sign of "complete object love" (Freud, 1914, p. 89).

## Unanswered prayers

All "true believers" would surely agree with Thomas Szasz's quip against mainstream psychiatry/psychoanalysis: "If you talk to God, you are praying. If God talks to you, you have schizophrenia" (1973, p. 101). Indeed, in all religions, certainly the Abrahamite ones, prayer is supposed to have efficacy, the ability to have a desired or intended result. Indeed, in the context of extreme suffering, prayer expresses the deep and abiding wish for salvation from one's pained condition. As one of the magisterial psalms of David reads:

> Save me, O God; For the waters are come in even unto the soul. I am sunk in deep mire, where there is no standing; I am come into deep waters, and the flood overwhelmeth me. I am weary with my crying; my throat is dried; Mine eyes fail while I wait for my God. (69:2–3)
>
> (Holy Scriptures, 1964, p. 823)

There is likely not a person in this world who cannot emotionally relate to this psalm on some level, for it evocatively depicts a dimension of being human in all of its poignant starkness. As the crazed and raging King Lear said on the heath, "Unaccommodated man is no more but such a poor, bare, forked animal as thou art" (*Lr.*, 3.4). Indeed, in the context of such "extreme" suffering, a believer consciously and unconsciously relates to his God in ways that are meant to help him endure and prevail over his suffering, however he construes it. Prayer, "a solemn request for help or expression of thanks addressed to God," as it is defined in the *Oxford Dictionary*,[10] plays an important role in keeping "the thin thread of conversation" (Berger, 1967, p. 17) going between man and God, the essential dialogue that is the basis for maintaining one's reality consciousness and "symbolic world." How does prayer become one of the important mediums for helping the believer endure and prevail over his suffering?

As Rabbi Sacks noted, during situations of extreme suffering, "the most profound of all spiritual experiences, the base of all others, is the knowledge that we are not alone" (2016b, p. 2): "Yeah, though I walk through the valley of the shadow of death, I will fear no evil, for Thou are with me" (Psalm 23:4) (*Holy Scriptures,* 1964, p. 791). Calling to mind a child's trusted relationship with his "psychological parent," the one who most symbolizes nurturance, stability and protectiveness, Sacks further notes, "God is holding us by the hand, sheltering us, lifting us when we fall, forgiving us when we fail, healing the wounds in our soul through the power of His love" (2016b, p. 2). Indeed, if one can emotionally connect to such a God, then one will have the will and ability to carry on amidst extreme suffering:

> Though we may fall, we fall into the arms of God. Though others may lose faith in us, and though we may even lose faith in ourselves, God

never loses faith in us. And though we may feel utterly alone, we are not. God is there, beside us, within us, urging us to stand and move on, for there is a task to do that we have not yet done and we were created to fulfill.

(Sacks, 2016b, p. 2)

Sacks is here reaffirming Freud's observation that a heartfelt belief in a theistic God, one who hears our prayers, affirms that there is an omnipotent, omniscient, omnipresent and most of all, an omnibenevolent God, an "illusory" and "wish-fulfilling" parenting figure in psychoanalytic language, who will help buffer us and transcend our fear, loneliness, pain and anguish.

Unraveling in a detailed way how the *homo religious* effectively "uses" prayer and other resources associated with his religious "symbolic world" to endure and prevail amidst extreme suffering is beyond the scope of this chapter. For example, empirical research has suggested that prayer can positively affect how one metabolizes physical pain, including chronic pain which is more aptly described as suffering: it can give a sense of meaning and purpose; it can enhance control and self-efficacy; it can act as a comforting diversion and distraction from one's distress; it can provide a way of giving and getting social support; and it can generate increased calmness and relaxation (Ladd & Spilka, 2012, p. 300). Rather than detail these intriguing findings, in this section I discuss how the problem of prayer's efficacy is dealt with by the typical believer when his heartfelt prayers distressingly appear not to be discernibly or adequately "answered."

### Struggling with God's unresponsiveness to our prayers

How a believer lives with their prayers not being satisfactorily answered depends on many psychological factors. Most importantly it depends on the nature of one's "perceived quality of relationship with God" (Ladd & Spilka, 2012, p. 298). The way a person tries to make intelligible his unanswered prayers tells us about their conscious and unconscious conception of their God image and their perception of how God interacts with the world. Given that prayer is a mode of relational communication with God, like any interpersonal communication, the satisfactoriness of the other's response will to some extent depend on what one expects from the other. Indeed, the greater the congruence between one's expectations and one's fate, the happier a person will be, and this is also true for the man/God relationship. So, for example, to oversimplify: if a child perceives his parents as essentially caring and loving, then he would expect a response to his request that would demonstrate kindness and concern. If his experience of his parents was that they were neglectful and abusive, he would expect an offensive and disparaging response. A "mature enough" child recognizes and accepts, if not begrudgingly, that sometimes his requests to his "good enough" parents are not gratified, frustrating as the word "no" is. Likewise, so this line of reasoning goes, the "enlightened believer" regards his requests to God as sometimes being denied (i.e., God is silent). The British novelist and believing Christian C.S. Lewis, in his essay "The Efficacy of Prayer," put this point just right:

> Prayer is request. The essence of request, as distinct from compulsion, is that it may or may not be granted. And if an infinitely wise Being listens to the requests of finite and foolish creatures, of course He will sometimes grant and sometimes refuse them.
>
> (Lewis, 2000, p. 238)

If human beings were typically so reasonable and composed, then Lewis's formulation would be the end of the matter. However, we psychoanalysts know that, especially in situations of "extreme" suffering, believers are not willing and able to accept "no" from God without considerable internal struggle and discomfort (and sometimes they remain hurt and angry at God for a lifetime). In fact, believers typically feel deeply troubled by God's silence to their ardently felt requests, especially when they are pleading for a reprieve from their suffering that feels so deserving. For example, what "believing" parent whose innocent child is dying from cancer would not feel that the "totally powerful and totally righteous God" should not intervene (Berger, 1967, p. 73)? Believers (and most people facing anomic terror) unconsciously, if not consciously, have to work very hard psychologically to carry on with a relatively intact faith and trust in their personal, just God. Remarkably, many believers remain steeped in their "symbolic world," angry and upset as they may be at God that their deeply felt and justified prayers were not answered. They do this, in part, because they feel they do not have another existentially viable option. As Abraham Lincoln famously admitted, "I have been driven many times to my knees by the overwhelming conviction that I had absolutely no other place to go" (Water, 2000, p. 764).

Indeed, similar to Lincoln, amidst intense suffering, finding and creating a self-sustaining "replacement world" feels radically ill-fated, if not impossible. Rather, a believer typically resorts to other strategies such as those described in cognitive dissonance theory. Reducing cognitive dissonance (intense uneasiness), says Leon Festinger, has the urgency of an instinct in the human mind similar to physical hunger. Just as hunger is a compelling motivation to be satiated, dissonance is a compelling motivation to explain inconsistency and remove dissonance. In other words, explanations act in the human mind in a manner that is similar to the way nutrients satiate physical hunger (Jenkins, 2013). As Berger noted, an explanation, a reason or justification given for a particular action or belief, reflects the "human craving for meaning that appears to have the force of an instinct. Men are congenitally compelled to impose a meaningful order upon reality," an activity of "world construction" (1967, p. 22). Put somewhat differently, there is a human tendency, if not compulsion, to clarify and make transparent those unclarified and opaque problems. This search for lucidity is rooted in the upsurge of "metaphysical anxiety" and emotional imbalance that threatens one's sense of reality. Such a feeling of being "adrift in an absurd world" is an internal disruption that needs to be put right (Geertz, 1973, pp. 101, 102).

For example, a believer can change the personal significance of his original belief or novel information. If a believer's conception of the existence of a responsive God that answers his prayers is contradicted by new information or evidence, i.e., God's silence, he can reduce the dissonance by deciding that the evidence is immaterial because the whole issue falls outside the realm of human intelligibility. He may tell himself that religion teaches us that living with God's inscrutability, mysteriousness and unknowability are at the heart of what it means to be *homo religious*. The point is that in this cognitive strategy, the believer does not actually satisfactorily resolve the inconsistency in his belief system, but rather, he consigns it to a domain of insignificance, a strategy that eradicates his sense of uneasiness.

A second kind of strategy is that the believer can look for evidence that challenges the validity and reliability of the new information. For example, he can persuade himself that the new information is simply not credible, or at least not definitive. For example, there is some empirical research data on the efficacy of prayer that suggests that in some contexts, prayers appear to be answered (Ladd & Spilka, 2013, pp. 299–300). Believers can "cherry pick" these scientific findings and draw on other domains of knowledge, such as personal testimonials, to reduce their dissonance about their original belief. In this way, the need and desire to reduce dissonance animates what is known as "confirmation bias," the human proclivity to interpret new evidence as confirmation of one's existing beliefs or theories.

Finally, a third dissonance-reducing strategy that a believer can use is to modify his original belief. For example, if evidence is presented that contradicts his belief that God answers our prayers, he can decide that the information is indeed correct and his prior belief was precipitous, premature or inadequately conceived. While this is not an often-used strategy for the typical believer, as it can undermine the subjective plausibility of his "symbolic world," some believers are capable of convincing themselves that God answers prayers in ways that he did not anticipate, or at a point in time when God is willing to solve many more difficulties for many more people than only the believer's request (Jenkins, 2013).

While these three strategies are only examples of the options that the typical believer can implement as he tries to consciously and unconsciously rationalize his dissatisfaction that God did not appear to answer his pained prayers, they do put into sharp focus the fact that, like with anyone ensconced in a "symbolic world," the believer fights hard not to experience his definition of reality as "fraudulent" or "fragile." That is, if one's "*ad hoc* cognitive and normative operating procedures" (Berger, 1967, p. 23) that constitute his "symbolic world" are seriously compromised or destroyed, his sense of reality and identity is thrown into a state of extreme conceptual disarray, causing terrifying anxiety and other shattering effects. Is there a reasonable avenue of flight from this awful feeling of chaos and "worldlessness" brought about when God does not appear to answer our prayers? Indeed, there may be at least a partial antidote to this anomic terror; but it involves, from the start, the transformation of our infantile view of God as the protective Parent, and the believer as the vulnerable child, as well as the behaviors that support such a way of being to one that reflects a "higher integration" and greater autonomy. Levinas calls this "a religion for adults" (1990, p. 11).

### Reconceptualizing the meaning of prayer

"The function of prayer is not to influence God," said the Axial-inspired Søren Kierkegaard, "but rather to change the nature of the one who prays" (Zackeim, 2015, p. x). Indeed, if keeping the "thin thread of conversation" (Berger, 1967, p. 17) going between man and God is what matters most in terms of symbolic "world maintenance," then the believer needs to change his understanding of what constitutes *his* contribution to the "conversation," as this is the only aspect that he can control. That is, the "terms of engagement" with God require a conceptual overhauling, one that is better aligned with how everyday reality seems to "hang together" and operate to the believer, in particular, the fact that God often appears not to answer our prayers when we are suffering.

As Levinas points out in his discussion of Hasidic Rabbi Hayyim Volozhiner's masterpiece, *Soul of Life* (*Nefesh ha'Hayyim*), prayer is the animating condition for ethical living, for being for the other before oneself (or at least *as much as* oneself): "Prayer never asks for anything for oneself; strictly speaking, it makes no demands at all, but is an elevation of the soul" (Levinas, 1989, p. 232). By "elevation of the soul" Levinas means that prayer potentiates in the believer an other-directed, other-regarding and other-serving way of being in everyday life. Such a view of prayer characterized by self "dis-inter-est" is a radical reorientation in terms of how the typical "enlightened believer" construes one of the two main functions of prayer – as a request for help. The other function of prayer is an expression of thanks, though the suffering believer may feel at indignant moments similar to Nietzsche, who quipped, "I cannot believe in a God who wants to be praised all the time" (Esar, 1995, p. 347). In particular, says Levinas, "prayer means that, instead of seeking one's own salvation, one secures that of others" (1989, p. 233). However, following Volozhiner, Levinas says that praying to end one's personal suffering is legitimate if it is a prayer to God who Himself suffers in the sufferings of man:

> There is a way in which the suffering self can pray: by praying for the suffering of God who suffers through my human suffering. I do not have

to pray for my suffering. God, prior to any demand, is already there with me.

(Levinas, 1989, p. 234)

For Levinas, at least in his explication of *Soul of Life*, "the meaning of suffering is surely the expiation of sin," a view that he says after Auschwitz is not acceptable to preach to others, "but does this prevent one from saying it to oneself?" (1989, p. 234). For Levinas, similar to St. Augustine, since man is ontologically guilty, there is always more we can and must do to help others. Such a critical self-reflection is necessary and inevitable. Thus, Levinas is putting forth a notion of "prayer without demand," an outlook that means that when one is suffering, our "torture" is "expiated precisely through" our awareness, or at least belief, of "the surplus of God's suffering over man's: God suffers in reparation for transgression" right up to the bitter end of one's suffering, "and the transgression," the guilt we feel, is "expiated" (ibid.). Levinas suggests that amidst our suffering, our prayers ought not be crudely self- and ego-centered. One's personal suffering is greatly "diminished" if it is God- and other-focused: "he can no longer feel [his suffering], in comparison with the suffering of God which is so much greater than his own" (ibid.).[11]

In this view, as Buber notes, authentic prayer still reflects the felt immediacy between man and God, it still involves the believer turning mind, heart and soul directly to God; however, more than asking like a child for instant release from one's suffering, he "ultimately asks for the manifestation of the divine Presence, for this Presence becoming dialogically perceivable" (Friedman, 2002, p. 159). That is, keeping the conversation going is what matters, despite the precariousness of all socially constructed worlds (Berger, 1967, p. 29). Authentic prayer, says Buber, even amidst suffering, means "the readiness of the whole man for this Presence, simple turned-towardness, unreserved spontaneity" (Friedman, 2002, p. 159). Most importantly, prayer conceived as an expression of "spiritual energy," as Buber calls it, must not remain introverted, self-centric and sufficient in and of itself, but ultimately must "overflow into social action" and communal enhancement (i.e., being for the other, suffering for the other) (Hodes, 1971, p. 78).

"Prayer, among sane people," wrote George Santayana, "has never superseded practical efforts to secure the desired end," and this is the best evidence that the sphere of expression is not being mistaken for concrete reality (Santayana & Smith, 1934, p. 50). It is through such a way of being-in-the-world via the heartfelt dialogic relation to the Eternal One that one can best make one's suffering sufferable. Another great Hasidic Rabbi, Levi Yitzhak of Berditchev, beautifully expressed this sentiment, an apt quotation to end this section:

Master of the Universe. I do not know what questions to ask. I do not expect You to reveal Your secrets to me. All I ask is that You show me one thing – what this moment means to me and what You demand of me. I do not ask why I suffer. I ask only this: Do I suffer for Your sake?

(Rabinowicz, 1982, p. 94)

Such a "prayer without demand," without infantile insistence for immediate relief from one's suffering, but which is other-directed, other-regarding and other-serving, is precisely what Levinas says constitutes a "religion for adults."

## The suffering of "losing" one's child to atheism, agnosticism, other religions or indifference

For the *homo religious* there is hardly anything that causes as much distress as having a child who one has raised to love and fear God (i.e., to be in awe of Him), to rejoice in Him and to live a religious lifestyle that instantiates those sentiments, who chooses to reject this and think and live differently. One only has to consider the typical "believing" Jewish, Christian or Muslim parent who feels rejected, ignored, abandoned and/or hated – in a word, heartbroken. Indeed, in Orthodox Judaism, if a son or daughter marries a non-Jew, the ultimate expression of rejection of his parent's religious world, the parent is supposed to say *kaddish*, the mourner's prayer, as if one's child is dead. While other religions do not go so far as this in their reaction to a child rejecting their religion, they all shun such behavior, and the "believing" parent whose child has gone "awry" typically feels very upset, sometimes for a lifetime. The social stigma of having such wayward and "off the path" children also plays a role in this upset. There are, of course, many different reasons – some "good" and some "bad" – why a child chooses to reject his parent's God/tradition/community and religious lifestyle. My focus here is on the nature of the parent's suffering – how the parent feels and responds.

To begin with, from the perspective of the "believing" parent, a child's choice to go his own religious way – whether in the form of atheism, agnosticism, conversion or simply indifference (each of these departures have their own unique phenomenologies and dynamics) – feels like a powerful repudiation of the parent, both a rejection of values and sensibilities, and a denial of the truth and validity of their belief system and lifestyle. Put starkly, a parent feels hugely narcissistically wounded, that is, his sense of self and self-esteem feels assaulted, leaving him hurt and angry. The key question is why this feels so narcissistically wounding.

To begin to answer this question we first need to take a short excursion into the reflections of Levinas on the existential meaning of "fecundity," the ability to produce children. It is through fecundity that the erotic charge between a man and woman takes on a radically different meaning, as does one's self- and self-world relation. The self is profoundly changed through bringing about the birth of a son or daughter within the context of a loving relationship. It is through the child that there is a degree of self-transcendence. Perhaps most importantly, the birth of a child summons the parent to a form of responsibility for the other that in certain ways, as most parents will say, requires considerably more selflessness, sacrifice and being for the other before oneself than does one's relationship to one's spouse or significant other:

> The fact of seeing the possibilities of the other as your own possibilities, of being able to escape the closure of your identity and what is bestowed on you and which nevertheless is yours – this is paternity [and maternity]. This future beyond my own being, this dimension constitutive of time, takes on a concrete content in paternity [and maternity].
>
> (Levinas 1985, p. 70)[12]

The point Levinas is making is that the child, or more accurately the relation to the child, has a duality of structure, for he represents alterity or otherness, but also one's self, all wrapped up in one. Levinas elaborates this "way of being other while being oneself":

> The son [or daughter] is not only my work, like a poem or an object, nor is he my property. Neither the categories of power nor those of knowledge describe my relation with the child. The fecundity of the I is neither a cause nor a determination. I do not have my child; I am my child. Paternity is a relation with a stranger who while being Other … is me, a relation of the I with a self which yet is not me. In this "I am" being is no longer Eleatic unity.[13] In existing itself there is multiplicity and a transcendence. In this transcendence the I is not swept away, since the son is not me; and yet I am my son. The fecundity of the I is its very transcendence. The biological origin of this concept nowise neutralizes the paradox of its meaning, and delineates a structure that goes beyond the biologically empirical.
>
> (Levinas, 1969, p. 77)

What Levinas is getting at is that the relation with the child puts us into a relation with a new structure of time, what he calls "infinite time." This is because the relation with the son or daughter is a relation with the other that is not a power, such as a thing to be used for instrumental purposes and then discarded. Rather, it is a relation of fecundity, a relation with the absolute future. Despite the inevitability of a parent's death, his or her existence is profoundly extended through his children (ibid., p. 268).

Infinite time "is the time in which the I exists without the finite limits of mortality" (Atterton & Calarco, 2005, p. 48). "The time in which being and infinitum is produced," says Levinas, "goes beyond the possible" (1969, p. 281). Infinite time, in a certain sense, is the possibility of a kind of everlasting youth, of newness, of eternal spring and hopefulness; it frees, or nearly frees, the self from the past in that, for example, one's mistakes, one's guilt-inducing omissions and commissions, take on new, more life-affirming meaning and purpose. I am reminded of a convicted felon I interviewed in a maximum-security prison who wanted court-ordered visitation with his four-year-old daughter, who he had seen only once or twice before he was incarcerated. He told me:

> The only thing that makes me want to survive in this jungle is the thought of reunion with "my baby." I am finished with a life of crime, all I want is to get out of this hellhole and be a good father to her, to let her know I did not forget her.

Infinite time also frees us, or at least lessens the frightening awareness of growing old and dying. Our good works, such as the goodness that we foster in our children – manifested in their living their lives in a manner that makes the world a better and more beautiful place – means, in a certain sense, that we live on. Fecundity thus brings about goodness in that it is through our children that we transmit important memories and insights, and instantiate obligations and responsibilities to those who come after us (Hutchens, 2004, p. 87). Levinas calls this "pardon" – a release or easing of burden from the past or from the mainly egological interiority that fecundity brings about (1969, p. 283).

   Thus, it is through the child that Eros evokes in the parent a different way of experiencing oneself and the world. According to Fryer, "in the child the I is drawn back to itself and its possible continuation in the other person who is both other than and yet still myself" (2004, p. 82). In other words, "Eros challenges traditional notions of subjectivity as the singular subject apart from other existents. Now subjectivity is bound up in an other who is not like myself, but who is myself, without sacrificing his otherness" (ibid.). Thus, the dual egoism and narcissism of the insular, loving couple is ruptured, giving way to self-transcendence in and through the child. Parents now dwell in "goodness," as they become in outlook and behavior decidedly other-directed, other-regarding and other-serving to the child.

   We are now better prepared to suggest why a child's repudiation of his parent's faith/tradition and religious lifestyle feels narcissistically wounding. One of the strongest urges adults have is to strive for "something more," "something better" and "something higher," what Robert Jay Lifton (1976) described as "symbolic immortality," an "experiential transcendence," that intense feeling when "time and death disappear." Such experiences of being enamored with existence centrally involve "losing oneself" and can occur in a number of enthralling contexts: in religious and secular forms of mysticisms; and in "song, dance, battle, sexual love, childbirth, athletic effort, mechanical flight, or in contemplating works of artistic or intellectual creation" (ibid., pp. 33–34). For the believer, it is having a child that continues the parent's religious world (i.e., "the thin thread of conversation" between man and God), perpetuating his life- and identity-defining values, beliefs and practices that more than anything represent his sense of immortality and transcendent strivings. Such parents are profoundly longing to be what Walter Benjamin called "witnesses for the future" (Bouretz, 2007, p. 173), and to have this denied them is, in psycho-analytic language, nothing less than a symbolic "castration."

Erik Erikson put this point just right in his discussion of the last stage of his psychosexual theory, that of "integrity vs. despair": "I am what survives me" (Hoare, 2002, p. 193). Erikson observed that if we view our lives as unproductive (e.g., not producing God-loving, God-fearing religious children to continue the legacy), feel guilt about our past (e.g., it is our fault that our child has gone awry) or feel that we did not accomplish our goals in life (e.g., raising religious children who will beget more religious children) we become very unhappy with life, an impotent feeling that can morph into a sense of despair that is marked by hopelessness and depression. Of course, there are much more reasonable and healthy ways of dealing with a child's repudiation of his parent's religious world – like embracing a view of "live and let live" – but the fact is that from the perspective of the believer, it is often an emo- tional ordeal, one that is especially hurtful and anger-inducing. This is in part because it feels as if God has outrageously inflicted undeserved and unjusti- fied suffering. This fate robs him of, or at least subverts in him, a "core" aspect of what is meaning-giving, affect-integrating and action-guiding about his faith and trust in God; namely, that once the believer dies, the best of what he has produced and accomplished – his God-loving, God-fearing and God-rejoicing children – will perpetuate his religious "world."

## Final thought

The believer, a magician of allegories and symbolism (Bouretz, 2007, p. 182), one who maintains his sense of fantasy and epiphany, may find God's answer to Job's pained and poignant question of why the good suffer and the wicked flourish as correct, but hardly intellectually or emotionally satisfying: "Don't ask! It's beyond your understanding" (Shengold, 1999, p. 258). Or alter- natively, as Martin Luther quipped, "Pray, and let God worry" (Gritsch, 2009, p. 94). Indeed, as Freud has argued, the believer struggles with his per- sonal suffering in many ways that are similar to a non-believer; namely, he desperately tries to make it go away, especially its more acutely painful aspects. As Shakespeare said in *Much Ado About Nothing*, "There was never yet philosopher that could endure the toothache patiently, however they have writ the style of gods and made a push at chance and sufferance" (5.1.37–40).

This being said, I have suggested that the believer is lodged in a "home" and "symbolic world" that has its own unique intellectual and emotional resources that can assist, however imperfectly, in "managing" suffering while maintaining the rudiments of autonomy, integration and humanity. After all, when all is said and done, what matters most to a suffering soul, to quote Shakespeare again, is to be willing and able to sustain, with at least a touch of stoicism, the plausibility of his world of meaning: "Men must endure. Their going hence, even as their coming hither: Ripeness is all" (*Lr.*, 5.2.9). What makes a believer's way of suffering unique is that it is intimately tied to, and metabolized through, a psychologically mediated dialogue with his God, a God who frequently responds to his questions and heartfelt pleas with what feels like silence or some other unsatisfying response. This is an essential aspect of the psychology of the believer: he suffers from a kind of perennial "heavenly homesickness" (Bouretz, 2007, p. 171). That is, he is willing and able to trustingly live with, and in, mystery, including his disturbing doubts that alternate between perceiving God's absence as presence and his presence as absence (Boss, 1999, p. 138).

Such an outlook is highly precarious, but that is the nature of the believer's world – he resides in a dimension of being that is metaphorically on the "narrow ridge" of "holy insecurity" (Hodes, 1971, p. 56). The key to living the "good life" with this dizzying insecurity is to be willing and able to be receptive, responsive and responsible to life and the world, including to the shocks of existence that must be borne to actualize the best one can be. As the great Bohemian Austrian poet and novelist Rainer Maria Rilke said:

> be patient toward all that is unsolved in your heart and try to love the questions themselves like locked rooms and like books that are written in a very foreign tongue ... And the point is, to live everything. Live the questions now. Perhaps you will then gradually, without noticing it, live along some day into the answer.
>
> (Hodes, 1971, p. 55)

## Notes

1  In *Totem and Taboo*, for example, Freud noted, "The god of each of them is formed in the likeness of the father, his personal relation to god depends on his relation to his father...at bottom God is nothing other than an exalted father" (1913, p. 147). Freud may have been influenced by Epictetus, the Stoic philosopher, who characterized God as the "caring father of human beings." According to Long, for Epictetus, God is theist, personalist and ethical (Long, 2002, p. 144, 157).

2  As Geertz noted, religion's "sacred symbols function to synthesize a people's ethos – the tone, character, and quality of their life, its moral and aesthetic style and mood – and their world view – the picture they have of the way things in sheer actuality are, their most comprehensive ideas of order" (1973, p. 89).

3  www.logicallyfallacious.com/tools/lp/Bo/LogicalFallacies/99/Genetic-Fallacy, retrieved 11/1/16.

4  www.thedailybeast.com/articles/2012/08/27/nobel-laureate-elie-wiesel-on-his-fear-of-being-the-last-holocaust-witness.html, retrieved 11/1/16; www.nytimes.com/1986/10/15/world/man-in-the-news-witness-to-evil-eliezer-weisel.html, retrieved 11/2/16.

5  P. Cary, personal communication, 3/21/01.
6  It should be mentioned that Melanie Klein has further developed Freud's classical views on guilt, claiming an innate sense of guilt that emanates from the mindfulness of the wish to obliterate what is also cherished, to resist what is capitulated to, namely, the "breast"/mother (Marcus, 2008, p. 53).
7  I have paraphrased Becker.
8  In this chapter I draw from Judaism, as this is the religion and culture I know from the "inside," especially psychologically speaking. I do, however, reference other religious traditions in passing.
9  It is also worth remembering, as Nietzsche noted, that the language game of "reason" is no more rational than "revelation."
10 https://en.oxforddictionaries.com/definition/prayer, retrieved 1/15/16.
11 Of course, psychoanalytically speaking, all prayers, even those that are otherfocused, like praying for a sick child, have a narcissistic gratification in that the health of sick child is so important to the parent.
12 Levinas uses paternity as his exemplar, though he seems to be actually speaking about parenthood. He has been criticized for this masculine bias in his philosophy.
13 Eleatic unity is the philosophy founded by Zeno of Elea and Parmenides maintaining the belief that there is one indivisible and unchanging reality.

## References

Akhtar, S. (2009). *Comprehensive Dictionary of Psychoanalysis*. London: Karnac.
Arendt, H. (1978). *Hannah Arendt: The Jew as Pariah*. R.H. Feldman (Ed.). New York: Grove.
Atterton, P., & Calarco, M. (2005). *On Levinas*. Belmont, CA: Wadsworth.
Becker, E. (1964). *The Revolution in Psychiatry*. New York: Free Press.
Becker, E. (1973). *The Denial of Death*. New York: Free Press.
Berger, P. (1967). *The Sacred Canopy: Elements of a Sociological Theory of Religion*. New York: Anchor.
Bettelheim, B. (1979). *Surviving and Other Essays*. New York: Knopf.
Bion, W. (1963). *Elements of Psychoanalysis*. London: Karnac.
Boss, P. (1999). *Ambiguous Loss: Learning to Live with Unresolved Grief*. Cambridge, MA: Harvard University Press.
Bouretz, P. (2007). Messianism and Modern Jewish Philosophy. In M.L. Morgan and P.E. Gordon (Eds.), *Modern Jewish Philosophy* (pp. 179–191). Cambridge: Cambridge University Press.
Buber, M. (1965). *The Knowledge of Man: Selected Essays*. M.S Friedman (Ed.). New York: Harper & Row.
Card, C. (2002). *The Atrocity Paradigm: A Theory of Evil*. Oxford, UK: Oxford University Press.
Cohen, R. (2016). Do Not Go Gentle. *New York Times*, 12/3/16, p. A23.
Des Pres, T. (1977). *The Survivor: An Anatomy of Life in the Death Camps*. New York: Pocket Books.
Donaldson, S. (2015). *Dimensions of Faith: Understanding Faith Through the Lens of Science and Religion*. Cambridge, UK: Lutterworth.
Durant, W. (1933). *The Story of Philosophy*. New York: Pocket Books.
Elwes, R.H.M. (1891). *The Chief Works of Benedict de Spinoza. Introduction: Tractatus Theologico-Politicus, Tractatus Politicus* (Vol. 1). London: George Bell & Sons.

Esar, E. (1995). *20,000 Quips and Quotes.* New York: Barnes & Noble.

Freud, S. (1913) [1953]. Totem and Taboo. In J. Strachey (Ed. & Trans.), *Standard Edition of the Complete Psychological Works of Sigmund Freud* (Vol. 13, pp. 1–162). London: Hogarth Press.

Freud, S. (1914) [1957]. On Narcissism: An Introduction. In J. Strachey (Ed. & Trans.), *The Standard Edition of the Complete Psychological Works of Sigmund Freud* (Vol. 14, pp. 67–102). London: Hogarth Press.

Freud, S. (1927) [1961]. The Future of Illusion. In J. Strachey (Ed. & Trans.), *The Standard Edition of the Complete Psychological Works of Sigmund Freud* (Vol. 21, pp. 5–56). London: Hogarth Press.

Friedman, M.S. (2002). *Martin Buber: The Life of Dialogue* (4th ed.). London: Routledge.

Fryer, D.R. (2004). *The Intervention of the Other: Ethical Subjectivity in Levinas and Lacan.* New York: Other Press.

Geertz, C. (1973). *The Interpretation of Cultures.* New York: Basic Books.

Giddens, A. (1984). *The Constitution of Society.* Berkeley: University of California Press.

Goffman, E. (1961). *Asylums.* Garden City, NY: Anchor.

Gritsch, E.W. (2009). Luther and Humor. In T.J. Wengert (Ed.), *The Pastoral Luther: Essays on Martin Luther's Practical Theology* (pp. 85–99). Grand Rapids, MI: Eerdmans.

Hall, T.W., & Fujikawa, A.M. (2013). God Image and the Sacred. In K.I. Pargament (Ed.), *APA Handbook of Psychology, Religion, and Spirituality: An Applied Psychology of Religion and Spirituality* (Vol. 1, pp. 277–292). Washington, DC: American Psychological Association.

Hoare, C.H. (2002). *Erikson on Development in Adulthood: New Insights from Unpublished Sources.* Oxford, UK: Oxford University Press.

Hodes, A. (1971). *Martin Buber: An Intimate Portrait.* New York: Viking.

*Holy Scriptures, The: A New Translation.* (1964). Philadelphia, PA: Jewish Publication Society of America.

Hutchens, B.C. (2004). *Levinas: A Guide for the Perplexed.* London: Continuum.

Jenkins, T. (2013). *Of Flying Saucers and Social Scientists: A Re-Reading of When Prophecy Fails and of Cognitive Dissonance.* London: Palgrave Macmillan.

Joas, H. (2012). The Axial Debate as Religious Discourse. In R.N. Bellah & H. Joas (Eds.), *The Axial Age and Its Consequences* (pp. 9–25). Cambridge, MA: Harvard University Press.

John, St. of the Cross (1619) [2003]. *Dark Night of the Soul.* E.A. Peers (Trans.). Mineola, NY: Dover.

Jones, J.W. (1991). *Contemporary Psychoanalysis and Religion.* New Haven, CT: Yale University Press.

Krystal, H. (1988). *Integration and Self Healing: Affect, Healing and Alexithymia.* London: Routledge.

Ladd, K.L., & Spilka, B. (2012). Prayer: A Review of the Empirical Literature. In K.I. Pargament (Ed.), *APA Handbook of Psychology, Religion, and Spirituality: An Applied Psychology of Religion and Spirituality* (Vol. 2, pp. 293–310). Washington, DC: American Psychological Association.

Levinas, E. (1969). *Totality and Infinity: an Essay on Exteriority.* A. Lingis (Trans.). Pittsburgh, PA: Duquesne University Press.

Levinas, E. (1985). *Ethics and Infinity: Conversations with Philippe Nemo.* R.A. Cohen (Trans.). Pittsburgh, PA: Duquesne University Press.

Levinas, E. (1989). Prayer without Demand. In S. Hand (Ed.), *The Levinas Reader* (pp. 227–234). Oxford, UK: Blackwell. (Original work published 1984)

Levinas, E. (1990). *Difficult Freedom: Essays on Judaism.* S. Hand (Trans.). Baltimore, MD: Johns Hopkins University Press.

Lewis, C.S. (2000). *C.S. Lewis Essay Collection and Other Short Pieces.* L. Walmsley (Ed.). New York: HarperCollins. (Original work published 1959)

Lifton, R.J. (1976). *The Life of the Self: Toward a New Psychology.* New York: Basic Books.

Long, A.A. (2002). *Epictetus: A Stoic and Socratic Guide to Life.* Oxford, UK: Oxford University Press.

Marcus, P. (2008). *Being for the Other: Emmanuel Levinas, Ethical Living and Psychoanalysis.* Milwaukee, WI: Marquette University Press.

Marcus, P., & Rosenberg, A. (Eds.). (1998). *Psychoanalytic Versions of the Human Condition: Philosophies of Life and their Impact on Practice.* New York: New York University Press.

May, R. (1958). Contributions of Existential Psychotherapy. In R. May, E. Angel, & H.F. Ellenberger (Eds.), *Existence: A New Dimension in Psychiatry and Psychology* (pp. 37–91). New York: Basic Books.

McGregor, P.J. (2016). *Heart to Heart: The Spiritual Christology of Joseph Ratzinger.* Eugene, OR: Pickwick.

Pattison, E.M. (1988). The Holocaust as Sin: Requirements in Psychoanalytic Theory for Human Evil and Mature Morality. In S.S. Luel & P. Marcus (Eds.), *Psychoanalytic Reflections on the Holocaust: Selected Essays* (pp. 71–94). New York: University of Denver and KTAV.

Rabinowicz, R.A. (Ed.). (1982). *Passover Haggadah: The Feast of Freedom* (2nd ed.). New York: Rabbinical Assembly.

Rizzuto, A.-M., & Shafranske, E.P. (2013). Addressing Religion and Spirituality in Treatment from a Psychodynamic Perspective. In K.I. Pargament (Ed.), *APA Handbook of Psychology, Religion, and Spirituality: An Applied Psychology of Religion and Spirituality* (Vol. 2, pp. 125–146). Washington, DC: American Psychological Association.

Rubenstein, R. (1966). *After Auschwitz: Radical Theology and Contemporary Judaism.* New York: Bobbs-Merrill.

Rycroft, C. (1995). *A Critical Dictionary of Psychoanalysis.* London: Penguin.

Sacks, J. (2016a). Rabbi Jonathan Sacks on Vayeira. *Shabbat Announcements,* Great Neck Synagogue, 11/19/16.

Sacks, J. (2016b). Rabbi Jonathan Sacks on Vayeitzei. *Shabbat Announcements,* Great Neck Synagogue, 12/10/16.

Santayana, G., & Smith, L.P. (1934). The Imaginative Nature of Religion. In *Little Essays Drawn from the Writings of George Santayana* (pp. 47–51). New York: Scribner's Sons.

Shakespeare, W. (1965). *The Complete Works of William Shakespeare.* New York: Avenel.

Shengold, L. (1999). *Soul Murder Revisited: Thoughts about Therapy, Hate, Love, and Memory.* New Haven, CT: Yale University Press.

Silberstein, L.J. (1989). *Martin Buber's Social and Religious Thought*. New York: New York University Press.

Szasz, T.S. (1973). *The Second Sin*. New York: Anchor.

Teresa, M., & Kolodiejchuk, B. (2007). *Mother Teresa: Come Be My Light: The Private Writings of the "Saint of Calcutta."* New York: Doubleday.

Thiessen, D. (1998). *A Sociological Compendium: Aphorisms, Sayings, Asides*. New Brunswick, NJ: Transaction.

Tillich, P. (1958). *The Dynamics of Faith*. New York: HarperCollins.

Tillich, P. (1968). *A History of Christian Thought*. C.E. Braaten (Ed.). New York: Simon & Schuster.

Tillich, P. (1991). *Paul Tillich: Theologian of the Boundaries*. M.K. Taylor (Ed.). Minneapolis, MN: Fortress.

Water, M.C. (2000). *The New Encyclopedia of Christian Quotations*. Grand Rapids, MI: Baker.

Welshon, R. (2004). *The Philosophy of Nietzsche*. Oxford, UK: Routledge.

Winnicott, D. (1965). *Maturational Processes and the Facilitating Environment*. New York: International Universities Press.

Wuthnow, R., Hunter, J.D., Bergesen, A., & Kurzweil, E. (1984). *Cultural Analysis: The Work of Peter L. Berger, Mary Douglas, Michel Foucault, and Jürgen Habermas*. Boston, MA: Routledge and Kegan Paul.

Zackeim, V. (Ed.) (2015). *Faith: Essays from Believers, Agnostics, and Atheists*. New York: Atria.

# Chapter 4

# The suffering of mental anguish

In a letter that aptly expresses a dark sentiment that most thoughtful people have felt from time to time, the elderly St. Augustine wrote, "Everyone should realize the misery which is part of human life extends from the tears of the newly born to the last breath of the soon to die" (Burt, 1999, p. 417). Indeed, this gloomy statement calls to mind Freud's tragicomic line (Marcus, 2013, p. 88) in *Studies on Hysteria* that the purpose of analysis is "transforming your hysterical [neurotic] misery into common [normal] unhappiness" (Breuer & Freud, 1955, p. 305). What Augustine and Freud are getting at is that life is a distress-filled existence from the cradle to the grave. Indeed, there are "limit-situations," as philosopher Karl Jaspers called them – existential "givens," like suffering, struggle, guilt and death, which one cannot avoid, let alone resolve or transcend (Cooper, 2017, p. 22). In fact, all suffering is a foretaste of death in the sense of feeling impotent, or passive, a kind of psychological materialization that calls to mind a corpse (Lingis, 2015, p. 237). The upsurge of awareness of our vulnerability, finitude and mortality is particularly ego-chilling. As psychoanalyst D.W. Winnicott quipped, "Death is a disaster which you have to put up with, because you're human" (Neve, 1992, p. 376).

These limiting existential factors can serve as the conditions of immobilization from anxiety, depression and other painful emotions, or for fashioning the "good life." While episodic anxiety and depression are part of the vicissitudes of everyday life, sometimes these feelings become so intense for so long that they morph into clinical conditions, these being the focus of hundreds of psychoanalytic and other volumes. As the Axial sages have taught, though human beings seem to be "hardwired" to experience bouts of intensely disturbing anxiety and depression, there are also skillful and wise ways of thinking and acting that tend to buffer a person from the most distressing aspects of these feeling states, or more accurately, these ways of being-in-the-world.[1] The *Bhagavad Gita*, for example, says, "For him who has conquered the mind, the mind is the best of friends, but for one who has failed to do so, his very mind will be the greatest enemy" (Prabhupada, 1972, p. 313). Not only do these protective ways of thinking and acting tend to maintain and potentiate personal autonomy, integration and humanity amidst suffering, they can also help a person grow and develop, even flourish, once they have "fought" through the worst aspects of their suffering.

Psychoanalysis has been masterful in depicting the range of these so-called neurotic ways of being-in-the-world that make one's life miserable. Indeed, a person almost always ultimately pays a high psychological price in the "real" and imagined world for behaving "unreasonably," for, as St. Augustine wrote in his *Confessions*, "The punishment of every disordered mind is its own disorder" (Wiley, 2002, p. 63). Most importantly, psychoanalysis has suggested what ideally has to be internally transformed, what "reasonable" thoughts and feelings need to animate one's decision making and behavior to effectively modulate, if not vanquish, inordinate anxiety, depression and other emotional impediments to living well.

This chapter is divided into Part A, on anxiety, and Part B, on depression. I first describe some of the existential limiting factors that beset all of us and incline us to experience our existence as distressed-filled. That is, we tend to promote the upsurge of anxiety and depression unless these existential limit factors, and the profound challenges they present, are "reasonably" metabolized and compassionately responded to. I then discuss a few "moral" aspects of anxiety and depression that have been underappreciated in the psychoanalytic literature and have bearing on the problem of fashioning the "good life." Following the great Axial sages as well as my two intellectual touchstones who have been animated by the Axial vision, Freud and Levinas, my claim is that the person bogged down by neurotic anxiety and depression is "ethically disabled," meaning they are "persistently and significantly alienated from the good" (Jacobs, 2001, pp. 1, 74). While what constitutes the "good" is of course perspectival, by "goodness" I mean, following Levinas, "a life of responsibility without concern for reciprocity," "a love without eros," "the order of being-for-the-Other," what Levinas and the Axial sages mean by holiness (1998a, pp. xv, ix).

In other words, such "ethically disabled" people have profound problems in living inextricably linked to their moral life; they are cognitively and emotionally impaired in their capacity for moral autonomy and integrity, a way of being that is energized by the commitment to "virtue ethic[s]" as they have been called (Jacobs, 2001).[2] As philosopher Jonathan Jacobs further notes, for such incapacitated people, "their characters are such that sound ethical considerations," such as being willing and able to be reliably other-directed, other-regarding and other-serving, are largely "inaccessible to them" (ibid., p. 1). They are, to quote Levinas, unwilling and unable to engage in acts of unforeseen, gratuitous kindness, those "acts of stupid, senseless goodness" (2001b, p. 89). Moreover, such people have a seriously truncated capacity for moral transformation, "for ethical self correction" (ibid.), as they are utterly wrapped up in themselves – self-centered, self-focused and other-excluding – as they desperately navigate the minefield of their minds (Spinelli, 2015, p. 105).

My focus on "moral psychology"[3] should not seem far-fetched and "preachy" to the typical psychoanalyst educated in Freud. Freud also wanted psychoanalysis to be an ethical enterprise (Marcus, 2008); he wanted analysts and analysands to be exemplary people in their moral life: "Our art," said Freud, "consists in making it possible for people to be moral and to deal with their wishes philosophically" (Hale, 1971, p. 121). Freud perhaps longed for psychoanalysis to be a way to help analysands make themselves into people characterized by moral excellence. The one just cited, four Freud quotes from letters to the American neurologist sympathetic to psychoanalysis, James Jackson Putnam, and one from one of Freud's technique papers suggest this is a plausible notion:

1    "That psychoanalysis has not made the analysts themselves better, nobler, or of stronger character remains a disappointment for me. Perhaps, I was wrong to expect it" (Hale, 1971, pp. 163–164).
2    "The unworthiness of human beings, including the analyst, always impressed me deeply, but why should analyzed men and women in fact be better. Analysis makes for integration but does not itself make for goodness" (ibid., p. 188).
3    "When I ask myself why I have always striven honestly to be considerate of others and if possible to be kind to them and why I did not give this up when I noticed that one is harmed by such behavior and is victimized because others are brutal and unreliable, I really have no answer. It surely was not the sensible thing to do" (ibid., pp. 189–90).
4    It is well known that Freud tried to live an exemplary ethical life and, without arrogance, believed that he did: "I consider myself a very moral human being, who can subscribe to the excellent maxim of Th. Visher: What is moral is always self-evident. I believe that in a sense of justice and consideration for one's fellow men, in discomfort at making others suffer or taking advantage of them, I can compete with the best men I have known. I have never done anything shameful or malicious, nor do I find in myself the temptation to do so" (ibid., p. 189). [4]
5    In light of Freud's strong ethical commitments and self-appraisal it is not surprising that he wrote in "On Psychotherapy" that an important qualification for the treating analyst is that "his own character be irreproachable" (1953, p. 267).

Freud seems to be saying that if one were "moral," "better, nobler," "of stronger character," if he was devoted to the valuative attachments of "goodness," "kind[ness]," "justice" and "consideration," he would be more likely to prevail amidst the harshness of life as an autonomous, integrated and humane person.[5] Perhaps most importantly for this chapter, this centrally includes being willing and able to make his "common unhappiness" as Freud characterized the human condition – one's inevitable suffering – more sufferable. Similar to the Axial sages, for Freud the fashioning of the "good life" required a well-developed sense of moral autonomy and integrity, which allows one to creatively surmount the personal suffering that is a constituent aspect of being human. It is to this subject that we now turn.

## Part A: anxiety

### The moral challenge of anxiety

"Anxiety is the dizziness of freedom," Kierkegaard wrote in his masterpiece, *The Concept of Anxiety*. Let's situate this quotation in its original context so that an important dimension of the "moral" aspect of anxiety, at least as I conceive it, is clear from the outset.

> Anxiety may be compared with dizziness. He whose eye happens to look down into the yawning abyss becomes dizzy. But what is the reason for this? It is just as much in his own eye as in the abyss, for suppose he had not looked down. Hence, anxiety is the dizziness of freedom, which emerges when the spirit wants to posit the synthesis and freedom looks down into its own possibility, laying hold of finiteness to support itself. Freedom succumbs to dizziness. Further than this, psychology cannot and will not go. In that very moment everything is changed, and freedom, when it again rises, sees that it is guilty. Between these two moments lies the leap, which no science has explained and which no science can explain. He who becomes guilty in anxiety becomes as ambiguously guilty as it is possible to become.
>
> (Kierkegaard, 1980, p. 61)

What Kierkegaard is getting at points to the moral "bedrock" of anxiety; namely, just as a person peers into the abyss and experiences dizziness, so too does freedom experience its own possibility. As Kierkegaard noted, "Freedom's possibility announces itself in anxiety" (ibid., p. 74). This is the deeply troubling moment when we realize that the possibility of relating to our self, our attitude toward our self, irrepressibly requires responsibility for our chosen actions. Moreover, says Kierkegaard, it is all-important that we discover this possibility of self-relating and not live our lives as if decision-making about our valuative attachments, that is, what we really care about, doesn't hugely matter. In this sense, anxiety always involves a moral value, a deeply held inner conviction that feels endangered.

Such self-awareness is thus discovered as we experience anxiety of this possibility of self-relating. To the extent that we do not sincerely reckon with this self-awareness and act accordingly in our everyday life, we feel "infinitely guilty," says Kierkegaard (ibid., p. 161).[6] This is why he famously noted, "Whoever has learned to be anxious in the right way has learned the ultimate" (ibid., p. 155).[7] The point, says Danish philosopher Arne Gron, is that anxiety signifies "that we cannot escape ourselves that we are somebody who relates," even if we attempt clever avenues of flight from this self-awareness. Anxiety is thus not only "the possibility of freedom; anxiety also becomes anxiety for this possibility." It is in this experience of anxiety, this "dizziness of freedom," that, says Kierkegaard, the possibility of "freedom succumbs" (Gron, 1994, p. 19). Put differently, the experience of anxiety can be either the handmaiden to impotence or the muse to creativity.

The experience of the "dizziness of freedom" is noticeable to the average person confronted by certain existential dichotomies, derivatives of those "limit-situations" mentioned earlier, that one ideally has to make conscious decisions about in terms of his attitude toward them.[8] This includes making no decision that is also a decision which, as Kierkegaard noted, uses one's freedom in the service of unfreedom. "Anxiety ... is an entangled freedom, where freedom is not free in itself" (1980, p. 49). In these instances, "anxiety is of all things the most selfish, and no concrete expression of freedom is as selfish" (ibid., p. 61). Before I discuss the experience of anxiety in more depth, I will mention three of the most common dichotomies that make most people anxious to varying degrees. The first is mainly focused on one's relationship to one's self, the second on others and the third on the world. Such dichotomies are hardly new notions to Axial sages, philosophers and existential psychologists (Cooper, 2017; Spinelli, 2015; Van Deurzen, 2012).

### Living as a "real" or "false" self

Drawing from the "theatre as life" metaphor (Marcus, with Marcus, 2011), R. D. Laing noted, "'A man without a mask' is very rare" (1959, p. 95). To some degree, we all have to wear a "mask" to navigate our daily lives, as a "false self" is an episodic social requirement that helps maintain the social glue of society. A "false self" refers to obliging and responding to the perceived demands of the social world at the expense of one's felt immediacy and spontaneity. Indeed, 2400 years before Laing and Winnicott, Socrates described the "false self," that is, how "an apparently healthy façade may conceal an unhealthy soul" as well as offering a timely doctrine of the "true self," one that is in harmony with itself (Symington, 1993, p. 39).

We all engage in what symbolic interactionist Erving Goffman (1959) called "impression management," consciously and unconsciously choreographed self-presentation meant to satisfy our real and imagined needs and goals. Boasting, flattery and ingratiation are three simple examples that people engage in to affirm their self-image and comply with social expectations (ibid.). An excessive amount of a "false self" often means that one lives mainly to please others (Winnicott, 1960), often neurotically, like the social chameleon. However, what drives this "role playing" is probably something more profound – namely, that most people are terrified of not measuring up, of being judged by others and themselves as "falling short" of the acceptable norm, even worse, as being a "failure" or a "loser." Heinz Kohut made this point just right: "We all want to enhance our self-esteem. We all want to shine ... there is a lot of hypocrisy about that" (Kohut et al., 1996, p. 73).

The problem is that for many anxious people, the "mask" becomes the reality consciousness of their inner lives. The "false front" becomes the basis for their gratifications of their deepest needs and desires, which has seriously deleterious ramifications in terms of their relationship with themselves, others and the world.[9] The person who lives as if the "mask," the inordinate role playing, is what he "really" is lives a life of "impersonation," as Laing evocatively calls it. The anxiety generated by the extreme of always having to put forth an effective "false" persona can be the basis for consciously and/or unconsciously feeling "inauthentic," and/or becoming what Karl Abraham (1955) was the first to psychoanalytically describe as an "impostor."[10] The "as-if" personality, the term that Helen Deutsch used to describe such character-disordered people, comes to mind: Such people give the onlooker "the inescapable impression that the individual's whole relationship to life has something about it which is lacking in genuineness and yet outwardly runs along 'as-if' it were complete" (1942, p. 302).

In contrast to the "false self" way of being-in-the-world, there is the person who chooses to be "real," whose acts are done in "good faith" and are "true" to the self – that is, to his needs, desires and self-expressions (Rycroft, 1995, p. 10). What is critical here is that for such a person there is no discrepancy between what he seems to be and what he is; and, perhaps most importantly, this inclines him to be receptive, responsive and responsible to others. In contrast, for the person lodged in a "false self" way of being, his life has a nervous and feverous pitch to it as he constantly tries to avoid being comprehended as the person he believes he actually is, namely, insecure, unsafe and unlovable (Laing, 1959, p. 94). As Winnicott noted, the function of the "false self" is to "search for conditions in which the true self can come into its own," and this is almost always consciously and/or unconsciously an anxiety-inducing undertaking (1960, p. 138). As the great Stoic philosopher, Marcus Aurelius, has noted in his *Meditations*, there is a much more productive and ennobling alterative to this "false self" way of being if one digs within oneself to reach goodness. For Aurelius this included the Stoic values of social duty and striving for the moral good. Like all Axial sages, Aurelius believed that any significant deepening and expansion of one's spiritual life must be heralded by positive changes in interhuman relations, in particular, changes that reflect an enhanced capacity to be other-directed, other-regarding and other-serving.

### Living "for oneself" vs. "for the other"

If the Axial religious philosophers are right, every person needs to decide whether his life and identity-defining moral convictions are lodged in an ethic that is mainly "for the other" or "for itself." Indeed, Martin Luther King, Jr., a man whose life and ideas were animated by the Axial vision, made this point just right: "Every man must decide whether he will walk in the light of creative altruism or in the darkness of destructive selfishness."[11] In general, the extent to which the "natural" inclinations of the selfishness of the self, the ego, dominate one's way of life – especially in one's interhuman relations – determines how likely one is to suffer in terms of guilty anxiety, depression and alienation. This is the basic, widely accepted spiritual /moral insight of all Axial thinkers. As Freud noted, "Narcissism is the universal and original state of things, from which object-love is then only later developed, without the narcissism necessarily disappearing on that account" (1933, p. 416). Levinas, too, believed that "Egotism is not an ugly vice on the part of the subject, but its ontology" (1996, pp. 70–71). Freud and Levinas agree, however, that overcoming or significantly modulating inherent selfishness, infantile narcissism and egocentricity is a very difficult task, but one that is a necessity on the "royal road" to the "good life."[12] In other words, while there is considerable anxiety involved in fashioning a self that is mainly other-directed, other-regarding and other-serving, this anxiety is in no way comparable in terms of the horror associated with the painful self-encirclement of selfishness, infantile narcissism and egocentricity. As Sophocles wrote in *Antigone*, "The only crime is pride," that is, malignant forms of self-love (2006).

### To be or not to be in control of our lives

The issue of control is one of the most common in psychoanalytic treatment. Analysands and psychotherapy patients are frequently complaining about feeling out of control, of being controlled by others or of wanting to control others. This is especially the case in contexts that are stressful, painful and require endurance, such as while coping with extended suffering. While western-based psychoanalysis aims to assist people with gaining control of their lives, an Axial outlook, especially one that is religious/spiritual, assists people with coming to terms with the limits of their control. When it comes to every major aspect of living – birth, who your parents are, who you fall in love with and the kind of work you choose,[13] your children's lives, illness, and death – one realizes the deeper and more decisive issue than trying to control one's life and world is learning to come to terms with how little control we actually have regarding things that matter. Chance, accident and other contingencies are hugely operative. Anxiety masks a powerful wish, and, as Freud noted, one rooted in the desire to reclaim one's lost childhood narcissism, the time when he existed as his own ideal.

The Axial sensibility can help a person internalize this rather harsh truth about reality while at the same time offering some hope, especially through a sacred/spiritual language that is embedded in a "sacred canopy." For example, by living in the present, moment by moment, even amid intense pain as the Buddha taught, as opposed to getting stuck in the past and dwelling on the future, the analysand can better endure his suffering. Suffering, says the Buddha, follows the same pattern, one that requires patience and a transcendent perspective. Suffering arises, dwells, changes and ultimately fades away. As the Taoist-sounding, motivational saying goes, the anxious person is lodged in the future, the depressed person in the past, and the peaceful person resides in the present.

### Anxiety as breakdown or breakthrough

Anxiety has long been regarded by psychoanalysts as perhaps the most common symptom among analysands, contributing to many of their worst problems in living.[14] Anxiety, that dreadful, self-absorbing feeling of worry or nervousness, or, in its extreme form, horror and panic, usually emanates from anticipation of a perceived threat, menace or danger, the basis of which is mainly "unknown or unrecognized" (Edgerton, 1994, p. 18). Nearly everyone has had such anxious experiences, and it is partly for this reason that Freud and others (Heidegger, 1962) have argued that anxiety is one of the foundational features of human existence.[15] Anxiety, as conventionally understood, has two interrelated aspects. It has a psychological or mental dimension, such as in tension and apprehension, and also a physiological or bodily dimension, such as in breathlessness and sweating. Anxiety, to the analyst, is not the same phenomenon as fear or what is sometimes called realistic anxiety. Whereas anxiety is connected to a danger that is unconscious, fear is a response to a consciously recognized, usually external, realistic danger. In general, most mental health professionals of diverse theoretical persuasions, including analysts, view anxiety as pathological when it seriously diminishes effectiveness in living, impairs the attainment of desired goals or fulfillment and/or blocks reasonable emotional equanimity and comfort.

In this section, I first briefly summarize two very different psychoanalytic views of the nature of psychopathology, anxiety manifestations in particular. My main purpose in doing so is to help contextualize what is the intriguing, though generally ignored, contribution of Levinas to the understanding of this important and common human experience, one that analysands and analysts frequently struggle with as they engage in the analytic encounter. It is mainly through unraveling Levinas's forbiddingly opaque notion of the "there is" – "the phenomenon of impersonal being," as he calls it (1985, p. 48) – that I hope to provide a complementary angle of vision on the source, expressions and meanings of certain forms of anxiety. Such a Levinasian angle of vision, can, I hope, deepen and expand the psychoanalytic understanding of this complex, multi-faceted and common human phenomenon. Moreover, by beginning to fill in the gap in the psychoanalyst's understanding of the origin, course and phenomenology of "anonymous existence," or "being in general" (Levinas, 2001a, pp. 44, 52), I hope to strengthen his ability to empathize with the analysand's "horror and panic" (Levinas, 1985, p. 49) that Levinas says constitutes the "there is," as well as to help the analysand derive some transformational insights from such a dreadful self-experience about the art of living the "good life."

I should stress from the outset that for Levinas, the "there is" is not simply a synonym for anxiety, as the term is commonly used. In fact, Levinas says the "there is" is neither a psychological problem nor even a subjective experience, at least not as it is usually construed. However, as I hope to convey, despite what Levinas says, his description of the "there is" and his interpretation of its meanings (none of which are easy to pin down, as in a certain sense the "there is" is ineffable) point to a mode of experience that is, for want of a better term, akin to (though not to be equated with) the experience of sudden, massive and decisive anxiety. This is anxiety not as it is psychoanalytically described and understood. The horror and panic of anonymous, impersonal being, the "there is," can be reasonably described as referring to a mode of being in which the individual is so overwhelmed by a unique form of unbearable anxiety, at least phenomenologically speaking, that he has access to a dimension of his being that is characterized by radical insomnia, by a horror of being. In this view, such intense anxiety may be understood as a central part of the psychological context that signals and prepares the way for the awful inevitability of the "there is."

This experience of extreme and largely inexplicable generalized anxiety, followed by the even more hellish "there is," followed by a return to normal consciousness, possibly with a degree of self-illumination, is the experiential process that I focus on in this section. It is this kind of horror and panic associated with the "there is" that Levinas probably felt at times in the Nazi forced labor camp that may be one of the important reasons that he wrote about the "there is" "for the most part" while a prisoner in the stalag (2001a, p. xxvii).

Finally, a note of caution and consolation. As Davis points out, Levinas's "there is" is trying to capture something that Levinas describes "as lying beyond any experiential or cognitive measure" (1996, p. 31), "neither nothingness nor being" (Levinas, 1985, p. 48). Like the entire Levinasian *oeuvre*, Levinas's poetic and evocative description of the "there is" is elliptical and paradoxical (ibid.). Moreover, it is sated with similes and comparisons meant to block the reader from assimilating the enigmatic "there is" into familiar modes of experience and understanding that, in the reader's mind, have ultimate clarity and explanatory supremacy. Rather, Levinas, like Socrates, is a gadfly. He wants to disrupt his readers' conventional modes of experiencing and thinking, to stimulate their skepticism so that they do not rush to premature closure about something that Levinas says can never be pinned down. Thus, the "there is" is an open-ended notion; and this fact, along with Levinas's obtuse literary style, makes any coherent explication of the "there is" exceedingly difficult for the explicator and rather hard going for the reader. It is less so, however, if one is mindful of the fact that the experience of reading Levinas, similar to being in an analysis, involves going on a long voyage of the mind and spirit. I therefore beg the reader's patience and ask him or her to "hang in there."

### Two divergent psychoanalytic conceptualizations to understanding anxiety: Sigmund Freud and W.R.D. Fairbairn

Freud had three theories of anxiety, though the last one is regarded as definitive (1933, 1959). The first theory asserted that anxiety was a result of repressed libido; the second that it was a repetition, an analogue of the birth trauma; and the third that anxiety had two fundamental forms, primary and signal anxiety (Rycroft, 1995, p. 8). Both primary and signal anxieties were regarded by Freud as responses of the ego to the heightening of instinctual pressure and emotional tension. Primary anxiety is the emotion associated with disintegration of the ego. In its extreme, such anxiety, what is called panic, is a feeling of utter helplessness, a transitory functional disorganization of the personality. Signal anxiety was conceived as an early warning system that alerts the ego to an imminent threat to its equilibrium and integrity. The purpose of signal anxiety, a form of self-monitoring, inner watchfulness and vigilance, is to make certain that by allowing the ego to implement defensive safeguards, debilitating primary anxiety is never experienced (ibid.).

Freud conceived anxiety to be related to a series of danger situations that are intrinsic to a child's growth and development (Moore & Fine, 1990, p. 25). As Moore and Fine succinctly describe it, the first of these threatening situations is the loss of the primary love object, most often the mother, the primary caregiver on whom the child is utterly dependent for survival. Next, as the child begins to experience the mother as a separate person with worth and importance, and object constancy has been attained (between ages 24 and 36 months, according to Mahler [in Mahler et al., 1973]), the fear of losing the mother's love becomes the child's paramount anxiety. During the Oedipal phase, says Freud, anxiety and fear associated with physical harm, that is, castration, assume center stage. Lastly, in the latency phase (between ages 6 and 12), the child's typical anxiety and fear is that the "internalized parental representations," the super-ego, will stop loving the child and will chastise, punish and abandon him.

As Moore and Fine further note (1990, p. 25), and Freud pointed out, though these particular fears and anxieties are associated with specific phases of psychosexual development, they can and do routinely exist in the adult ego and personality. Most importantly, in a neurotic adult, the main unconscious fear and anxiety is that one of these childhood danger situations will be re-experienced. For the classical analyst, anxiety reactions and neurotic symptoms are the ego's attempts to prevent these traumatizing unconscious anxieties from becoming psychic eventualities. The focus of treatment is to make the unconscious anxieties conscious and thereby strengthen the ego's ability to ward off and control debilitating anxiety, thus protecting the integrity of the personality.

Freud's theory of anxiety has a relational thrust to it: like Levinas, he is, in part, focused on the meaning of the "other," especially the "m/other" in human existence; but it is mainly through the emergence of relational and self-psychology that intersubjectivity takes center stage. It is for this reason that I have chosen to review, in addition to Freud, one of the seminal British object relational theorist's accounts of the development of psychopathology, including anxiety manifestations and conditions, before I consider Levinas's notion of the "there is."

"Psychology," says W.R.D. Fairbairn, is the "study of the relationships of the individual to his objects" (1952, p. 60). Fairbairn's reconceptualization of psychoanalysis deviated from Freudian theory in at least two important ways. First, as Moore and Fine point out, Fairbairn viewed the "ego as a structure" that existed from birth rather than emanating from the id as a consequence of its interactions with reality (Moore & Fine, 1990, pp. 71–73). The ego was self-energizing; it did not derive its energy "from the id; it was a dynamic structure." Fairbairn's rejection of the notion of a separate id was in part rooted in his view that "libido is a function of the ego" and aggression is a response to real-life neglect, interference and frustration of the individual's attempt to generate satisfying connections with others. Fairbairn also deviated from Freud in his assertion that "libido is object-seeking, not pleasure-seeking"; its goal was not the discharge of tension but the creation of gratifying relations with others. In other words, for Fairbairn there is a fundamental human striving to relate and connect to others, and the infant therefore is "hardwired" toward relationships from birth.

This relations-seeking and relations-maintenance has adaptive value in terms of biological survival (ibid.). As James Grotstein notes, for Fairbairn, "the human being was born and lived his lifetime with such an inescapable need for the object, that this object dependence informed all stages of development, from immature to mature dependency" (1998, p. 162). Moreover, for Fairbairn the inevitable frustrations and inadequacies in the mother–infant relationship lead to "the internalization of an object" that is gratifying and ungratifying (Moore & Fine, 1990, p. 72). Anxiety, insecurity and ambivalence are stimulated in the infant, leading to the activation of defenses, especially splitting, which Fairbairn viewed as a "universal mental phenomenon necessary" to manage frustration, dissatisfaction and over-stimulation in early relationships (ibid.). Says Grotstein, "the human condition predicates man as having a schizoid nature by virtue of the splitting disassociations that inevitably characterize the formation of the endopsychic structure" (the unitary all-embracing psychic structure Fairbairn called the ego) (Grotstein, 1998, p. 162). For Fairbairn, schizoid persons desire loving connections and affectionate attachments to objects; however, their internal worlds are so animated by violent assaults from split-off, destructive objects that real life interpersonal relationships are nearly impossible.

For Fairbairn, psychopathology, including anxiety manifestations and conditions, is the "study of the relationships of the ego to its internalized objects" (1952, p. 60). The internalized objects within Fairbairn's perspective are, by their very nature, psychopathological structures. Psychopathology for Fairbairn, unlike Freud (who mainly saw it as a consequence of conflict over pleasure-seeking impulses), was rooted in disturbances and interferences in relationships to others. Understanding the infant's experiences with his early significant others was thus crucial for understanding healthy and unhealthy development. For Fairbairn, intimates Grotstein, maternal deprivation in particular was the basis for psychopathology. Fairbairn believed that psychopathology, including anxiety and panic, was best conceptualized as the ego's efforts to maintain old connections and yearnings represented by internal objects. The main problematic that undergirds all psychopathology for Fairbairn is between the developmental inclination toward mature dependence and more differentiated and satisfying relations, and the childish refusal to relinquish infantile dependence and connections to undifferentiated objects, emanating from the terror of losing connection of any kind.

As we will soon see, Levinas's first inkling of the "there is" was when he was a child separated from his parents in a common, seemingly non-traumatic familial context. Says Grotstein, "In his emphasis on the importance of introjective over projective identification":

> [Fairbairn] formulated object relations theory as being fundamentally traumatic, that is, objects are internalized only when they are felt to be endangering. Thus, strictly speaking, the term "object relations" constitutes a default category of failed interpersonal relation where the responsibility lies with the external parental objects.
>
> (Grotstein, 1998, pp. 162–163)

Thus, for Fairbairn, "only bad objects are internalized; good objects do not have to be because they are satisfying" (ibid., p. 163). Psychopathology, such as anxiety and panic, for Fairbairn, emanates from the ego's self-fragmentation as it tries to maintain the connection to the object (e.g., a significant other) and control its unsatisfying elements.

Finally, it is worth noting that psychoanalytic therapy for Fairbairn is best understood in terms of how it differs from Freud. Unlike Freud, who believed that the analytic experience is mainly constituted by the working through of unconscious conflict about one's id impulses, Fairbairn thought it should aim at reconstituting the individual's capacity to form and maintain authentic, real relationships with others. "Mature dependence," Fairbairn's term for the theoretically possible but practically unreachable ideal state of emotional health, is manifested in terms of the individual's ability to sustain intimate, mutual connections to other people. Moreover, says Grotstein, the individual no longer has the need to introject and identify with the realistic badness of one's early and later objects so as to preserve his needed goodness. In the healthy person, there is no need to self-fragment in order to sustain connection and loyalty to the contradictory and irreconcilable aspects of significant objects, that is, of valued, cherished others.

Thus, we have two psychoanalytic ways of describing and formulating the experience of anxiety. For Freud, anxiety reactions and neurotic symptoms are compromise formations, the ego's feeble efforts to safeguard the person from re-experiencing childhood traumatizing unconscious threats to its integrity. For Fairbairn, anxiety reflects the ego's inadequate efforts to maintain old connections and yearnings represented by internal objects. Both of these formulations of anxiety, correctly I think, describe it as an unavoidable disruption of comfortable consciousness by extremely unpleasant affect, or worse, by horror and panic. What I hope to suggest is that Levinas's notion of the "there is," impersonal being, gives psychoanalysis a point of entry into a complementary understanding of a primal human anxiety, with its diverse manifestations, that can blunt the development of "authentic" self-identity and the capacity to love. Like Freud, Levinas seems cognizant of the inevitability of anxiety, that is, the inevitability of traumatic disruptions of consciousness emanating from both within the person (e.g., guilt for a real or imagined misdeed) and/or from the outside world (e.g., the death of a loved one). While Freud focuses on anxiety related to conflict over the sexual and aggressive drives, and Fairbairn to the disturbance and interference of relationships with significant others, Levinas posits that it is only from a radical otherness – something that can neither emanate from nor be assimilated into the conventional ego of Freudian and other forms of psychoanalysis (Gantt & Williams, 2002, p. 8) – that "authentic" self-identity and the capacity to love, mainly construed as a responsibility for the other mode of being, can develop.

## The "there is"

The "there is" is one of Levinas's most enigmatic philosophical abstractions, a kind of hypothetical construct, a "thought experiment" meant to evoke a dimension of being, of deeply internal experience, that is central to the Levinasian project. The notion of the "there is" is "elemental," a key notion that helps animate Levinas's efforts to further his project of describing and explicating "how our encounter with the Other enters into the drama of consciousness" (Davis, 1996, p. 23). Levinas's notion of the "there is" attempts to describe the relationship between the burden of existing and the human other that demands an ethical response, this being the basis for fashioning the "good life" as I have described it.

Finally, the "there is" gives us an inkling of what Alford surmises is Levinas's greatest fear, and indeed, many people's fear to one degree or another, "that love for the being of another will trap the human in being" (Alford, 2002, p. 57). This fear of entrapment within oneself, without escape, hints at what Levinas is getting at. Such a mode of experience, with its attendant hellish anxiety, horror and panic, its "egocentric interiority" (Levinas, 1987b, p. 101) and imprisoning, morbid narcissistic self-absorption, is what I believe Levinas sees as the main obstacle that prevents the individual from loving, from embracing a "responsibility for the other" existential orientation. These are the basis of the "good life" as he and I conceive it. "Love," a word Levinas deeply distrusts and thinks is compromised, which he prefers to call "being-for-the-other," is in fact the "escape" from the "there is," the only way "to stop the anonymous and senseless rumbling of being" (1985, p. 52). Both Freud and Fairbairn would probably be sympathetic to this claim.

### The phenomenological context of the "there is"

Let us begin with Levinas's descriptions of the "there is":

> My reflection on this subject starts with childhood memories. One sleeps alone, the adults continue life; the child feels the silence of his bedroom as "rumbling." It is something resembling what one hears when one puts an empty shell close to the ear, as if the emptiness were full, as if the silence were a noise. It is something one can also feel when one thinks that even if there were nothing, the fact that "there is" is undeniable. Not that there is this or that; but the very scene of being is open: there is. In the absolute emptiness that one can imagine before creation – there is ... neither nothingness nor being. I sometimes use the expression: the excluded middle. One cannot neither say of this "there is" which persists that it is an event of being. One can say that it is nothingness, even though there is nothing. *Existence and Existents* tries to describe this horrible thing, and moreover describes it as horror and panic.
>
> (Levinas, 1985, pp. 48–49)

Elsewhere, Levinas further describes the "there is," again reminiscing about childhood:

> The "there is" is unbearable in its indifference. Not anguish [as in Heidegger's *es gibt*], but horror, the horror of the unceasing, of a monotony deprived of meaning. Horrible insomnia. When you were a child and someone tore you away from the life of the adults and put you to bed a bit too early, isolated in the silence, you heard the absurd tie in its monotony as if the curtains rustled without moving. My efforts ... consist in investigating the experience of the exit from this anonymous "nonsense."
>
> (Levinas, 2001b, pp. 45–46)

Finally, Levinas draws from French writer and philosopher Maurice Blanchot to describe the "there is":

> He has a number of very suggestive formulas; he speaks of the "hustle-bustle" of being, of its "clamor," its "murmur," of a night in a hotel room where, behind the partition, "it does not stop stirring"; "one does not know what they are doing next door." This is something very close to the "there is."
>
> (Levinas, 1985, p. 50)

For now, I want to emphasize what is striking about Levinas's descriptions. In two of three instances, he refers to experiences of separation from adults, probably his parents, and the lonely and pained experience of being excluded from their palpably bountiful, pleasurable and meaningful lives. The third instance also speaks to being excluded from the stirrings of life and pleasure that Levinas fantasizes are occurring behind the partition, next door. Thus, according to Levinas's descriptions, the "there is" emerges within the psychological context of felt radical disconnection, distance and loneliness, the opposite of the phenomenology of love, with its strong feelings of connection, closeness and togetherness.

Levinas points out that the "there is" refers to no identifiable subject, but rather it describes what he calls "existing without existents" (1989, p. 44) (roughly the difference, following Heidegger, between Being and being). By this is meant an anonymous modality of existing prior to the emergence of the individual human subject. Levinas's concern is how the self emerges out of the "there is," that is, roughly, how personal identity evolves into a self-determining, self-actualizing "for the other" person. However, such individuation is only "authentic" and worthwhile to the extent that it resists subjugating its "concrete subjectivity," its individuality, to the violence done to it by two sources: by the philosophical paradigm of rationality, with its tendency to "metaphysical reductionism" and totalization; and by the violence done by the developing self to itself (Hutchens, 2004, pp. 36–38). This discussion of the "there is" mainly pertains to the second form of violence – for instance, how individuals avoid responsibility for and to the other, how they truncate their ties to empathy and blunt their capacity to love. Such an outlook and behavior is the source of much personal misery.

Levinas, according to philosopher A.T. Peperzak, indicates that the "there is" is "a treacherous semblance of nothingness, a hiding place of mythical powers without face, an indeterminate and opaque density without orientation or meaning, a senseless and therefore terrifying chaos" (1993, p. 163). The "there is," says Levinas, pre-exists nothingness; it is evoked in the terrifying silence facing the "vigilant insomniac." The vigilant insomniac "is and is not an I" who cannot manage to fall asleep (Hand, 1996, p. 29). As we have seen, for Levinas, the child who in his bed senses the night dragging on has an experience of horror that "is not an anxiety" (1985, p. 49), at least not in the psychoanalytic sense. Rather, it is something even more terrifying and menacing, though Levinas only hints at this difference:

> The impossibility of escaping wakefulness is something "objective," independent of my initiative. This impersonality absorbs my consciousness; consciousness is depersonalized. I do not stay awake; "it" stays awake. Perhaps death is an absolute negation wherein "the music ends" ... But in the maddening "experience" of the "there is" one has the impression of a total impossibility of escaping, of "stopping the music."
>
> (ibid.)

The "there is," says Levinas, thus signifies the end of objectivizing consciousness, as it is not an object of perception or conscious thought (though Levinas's childhood examples seem to suggest otherwise), and cannot be comprehended or intentionally created. According to him, it is impossible to avoid the experience of the "there is" because one is immersed and inundated in it. This inescapability, experienced as dread and panic, suggests Levinas, signifies "the impossibility of death ... the impossibility of escaping from an anonymous and uncorruptible [sic] existence" (Levinas, 1989, p. 33). For Levinas, the "there is" is not a psychological experience – it is not a question of "states of the soul" (1985, p. 50) as one is usually construed – because "it is subjectivity itself which has fled" (Alford, 2002, p. 57). This is because all that constitutes an experience as psychological – that is, subjectively knowable and intelligible – is besieged with the horror and panic of mere existence. Consciousness, in other words, has been objectified; it has become a thing, an it, and personal identity has become swamped, swallowed up by it (ibid., p. 58).

What Levinas is getting at is a reversal of the way in which Heidegger conceptualizes this type of subjective experience, the es gibt (the "there is"). The Heideggerian es gibt is generosity and abundance; it refers to "the donation by Being to beings of light, freedom and truth" (Davis, 1996, p. 129). In contrast to the "there is" as abundance and diffuse goodness, the "there is" is unbearable in its indifference. Before the generosity of Being, says Levinas, there is a "chaotic indeterminacy" to being that comes before all giving, "creativity and goodness" (Peperzak, 1997, p. 3). Heidegger's es gibt, arguing from beings to Being, is mainly rooted in the fear of pure nothingness, of death. In contrast, for Levinas the experience of the "there is" is the terrifying feeling that there is no way of escaping from mere being; there is "no exit" from existence, not even suicide, as I shall shortly explain. In other words, says Levinas, in contrast to Heidegger's use of the term "there is," the horror of the night of the vigilant insomniac is not merely anxiety about nothingness and the fear of death. Rather, "there is horror of ... the fact that tomorrow one still has to live, a tomorrow contained in the infinity of today. There is horror of immortality, perpetuity of the drama of existence, necessity of forever taking on his burden" (Levinas, 1989, pp. 34–35). Levinas says elsewhere, "Anxiety, according to Heidegger, is the experience of nothingness. Is it not, on the contrary – if by death one means nothingness – the fact that it is impossible to die?" (1987b, p. 51).

Levinas is contrasting the horror of the night to Heideggerian anxiety, fear of being, to Heideggerian fear of nothingness. The primordial anxiety and fear for Levinas is mere being, existing forever, with no escape, trapped in the nocturnal horror of existence that is prior to the emergence of consciousness, into, perhaps, a kind of persecutory, psychotic-like regression into a pre-verbal, primary narcissism.

Before further explicating Levinas's notion of the "there is" and showing how it can enhance the psychoanalytic understanding of anxiety and a person's successful efforts at fashioning the "good life," I want to elucidate another unwieldy term: "hypostasis" (of the self, coming into existence) – a process that is an essential part of Levinas's description of the "there is" (1989, pp. 51–57; 2001a, pp. 61–100).[16] Hypostasis of the self is Levinas's attempt to explain how "the self assumes a self-reflective and self-determining form" (Hutchens, 2004, p. 43). It is as close to a developmental theory accounting for the birth of personal identity, the self, as there is in Levinas; however, he does not avail himself of the insights of psychoanalytic developmental theory or the research literature on child development, and thus some of what he describes is not congruent with this received knowledge about the birth and development of human identity.[17]

## The "there is" and the emergence of the self

For Levinas, as Hutchens points out, in the beginning there is the "there is": "the self is anonymous and indeterminate ... without being anything," and motivated "to become conscious and present to itself" (Hutchens, 2004, p. 43). Neither "subjective nor substantive," the self then withdraws and shrinks back from this "there is" state as it strives for definition, identity and constancy. This dynamic process of hypostasis entails, in Levinas's language, "becoming something," which means evolving into an existent (being) from simple, plain "mere existence" (Being).

However, the hypostasizing self struggles, or "works to exist" (Hutchens, 2004, p. 44) to become more than simply an existent, as if existing were an effort necessary of any self. Originally in a state of isolation and solitude, there is something in its anonymous striving and impersonal work of existing that prompts its existence as a self. What this "something" is, Levinas does not say. This work to exist, he says, allows the self to depart from its anonymous "there is" existence and become a determinative, separate and present self. "Hypostasis is the emergence of the uniqueness of the self," the self-empowerment that permits an avenue of flight from the dreaded impersonality and anonymity of the "there is" (Hutchens, 2004, p. 44; Levinas, 1985,

p. 48). The self thus evolves and appropriates consciousness that reflects specificity and "localization" (Levinas, 2001a, p. 66). It is by the fact of being consciousness that the self views itself as disengaged, as separate from impersonal existence. The self, in other words, comes to existence out of itself. It relinquishes its objectivity and develops itself through the subjective processes and procedures of consciousness.

However, critical to this discussion, the self is still aware of the "incessant murmur" and "rustling" of anonymous existence and can never totally relinquish the ominous "rumbling" of "there is" (Levinas, 1998b, p. 164). The self must declare and affirm itself in this anonymity, assuming determination by being watchful over, and mindful of, itself. Although, continues Hutchens, the self never stops being unique and a lone being "in this process of self-determination," it never completely inoculates itself to the dread of being within the terrifying "rustling" of impersonal existence. As the self creates a space for itself and situates itself in that space as a singular and developing self, it is, says Hutchens, burdened with an "I," a fleshy body, including a brain capable of feeling and perception. Such an acquisition involves "hosting a guest entrusted to it, which is conscience" (2004, p. 44).

Conscience, for Levinas, at least on the level of knowing, is what mainly constitutes consciousness (Kunz, 2002, p. 127). It is the recognition of our obligations to all others. It is the mindfulness of the fact that my responsibilities are allocated to me, for example, as wife to husband, parent to child, as a neighbor, a colleague, a countryman and a fellow human being (ibid.). It is, in its adult expression, the mindfulness of my obligation to embrace *Menschlichkeit*, to be a compassionate and kind person, and the awareness of the guilt of not having been so.[18] "The interiority of mental life is, perhaps, originally this," what Levinas calls "bad conscience." Bad conscience is ignoring the obligation to not leave the other alone in the face of his suffering and death. More generally, and calling to mind Socrates's valuative attachments, it is denying the "possibility of dreading injustice more than death, of preferring the injustice undergone to the injustice committed and which justifies being by that which assures it" (Levinas, 1998a, pp. 175, 177). Finally, Levinas proclaims, "The true inner life is ... the obligation to lodge the whole of humankind in the shelter – exposed to all the winds – of conscience" (1996, p. 122). Conscience, the ethical sensibility, means that one does not shy away from seeing the distress of others and of feeling responsible for making things better for them.[19]

As Hutchens points out, for Levinas the next sub-phase of the hypostasis of the self, of self-development, is that the self becomes split into two, a divided self:

> The self then divides itself into a subject of thinking and a "psyche" upon which it reflects consciously. Hypostasis "doubles up" the self: on the one hand, it is always reflecting upon itself in an unchanging way, that is it

"remains the same in its very alterations" and on the other hand, what it is conscious of undergoes alterations. Identity is always being changed by the processes of being self-conscious and yet what does the identifying does not change. The self is in flux, but never loses itself in flux. Repulsed by the changes it necessarily undergoes, the self retreats into itself, away from the world to which it is exposed as it changes. It withdraws into an insular self-sufficiency in order to be at peace with itself.

(Hutchens, 2004, p. 44)

For Levinas, while the self strives to be safe, self-sustaining and self-sufficient within its narcissistic fortress, within its protective cocoon, the reality is that it can never be completely self-determined. This is because the body, mind and spirit are vulnerable to assaults from within, such as from ontological anxiety and guilt, and from without, such as from the demanding, challenging and often harsh external world. Despite all of its feeble, neurotic and absurd efforts at self-determination and self-sufficiency, those forms of pathological narcissism that are meant to sustain the analysand's weak, fragmentation-prone self, the self is, in Levinas's language, still plagued, haunted by the rumbling of the horror of being, the "there is." It is only through engaging that which is strange, alien and external to this narcissistic self that one is able to diminish the toxic effects of the empowering, though normalizing, homo-genizing and totalizing rational procedures described earlier. Most impor-tantly, however, it is through the ethical response to the human face, responsibility to the other, that one can blunt, if not avoid, the "there is" and achieve a modicum of what analysands call peace of mind.

### The "take home message" for psychoanalysis about the "there is"

I am aware that this discussion of the "there is" has been a long and complex one that the reader may feel has, as the saying goes, generated a lot of heat but little light. Some of what Levinas is talking about has similarities to familiar psychoanalytic notions such as depersonalization, the feelings and thoughts of unreality pertaining either to the self, the outside world, or both; derealization, the feelings and thoughts of alienation or detachment from one's environment that often occurs simultaneously with depersonalization; or loneliness, that feeling of being companionless and solitary. All seem to cap-ture something of the "there is." Moreover, certain descriptions of ontological insecurity – for example, the feeling that one is threatened by non-being – also call to mind aspects of the "there is," as does Sartre's "nausea" (1949).[20] Indeed, Rollo May's contribution (1958); R.D. Laing's (1959) brilliant descriptions of engulfment, with its subversion, if not eradication of identity; implosion, the apprehension that at any instant the outside world will pour in and "obliterate all identity as a gas will rush in and obliterate a vacuum"; and petrifaction, a version of fear and horror that one will be transformed into an inanimate object like a rock or changed into an automaton devoid of feelings, subjectivity and self-awareness, all resonate with Levinas's concept of the "there is."

While phenomenological purists will continue to debate the nature of the "there is" and attempt to discern its differences from and similarities to certain forms of anxiety, depersonalization et cetera, for our purposes it is the connection between the experience of the "there is" and the development of "authentic" self-identity and the deep and expansive capacity to love, the basis for fashioning the "good life," that I want to make clear. The fact that Levinas lacks any kind of psychologically sophisticated developmental theory, appreciation of dynamic unconscious processes and internalized object relations makes mining his insights about personal identity and the capacity to love difficult to discern and explain, psychoanalytically speaking.

Most striking about Levinas's descriptions of the "there is" in his childhood and hotel examples is the fact that they seem to be associated with feelings of extreme abandonment and aloneness, a painful narcissistic, autistic-like, frozen mode of self-experience. Such a state, a kind of free fall into the void, is rooted in the profound despair of not having one's imagined life-sustaining needs and wishes satisfied by the outside world (and internalized object world), usually one's significant other(s). The "there is" experience is characterized by feelings of internal loss, emptiness and rage for not having one's infantile, narcissistic wishes to possess, control and feed off of the loved object gratified, regardless of its impact on the object, the other. As Melanie Klein has described, such wishes to ruthlessly and aggressively obtain what one desires and needs leads to a depressive feeling that one has annihilated one's own good object (1948). The imagined loss of one's life-sustaining external and internal objects leads to the feelings of pain, loss and guilt associated with Klein's depressive position, and, in my view, to some extent with the "there is." In this formulation, the love and concern for others is mainly driven by the anxiety of being abandoned and alone and, secondarily, by guilt for one's aggression toward one's ambivalently loved object, as in "I have destroyed those who care for and love me; how will I survive?" (Alford, 1998, pp. 123–124). The "there is" is being "without there being any objects. The being in every silence, every non-thought, every way of withdrawing from existence" (Levinas, 2000, p. 98).

The "there is" can be viewed as a primitive defense, a last-ditch attempt to sustain oneself psychically by retreating into a solipsistic enclosure.[21] Such an enclosure, a narcissistic web of being, is both a tomb and a womb-like place. On the one hand, it reflects the horror and panic of feeling radically abandoned and trapped in being, that is, trapped in an endless, solitary, linguistically deprived and Godless awfulness. On the other hand, the enclosure is a closed system in which, paradoxically, night, ambiguity and indeterminateness shield oneself from the even more threatening and painful demands of relatedness, intersubjective engagement and active partaking in life, giving and receiving love conceived as responsibility for and to the other. In other words, as Ferenczi and Dupont noted, a less searing form of "pain" can be "the alleviation of other greater pains," which is the basis for some forms of masochism (qtd. in Orange, 2011, p. 195).

There is a second "higher-level" aspect of the "there is" that I want to put into sharper focus that also has direct bearing on psychoanalysis. The "there is," says Levinas, is "the consciousness of having no way out" (2003, p. 2),[22] of being riveted, chained to existence, in horror and panic. Not even suicide is viewed as an escape from the dread and pain of existence. It is hard to imagine falling into such a dire state in which not even death is viewed as a desirable option or a form of relief. As I have observed in analysands, there are certain subjective states that not even the fantasized womb-like, shielding feeling of being anesthetized or asleep appears as a way out of the pain. Levinas is thus claiming that built into the human condition is the proclivity to experience a form of existential pain that is so bad, so inescapable, that even suicide does not feel like a plausible way to stop the pain. Psychoanalytically speaking, the "there is" as horror and panic is a trauma for consciousness and an impossibility for symbolization. It cannot be avoided in the same way as being cannot be avoided (Lechte, 1994, p. 116).

In most people, such a distressing state is largely ineffable, never consciously experienced, at least not in a "pure" form. Perhaps, rephrasing psychoanalyst Joseph Sandler (1960), we can say that the "there is" is something of a "background of unsafety." For others, the "there is" comes over them like an emotional storm; and still for others, it is only the derivatives of the "there is," extreme anxiety and panic, that are felt. Fatigue, indolence and insomnia, says Levinas, also contain the shadow of the "there is" (2001b, p. 45). For Levinas, suicide is not a viable avenue of escape. The nature of the experience is that it is "impossible to die" (1989, pp. 50–51). Levinas does not tell us why, though, as Alford points out, suicide assumes a pained subjectivity revolting against an absurd and meaningless existence (2002, p. 63).[23]

Of course, in a certain sense, Levinas is wrong. Death, as far as we know, does end the pain. However, to the person amidst the "there is," there is the deeply felt sense that even if one were to die, palpable life would not end, the music would not stop. Perhaps we can say, following Levinas, that such a person feels that even if one were to die, the dire consequences of one's selfishness and malignant narcissism, callousness, misdeeds and other shortcomings – especially toward those we think we care about and love – will continue to ripple negatively through the lives of those we leave behind.

The conscious and/or unconscious awareness of our "genuine guilt," as I call it in Chapter 3 on faith, for having denied and ignored our responsibilities for and to the other is in a certain sense felt as an inescapable self-accusation that not even death can obliterate. Moreover, sometimes such a state of mind includes a notion that after one dies one is still held accountable to God or some other cosmic judge, or, as Hamlet said, "perchance to dream." Thus, the circle of fire is closed; there is no exit from the horror of being, of My being Me. Insomnia is what Levinas calls the seemingly without-end, self-shattering, anxious and panicked awareness that one has irrevocably inflicted injury on loved ones and there is no way of making reparations or putting things right. Thus, I am claiming that while, phenomenologically speaking, the "there is" experience resembles feeling trapped in the horror and panic of mere being, its potential meaning and significance after one re-enters normal, self-reflective, self-critical consciousness includes a feeling of bad conscience, of culpability.

This is not the conscience of Freud's superego, the internalization of parental and societal values, demands and prohibitions. Levinas's conscience goes deeper, as it is based on the experience that the face of the other calls my selfish, egotistical and generally self-centric way of being into ultimate question. The "there is" is burning into the soul of the individual who experiences the accusation and the warning that unless one breaks free from one's morbid ego-centeredness and destructive narcissistic desires, one is doomed to the hellish solitary confinement, the horror and panic, of being trapped in a maze of grotesque happenings of guilt without escape. One feels blameworthy and accountable, condemned to a life sentence without parole.

Crucial to his conceptualization of the "there is," the possibility of escape from the horror of the "there is" means embracing a different mode of being in the world, what Levinas calls "otherwise than being."[24] "Otherwise than being" is Levinas's way of describing love, understood as "responsibility for the other," "being-for-the-other." It is through love, "in the form of such a relation that the deliverance from 'there is' appeared to me" (Levinas, 1985, p. 52). He continues:

> The true bearer of being, the true exit from the "there is" is in obligation, in the "for the Other," which introduces a meaning into the nonsense of the "there is." The I subordinated to the other. In the ethical event, someone appears who is the subject par excellence. That is the kernel of all I would say later.
>
> (Levinas, 2001b, pp. 45–46)

Levinas is suggesting that the way out of the desolate solipsism and narcissism of the "there is" is through love that connects the person to an open future infused with potentialities and possibilities.

Love, then, understood first and foremost as "for the other," before oneself, is the antidote to the horror and panic of the "there is," and to the wide range of anxieties and other forms of suffering that are manifestations of, and emanate from, the "there is." The redemptive value of love is phenomenologically evident when one contrasts its adjectival differences with the "there is." The "there is," compared to love, is experienced as anonymous versus individuating; imprisoning/entrapping versus free/wandering; near psychic-death versus psychic rebirth; bitter heaviness of being versus sweet lightness of being; self-centric/self-interested/selfish versus fiercely other-related/other-regarding/other-serving; and, finally, amidst the "there is," the world is experienced as a wall, whereas in love it is experienced as an open gate.

Levinas's dialectical formulation between the "there is" and "love" is easily linked to Freud's and Fairbairn's conceptualizations about anxiety and psychopathology that we discussed earlier. For Levinas, Freud, Fairbairn and other psychoanalytic theorists, "authentic" self-identity, "maturity" and "health," in psychoanalytic language, are best manifested and expressed in the capacity to love deeply and widely. This capacity is, in part, rooted in ridding oneself of one's self-absorbing, internalized unconscious childhood conflicts over one's sexual and aggressive drives (Freud), as well as the self deficits (e.g., in self-coherence, self-continuity and self-esteem), mainly emanating from inadequate early parenting and caretaking (Fairbairn). Only through "working through" these life, pleasure, relationship and meaning-denying conflicts, and repairing the developmental deficits that often underlie them, is it likely that one can evolve into a person capable of being "otherwise than being" – in Levinas's terms, a person capable of "leaving oneself ... being occupied with the other, that is with his suffering and death, before being occupied with one's own death" (2001b, p. 46). Exactly how Levinas understands this extraordinary form of being in the world, the inter-human relations in which one embraces the "ethical order" – what he calls the "order of love," the "order of compassion" (ibid., p. 50) – has been discussed in Chapter 2 on love. My "take-home message" about the "there is," about "mastering" anxiety on the way to fashioning the "good life," is aptly captured by a quote attributed by some to Lao Tzu: "Being deeply loved by someone gives you strength, while loving someone deeply gives you courage" (Golding & Hughes, 2012, p. 20).

## Part B: depression

### When the world begins to darken: depression

"The depressed person is a radical, sullen atheist," said social theorist/psychoanalyst Julia Kristeva (1989, p. 5). What she is getting at is that by not accepting loss (i.e., engaging in and "completing" the mourning process) – whether for a beloved person, animal, thing or ideal, or simply not dealing with the unavoidable letdowns, exasperations and setbacks that are part of everyday life with others that temporarily reduce self-esteem and self-worth – the depressed person is unwilling and unable to move forward by renewing that illusionary, though necessary faith that they reside in an ethically caring universe.[25] For the literally "religious" aspirant such faith is, in part, rooted in two powerful emotions that animate his faith: that he is ultimately dust and ashes, "food for the worms" as Ernest Becker evocatively put it (1973, p. 87);

and he is created in God's image, capable of infusing the world with Beauty, Truth and Goodness. The balance between these two emotions is what gives the "religious" aspirant humility and pride that allows him to press on amidst suffering (Appelfeld, 1994, p. 23).

Where the "religious" aspirant can affirm this belief as deep and abiding trust that he lives in a nurturing universe, the depressed person cannot engage in this restorative way of feeling and thinking and is left trapped in a kind of "metaphysical pathos," a way of being that over time can greatly annoy those around him and further estrange him (Barlow, 1999, p. xx). Most importantly, because the self of a "religious" aspirant is willing and able to experience his belief as trust, he tends to be more receptive to love, to being other-directed, other-regarding and other-serving, while an "atheistic" self tends to be the opposite, utterly wrapped up in his misery. Kristeva, in true Lacanian fashion, is referring to identifying with the "imaginary father," the representation that provides great significance to the "symbolic father" and thus shields the fantasized father against the devastating impact of the omnipotent archaic mother. In other words, the depressed person cannot identify with the idealized and loving "imaginary father," the one who serves as a consolation for the varieties of loss and emptiness that we all must reckon with throughout our lives (Caruana, 2015).

In this section, I present three of the limit-conditions – the existential "givens" that tend to be the conditions of possibility for experiencing psychological depression (in contrast to biochemically-induced depression)[26] – followed by a Levinasian analysis of some of the "moral" aspects of depression that are underappreciated in the psychoanalytic *oeuvre* that all of us are prone to experience in our life as we attempt to fashion the "good life." Indeed, three of the major non-psychoanalytic, psychological theoretical frameworks aptly depict the different conditions of possibility for the upsurge of depressive feelings, what positive psychologist Martin Seligman called the "common cold of psychological disorders" (Hautzinger, 1989, p. 268).

### The behavioral perspective

Behavioral theory focuses on the critical importance of the environment in "shaping" human behavior ("shaping," also known as "successive approximation," is a conditioning paradigm that involves reinforcing the "target" behavior, such as modifying aberrant behavior or generating appropriate behavior). Operant conditioning, for example, claims that depression is brought about when environmental reinforcement is taken away. This claim appears to be prima facie true when we consider some of the common life events that often precede depression: separation/divorce, illness or death of a close friend or family member, emotional/physical neglect or abuse, social isolation, and failing a class or some other kind of important assessment. For example, when a loved one dies, a significant source of positive reinforcement is extinguished. This typically induces sadness, a loss of motivation and inactivity, social withdrawal and difficulties concentrating. The primary source of reinforcement becomes the sympathy, attention and support of family and close friends. From the behavioral perspective, what is going on here is that "maladaptive behavior" – such as whimpering, grumbling, dependency and, in the extreme, suicidal verbalizations – becomes reinforcing. Typically, over time this behavior estranges close friends, which further reduces reinforcement and thus intensifies social isolation, distress and the feeling of misery.

Depression is a vicious cycle, a downward spiral that severely reduces self-esteem and self-efficacy and markedly taints one's self-concept and overall outlook.[27] What behavioral theory puts into sharp focus about depression is that we are terribly vulnerable to the vicissitudes of the external world in terms of how we feel, think and act. Put differently, human behavior, including forms of mental anguish like depression and anxiety, is best understood by never forgetting that we are exquisitely context-dependent and setting-specific beings. As the existentialists have taught us, human beings are "embedded within their world," and therefore the emphasis in treatment should be on the challenges and problems they struggle with in relationship to the "outside" world (Cooper, 2015, p. 57). Contextualism, as it is called in psychology, means that all behavior is best understood as "act-in-context or the historical event," that is, the function of behavior is always historically situated.[28]

This may appear to be stating the obvious, but there is a very important aspect of this claim that has an underappreciated bearing on psychoanalytic views of depression and anxiety. Drawing from an example from life in extremity – that is, prisoner behavior in the Nazi concentration camp where the "shattering of the self was one of the deepest forms of damage" (Appelfeld, 1994, p. 22) – I want to suggest how under-theorized the environment has been, and still is, in psychoanalytic theory. Most importantly, such a theoretical neglect of the role of the environment in understanding behavior has constraining consequences for how psychoanalysis understands itself, and, therefore, how it views mental anguish, including depression and anxiety, and how best to help analysands manage, if not master, it.

While there has been progress in theorizing the environment in psychoanalytic studies recently, what former president of the American Psychoanalytic Association Robert Wallerstein said in 1973 in many ways is still true today, that the study of so-called "reality" has been "relatively neglected or taken for granted in usual psychoanalytic discourse" (Kabatznick & Marcus, 1986, p. 121). Wallerstein believed that this neglect is implicit in the long-standing belief of a fixed world "out there" of an unvarying "average expectable environment" (ibid.). Indeed, in general, as Erikson believed, psychoanalysis has regarded the introspective subjective, the metasubjective and the inter-subjective as more important than the objective (Hoare, 2004, p. 86), while

Loewald noted that, "objectivity, rationality, and reality themselves are not what we thought them to be" (1979, p. 773).

More recently, psychodynamic psychologist Tamara McClintock Greenberg noted that, "within mainstream psychoanalysis, there has been relatively little emphasis on 'real events,' including the effects of adult-onset trauma," such as illness in old age (2016, p. 43). For example, three famous experimental social psychological studies that are pertinent to "moral psychology" – Solomon Asch's classic experiment on social pressure/conformity (i.e., telling the truth vs. lying), the "bystander" experiments by Bibb Latané and John Darley on altruism versus self-interest and Stanley Milgram's study of obeying or refusing authority – all challenge psychoanalysis to generate a more robust psychology of "everyday" situational behavior that gives greater consideration to the role of reality alongside fantasy and wish in understanding vitally important types of human behavior (Kabatznick & Marcus, 1986, p. 115). For, as the celebrated Israeli novelist/Holocaust survivor Aharon Appelfeld told Philip Roth in an interview, "Reality, as you know, is always stronger than the human imagination. Not only that, reality can permit itself to be unbelievable, inexplicable, out of all proportion. The created work [i.e., fantasy/imagination], to my regret, cannot permit itself all that" without suffering serious, "real-life" consequences (Appelfeld, 1994, p. 68). This being said, it is important to remember that while man is a context-dependent and setting-specific being, he also imaginatively hungers to transcend context and setting, leaning into the future, desiring something "more," "higher" and "better."

Bruno Bettelheim, a Holocaust survivor, argued in *The Informed Heart* that psychoanalytic theory (i.e., classical theory) was inadequate in explaining "what constitutes a well integrated personality" in the radically extreme social environment of the camps, or "which behavior is preferable, or which personality more adequate" (1960, p. 20). Bettelheim observed that some of the prisoners who maintained their "old personality structure, stuck to their values in the face of extreme hardships, and as persons were hardly touched by the camp experience" were people whom psychoanalysts would have viewed "as extremely neurotic or plainly delusional, and therefore apt to fall apart, as persons, under stress" (ibid.). Such were the Jehovah's Witnesses (and others with strong religious and moral convictions, like devout Jews, Catholic priests and Communists), "who not only showed unusual heights of human dignity and moral behavior, but seemed protected against the same camp experience that soon destroyed persons considered very well integrated by my psychoanalytic friends and myself" (ibid.).

Those persons who, according to psychoanalytic theory, should have stood up best under the harshness of the camp experience – such as the secular "intellectuals, the liberals, the humanists, the professors of sociology, and the like" as Elie Wiesel described them (1974, p. 273) – were often the first to cave to the extreme stress. They became regressed, that is, depressed, anxious and, most importantly, morally corrupted, as they identified with Nazi values. Behavior in the camps could not be explained based on past life history and former personality, or on those aspects of personality that at the time seemed significant in the then current psychoanalytic thinking. Bettelheim points out that this conclusion emanated, in part, from his own personal experience of disappointment with psychoanalysis as a self-sustaining frame of reference in the camps. He writes:

> Most surprising of all, psychoanalysis which I had come to view as the best key to all human problems offered no suggestion or help toward the solution of how to survive and survive halfway decently in the camps. For that I had to fall back on qualities that in my psychoanalytic experience and thinking were of little importance, if not of negative valence, while those qualities I had learned to stress were often as much of a hindrance as a help.
>
> (Bettelheim, 1960, pp. 15–16)

What Bettelheim ultimately showed in both his early and later studies on the concentration camp experience was that psychoanalysis, which included various post-Freudian versions as self-psychologists/Holocaust survivors Paul and Anna Ornstein told me (personal communication, 1989), was inadequate to explain why and how inmates maintained their autonomy, integration and, most importantly, their humanity during their horrendous ordeal. Bettelheim argued that this theoretical and practical deficit was because psychoanalysis did not give enough theoretical importance to the powerful influence of the social environment in changing the individual. He came to realize that psychoanalysis, as a treatment modality, was not the most potent influence to bring about personality change. Rather, an extreme environment such as the camps could more swiftly and invasively shape the person for better or worse. Says Bettelheim, "The impact of the concentration camp ... within a few weeks, did for me what years of useful and quite successful analysis had not done" (1960, p. 12). Psychoanalyst Franz Alexander, one of the originators of psychoanalytic psychosomatic medicine and criminology, has noted that Bettelheim "recognized that psychoanalysis was conceived in times of stability and did not pay sufficient attention to the environmental influences on shaping personality" (1961, p. 42). He thus asserted that psychoanalytic theory needed to be changed.

According to Bettelheim, what was necessary to help reshape psychoanalytic theory to effectively illuminate situations of extremity, which arguably includes a seriously depressed/anxious person who views himself as in an "extreme" situation, was the development of a theory that took the powerful role of the social environment into consideration along with the vicissitudes of the sexual and aggressive drives and early life history. Says Bettelheim:

I only wish to suggest that the psychoanalytic theory of personality is deficient in suggesting what makes for a "desirable," well integrated personality; and this because it overstresses the importance of the inner life to the neglect of the total man as he deals with his human and social environment.

(1960, p. 21)

Even more to the point, Bettelheim noted, "What psychoanalysis has already achieved for the personality within a stable social context must now be done for personality and social context in their interaction, when both of them are changing" (ibid., p. 37), like in the concentration camp. Bettelheim thus seemed to recognize deficiencies in psychoanalytic personality theory that, as he intimates, forced him to try to modify his psychoanalytic perspective with insights from the field of social psychology (e.g., the role of the social environment in changing personality). What Bettelheim was identifying as problematic in psychoanalytic theory is still a theoretical, clinical and practical conundrum that has not been adequately addressed by the psychoanalytic community. Psychoanalysis has not drawn from social psychology and sociology in a sophisticated way to develop a theory that can make better sense out of behavior in radically unstable social environments. While most of us have mercifully not endured concentration camps or other such "extreme" situations, the conditions of possibility that tend to bring about depression are often correlated with the real and imagined utter "outrageousness" of an external world that radically subverts one's autonomy, integration and humanity. To better grasp how such people consciously and unconsciously build their private "concentration camp" for themselves (Appelfeld, 1994, p. 17) requires that we have a better understanding of the role of powerfully toxic "real" environments in propelling them into their depressive abyss.[29]

## The cognitive perspective

The cognitive perspective on depression emphasizes the role of a person's beliefs rather than their behavior, as described above, in generating depression. Depression is a consequence of systematic negative bias in thought processes. Flawed cognitions cause the emotional, behavioral and sometimes physical symptoms that constitute depression as conventionally described. Aaron Beck, for example, described these defective cognitions in terms of three main faulty mechanisms (the cognitive triad): negative automatic thinking about the self, world and future; negative self-schemas (i.e., beliefs about oneself); and mistakes in logic and information processing (Beck et al., 1979). For instance, a depressed person tends to regard himself as helpless, worthless and inadequate. He views events in the world in an unrealistically negative and pessimistic manner, and interprets the world as full of impediments that cannot be effectively managed or surmounted. Lastly, the depressed person regards the future as utterly hopeless, mainly because they believe that their worthlessness and inadequacy guarantees that their situation will never get better.[30] With such a self-defeating way of thinking it is no wonder that such a person feels hopeless.[31]

It is hard not to recognize the validity of the cognitive perspective, the role of flawed beliefs, in explaining what tends to induce depressive feelings in the average person. Indeed, there seems to be a "hardwired" tendency to think in biased, distorted, illogical and other defective ways, such that a technique-oriented, psycho-educational intervention like Cognitive Behavioral Therapy (CBT) is helpful. However, what the cognitive perspective underemphasizes is the limited way it conceptualizes the "self" as it relates to beliefs and, most importantly, to moral values. The cognitive perspective does not adequately theorize the role of moral values in both inducing and fending off depression in such a way that one can maintain one's autonomy, integration and humanity amidst suffering. For the cognitive therapist, the "self" is equated with the self-concept, the view of the self that is fashioned from the beliefs one maintains about oneself and the responses of others. Moreover, the self is viewed as a self-enclosed entity; it is in the person's "head," rather than inextricably embedded in the social world (Cooper, 2015, p. 57). While this is a "good" conception, it is not a "complete" one, for it mistakenly assumes that the depressive thoughts always cause depression rather than them being a consequence of other self-undermining limitations associated with a bogged-down way of being-in-the-world.[32]

For the depressive, the rigid, structure-bound and nihilistic outlook of extreme self-absorption, self-indulgence and self-glorification keeps him willingly lodged in his airless bubble, and therefore tragically prevents him from reclaiming his autonomy, integration and humanity during his depressive ordeal. The self is "webs of beliefs and desires, or sentential attitudes – webs which continually reweave themselves so as to accommodate new sentential attitudes" (Rorty, 1990, p. 93). Furthermore, this web of belief stimulates the organism into actions, which produce new beliefs to be woven into the webs, which in turn produce actions, and so on for as long as the organism survives. In other words, says Rorty, "there is no self distinct from the self-reweaving web. All there is to a human self is just that web" (ibid.).

Psychoanalyst Roy Schaefer formulates the self in a similar manner when he writes that the self is "an experiential phenomenon, a set of more or less stable and emotionally felt ways of telling oneself about one's being and one's continuity throughout change ... the self is a thought, not an agent ... a kind of retelling about one's individuality" (1978, pp. 84, 86). Thus, the self is not a fixed, static structure, as cognitive therapists tend to theorize it, but rather is relative, contingent, conditional and variable. It has to be routinely fashioned and sustained in the reflexive activities of the individual. Formulating the "self" this way helps us to understand why the key to mental survival in the concentration camps as an autonomous and integrated person was to cling to one's internal sense of selfhood by acting out one's moral values and inner convictions. For it is precisely moral values and inner convictions that are the "self," that network of beliefs, desires and emotions that matter most in terms of "remaining human" throughout the prisoner's ordeal.[33]

Moral values provide an orientation to action; they are, as Kluckhohn has written, "conceptions, explicit or implicit, distinctive of an individual or characteristic of a group, of the desirable which influence the selection from available modes, means, and ends of action" (1951, p. 388). The prisoners with strongly held,[34] consistent, flexibly applied, transcendent values – like Jehovah Witnesses, devout Jews, Catholic priests and diehard Communists – were best at enduring the daily grind of camp life and "remaining human," in part because they had direction to their lives in extremity. For these inmates, acting on these moral values could involve a wide range of behavior – from acts of dramatic self-assertion (e.g., physical resistance) to exerting attitudinal freedom (e.g., viewing one's circumstances in a non-debasing manner). Such inmates were less likely to regress, to give in to depression, anxiety and moral corruption that aped Nazi values. The point is that in the camps, what one did to support self-esteem was not fixed. As long as one had a relatively intact sense of self, that is, one's strongly held transcendent moral values and inner convictions, a wide range of behavior may have been necessary for an inmate to maintain his autonomy, integration and humanity in the changing, morally ambiguous circumstances of camp conditions. Finally, in terms of the average person trying to endure and surmount his depressive ordeal (his "total institution"), Goffman's important observation surely has some relevance: "Strong religious and political convictions [i.e., transcendent moral values and inner convictions] have served to insulate the true believer against the assaults of a total institution" (1961, p. 66).[35]

### Learned helplessness

Martin Seligman's concept of "learned helplessness" has been used to explain the causation of forms of depression. It has been succinctly defined as:

> a mental state in which an organism forced to bear aversive stimuli, or stimuli that are painful or otherwise unpleasant, becomes unable or unwilling to avoid subsequent encounters with those stimuli, even if they are "escapable," presumably because it has learned that it cannot control the situation.[36]

The simple but compelling idea here is that a person no longer attempts to escape a painful situation after he has initiated numerous failed escapes. Depression comes about when a person suffers from this marked sense of powerlessness, emanating from a traumatic event or persistent lack of success. As psychologist Kathryn Hahner (1989) points out, in a later "reformulated" version of Seligman's theory, he drew from attribution theory (i.e., the way people attribute causality to events). According to Seligman, "when a person finds that he is helpless, he asks why he is helpless. The causal attribution he makes then determines the generality and chronicity of his helplessness deficits as well as his later self-esteem" (Abramson et al., 1978, p. 50). That is, the causal attribution will determine whether a person feels depressed or not, and if he does feel depressed, to what degree (ibid.). As Hahner explains, Seligman's "reformulated" theory argued "that the basis of depression and helplessness deficits is a person's causal attribution to the self for bad events – an internal attribution ('It's my fault')." Moreover, the theory "also predicts that depressed people will make more global attributions ('It's like this in every situation')" (1989, n.p.). Finally, says Hahner, a depressed person "will make more 'stable' attributions; i.e., things are seen as always staying the same" (ibid.). The "reformulated" theory claims that depressed persons make internal attributions for what they view as bad events and are deeply pessimistic about the future. While Seligman has argued that his theory differs from Beck's, its main findings surely resonate with Beck's (ibid.). What is important for us here is that Seligman puts into sharp focus a human proclivity: internal attributions for bad events, especially when linked to perceived lack of control, create the conditions of possibility for the upsurge of depressing feelings.

As I will argue in the following section, what was true in the concentration camp is also true for those in the grip of depression: to quote sociologist/ Auschwitz survivor Anna Pawełczyńska, "models and values that are deeply internalized," especially those that are other-directed, other-regarding and other-serving, "create the strength to resist every alien system which denies those values" (1979, p. 137).[37] Such an "alien system" can include the powerful interpretive grip that a depression has on a suffering person's outlook and behavior, a form of "total institution" that is reinforced to some degree by real or imagined external, situational factors. In other words, by having a consistent set of flexibly implemented, transcending values and strong beliefs that one adheres to, one is best able to protect their autonomy, integration and humanity, the very qualities of mind, heart and spirit that are eroded in persistent depression. It is to this subject that I now turn.

*Psychoanalytic reflections on the moral meanings of depression*

Let's begin with a quotation from the unconventional Christian believer Kierkegaard's masterpiece *Either/Or* to spotlight one of the most significant moral aspects of the experience of depression, namely that it is highly narcissistic:

> In addition to my other numerous acquaintances, I have one more intimate confidant – my depression. In the midst of my joy, in the midst of my work, he beckons to me, calls me aside, even though physically I

remain on the spot. My depression is the most faithful mistress I have known – no wonder, then, that I return the love.

(1987, p. 20)

Kierkegaard's testimonial aptly reflects the intensely erotically charged interest in oneself that is associated with the phenomenology of depression. Indeed, way before Freud, his beloved novelist Dostoyevsky made the same point, that "man is sometimes extraordinarily passionately in love with suffering, and that is a fact" (1864, Ch. IX). Depression, what Kierkegaard roughly means by "despair," is "sickness unto death." The latter phrase describes the dread that a person feels that his life will be spiritually empty and meaningless (i.e., in religious language, "eternal death," the wretched fate of the wicked in hell), rather than attain the "eternal life" (the fate of the righteous) that faith in God provides as Jesus has promised. For Kierkegaard, despair is tied to his conception of the "self," though both are murky notions in his Christian psychological reflections. To become a "self," perhaps better thought of as an "authentic self," involves struggling with the greatest impediment to such "higher" spiritual and psychological integration, namely sin. Sin for Kierkegaard is also a murky term, but in its most basic manifestation it means engaging in immoral acts judged to be transgression against divine law. Ironically, however, becoming aware of and taking responsibility for sin and converting it to goodness is the "royal road" to faith, the surest "antidote" to despair. As philosopher William McDonald further notes, for Kierkegaard, the "human being" is a synthesis of various components of the physical and the spiritual: the finite and infinite, temporal and eternal, necessity and freedom, and body and soul.[38]

In contrast to the "human being," the "self" is the active process of relating these components of synthesis to each other. The "self," says McDonald, is the work of sustaining the proper balance of the synthesis, while despair is the opposite, an imbalance in the synthesis of the spirit/body relation.[39] Kierkegaard provides a simple example: he describes a person whose way of being-in-the-world is markedly characterized by fantasy and imagination, by the non-rationalist/spontaneous outlook of the Dionysian, as Nietzsche called it, and therefore is not properly responsive to the Beauty, Truth and Goodness of the "real" world around him. Similarly, a person whose way of being-in-the-world is overly practical and concrete, dominated by the rationalist/linearity of the Apollonian outlook, never engages the spiritual realm or the freedom of the spirit and the joy of living that it evokes. Both sorts of people are in despair because they are not experiencing with the fullness of their being praiseworthy features of human experience, and thus are failing to be actualized human beings in the fullest and best way. However, this balancing task is not achievable by a person's skillful actions alone (i.e., faith is necessary), hence the various forms of despair: "Willing to be a self ... Not willing to be a self ... Being unaware of the possibility of being a self" (McDonald, n.p.).

Finally, there is the worst form of despair: sin-consciousness, which is the awareness that one is radically morally flawed, especially in actions, compared to the all-good, forgiving God.[40] Perhaps most importantly, it is accompanied by feeling anxious and guilty for not choosing to do anything that is self-correcting in light of this awareness of one's moral flaws. In other words, says McDonald, Christian faith, believing that God is the ultimate ground of the self-relation, is the way out of despair. Once one owns up to one's sinfulness, an admission that evokes an upsurge of God-consciousness according to Kierkegaard, one will be willing and able to receive God's gracious forgiveness and strive to be and do better.[41] Moreover, as McDonald emphasizes, this sin/God consciousness includes the "higher" self-integration that is correlated with the mindfulness of one's dependence on God, the wholly and holy Other, the basis for living the "good life" as I have called it (ibid.).

Finally, to make matters even more complicated, for Kierkegaard, while faith is the opposite of sin, it is "absurd," that is, not rational, to believe that God cares about our puny little lives, and it is nonsensical to believe that one can enter into a direct dialogue with God (e.g., how would one know for sure that it was God talking?). This being said, it is precisely this leap of faith that is necessary to have a transformative personal relation with God. For this relation is the most fertile psychological/spiritual breeding ground (though a "groundless ground") for the growth of moral excellence, for righteousness, the qualitative change of mind, heart and spirit that is the basis for fashioning the "good life."

I have provided this summary of Kierkegaard's Christian view of despair to provide a point of entry into the heart of my psychoanalytically oriented discussion about the moral aspects of depression – namely, that to an under-appreciated extent, depression is a reaction to personal decisions and moral choices. The depressed person is consciously and unconsciously unwilling and unable to create an enlarged sense of self, to expand and deepen his capacity for love, and to embrace a spiritual, transcendent relationship with life. Rather, such a person is bound to their sense of self, to a repressed/restricted/fragmented self, and they deny and resist their potential to grow, develop and refashion themselves via creative, life-affirming practices (Schneider & Krug, 2010, pp. 16, 18 22, 117). In short, the depressed person is "bound, tied and gagged" by the ill-conceived self, other and world constructs by which he has strangely and painfully chosen to live.

Indeed, psychologist Sonja Lyubomirsky (2005) described the "happiness set point" in her book on the "how of happiness," suggesting that 50 percent of happiness is genetically predetermined, while 10 percent is due to life circumstances, and 40 percent is the result of personal outlook, that is, decisions and moral choices. Kierkegaard provides two straightforward examples of this point as it relates to despair: Consider a person who longs to be Caesar but never reaches his objective. Such a person seems to be in despair over something, that is, of not being Caesar. However, what he is "really" feeling despair about is himself. That is, he longs to be something that he is not, in this case Caesar, and he longs not to be himself, since he is not Caesar. In a second example, a woman whose paramour has died or has betrayed her may seem to be in despair because of her paramour; but what she is "really" in despair about is herself, that is, she longs to still be her paramour's beloved. In both of these simple examples, we see "the cunning and sophistry" of despair, as Kierkegaard terms it, and, most importantly, the fact that all forms of despair, at least generally speaking, are an "unwillingness to live up to the expectation of selfhood" (Hannay, 1998, pp. 330, 338). Such a person abandons all hope of being free of his morbid narcissistic self. His calcified self-relation is one that closes him off to the summoning and transformative "voice" of the infinite, to the trace of the transcendent that the Axial sages claimed, "commanding" us to be other-directed, other-regarding and other-serving, a way of being that is both equated with and potentiating of the "good life."

## The "three poisons" of depression

The Buddha pointed out that the three key virtues that constitute the "good life" – humility, charity and truthfulness – were impeded from being culti-vated in the average person because he had not surmounted three impedi-ments, the "three poisons" of greed, hatred and delusion. To the extent that these poisons are mastered, transformed or eliminated, selflessness (humility), compassion (charity) and seeing things in their "suchness" (truthfulness) replace them (Smith, 1991, p, 387). In a manner that calls to mind the insights of the Buddha, Jean Améry, the celebrated French essayist and Nazi death-camp survivor (also a "torture" victim), succinctly describes the phe-nomenology of the depressive in terms of its three features that "poison" the self: "The past is disgraceful, the present painful, the future non-existent" (1999, p. 56).[42] I will briefly unpack Améry's description in a slightly different order – the present, the past and the future.

### PRESENT PAINFUL

The "moral emotions" that psychiatric researchers have called shame, guilt and indignation are of course pertinent to understanding the negative moral processes involved in the burgeoning of depression. Likewise, the "moral emotions" of certain forms of prosocial pride and gratitude suggest a life-saving counterpoint to depression (Pulco et al., 2013, p. 310). While aspects of the phenomenology of depressive suffering are familiar to most people from the various published memoirs, testimonials and even personal experiences, it has been beautifully described by the American novelist David Foster Wallace (1996), who explains that "psychotically depressed" persons do not attempt suicide because death appeals to them; they do so because life feels unendurable, like a trap from which one must escape. While Wallace is discussing the psychotically depressed person, his words resonate with those people who may feel less depressed but can still relate to the agony of believing and feeling there is no satisfying exit from one's tortured mind. Indeed, such an internal scenario calls to mind the biblical account of the Exodus, of the freedom-seeking Israelite slaves fleeing the murderous Egyptians only to find themselves at the edge of the swollen Red Sea with nowhere to run or hide and facing sure death through drowning. The difference between Wallace's and the biblical account is of course that the Israelites were miraculously saved from their death when a divinely inspired Moses split the Red Sea and the Egyptians in pursuit were drowned.

One of the key points of the Exodus story that speaks to the phenomenology of depression and its "antidote" is that amidst one's enslavement and bondage to depression, one must emulate God's behavior: That is, just as God "remembered" His covenant with the Israelites, and was responsive and responsible to their suffering by intervening in their life and death ordeal, so must the depressed person "remember" his "covenant" with those he loves (and, by extension, embrace life without reserve, honor what is "good" about being alive and work to perfect the world), by being responsive to and responsible for the suffering of those significant others who are pained and in other ways negatively impacted by his condition. As the great Axial-inspired Sufi poet/mystic Rumi has noted (2005), refusal to praise is linked to depression. To praise means to be open and responsive with the fullness of one's whole being to the self-transcendent Beauty, Truth and Goodness that are literally right before one's eyes. Indeed, to have the will and ability to view one's depressive suffering as Rumi advocates, as a question of freedom and responsibility for the other, including letting oneself be bathed in the Beauty, Truth and especially Goodness of the other, can often evoke the spontaneous gratitude that the religious aspirant calls divine "grace."

There have been many psychoanalytic theories to account for depressive suffering, and, depending on the totality of life circumstances associated with a particular patient's form of depression, each one of them is illuminating and helpful to the clinician trying to assist these pained patients. For example, Karl Abraham (1927) emphasized the depressive as fixated in the oral-sadistic phase.[43] As a result he is highly ambivalent toward significant others, and thus is truncated in his ability to love. Most importantly, the extreme contempt underlying this incapacity to love generates intense anxiety that is repressed and then projected onto and into the world. As a consequence of these projections, the individual feels unloved and unlovable, alienated and hated – in short, depressed.

Freud (1917 [1957]) regarded melancholic depression as a pathological type of mourning for the lost "object." The lost object is not conceived as a "real-life" person but an "internal object" (roughly how another person is experienced, represented and remembered by the person engaging in the objectification). Similar to Abraham, Freud claimed that the depressed individual has tremendous ambivalence toward the internal object, one that he was both highly dependent on but also felt antagonistic toward. In this view, the depression is rooted in two imaginings – that he has killed off the internal object, leading to an upsurge of self-blame and reduced self-esteem; and that he is unable to survive, let alone flourish, without the object; hence, he feels depressed (Rycroft, 1995, p. 35). Sandor Rado (1928) claimed that the depressive is narcissistically vulnerable; that is, he has an inordinate need to be loved by an adoring mother (or caregiver) and is angry that receiving this infantile love on demand is no longer possible. Unwilling and unable to accept this narcissistically hurtful/enraging fact, his regret and depression are his last-ditch attempt to gain such infantile love. As philosopher George Santayana noted, "depression is rage spread thin" (Aguirre, 2008, p. 5). Melanie Klein (1984) argued that depression is rooted in the "depressive position," when the infant or patient recognizes that his ambivalence, his love and hate, is directed toward the same object, the mother or primary caregiver, and thus intense guilt is generated. This leads to him wanting to shield his mother from his hatred and undo the fantasized damage he has inflicted on her. For Klein, such guilt-reducing actions are conceived as forms of reparation, and the depressed patient is stuck in the "depressive position." Finally, John Bowlby's (1963) theory of attachment links depression to "real-life" maternal deprivation. For example, short-term abandonment of a child by his mother (or other attachment figure) leads to the sequence of protest (e.g., crying, screaming and anger meant to block separation); despair (e.g., withdrawing into quiet desperation and ignoring non-maternal attempts to be comforted); and detachment (e.g., engaging others combined with angry rejection of the mother/caregiver when she returns). For Bowlby, depression is mainly related to the person redirecting his anger at his "real-life" abandoning mother/primary caregiver to himself.

While all of these theories brilliantly spotlight aspects of the phenomenology of depression, they underappreciate what I believe is morally central to the condition and which I have already insinuated in my Kierkegaardian musings – namely, that the "bedrock" of the experience of depression is the highly erotically charged narcissistic self-relation that does not allow for much "other awareness" (Cooper, 2015, p. 179), let alone ethically animated other-directedness. That is, from the point of view of moral psychology, the depressed person disavows his freedom and possibilities. Put starkly, he becomes unconscious of his decision to deny his freedom and responsibility to the other, propelling him into an extremely dysfunctional identification with the limits of his inordinately narcissistically animated selfhood, often characterized by a suppressed/repressed, constricted/fragmented way of living (Schneider & Krug, 2010, pp. 14, 117).

When Améry described the depressive's relationship to the present as "painful," he was pointing to what it feels like to be trapped in an encapsulated self, in a totalizing system of closed-mindedness, to be unwilling and unable to liberate oneself from the inner maze of grotesque happenings, especially the relentless self-recriminations. This somewhat accounts for the "going around in circles" feeling of the depressed person's presentation in treatment.[44] To make matters even worse, the depressed person is often quasi-aware of the largely self-chosen, self-made nature of his internal "concentration camp," causing waves of shame, guilt and anxiety. Playing off the evocative philosophy of Leibnitz, such an imprisoned person is like a "windowless monad," a single and simple entity (i.e., a solipsistic being) that is incapable of having a direct causal and perceptual relationship with any other monad (i.e., person). This self-limiting way of being is the basis for the utter "forsakenness" (Yalom, 1989, p. 150), the sense that one resides in a real or imagined loveless hell, including the hell of being at the mercy of a neglectful, abusive universe as depressives typically construe it.

## PAST DISGRACEFUL

The Axial philosopher Plato put his finger on the depressed person's sense of disgracefulness, what psychoanalysts usually refer to as shame. In his dialogue *Gorgias*, Plato writes, "Then not only custom, but also nature affirms that to do is more disgraceful than to suffer injustice, and that justice is equality" (read equality as honoring the dignity and goodness of the other; 2008).[45] To do real or imagined "injustice," that is, to feel shame and guilt for failing oneself and others, is precisely what the depressive feels.

While shame and guilt both reflect "moral angst," they have been conceptualized differently. As experimental personality researchers have noted, shame centers on the self, while guilt centers on behavior. Shame emerges when people negatively appraise the global self ("I am bad"), while guilt emerges when people negatively appraise a specific behavior ("I did something bad"). Moreover, shame has been found to be a more painful and distressing feeling because, in light of failure and transgression, the whole self is judged as deficient and imperfect, leading to feelings of worthlessness and powerlessness, and the wish to vanish. Shamed people often ruminate on how defectively they are viewed by others (Tangney & Mahek, 2004). Psychoanalytically speaking, shame is lodged in the painful feeling of failure for not behaving in a manner that is in accordance with one's expectations of one's ego-ideal, while guilt emerges when a person feels he has violated a prohibition of, say, a moral system emanating from outside the self, though embedded in the super-ego. While the shame-filled person withdraws into a system of hideouts because of his "sins," the guilty person typically feels compelled to "confess" his "sins" (Akhtar, 2009, p. 264). Of course, both shame and guilt are operative in most depressives; they co-produce each other in certain contexts, or shame is assimilated into guilt, et cetera.[46] However, here I want to briefly focus on the shame element because it is underappreciated in terms of what may be most morally tragic about depression, but also suggestive of how to surmount its most painful aspects.

"Shame is a soul eating emotion," said Carl Jung (Sanderson, 2015, p. 11). Indeed, as Kilborne noted, unresolved shame conflicts are especially tragic in that the person is ensnared in a painful paradox "between the longing to be recognized and the terror of being seen" (2004, pp. 465, 472). That is, there is an "inability to make a vital connection to anyone" (hence the depressive's "closedness,"[47] avoidant attachment patterns and social isolation) "together with shame also over omnipotent wishes organized in response to a fear of never being seen or found," hence the defensive narcissistic self-absorption, reversing self-shame into shaming others, self-serving playing "fast and loose" with the "facts" of reality, and other kinds of deceptions (ibid., p. 479; Akhtar, 2009, p. 264).

My point is that the depressed person feels intense humiliation because he has betrayed himself by betraying those who are dependent on him, whom he loves and for whom he is responsible. The narcissistic self-relation, the lynchpin of depression, evokes shame/humiliation because he recognizes that he is unwilling and unable to be other-directed, other-regarding and other-serving, as he believes he should be. Richard Rorty captures the destructive impact such humiliation has on people's inner monologue:

> Now that I have believed or desired this [read: being for oneself rather than for the other] I can never be what I hoped to be, what I thought I was. The story I have been telling myself about myself – my picture of myself as honest, or loyal, or devout – no longer makes sense. I no longer have a self to make sense of. There is no world in which I can picture myself living, because there is no vocabulary in which I can tell a coherent story of myself.
>
> (1989, p. 179)

In other words, in the mind of the depressive, humiliation means he is not able to integrate events that occurred, acts of omission and commission, and sort them into the ongoing, let alone acceptable, story about the self. Thus, as with the prisoner in the concentration camp who did not remain faithful to his former system of moral values in imprisoned life, the depressive lives with a soul-destroying feeling of shame and guilt that ultimately undermines his autonomy, integration and humanity. As such, he withdraws into his solipsistic, protective cocoon. Ironically, to make matters worse, he longs to resurrect himself in his own eyes and the eyes of others. That is, he craves feeling self-worthy and lovable to others, a vital validation from a world that he protractedly doubts will ever be forthcoming as he desperately needs and wants. As Erik H. Erikson noted, "doubt is the brother of shame" (qtd. in Singh, 2000, p. 48). It is precisely this anxiety-ridden doubt that makes the future appear so dark, gloomy, and impossible to bear to the depressive.

"Everything begins with the future," Heidegger wrote (2001, p. 159). What he meant by this is that human beings are not merely caused beings, motivated from the past as Freud has so brilliantly taught us, but they are equally animated "by future goals, meanings and possibilities" (Cooper, 2017, p. 21). That is, "we pull ourselves from ahead, rather than being pushed from behind" as the existentialists have claimed (ibid.). Of course, it is clear to most thoughtful people that *both* the past and the future influence our behavior in varying ways depending on the circumstances. As I have earlier noted, humans are at once historically situated and context-dependent, and future-directed and context-transcending. The depressed person is both unwilling and unable to imagine, let alone embrace, a prospective consciousness that is characterized by life-affirming dignity, hope and faith. Rather, he is lodged in a retrospective consciousness characterized by life-denying shame, guilt and anxious doubt. As is common psychological knowledge, where there is shame and guilt, when one feels like a "sinner" and "criminal," there must be punishment. Indeed, the depressed person profoundly feels that he has failed himself because he has failed those he loves and, hence, the crime seeks the punishment. In the self-accusative world of the depressive, this punishment takes the many forms that psychoanalysts have aptly described in their depictions and formulations of depressive suffering. However, what is most important for our discussion is that the punishment is characterized by a kind of self-imposed "banishment" and "exile" – removing oneself from the human community in real and imagined ways (hence the social withdrawal and internal desolation that is typical of the depressive) – into the self-created agony and terror of the "concentration camp" of their own minds.

### "Liberation" from depressive suffering

Finding one's way out of depressive suffering is an extremely difficult task. Some of the most challenging psychoanalytic work is to help a depressed person "liberate" himself from his painful ordeal. As the spectacularly gloomy singer/songwriter Leonard Cohen noted in 1988 about his bout with clinical depression, "One has a sense that a catastrophe has occurred in the psychic landscape."[48] Taking my lead from observations made by concentration camp prisoners who were better able to maintain their autonomy integration and humanity during their extreme ordeal, I believe there are some important moral insights from the "kingdom of night" that have a bearing on how to help a depressed person find his way out of his self-made, self-chosen "concentration camp." While this subject deserves a book, I will only here make three general comments that I hope are suggestive of what points in the direction of relief, if not being the "antidote" to depressive suffering.

Camp survivor/logotherapist Viktor Frankl noted, "In this living labora-tory we watched and witnessed some of our comrades behave like swine while others behaved like saints. Man has both potentialities within himself: which one is actualized depends on decisions" (1984, p. 157). Frankl is emphasizing what is often underappreciated by analysts and underutilized by depressed analysands – namely, that while humans do not have unimpeded freedom (as there are limit-situations to existence), they are basically free. As Nietzsche said, "Will a self and you will become a self" (Van Deurzen, 2012, p. 239). That is, the way out of depression requires the vigorous mobilization of the will, the ability to embrace an inner attitude characterized by courage and resolve, "a willingness to stand naked in the storm of life," as Ernest Becker evocatively put it (Cooper, 2017, p. 32). Indeed, as experimental personality researchers have pointed out, the will, conceived as a potentially "healthy" agentic capacity, "deserves to be taken seriously as a scientific construct" (Kuhl & Koole, 2004, pp. 424, 423).[49] Put differently, the depressed person must be willing and able to "fight like hell" against his condition, a way of being that calls to mind the bravery and determination of all great military strategists/soldiers who try to defeat a cunning and brutal enemy (Marcus, 2014). As the Axial-inspired Muhammad the Prophet noted, "We have returned from the Lesser Holy War [with the external enemy] to the Greater Holy War [with the selfish passions]" (Marcus, 2003, p. 159).

A second moral consideration that may be helpful in dislodging depres-sive suffering is to increase awareness of the person's life-denying way of being-in-the-world that closes off other life-affirming possibilities. These are the realms of "un-freedom" (Cooper, 2017, p. 71), those unconscious deci-sions, repressed hopes and unavowed insights that keep someone imprisoned in an extremely restricted, shame- and guilt-driven existence (ibid.). The largely morbid, narcissistic self-relation has to give way to some internal "space" for something radically otherwise, to a different way of construing and imagining one's condition of possibilities. It is crucial that one have the will and ability to "think differently" about oneself and one's circumstances. Foucault made this same point superbly when he discussed the role of "cri-tique" in changing how people fashion their subjectivity in light of residing in an oppressive, normalizing socio-intellectual reality that has become deeply internalized.

> Critique is not a matter of saying that things are not right as they are [the depressive's complaint]. It is a matter of pointing out on what kinds of assumptions, what kinds of familiar, unchallenged, unconsidered modes of thought the practices [the depressive way of being] we accept rest.
>
> (Foucault, 1988, p. 35)

A "permanent critique" of ourselves refers to the critical and analytic modes of self-reflection about the limits that make us the people we are. It is through critique that Foucault hoped to facilitate greater critical self-reflection about these practices, especially their potential danger. Such self- and life-reflective thought does not come easily because it is Socratic in character, it is "paralyzing, stinging, moral and maieutic" (Calcagno, 2015, p. 121). In the depressive's case, this centrally involves critiquing the morbid narcissistic self-relation, with its ill-conceived and ill-fated meaning-giving, affect-integrating and action-guiding infrastructure. What Foucault and Freud are saying is that if you "change something in the minds of people," their "mode of thought" as Foucault described it – and not simply a particular irrational idea, as cognitive behaviorists believe – they realize that they "are much freer than they feel," and a deep transformation in how they reside in the world can begin to occur (Foucault, 1988, p. 35). Indeed, this upsurge of newfound freedom is crucial to living through one's depression and becoming positively transformed by it. In his discussion of the extent an individual can resist tyrannical violence, Levinas puts this point just right as it applies to surmounting the tyrannical violence of experienced depression: In "freedom of thought [one] preserves an unlimited power of refusal," and "what does remain free is the capacity to foresee one's own degradation, and arm oneself against it" (1987a, p. 17).

Finally, from the moral psychological point of view, once the depressed person's will has been mobilized and his freedom to think, feel and act is expanded and deepened, or at least "loosened up," he needs to embrace with the fullness of his being the key valuative attachment that in the camps mainly determined who survived as a "person," with their autonomy, integration and humanity relatively intact. By attaching oneself to an other-directed, other-regarding and other-serving ethic of responsibility – a way of thinking, feeling and acting that both personifies and potentiates transcendence – one is most likely to have the will and ability to vanquish one's depressive suffering. This may appear to be a far-fetched idea when one considers the extremely sedimented self (Spinelli, 2015) that is typical of the depressive, who vigorously resists embracing anything non-self-centric, let alone an ethic of responsibility for, and to, the other. However, as all Axial religious sages proclaimed, the most robust way to experience a trace of God, the Absolute Other, is to give to others "until it hurts," and this has special bearing on the depressed person who is trapped in his calcified, morbid, narcissistic self-relation. As Rabbi Sacks has pointed out, "the very act of giving flows from, or leads to, the understanding that what we give is part of what we were given," by God if one is a believer, but also by those who care about and love us, and far beyond (2017, p. 2). That is, giving of oneself, including in the broadest sense – such as being open and responsive to the Beauty, Truth and Goodness in the wider world – is a way of saying thanks. It is an act of profound gratitude, one that eludes the person amidst his steadfastly held depressive suffering.

## Final comment

Given the inevitability of rather extreme mental anguish in everyday life, the reader may be in gloomy agreement with philosopher Schopenhauer: "The shortness of life, so often lamented may perhaps be the very best thing about it … No man, if he be sincere and at the same time in possession of his faculties, will ever wish to go through it again" (Cooper, 2017, p. 197). However, while mental anguish, including as it manifests itself in extreme anxiety and depression, may begin catastrophically as "breakdown," it can end wondrously as "breakthrough."[50] Indeed, the Nobel Prize-winning author Hermann Hesse made this point beautifully in his Buddhist-inspired, spiritual tale *Siddhartha* (1951) when he explained that he had to reach his lowest point in order to experience his highest point. Hesse is describing what is the deep and abiding hope of any person who is amidst extreme emotional turmoil: to be released from his distressing entrapment and emerge a better, stronger and more skillful person, infused with practical wisdom about how to live the "good life." As I have suggested throughout this chapter, to earn such "grace," as Hesse called it, requires a lot of "hard work" on oneself – that is, "working through" all of the "usual suspects" described by psychoanalysts in their accounts of anxiety and depression. This being said, what I hope I have convinced the reader is worth seriously considering is that for this life-affirming psychological clearance and clarification to occur, one must embrace the "Openness to the Open" (Cain, 1995, p. 121). Such a way of being-in-the-world involves "simultaneously throwing one's self open and offering one's self up" (Marcel, 1965, p. 188). That is, such a process of creative receptivity as Marcel calls it, of giving oneself with the fullness of one's whole being, involves a significant scaling back of one's inordinate, if not morbid narcissism, and the defensive regime that protects the enfeebled, calcified and barren self. It means wholeheartedly engaging the mystery of being, embracing the "saving light" (Marcel, 2005, p. 53) of gratitude for being willing and able to give and receive love.[51]

## Notes

1 By being-in-the-world I mean to emphasize that the human being is best conceptualized as an individual unity of thought, feeling/kinesthetic and action, engaged in the lived actuality of his everyday life.

2 Erik H. Erikson has called the ego strengths that emerge from each phase of the life cycle "virtues," as he was greatly influenced by Taoist and Confucian mysticism, of "The Way," most associated with Lao-Tsu. For Erikson, virtue meant "ego strength, character and ethical vitality" (Hoare, 2002, p. 104).

3 Jonathan Lear has given a serviceable definition of "moral psychology": "the name of a commitment to a rigorous and truthful account of the psyche that is itself trying to promote what it finds to be good about human being" (2014, p. 470).

4 Freud sounds similar to Socrates, who allegedly remarked, "I have never knowingly harmed any man, or sinned against God" (Johnson, 2011, p. 111).

5 The "ethical turn" has been recently discussed by a few relational psychoanalysts. One of the best books was written by Donna M. Orange (2011), a philosopher and psychoanalyst, who uses Gadamer and Levinas as her intellectual points of entry. My book on Levinas, ethical living and psychoanalysis, is also worth perusing (Marcus, 2008).

6 For Kierkegaard guilt is an ontological category, a "given" of human existence; however, when ontological guilt is not properly reckoned with, it upsurges and intensifies, often morphing into neurotic anxiety.

7 Tillich points out the dire consequences of not reckoning with nonbeing: "He who does not succeed in taking his anxiety courageously upon himself can succeed in avoiding the extreme situation of despair by escaping into neurosis. He still affirms himself but on a limited scale. Neurosis is his way of avoiding nonbeing by avoiding being" (1950, p. 66).

8 The problem of "choice" is an extremely complex one, both psychologically and philosophically, especially in light of the recent neuropsychological findings that "suggests that the experience of choice may be an illusion, and that decisional activity is occurring in our brains long before we are aware of making a choice" (Cooper, 2017, p. 38). Still, as Heidegger pointed out, while we can never abstract ourselves from the social context we are lodged in, we can "choose to choose" what we regard as important and implement those social practices in our own unique manner (ibid., p. 32).

9 The great American singer and actress Judy Garland put this point just right: "In the silence of night I have often wished for just a few words of love from one man, rather than the applause of thousands of people" (www.thenational.ae/arts-culture/paying-a-perfect-compliment, retrieved 1/10/17).

10 The evocative existential terms "inauthentic" and "authentic" turn up throughout this chapter. Exactly what these terms mean and how one makes a judgment about what constitutes such experience and behavior is hardly clear among the psychoanalytic, psychological and philosophical scholars. For the purposes of this chapter I refer to the authentic/inauthentic distinction as "between acts which are done in good and bad faith, which are true and false to the self" (Rycroft, 1995 p. 11). As Jaspers put it, authentic living is "becoming oneself while suffering defeat" (Van Deurzen, 2012, p. 60).

11 www.civilrightsdefence.org.nz/tuhoe/mlk.html, retrieved 1/13/17.

12 Freud indicated that he "suspects" that "this narcissistic organization is never wholly abandoned" and typically "a human being remains to some extent narcissistic even after he has found external objects for his libido" (1958, p. 89).

13 See Marcus (2017) for an explication of Freud's suggestion as it relates to the psychology of work.

14 An earlier version of this material is drawn from my books on Levinas (Marcus, 2008; Marcus, 2010).

15 Spinelli notes some of the differences between Freud and existential psychology on the subject of foundational anxiety: The experience of anxiety is not the result of insufficiently satisfied instinctual demands, nor the product of conflicting drives, nor the consequence of inadequately formed infantile relations, nor a function of miscomprehended, incomplete or improper learning experiences; rather, it is the consequence of efforts to cope with, reduce or avoid the unavoidable existential anxiety (e.g., the fear of dying and living) that is intrinsic to human existence (2015, p. 106).

16 Hypostasis is a term that Levinas uses mainly in his early writings. It can be defined, Wyschogrod further says, as "the appearance of something that arises from anonymous being and that now carries being as its attribute" (2000, p. 244).

17 A critique of Levinas's developmental theory, as I have loosely called it, from the point of view of psychoanalytic and other developmental theories and findings is beyond the scope of this discussion. I only mention this point as a cautionary note.

18 Levinas has a lovely metaphor to capture this notion of ethical subjectivity. He says that a "curvature of intersubjective space" exists in which the other is located at the higher point, that is, the needs of the other are more important than my own. "The 'curvature of intersubjective space' signifies the divine intention of all truth" (1969, p. 291). Moreover, "'the curvature of space' is, perhaps, the very presence of God" (ibid.).

19 Erik H. Erikson has a somewhat different notion of ethics, one that may resonate more with mainstream psychoanalytic thought: "Ethics says ... that the worst crime is the crushing of the human spirit ['virtue' or 'soul']" (Hoare, 2002, p. 48). This is ethics as "soul murder." Erikson also noted that while "morals tells us what to say 'no' to, ethics expresses what we say 'yes' to" (ibid., p. 73). Finally, said Erikson, ethics is the "final ego-ideal of adulthood," one that exemplifies social justice and truth in action (ibid., p. 176).

20 Levinas discusses nausea in his slim volume, *On Escape/De l'évasion* (2003). Sartre's first version of his novel goes back to 1931; while Levinas's essay was written in 1935, it is not clear if either author influenced the other in their formulation of the "there is." It is worth noting that Sartre's and Levinas's uses of the term nausea are quite different. For Sartre, nausea emanated from the horror of nothingness that threatened the autonomous self, whereas for Levinas, nausea depicted the failure to escape from the bounty and plenitude of being. The real-life implications of these differing viewpoints, however, are not so clear.

21 Levinas is not entirely clear whether the "there is" is mainly a retreat, "a hiding place" (Peperzak), a "withdrawing from existence" (Alford) or the origin, the beginning of existence.

22 As Samuel Moyn suggests, Heidegger's influence is evident here. While Levinas ultimately rejected Heidegger, he never discarded the view that "man's essence ... lies in a kind of bondage." Moyn is quoting from Levinas (see Moyn, 2006, p. 103).

23 The evocative term "absurd" is used in this chapter from time to time. Following Camus, by "absurd" I mean that human existence has no absolute or ultimate foundation; rather, as the famous phrase says, human existence is "interpretation all the way down" (Cooper, 2015, p. 152). Thus, the human project is to create credible meanings and purposes.

24 In this context, embracing "otherwise than being" implies that it is something that one can in a certain sense choose. However, for Levinas any "choice" is a "second order" choice as we are all subject to the otherwise (*autrement*); it is a condition of possibility for any encounter with another.

25 As American film director Stanley Kubrick noted in an interview, "the most terrifying fact about the universe is not that it is hostile but that it is indifferent; but if we can come to terms with this indifference and accept the challenges of life within the boundaries of death – however mutable man may be able to make them – our existence as a species can have genuine meaning" (Solomon et al., 2004, p. 28).

26 Yalom (1980), one of the most prominent existential psychiatrists, regards death, freedom, isolation and meaninglessness to be the "givens," the "ultimate concerns" of human existence.

27 www.nimh.nih.gov/health/topics/depression/index.shtml, retrieved 4/25/17.

28 https://contextualscience.org/contextualism, retrieved 2/1/17.

29 While I am suggesting that "reality" has a huge influence on behavior, I am aware that it is always mediated through a person's unique outlook and way of

metabolizing experience. This includes drawing from conscious and unconscious resources. Hence some people are more skillful at "managing" the more "extreme" aspects of toxic reality than others, what Erikson called "contextual mastery" (Hoare, 2002, p. 74). As Greenberg noted, "reality," or at least "certain kinds of external or practical concerns," have "not been integrated very well into [psychoanalytic] theory" (2016, p. 9), a subject about which I am currently writing a book.

30  www.nimh.nih.gov/health/topics/depression/index.shtml, retrieved 4/25/17.

31  While cognitive therapists believe that psychological suffering is due to clients not perceiving reality correctly, some have argued that they suffer because they perceive reality too accurately; that is, they are not able to prophylactically deceive themselves when necessary (Holzhey-Kunz, 2016). Indeed, the great Axial sages, and Freud, were aware that a certain amount of benign delusion or self-swindling is necessary to face the harshness of everyday life, though the danger of this morphing into malignant "bad faith" or self-alienation is always present.

32  Some doubt has been raised about the alleged vital link between depression and systematic logical mistakes in appraising the self, world and future. For example, Spinelli cites one important 1994 study that showed that "depressed people's ratings of their own social performance were more in accord with the views of independent judges than are those of the non-depressed." Moreover, "the general logical problem-solving capability of depressed individuals remained largely unimpaired while non-depressed individuals may demonstrate quite marked errors in logical reasoning" (2015, p. 83).

33  "Remaining human," that is, maintaining a modicum of one's autonomy, integration and humanity, a term used by Elie Wiesel and other concentration camp survivors (and Holocaust scholars) was the most important challenge during incarceration since physical survival was mainly a matter of luck. To the extent one was able to "remain human" the greater the chance that one would not be psychologically destroyed, including taking on Nazi values and behavior. Exactly what instantiates "remaining human" in the camps, or for that matter in any social context, is a complex philosophical and psychological problem that I have taken up elsewhere (Marcus, 1999, pp. 64–65).

34  All personally ascribed to values are highly emotionally infused, which is what makes values so animating and potentiating.

35  According to Ernest Jones, Freud held a somewhat similar view. Jones says that one of Freud's favorite sayings was "a man is strong so long as he represents a strong idea" (Phillips, 1994, p. 113).

36  www.britannica.com/topic/learned-helplessness, retrieved 2/6/17.

37  Kierkegaard noted in his "Journals," "the thing [to live the 'good life'] is to find a truth which is true for me, to find the idea for which I can live and die" (1938). As Erikson explained, such "choices and decisions" will tend to bring about "a more" passionately felt "final self-definition, to irreversible role pattern, and thus to commitments 'for life'" (Hoare, 2002, p. 178).

38  www.iep.utm.edu/kierkega, retrieved 2/9/17.

39  Says Kierkegaard, "The self is a relation that relates itself to itself or is the relation's relating itself to itself" (1980, p. 13).

40  Erikson, greatly influenced by Kierkegaard, wrote that he believed in "original sin." For example, the human being "is the biggest liar in the universe." As a psychoanalyst he regarded such "original sin" as a sign of the adult's "curse." Being "guilty of guilt," said Erikson, was a developmental sin (Hoare, 2002, pp. 106, 58).

41  As Paul Tillich noted, sometimes this mysterious sense of forgiveness is a kind of acceptance even though one cannot precisely locate or demonstrate the source of the unconditional love (Cooper, 2017, p. 34).

42  The experience of temporality, past, present, future, is never straightforward or linear; rather, it is always interpretively dialectical, interwoven and complex. For example, how one recollects the past is to some extent determined by the present. Likewise, the present is experienced differently if the future looks hopeful, and how one feels about the future depends on how one feels about the present. In a certain sense, the way one relates to temporality is perhaps best viewed as forms of presence that always include present-past-future elements. Heidegger made this point succinctly when he observed that temporality is "a future which makes present in the process of having been" (1962, p. 374).

43  I have drawn from Akhtar (2009, p. 74) in organizing this brief review of theories of depression.

44  Research suggests that the limbic system might be implicated here. That is, when a specific emotion, like depression or anxiety, is permitted to keep looping around, the emotion gets habituated doing just that, and the discharge of that emotion will become increasingly likely rather than less likely (Van Deurzen, 2012, p. 146).

45  Aristotle is paraphrasing Socrates, who said in *Crito*, "It is never right to do wrong, or to requite wrong with wrong, or when we suffer evil to defend ourselves by doing evil in return" (Johnson, 2011, p. 114).

46  The existential claim that "guilt is our own sense of falling short" while "shame is to fall short in another's eyes" (Van Deurzen, 2012, p. 189) certainly is true in certain contexts, but from a psychoanalytic point of view, it oversimplifies how the psyche works.

47  "Closedness" versus openness are ways of relating to the world that existentialist Medard Boss (1979) has aptly described. Where focusing on the patient's "closedness" is geared toward helping him see how he restricts his way of being-in-the-world, and thus his possibilities for living better, Freud's unconscious is more focused on the camouflaged motives for the "closedness" (Cooper, 2017, p. 49).

48  *International Herald Tribune*, Paris, 12/4/88.

49  While the role of the will has been undertheorized in psychoanalytic theory, there has been some interesting work done, for example, Rank (1945). Alfred Adler and Erich Fromm also used the notion of the will in their work. Rollo May defined the will as "the capacity to organise one's self so that movement in a certain direction or towards a certain goal may take place" (1969, p. 218). The effective use of the will requires considerable flexibility, improvisation and adaptability.

50  Some psychiatrists have claimed that the "depressive position" can have an adaptive advantage that is rooted in human evolution. For example, Burton notes that "the time, space and solitude that the depressive position affords prevent us from making rash decisions, enables us to reconnect with the bigger picture, and encourage us to reassess our social relationships, think about those who matter most to us, and relate to them more meaningfully and with greater compassion" (2015, pp. 143–144). In this view, "the depressive position evolved as a signal that something is seriously wrong and needs working through and changing, or, at the very least processing and understanding" (ibid.). The "depressive position" can compel us to renounce a Pollyanna type of optimism and remove the rose-tinted glasses that help us avoid reality, stand back at a distance and reconsider and prioritize our needs, and fashion more accomplishable, realistic plans for fulfilling them. From an existential perspective, says Burton, the "depressive position" forces us to become more mindful of our mortality and freedom, and challenges us to creatively use that freedom within the context of our mortality (ibid.).

51  It is worth noting the paradox of love, that "even completely 'self-emptying' love can lead to a certain 'filling' of the self" (Gschwandtner, 2015, p. 77). If you are a "believer," Rumi's words will resonate with the above paradox: "When you forget your self, you are remembered by God" (2005, p. 174).

## References

Abraham, K. (1927). Notes on the psychoanalytic investigation and treatment of manic-depressive insanity and allied conditions. In *Selected Papers on Psycho-analysis* (pp. 137–156). London: Hogarth Press. (Original work published 1911)

Abraham, K. (1955). The history of the impostor in light of psychoanalytic knowledge. In *Clinical Papers and Essays on Psychoanalysis* (pp. 291–305). New York: Brunner-Mazel. (Original work published 1925)

Abramson, L.Y., Seligman, M.E.P., & Teasdale, J.D. (1978). Learned helplessness in humans: Critique and reformulation. *Journal of Abnormal Psychology*, 87, 49–74.

Aguirre, B.A. (2008). *Depression*. Westport, CT: Greenwood.

Akhtar, S. (2009). *Comprehensive Dictionary of Psychoanalysis*. London: Karnac.

Alexander, F. (1961). Mass Man in Death Camp and Society. *New York Times Book Review*, 10/8/61, p. 42.

Alford, C.F. (1998). Melanie Klein and the Nature of Good and Evil. In P. Marcus & A. Rosenberg (Eds.), *Psychoanalytic Versions of the Human Condition: Philosophies of Life and Their Impact on Practice* (pp. 123–124). New York: New York University Press.

Alford, C.F. (2002). *Levinas, the Frankfurt School and Psychoanalysis*. Ithaca, NY: Cornell University Press.

Améry, J. (1999). *On Suicide: A Discourse on Voluntary Death*. J.D. Barlow (Trans.). Bloomington: Indiana University Press.

Appelfeld, A. (1994). *Beyond Despair: Three Lectures and a Conversation with Philip Roth*. J.M. Green (Trans.). New York: International Publishing.

Barlow, J.D. (1999). Translator's Introduction. In J. Améry, *On Suicide: A Discourse on Voluntary Death* (pp. xi–xxi). Bloomington: Indiana University Press.

Beck, A.T., Rush, A.J., Shaw, B.F., & Emery, G. (1979). *Cognitive Therapy of Depression*. New York: Guilford.

Becker, E. (1973). *The Denial of Death*. New York: Free Press.

Bettelheim, B. (1960). *The Informed Heart: Autonomy in a Mass Age*. New York: Free Press.

Boss, M. (1979). *Existential Foundations of Medicine and Psychology*. S. Conway & A. Cleaves (Trans.). Northvale, NJ: Jason Aronson.

Bowlby, J. (1963). Pathological Mourning and Childhood Mourning. *American Psychoanalytic Association*, 11, 500–541.

Breuer, J., & Freud, S. (1955). Studies on Hysteria. In J. Strachey (Ed. & Trans.), *The Standard Edition of the Complete Psychological Works of Sigmund Freud* (Vol. 2, pp. 1–312). London: Hogarth Press. (Original work published 1893)

Burt, D.X. (1999). Health, Sickness. In A.D. Fitzgerald (Ed.), *Augustine Through the Ages: An Encyclopedia* (pp. 416–419). Grand Rapids, MI: Eerdmans.

Burton, N. (2015). *Heaven and Hell: The Psychology of the Emotions*. Devon, UK: Acheron.

Cain, S. (1995). *Gabriel Marcel's Theory of Religious Experience*. New York: Peter Lang.

Calcagno, A. (2015). Finding a Place for Desire in the Life of the Mind: Arendt and Augustine. In D. Enns and A. Calcagno (Eds.), *Thinking About Love: Essays in Contemporary Continental Philosophy* (pp. 114–127). University Park: Pennsylvania State University Press.

Caruana, J. (2015). The Subject in Crisis: Julia Kristeva on Love, Faith, and Nihilism. In D. Enns and A. Calcagno (Eds.), *Thinking About Love: Essays in Contemporary Continental Philosophy* (pp. 46–60). University Park: Pennsylvania State University Press.

Cooper, M. (2015). *Existential Psychotherapy and Counseling: Contributions to a Pluralistic Practice*. Los Angeles: Sage.

Cooper, M. (2017). *Existential Therapies* (2nd ed.). Los Angeles: Sage.

Davis, C. (1996). *Levinas: An Introduction*. Cambridge, UK: Polity.

Deutsch, H. (1942). Some Forms of Emotional Disturbance and their Relationship to Schizophrenia. *Psychoanalytic Quarterly, 11*, 301–321.

Dostoyevsky, F. (1864). *Notes from the Underground*. Retrieved from www.gutenberg. org/files/600/600-h/600-h.htm

Edgerton, J.E. (Ed.). (1994). *American Psychiatric Glossary* (7th ed.). Washington, DC: American Psychiatric Press.

Fairbairn, W.R.D. (1952). Repression and the Return of Bad Objects (with Special References to the "War Neurosis." In *Object Relations Theory of the Personality*. New York: Basic Books.

Foucault, M. (1988). Technologies of the Self. In L.H. Martin, H. Gutman, & P.H. Hutton (Eds.), *Technologies of the Self* (pp. 16–49). Amherst: University of Massachusetts Press.

Frankl, V. E. (1984). *Man's Search for Meaning* (revised and updated ed.). New York: Washington Square.

Freud, S. (1933). Introductory Lectures on Psychoanalysis. In J. Strachey (Ed. & Trans.), *The Standard Edition of the Complete Psychological Works of Sigmund Freud* (Vol. 16, pp. 243–463). London: Hogarth Press. (Original work published 1916)

Freud, S. (1953). On Psychotherapy. In J. Strachey (Ed. & Trans.), *The Standard Edition of the Complete Psychological Works of Sigmund Freud* (Vol. 7, pp. 257–268). London: Hogarth Press. (Original work published 1905)

Freud, S. (1957). Mourning and Melancholia. In J. Strachey (Ed. & Trans.), *The Standard Edition of the Complete Psychological Works of Sigmund Freud* (Vol. 14, pp. 237–260). London: Hogarth Press. (Original work published 1917)

Freud, S. (1958). Totem and Taboo. In J. Strachey (Ed. & Trans.), *The Standard Edition of the Complete Psychological Works of Sigmund Freud* (Vol. 13, pp. 1–190). London: Hogarth Press. (Original work published 1913)

Freud, S. (1959). Inhibitions, Symptoms and Anxiety. In J. Strachey (Ed. & Trans.), *The Standard Edition of the Complete Psychological Works of Sigmund Freud* (Vol. 20, pp. 87–175). London: Hogarth Press. (Original work published 1926)

Goffman, E. (1959). *The Presentation of Self in Everyday Life*. New York: Doubleday.

Goffman, E. (1961). *Asylums*. New York: Anchor.

Golding, K.S., & Hughes, D.A. (2012). *Creating Loving Attachments: Parenting with PACE to Nurture Confidence and Security in Troubled Children*. London: Jessica Kingsley.

Greenberg, T.M. (2016). *Psychodynamic Perspectives on Aging and Illness* (2nd ed.). Heidelberg: Springer.

Gron, A. (1994). *The Concept of Anxiety in Soren Kierkegaard*. J.B.L. Knox (Trans.). Macon, GA: Macon University Press.

Grotstein, J.S. (1998). W.R.D. Fairbairn and His Growing Significance for Current Psychoanalysis and Psychotherapy. In P. Marcus & A. Rosenberg (Eds.), *Psychoanalytic Versions of the Human Condition: Philosophies of Life and Their Impact on Practice* (pp. 161–182). New York: New York University Press. (Original work published 1988)

Gschwandtner, C.M. (2015). The Phenomenon of Kenotic Love in Continental Philosophy of Religion. In D. Enns and A. Calcagno (Eds.), *Thinking About Love: Essays in Contemporary Continental Philosophy* (pp. 63–80). University Park: Pennsylvania State University Press.

Hahner, K. (1989). Learned Helplessness: A Critique of Research and Theory. *Perspectives on Animal Research*, 1. Retrieved 2/6/17 from www.safermedicines.org/reports/Perspectives/vol_1_1989/Learned%20Helplessness.html.

Hale, N.G. (Ed.). (1971). *James Jackson Putnam and Psychoanalysis: Letters between Putnam and Sigmund Freud, Ernest Jones, William James, Sandor Ferenczi and Morton Prince, 1877–1917*. J.B. Heller (Trans.). Cambridge, UK: Cambridge University Press.

Hand, S. (Ed.). (1996). *Facing the Other: The Ethics of Emanuel Levinas*. Richmond, UK: Curzon.

Hannay, A. (1998). Kierkegaard and the Variety of Despair. In A. Hannay & G.D. Marinao (Eds.), *The Cambridge Companion to Kierkegaard* (pp. 329–348). Cambridge, UK: Cambridge University Press.

Hautzinger, M. (1989). An Integrative Theory of Depression. In J.M. Hooley, J.M. Neale, & G.C. Davison (Eds.), *Readings in Abnormal Psychology* (pp. 264–284). New York: Wiley.

Heidegger, M. (1962). *Being and Time*. J. Macquarie & E. Robinson (Trans.). Oxford, UK: Blackwell.

Heidegger, M. (2001). *Zollikon Seminars: Protocols-Conversations-Letters*. F. Mayr & R. Askay (Trans.). Evanston, IL: Northwestern University Press.

Hesse, H. (1951). *Siddhartha*. H. Rosner (Trans.). New York: New Directions.

Hoare, C.H. (2002). *Erikson on Development in Adulthood: New Insights from the Unpublished Papers*. Oxford: Oxford University Press.

Holzhey-Kunz, A. (2016). Why the Distinction between Ontic and Ontological Trauma Matters for Existential Therapist. *Existential Analysis*, 27(1), 16–27.

Hutchens, B.C. (2004). *Levinas: A Guide for the Perplexed*. London: Continuum.

Jacobs, J. (2001). *Choosing Character: Responsibility for Virtue and Vice*. Ithaca, NY: Cornell University Press.

Johnson, P. (2011). *Socrates: A Man for Our Times*. New York: Viking.

Kabatznick, R., & Marcus, P. (1986). Psychoanalysis and Social Psychology. *Journal of the American Academy of Psychoanalytic Dynamic Psychiatry*, 14(1), 115–123.

Kierkegaard, S. (1938). *Journals*. A. Dru (Ed. & Trans.). London: Oxford University Press. (Original work published 1834–1854)

Kierkegaard, S. (1980). *The Concept of Anxiety: A Simple Psychologically Orienting Deliberation on the Dogmatic Issue of Hereditary Sin*. R. Thomte & A.B. Anderson (Ed. & Trans.). Princeton, NJ: Princeton University Press. (Original work published 1844)

Kierkegaard, S. (1987). *Either/Or*. Part 1. H.V. Hong & E.H. Hong (Trans.). Princeton, NJ: Princeton University Press. (Original work published 1843)

Kilborne, B. (2004).Shame Conflicts and Tragedy in The Scarlet Letter. *Journal of the American Psychoanalytic Association*, 53(2), 465–483.

Klein, M. (1948). *Contributions to PsychoAnalysis, 1921–45*. London: Hogarth Press.

Klein, M. (1984). A Contribution to the Psychogenesis of Manic-Depressive States. In *Love, Guilt, and Reparation and Other Works, 1921–1945* (pp. 262–269). New York: Free Press. (Original work published 1934)

Kluckhohn, C. (1951). Values and Value Orientation in the Theory of Action: An Exploration in Definition and Classification. In T. Parsons & E.A. Shils (Eds.), *Toward a General Theory of Action* (pp. 388–433). Cambridge, MA: Harvard University Press.

Kohut, H., Tolpin, P., & Tolpin, M. (1996). *Heinz Kohut: The Chicago Institute Lectures*. Hillsdale, NJ: Analytic.

Kristeva, J. (1989). *Black Sun: Depression and Melancholia*. L.S. Roudiez (Trans.). New York: Columbia University Press.

Kuhl, J., & Koole, S. (2004). Workings of the Will: A Functional Approach. In J. Greenberg, S.L. Koole, & T. Pyszczynski (Eds.), *Handbook of Experimental Existential Psychology* (pp. 411–430). New York: Guilford.

Kunz, G. (2002). Simplicity, Humility, Patience. In E.E. Gantt & R.N. Williams (Eds.), *Psychology for the Other: Levinas, Ethics, and the Practice of Psychology* (pp. 118–142). Pittsburgh, PA: Duquesne University Press.

Laing, R.D. (1959). *The Divided Self*. Baltimore, MD: Penguin.

Lear, J. (2014). Mourning and Moral Psychology. *Psychoanalytic Psychology*, 31(4), 470–481.

Lechte, J. (1994). *Fifty Key Contemporary Thinkers: From Structuralism to Postmodernity*. New York: Routledge.

Levinas, E. (1969). *Totality and Infinity*. A. Ligis (Trans.). Pittsburgh, PA: Duquesne University Press.

Levinas, E. (1985). *Ethics and Infinity: Conversations with Philippe Nemo*. R.A. Cohen (Trans.). Pittsburgh, PA: Duquesne University Press.

Levinas, E. (1987a). *Collected Philosophical Papers*. A. Lingis (Trans.). Dordrecht-Boston: Nijhoff.

Levinas, E. (1987b). *Time and the Other*. R.A. Cohen (Trans.). Pittsburgh, PA: Duquesne University Press.

Levinas, E. (1989). There is: Existence without Existents. In S. Hand (Ed.), *The Levinas Reader* (pp. 29–36). Oxford: Blackwell.

Levinas, E. (1996). *Proper Names*. M.B. Smith (Trans.). Stanford, CA: Stanford University Press.

Levinas, E. (1998a). *Of God Who Comes To Mind*. B. Bergo (Trans.). Stanford, CA: Stanford University Press.

Levinas, E. (1998b). *Otherwise Than Being: Or Beyond Essence*. A. Lingis (Trans.). Pittsburgh, PA: Duquesne University Press.

Levinas, E. (2000). *Alterity and Transcendence*. M.B. Smith (Trans.). New York: Columbia University Press.

Levinas, E. (2001a). *Existence and Existents*. A. Lingis (Trans.). Pittsburgh, PA: Duquesne University Press.

Levinas, E. (2001b). *Is It Righteous To Be? Interviews with Emmanuel Levinas*. J. Robbins (Ed.). Stanford, CA: Stanford University Press.

Levinas, E. (2003). *On Escape/De l'évasion*. B. Bergo (Trans.). Stanford, CA: Stanford University Press. (Original work published 1935)

Lingis, A. (2015). The Babies in Trees. In D. Ennis & A. Calcagno (Eds.), *Thinking About Love: Essays in Contemporary Continental Philosophy* (pp. 235–245). University Park: Pennsylvania State University Press.

Loewald, H. (1979). The Waning of the Oedipus Complex. *Journal of the American Psychoanalytic Association*, 37, 751–775.

Lyubomirsky, S. (2005). *The How of Happiness: A New Approach to Getting the Life You Want*. New York: Penguin.

Mahler, M.S., Pine, F., & Bergman, A. (1973). *The Psychological Birth of the Human Infant*. New York: Basic Books.

Marcel, G. (1965). *Being and Having: An Existentialist Diary*. K. Farrer (Trans.). New York: Harper & Row.

Marcel, G. (2005). *Music and Philosophy*. S. Maddux & R.E. Wood (Trans.). Milwaukee, WI: Marquette University Press.

Marcus, P. (1999). *Autonomy in the Extreme Situation: Bruno Bettelheim, the Nazi Concentration Camps and the Mass Society*. Westport, CT: Praeger.

Marcus, P. (2003). *Ancient Religious Wisdom, Spirituality, and Psychoanalysis*. Westport, CT: Praeger.

Marcus, P. (2008). *Being for the Other: Emmanuel Levinas, Ethical Living and Psychoanalysis*. Milwaukee, WI: Marquette University Press.

Marcus, P. (2010). *In Search of the Good Life: Emmanuel Levinas, Psychoanalysis, and the Art of Living*. London: Karnac.

Marcus, P. (2013). *How to Laugh Your Way through Life*. London: Karnac.

Marcus, P. (2014). *They Shall Beat Their Swords into Plowshares: Military Strategy, Psychoanalysis and the Art of Living*. Milwaukee, WI: Marquette University Press.

Marcus, P. (2017). *The Psychoanalysis of Career Choice, Job Performance and Satisfaction: How to Flourish in the Workplace*. New York: Routledge.

Marcus, P., with Marcus, G. (2011). *Theater as Life: Practical Wisdom Drawn from Great Acting Teachers, Actors and Actresses*. Milwaukee, WI: Marquette University Press.

May, R. (1958). Contributions of Existential Psychotherapy. In R. May, E. Angel, & H.F. Ellenberger (Eds.), *Existence: A New Dimension in Psychiatry and Psychology* (pp. 37–91). New York: Clarion.

May, R. (1969). *Love and Will*. New York: Norton.

McDonald, W. Søren Kierkegaard (1813–1855). *Internet Encyclopedia of Philosophy*. Retrieved 2/9/17 from www.iep.utm.edu/kierkega/www.iep.utm.edu/kierkega/.

Moore, B.E., & Fine, B.D. (Eds.). (1990). *Psychoanalytic Terms and Concepts*. New Haven, CT: American Psychoanalytic Association and Yale University Press.

Moyn, S. (2006). *Origins of the Other: Emmanuel Levinas between Revelation and Ethics*. Ithaca, NY: Cornell University Press.

Neve, M. (1992). Clare Winnicott talks to Michael Neve. *Free Associations*, 3, 167–184.

Orange, D.M. (2011). *The Suffering Stranger: Hermeneutics for Everyday Clinical Practice*. New York: Routledge.

Pawełczyńska, A. (1979). *Values and Violence in Auschwitz: A Sociological Analysis*. C.S. Leach (Trans.). Berkeley: University of California Press.

Peperzak, A. (1993). *To the Other: An Introduction to the Philosophy of Emmanuel Levinas*. Lafayette, IN: Purdue University Press.

Peperzak, A. (1997). *Beyond: The Philosophy of Levinas*. Evanston, IL: Northwestern University Press.

Phillips, A. (1994). *On Flirtation: Psychoanalytic Essays on the Uncommitted Life.* Cambridge, MA: Harvard University Press.

Plato. (2008). *Gorgias.* B. Jowett (Trans.). Retrieved from www.gutenberg.org/files/ 1672/1672-h/1672-h.htm

Prabhupada, A.C.B.S. (Trans.). (1972). *Bhagavad Gita as it is.* New York: Macmillan.

Pulco, E., Zahn, R., & Elliot, R. (2013). The Role of Self-Blaming Moral Emotions in Major Depression and their Impact on Social-Economical Decision Making. *Frontiers in Psychology,* 4, 310. https://doi.org/10.3389/fpsyg.2013.00310

Rado, S. (1928). The Problems of Melancholia. *International Journal of Psychoanalysis,* 9, 420–438.

Rank, O. (1945). *Will Therapy and Truth and Reality.* New York: Knopf.

Rorty, R. (1989). *Contingency, Irony, and Solidarity.* Cambridge, UK: Cambridge University Press.

Rorty, R. (1990). *Objectivity, Relativism, and Truth.* Cambridge, UK: Cambridge University Press.

Rumi, M.J. (2005). *The Rumi Collection.* K. Helminski (Ed.). Boston: Shambhala.

Rycroft, C. (1995). *A Critical Dictionary of Psychoanalysis.* London: Penguin.

Sacks, J. (2017). Terumah. *Shabbat Announcements,* 3/4/17, pp. 1–2.

Sanderson, C. (2015). *Counselling Skills for Working with Shame.* London: Jessica Kingsley.

Sandler, J. (1960). The Background of Safety. *International Journal of Psychoanalysis,* 41, 352–365.

Sartre, J.-P. (1949). *Nausea,* L. Alexander (Trans.). New York: New Directions.

Schaefer, R. (1978). *Language and Insight.* New Haven, CT: Yale University Press.

Schneider, K.J., & Krug, O.T. (2010). *Existential-Humanistic Therapy.* Washington, DC: American Psychological Association.

Smith, H. (1991). *The World's Religions: Our Great Wisdom Traditions.* New York: Harper San Francisco.

Solomon, D., Greenberg, J., & Pyszczynski, T. (2004). The Cultural Animal: Twenty Years of Terror Management Theory and Research. In J. Greenberg, S.L. Koole, & T. Pyszczynski (Eds.), *Handbook of Experimental Existential Psychology* (pp. 13–34). New York: Guilford.

Sophocles. (2006). *The Oedipus Trilogy.* F. Storr (Trans.). Retrieved from www.gutenberg.org/files/31/31-h/31-h.htm

Spinelli, E. (2015). *Practising Existential Psychotherapy: The Relational World* (2nd ed.). London: Sage.

Symington, N. (1993). *Emotion and Spirit: Questioning the Claims of Psychoanalysis and Religion.* New York: St. Martin's.

Tangney, J.P., & Mahek, D.J. (2004). In Search of the Moral Person: Do You Have To Feel Really Bad to Be Good? In J. Greenberg, S.L. Koole, & T. Pyszczynski (Eds.), *Handbook of Experimental Existential Psychology* (pp. 158–186). New York: Guilford.

Tillich, P. (1950). *The Courage to Be.* New Haven, CT: Yale University Press.

Van Deurzen, E. (2012). *Existential Counseling and Psychotherapy Practice* (3rd ed.). London: Sage.

Wallace, D.F. (1996). *The Infinite Jest.* New York: Little, Brown.

Wiesel, E. (1974). Talking and Writing and Keeping Silent. In F.H. Littell & H.G. Locke (Eds.), *The German Church Struggle and the Holocaust* (pp. 269–277). Bloomington, IN: Wayne State University Press.

Wiley, T. (2002). *Original Sin: Origins, Development, Contemporary Meanings.* New York: Paulist Press.

Winnicott, D.W. (1960). Ego-Distortion in Terms of True and False Self. In *Maturational Processes and the Facilitating Environment* (pp. 53–63). New York: International Universities Press.

Wyschogrod, E. (2000). *Emmanuel Levinas: The Problem of Ethical Metaphysics* (2nd ed.). New York: Fordham University Press.

Yalom, I. (1980). *Existential Psychotherapy.* New York: Basic Books.

Yalom, I. (1989). *Love's Executioner.* New York: Basic Books.

# Chapter 5

# The suffering of old age

"For certainly old age has a great sense of calm and freedom," said Plato, "when the passions relax their hold, then, as Sophocles says, you have escaped from the control not of one master only, but from many" (Plato, 1871, p. 147). Plato must been having a very good day when he said this. Indeed, it is a "blessing," as the religious aspirants say, to experience old age with such a "sweet lightness of being," as French-Czech writer Milan Kundera famously called it (2009, p. 30). However, from my experiences as a psychoanalyst for over thirty years, and now being age 65, the words of American novelist Philip Roth perhaps better capture how many people in our era experience old age – that old age is not a battle but a massacre (2006). Of course, to some extent both Plato and Roth are right; there is a double structure to old age. On the one hand, there is an increased freedom that emanates from the waning demands of sexual instincts and liberation that comes with feeling less concern about social judgment. On the other hand, there is also a sense of the tragic adversity from the worst aspects of aging such as physical/mental diminishment and greater mortality saliency. It is the wise elder who does not waste time regretting what could have been or should have been, or being worried about what will be, but who gets on with the "business of living." The art of living the "good life" requires everyday skillfulness to fend off the "narcissistic melancholy" (Améry, 1994, p. 32) and insidious anxiety associated with aspects of old age, though it is much easier said than done.

Playing off philosopher Ludwig Wittgenstein's famous aphorism from the *Tractatus*, "The world of a happy person is different world from that of the unhappy person" (1999, 6.43), I draw from the brilliant work of Austrian essayist/Auschwitz survivor Jean Améry, who in his study of the Nazi concentration camps compared two groups of inmates – the "believers" (e.g., deeply religious persons and militant Marxists) and the "intellectuals" (e.g., the humanists and the liberals) – in terms of how they fared in maintaining their autonomy, integration and, most importantly, their humanity in the face of the Nazi assault. As Améry noted, those inmates with strong beliefs or ideology had "a firm foothold in the world from which they spiritually unhinged the SS state ... They survived better or died with more dignity than their irreligious or unpolitical intellectual comrades" (1980, p. 13). Death camp survivors Primo Levi, Elie Wiesel and Anna Pawełczyńska, and concentration camp survivor Bruno Bettelheim, agreed with Améry on this point, as did many other survivors (Marcus, 1999, p. 88). In his study of aging, Améry makes an astonishing claim as reported by his translator: "He found the terror of his experiences at Auschwitz to be qualitatively different and, incredible to say, less filled with internal *horror* and *anguish* than the experience of aging" (Barlow, 1994, p. xi). The claim that aging felt worse to Améry than Auschwitz will certainly appear extreme if not outrageously grotesque to many people, though given that he did view old age this way, it is not altogether surprising that at age 66 Améry killed himself (as did Levi, Bettelheim, Paul Celan, Peter Szondi, Tadeusz Borowski and other less well-known survivors).[1]

By comparing elderly "believers" (mainly Axial-inspired religious/spiritual ones) and "intellectuals" (mainly skeptic-humanistic secular ones) as they relate to key challenges of old age I hope to put into sharp focus some of the underappreciated aspects of this phase of life that are pertinent to the psychoanalytically animated geropsychology. As Greenberg (2016, p. 8) pointed out, while Freud believed that analysis of people over age 50 was ill-fated due to their inordinate "accumulation of material" and lack of "elasticity of the mental processes," there have been a few illuminating psychoanalytic studies of this phase and specific problems pertinent to the elderly (Davenhill, 2007; Erikson, 1950; Lax, 2007). However, says Greenberg, "in general ... until recently there has been little psychoanalytic or psychodynamic literature on work with older adults" (2006, p. 8). Following Améry (1994), I will organize this chapter around the following set of existential issues related to growing older:

1   the troubling changes in how one experiences time;
2   self-alienation, especially from one's own body;
3   the sense that one can no longer live according to one's potentialities or possibilities;
4   the loss of the will and ability to adequately comprehend new developments in the arts and the shifting values of society;
5   increased mortality awareness.

Before getting to the heart of this chapter, I want to remind the reader that the so-called elderly "believers" and "intellectuals" are merely conceptual "ideal types" meant to animate aspects of how different people with divergent outlooks can respond to the challenges of old age. In real life, the experience of getting older is hardly so conceptually and practically "neat and tidy"; rather, it requires considerable practical wisdom to effectively navigate, let alone gracefully. As Carl Jung paradoxically noted, "From the middle of life onward, only he remains vitally alive who is ready to die with life" (Hockley, 2001, p. 144). It is this death awareness that upsurges in middle age and intensifies in old age that provides the experiential and conceptual frame for living everyday life with the fullness of one's whole being.

## The experience of time

"A day comes," said Albert Camus, "when a man notices ... [h]e belongs to time, and by the horror that seizes him, he recognizes his worst enemy" (Pillemer, 2011, p. 127). Indeed, while as far as we know, nonhuman animals live their creaturely existence in the immediate present, humans, for worse or for better, have the capacity to apprehend the past and the future, even to sense the eternal as religious "believers" have claimed. As Ernest Becker noted, to comprehend time is crucial for humans, as it generates a context in which goals and goal-related behavior can exist (Vohs & Baumeister, 2004, p. 497). Time, in other words, is a type of "inner sense," a vehicle for a person to perceive himself and his circumstances (Améry, 1994, p. 8). It should be emphasized that this is not the time of the physicist but rather "lived time" or subjective time (ibid., p. 5), which is my concern in this chapter. For the elderly, the experience of time is especially challenging because of psychological and other types of "resource-depletion" (Vohs & Baumeister, 2004, p. 497), clusters of deficits and vulnerabilities that call to mind the constraining but also enabling aspects of time evoked in Shakespeare's line from *Henry IV Part 2* (1.3): "We are time's subjects, and time bids be gone."

An important aspect of the typical elder's relationship to time was evocatively captured by Améry, who wrote, "Time has passed, flowed, rolled on, blown away, and we pass with it – what I am saying? – like smoke in a strong wind" (1994, p. 4). Elders react differently to this passing-time awareness: for some, their existence becomes more poignant or maudlin; for others, it becomes more terrifying and anguished; and still for others, let's call them the "lucky ones," it becomes the basis for an upsurge of embracing life without reserve (e.g., recall Robert Browning's immortal poetic words from *Rabbi ben Ezra*, "Grow old along with me! The best is yet to be, the last of life, for which the first was made"[2]). One of the troubling aspects of this passing-time awareness is that it can lead to a sense of regret, a feeling that often begins with one's first look into the bathroom mirror upon awakening as we confront an aging body. Beyond this mindfulness of this distressing passage of "our lived time" we face every morning (Améry, 1994, p. 4), what do people typically regret when they are older?

### Regrets

The psychoanalytically and psychologically underexplored emotion of regret has been aptly defined by Janet Landman: "a more or less painful cognitive and emotional state of feeling sorry for misfortunes, limitations, losses, transgressions, shortcomings, or mistakes" (1993, p. 36). Unsurprisingly, according to Landman, how a person experiences regret mainly depends on one's outlook and cultural values. While regret is often regarded as a negative emotion, "obsessively recycling, replaying, and rehashing mistakes, losses, and misfortunes," what boils down to "an exercise in lamentation or immobility," it can also have a wide range of constructive, utilitarian and/or ethical functions for the morally serious agent (ibid., pp. 15, 21).

The psychology of regret is a hugely complex subject, in part because nearly everyone has serious, long-lasting things they regret doing – such as failing as a spouse/significant other or parent, an extramarital affair, a dishonest business transaction, an addiction (including "workaholism"), etc. The types of serious life regrets are as numerous as there are people. As Cornell University gerontologist Karl Pillemer (2011) has reported in his Legacy Project research, in general, the above "big ticket" items are not what many elders regret most when asked; rather, when elders reflected on their lives, Pillemer heard variations of "I would have spent less time worrying" and "I regret that I worried so much about everything." Indeed, many elders felt that if given one "do-over" in life, they would want all the time back they spent worrying anxiously about the future (Pillemer, 2016).

While these findings are of great interest, what is less appreciated is the fact that for many elders, their regrets are less about what they did than what they did not do, a feeling of sorrow that calls to mind Robert Frost's ambiguous and ironic masterpiece, "The Road Not Taken" (1916). Pillemer, for example, indicated that other major life regrets reported by elders spoke to the painful awareness of the irreversibility of lived time: missed opportunities, especially not traveling more with one's significant other while still healthy; not having shared deeper feelings with important people while they were still alive; not telling the truth when it really mattered; and not choosing the right life partner (Pillemer, 2011, p. 194). Indeed, sages inspired by the Axial outlook were well aware of Frost's sentiment and Pillemer's findings as played out in ordinary life. For example, in the Talmud, Rabbi Chizkiah declares, "A person will have to answer for everything that his eye beheld and he did not consume" (Jerusalem Talmud, Kiddushin 4:12).[3]

This being said, one must remember that these different types of regret are two sides of the same coin. That is, an action that was regretfully done, say engaging in an extramarital affair, is also an action regretfully not done, like properly loving one's spouse by being faithful. Hence, the guilt and other negative emotions that such flawed partners feel has a dialectically related double structure that is difficult to come to terms with or internally "put right." Loewald aptly described such "putting right" using a term most associated with religion, namely "atonement." "'Atone' literally … means to become or cause to become at one, to reconcile, to bring to concord or harmony" (2000, p. 390). Atonement is frequently linked with acts of internal and external reparation that bring about a sense of "forgiveness" (Rosen, 1993), which completes the "putting right" process.

I am reminded of a poignant clinical example of "the road not taken" concerning a good-hearted, brilliantly capable, though very neurotic man in his mid-fifties who I still treat in psychotherapy.[4] He remained in a terribly abusive marriage with a very "crazy" and destructive woman (who probably had a "borderline" personality) for over twenty-five years. They literally verbally fought every day in a manner that called to mind the sadomasochistic dynamics of Strindberg's *Dance of Death*, the story of a husband and wife who could not live with, or without, each other. However, my patient found an imaginative respite from the horror of his torturous and "sick" marriage, as he called it, by fantasizing about seeking out a woman he loved from his college days, the woman he gave up to marry his wife, who at the time in his twisted way of thinking seemed like the better option. After working with him for a few years, he re-found the beloved girlfriend of his college days, they began an affair, he left his marriage with great difficulty (e.g., guilt, anxiety) and, after nightmarish divorce litigation, they moved in with each other and have for the most part lived happily ever after. When he began to emotionally metabolize and mourn the fact that he had spent twenty-five years, nearly half of his life, in a horrid marriage for all of the wrong reasons, that he could have, and should have, left his wife in the first year of the marriage and re-found the woman he rejected (literally the "woman of his dreams"), this painful awareness of the irreversibility of lived time, combined with him facing the extreme masochism and stupidity animating his decision to remain in the marriage, evoked a relentless self-fury that was palpable. His three children suffered (and continue to) because of him remaining in the wretched marriage and without his protection of them from their destructive mother (and the "war zone" of their marriage). This fact has made his guilt that much worse, and he is prone to unconsciously seek out forms of punishment still now. Exactly how one "reasonably" lives with such searing regrets pertaining to the passage of time and his guilt-inducing role in his personal and familial implosion is what the treatment is now focusing on. Indeed, memories can be burdensome.

Regret has not received much psychoanalytic investigation for a number of reasons (Akhtar, 2009, p. 243). The term regret, like its emotional cousins – guilt, shame and remorse – is unclearly defined, let alone easily distinguishable. Indeed, the most basic concepts in psychoanalysis are still radically contested (Marcus & Rosenberg, 1998). Moreover, like most emotions, regret is usually experienced as part of an assemblage of diverse emotions, making clarifying the unique meaning of the emotion extremely difficult to discern, let alone grasp how it relates to its "swirling around" emotional cousins. Research has shown that emotions are inclined to be experienced in "clusters, especially positive and negative clusters, rather than in isolation," and therefore, it stands to reason that regret, remorse, guilt, disappointment and sadness often are experienced together (Landman, 1993, p. 56).

This being said, what I want to emphasize is that inordinate regret can have an especially negative impact in old age because it is highly narcissistic by definition, and therefore animates one's general outlook and behavior in destructive ways. Regret about missed opportunities, destructive actions or vital words left unspoken can leave one despondently self-focused. Extreme regret can thus be the basis for waves of anhedonia, depression and suicidal wishes (Akhtar, 2009, p. 244). As Erikson noted, the final stage of the life cycle (age 65 and over) – what he called "ego integrity vs. despair" – centered on the elder judging his life to have been either meaningful and satisfying or insignificant and regretful. Most importantly, to become the wise, caring adult associated with ego-integrity, one who cultivates and supports those with, and for whom, one is closely involved and for which one ultimately feels responsible, involves the willingness and ability to live in a "post-narcissistic" manner, as Erikson called it. This means caring so profoundly about others that one's own needs and desires are secondary (Hoare, 2002, p. 186). In this context, nagging life regrets are one of the main impediments to achieving the decentering that is a precondition for achieving ego integrity in an elder, the "blessed" wisdom of functioning and flourishing in old age.

In contrast to regret as a negative experience, regrets, like other moral emotions, can function as "a guardian of our goodness." That is, as Landman explains, regret can generate life-affirming awareness of our flawed character and the fact that what we are, as a person, is defined by what we are not. By engaging in critical reflection about the disconnect between what we are and "ought" to be, and initiating actions geared toward self-correction, the toxic potential of regret can be foreclosed, bypassing its corrosive impact on one's general outlook and behavior (Landman, 1993, p. 28). Such an application of critical intelligence to the regressive, self-directed aspects of this moral emotion can transform it into something progressive, and other-directed, toward a transcendent way of being that points to something "more," "higher" and "better." The Welsh-born poet and Anglican priest George Herbert put this point just right when he wrote, "living well is the best revenge" against regret (ibid., p. 239). In my preferred phrasing, this means that living the "good life," one that is devoted to potentiating Beauty, Truth and especially Goodness in ordinary existence, is the best remedy for all forms of regret.

### Nostalgic reverie

Another aspect of the experience of lived time in elders is an intensification of nostalgic feelings and thoughts. Nostalgia, a word from the Greek *nóstos*, means "longing for return/homecoming" and is most associated with the *Odyssey*, in which Odysseus strives with enormous effort for his and his companions' own *nóstos* (Vandiver, 1999, p. 57). The other Greek root of nostalgia, *álgos*, means ache or pain. Like all emotions, depending on the context of the totality of "real" and imagined circumstances, nostalgia is "a sentimental longing or wistful affection for a period in the past," and can have both enabling and constraining functions, positive or negative psychological effects.[5] Also worth mentioning is that while nostalgia is generally regarded by psychology researchers as a "predominantly positive, self relevant emotion" (Sedikides et al., 2004, p. 202), a robust "resource for the self" (Vess et al., 2012, p. 273), it is often activated by menacing events such as the death of a significant other, a decline in health, a relationship break-up, or unemployment and its resultant income loss and downward modification of lifestyle. Nostalgia can also be a purposeful reaction to troubling emotional states such as sadness, loneliness, anxiety and alienation; and, as Marcel Proust famously described in his depiction of involuntary memory in the madeleine scene in *Time Regained*, it can be stirred up by a chance encounter with an old photograph, letter or song (Sedikides et al., 2004, p. 210).

On the enabling, positive side, nostalgia has a number of adaptive purposes. It can upgrade one's mood even though it may be activated within the context of troubling emotions like loss and distress. Researchers have found that "nostalgia proneness" can have a number of psychological benefits (Batcho, 2011). For example, in general, while nostalgia-prone people are no more happy or sad than the less nostalgia-prone, they are inclined to feel emotions more forcefully, implying that they are more open and receptive to here-and-now experiences. They are also inclined to regard interpersonal relationships as more important in their everyday lives in a variety of ways. In terms of their self-conception, they are more attuned to how others have assisted them in fashioning their identity. When recalling their past, they are more prone to recollect experiences in which other people are central to the happening. For instance, a more nostalgia-prone person will quite likely be more willing and able to recall going fishing with his father, while a less nostalgia-prone person might be more prone to remember going fishing alone. In other words, nostalgia proneness potentiates improved ways of coping, including implementing more effective strategies and tactics to manage everyday problems in living, such as "reframing" them more favorably (Batcho, 2011). Also worth noting, one study found that calling to mind "heartwarming" positive memories had a literal homeostatic function that tended to increase physiological comfort, in particular, the perception of physical warmth (Zhou et al., 2012).

While nostalgia can be prompted by a sense of loneliness, it can ironically facilitate greater social relatedness, or what researchers call social connectedness. For example, nostalgic sentiments usually are linked to recollections that include significant others, and calling to mind these close attachments tends to increase the sense of social relatedness and confidence that one has access to a caring matrix. In nostalgic musings, "the mind is peopled," often with safe and secure attachments (Sedikides et al., 2004, p. 207). Such an increased mindfulness of relational connections gives one a sense of greater personal belongingness that enhances self-esteem and improves self-concept, and can act as a kind of "celebration of life – both past and present" (ibid.).

Nostalgia can increase self-esteem in another way. One study indicated that people capable of nostalgic recall had greater access to favorable self-char-acteristics (e.g., reduced loneliness and increased positive self-affirmation) compared to a control group of those who were anticipating a positive future experience. In a second study, it was found that those people who were not able to engage in nostalgic recall tended to be more narcissistic, an effect that was significantly modulated when these people engaged in nostalgic recall (Vess et al., 2012). This finding suggests that to the extent that one can be other-directed, other-regarding and other-serving, even in fantasy (i.e., ima-ginings of the past), the greater the likelihood that one will feel better about who one is. Researchers have further shown that this upsurge in self-esteem and improved self-concept is further enhanced if such behavior were actua-lized in "real life," such as in work contexts. For example, research in proso-cial motivation (e.g., generosity of spirit) has shown a positive influence on employee work behavior and performance, which enhanced self-esteem and self-concept (Marcus, 2017, p. 68).

Perhaps most importantly for our discussion of old age, nostalgic reflection tends to strengthen one's meaning structures "through the identification with the cultural worldview" (Sedikides et al., 2004, p. 207). That is, nostalgia shores up one's defenses against assaults on one's narrative of self-identity, as well as "jump starting" an individual's desire to "put things right." For example, nostalgic reflection calls to mind the positive significance of cultural traditions and rituals that one has felt meaningfully part of, such as religious holidays, Thanksgiving dinners, parades, school fares or the wide range of collection hobbies of baseball cards, movies and war memorabilia. This nos-talgically animated behavior enhances one's sense of "cultural belongingness" while at the same time providing direction and the sense that one's life is meaningful in the larger social/cultural context. Through this nostalgic reflection, the life-affirming continuity of one's narrative of self-identity is reinforced with the many benefits that such a feeling provides, especially the greater sense of self-mastery and control during the more challenging times in one's life (ibid.).

Finally, researchers have found that nostalgic reflections tend to prompt people to be more willing and able to involve themselves in activities that advance psychological growth, in part because the nostalgic recall improved their mood. Moreover, such nostalgically prone people have an increase in perceived self-efficacy; that is, they regard themselves as the kind of people who are growth-oriented in outlook and behavior, in part because their self-esteem was increased (Baldwin & Landau, 2014). In general, nostalgia has the ability to facilitate security in a world that is perceived as threatening and uncertain, and it can bring about growth and development (ibid.). The indi-vidual's nostalgic recalls can serve either of these two psychological needs, depending on which one is evoked before the nostalgic experience (ibid.). What seems plausible is that nostalgic reminiscence can have a therapeutic effect, including for the elderly. That is, "revisiting a healthy past can offer hope for a better future by reminding a person that what was possible once can be possible again" (Batcho, 2013, p. 365).

For the aging person and elder, admittedly with some skillful psychological retrofitting, such nostalgic efforts can be near redemptive in terms of enhancing one's will and ability to "press on" with a positive outlook into a challenging future. On the constraining, negative side of nostalgia, it can be used defensively as a form of "bad faith" or self-delusion in that it grossly distorts the historical record of one's personal life, such as self-servingly remembering events to preserve a more favorable view of oneself than was actually the case. If such nostalgia becomes chronic it can backfire. Freud's concept of "screen memories" is pertinent here. A "screen memory" is a remembered detail of childhood that signifies important emotional experiences that have become repressed. Though these remembered details feel very real, like in a dream, they are frequently out of sync with the chronology of the memory, and thus their psychological significance lies in the symbolic link to the repressed elements of the historical happening. A "screen memory" can therefore be regarded as a compromise formation between the wish to remember (that is, to know) and the wish to forget (that is, to not know) (Greenson, 1958).

Such an ambivalent and ambiguous self-relation is especially salient in old age as one strives for what Erik Erikson called in his unpublished papers "integrality," the ability to sustain a sense of wholeness in the face of physical and mental deterioration. Indeed, the art of living the "good life" in old age – including finding and creating enduring meaning, sustaining self-coherence and integrating one's complete life narrative – depends on the capacity to integrate a lifetime of memories (Hoare, 2002). This "project" of old age can easily get derailed by engaging in nostalgic reverie as a form of self-deception. The aging southern belle, Blanche DuBois, of Tennessee Williams's *A Streetcar Named Desire* (1947), powerfully depicts this avenue of flight from reality, including its dire psychological and real-life consequences.

Boym (2001) has further elaborated the self-deceiving potential of nostalgic reverie in describing two forms of nostalgia: one is life-affirming and the other life-denying. "Restorative nostalgia" emphasizes *nóstos* (home) and aims for a transhistorical reconstruction of the lost home.[6] Homesickness, an anxiety/depression felt, for example, by children when they have left home to go to camp, is a common example. Psychoanalytically speaking, homesickness, like all forms of nostalgic reverie, is rooted in the fantasized wish to return to the blissful nurturance and stability associated with the mother's real and/or imagined breast (Sterba, 1940), or the oceanic feeling linked to existence prior to birth (Fenichel, 1945). In either case, most psychoanalytically oriented writers regard nostalgia as lodged in incomplete mourning related to infantile trauma to the mother–child dyad. The goal, therefore, is the reclamation of an idealized past (Akhtar, 2009, p. 191), the longing for an ultra-satisfying fanciful place or dreamland. One thinks of some elder's futile craving for youth, especially its appearance, freshness, vigor and spirit that is decades behind them, impossible to be reinstated.

In contrast, reflective nostalgia flourishes in *álgos*, the longing itself, and postpones the homecoming, "wistfully, ironically, desperately" (Boym, 2001). While restorative nostalgia does not view itself as nostalgic, but rather as a matter of truth and tradition, reflective nostalgia resides in the ambivalences and ambiguities of human longing and belonging, and unflinchingly faces the contradictions and paradoxes of experience and modernity itself. Restorative nostalgia "protects the absolute truth" as in national and religious revivals, "while reflective nostalgia calls it into doubt," and hence it tends to be ironic, humorous, compassionate and critical.[7]

For some elders, rather than accepting the reality of the past being past and enjoying the good feeling aroused by the memory, they become anxious about the passage of time, and they try to reenact the special past experience in present life. As they are not willing or able to accept the irreversibility of lived time – that is, the details of their autobiographical past – they cannot derive the joy evoked when one appreciates one's past with some aesthetic sensibility, like when one engages a great painting, book or movie. The distinction between "good" nostalgia (reflective) and "bad" nostalgia (restorative) has little to do with the "real" content of our recollected autobiographical past; rather, it has to do with the expectations about how those recollections can serve us in real life. In this sense, what is most important is not the "real" past, "what actually happened" back then,[8] as much as our perspective toward the past, which to a significant degree boils down to how we choose to view it.

Finally, there is nostalgic reminiscence that reflects both the wish to remember (especially what was good) and the wish to forget (especially what was bad), which is typical of traumatized individuals who seem unwilling and unable to have one with the other. I am reminded of Primo Levi's warning against "the dangers of looking back," the risk of recalling "dangerous waters" for Holocaust survivors and other similarly traumatized individuals (Rosenblum, 2009, p. 1336). Such trauma survivors want to recall their life before imprisonment, as well as some of the life-affirming experiences during their ordeal (the "good" memories); however, they are also inundated with the painful memories of the *lager*, memories that they do not want to remember but also want to revisit and "come to terms with," if that is even possible. Such double-edged looking back can be devastating, says Levi, as it usually evokes an upsurge of depression, even suicidal wishes or acts (ibid.). What Levi is putting into sharp focus for the typical elder is the fact that nostalgia can carry with it threatening "surprises" that can turn one's nostalgic reminiscence into a nightmare of regret, guilt, shame and disorienting fury. Such moments confirm Heidegger's insight that "time traveling" is the nature of conscious experience, and this can be a perilous journey. That is, existence ("Being") is paradoxically and ironically infused by non-Being: it is "the no-longer (Past) and the not-yet (Future)" that have such a strong interpretive grip on our conscious thoughts, concerns and feelings (Barrett, 1958, p. 226). Cohn aptly summarized this important Heideggerian point as, "the past is still present in a present that anticipates the future" (Spinelli, 2015, p. 55). In some instances, the past can shockingly intrude into the elder's well-intentioned nostalgic reminiscence and create internal havoc.

Depending on the tradition that the elder religious/spiritual aspirant is lodged in, he has his own unique way of experiencing time, regrets and nostalgia, which gives him an enviable way of reckoning with the passage of time, on the way to death. While this is a complex subject, I will simply remind the reader what the great Axial Taoist sage/philosopher Chuang Tzu alleged: the more one can view the world as in constant, though rhythmic flux and transformation, the more one will cultivate a potentiating, strengthening and comforting mystical identification with existence and the world as a totality. For example, in Taoist tradition it is believed that in the human body and spirit there exists simultaneously a wintertime, when something is dying and falling away, and a springtime, when something new is coming to life. When the "believer" is willing and able to reside on that threshold, he is in sync with the rhythm of his destiny (O'Donohue, 1998, p. 231). As Wittgenstein noted, there is a profound connection between what is unspeakable and what is mystical: "There are, indeed, things that cannot be put into words. They make themselves manifest. They are what is mystical ... The mystical is the fact that the world is" (Hadot, 2009, p. 80). For Chuang Tzu, as with other Axial thinkers like Ecclesiastes, by identifying with the vital, repetitive and eternal rhythms of Nature (which are divinely inspired), the individual participates in the infinity of the universe. Thus, in terms of the religious/spiritual elder's personal experience of time, regrets and nostalgia, so often lived in the context of *Sturm und Drang* and suffering, he understands that ultimately he, too, is merely a part of the cycle of change. It is this awareness that gives him a degree of life-affirming transcendence (Marcus, 2003).

## Self-alienation from one's body

Freud was age 74 when he famously wrote in *Civilization and its Discontents* that "the sexual life of civilized man is notwithstanding severely impaired; it sometimes gives the impression of being in process of involution [atrophy] as a function, just as our teeth and hair seem to be as organs" (1961a, p. 105). It is hard not to wonder whether when Freud wrote this passage, the fact that he was an old man dealing with his organism's breakdown didn't influence his troubling though correct formulation. Indeed, nearly all elders will tell you that as they age, their body is experienced as a "stranger to oneself" (Améry, 1994, p. 26), no matter how much effort one puts into keeping it healthy and fit. Researchers have noted that high on the list of advice that elders give to live well is "act now like you will need your body for a hundred years." That is, says Pillemer, "Stop using 'I don't care how long I live' as an excuse for bad health habits." Ill-conceived, ill-fated behaviors such as smoking, poor eating habits and lack of exercise "are less likely to kill you than to sentence you to years or decades of chronic disease," which can make everyday life miserable (2011, p. 160). Freud, for example, was a heavy smoker with a twenty-cigar a day habit. In 1923 (at age 67), he was diagnosed with squamous cell carcinoma of the palate, for which he underwent a painful ordeal for 16 years. During this period, he vigorously refused to quit smoking. Freud consulted many specialists during the course of his oral cancer (otolaryngologists, oral and maxillofacial surgeons, prosthodontists and general surgeons), and he underwent thirty-four surgical procedures before his death in 1939 (age 83) through euthanasia (Adeyemo, 2004). In a letter to his colleague and friend Max Eitingon on March 22, 1924, a depressed Freud wrote:

> I am no longer the same man. In reality, I am tired and in need of rest, can scarcely get through my six hours of analytic work, and however cannot think of doing anything else. The right thing to do would be to give up all work and obligations and wait in a quiet corner for the natural end.
>
> (Schur, 1972, p. 377)

While Freud's story is extreme, the fact is that elders typically enter into a very complex and deeply troubling relationship with the body as the aging process takes hold in consciousness.

### Looking into the mirror

The brilliant writer/philosopher Simone de Beauvoir did not seem to follow the practical wisdom of the great Axial philosopher Confucius when she gazed at her aging face in the mirror: "We should feel sorrow," said Confucius, "but not sink under affliction; the heart of a wise man [or wise woman] should resemble a mirror, which reflects every object without being sullied by it" (Hupfeld, 1897, p. 578). Indeed, de Beauvoir, who has written so spectacularly about "the force of circumstances," especially as it pertains to aging, noted with stunned emotion when looking into the mirror:

> I often stop, flabbergasted, at the sight of this incredible thing that serves as a face. I loathe my appearance now: the eyebrows slipping down toward the bags underneath, the excessive fullness of the cheeks, and that air of sadness around the mouth that wrinkles always bring ... I see my face as it was, attacked by the pox of time for which there is no cure.
>
> (de Beauvoir, 1965, p. 656, quoted in Améry, 1994, p. 28)[9]

De Beauvoir's confession surely resonates with most elders who have had a similar experience of looking into the mirror and feeling that the "devil's shadow" is behind the glass. As Améry noted, when an elder looks into the mirror, he is suddenly faced with the shock and "horror that we are both ego and non-ego"; we are our "self" and not our "self," calling into question one's customary sense of oneself as an acceptable, if not lovable, integrated being (1994, p. 29).

What Améry is getting at is that the elder's confrontation with the mirror image evokes a double structured, ambivalent and paradoxical reaction: on the one hand, there is a familiar self-satisfaction connected to having endured (surviving as an embodied being), and the wish to continue to flourish in life (as a psychological being). This sentiment is often contained in the assertion "I know I am old, but I feel young"; on the other hand, there is an alienating sense of exhaustion at the thought of having to carry on living and being oneself. This sentiment is often contained in the assertion "I am tired of living, I am tired of myself." The elder's infatuation with his mirror image, says Améry, "is no longer unequivocal but is precisely a weary love in which the weariness loves itself and the love is deeply weary of it" 1994, p. 30). Indeed, the troubling paradox is the fact that the elder's mirror image signifies extreme familiarity and alienation at the same time – "I am more myself, undeniably an old person with an atrophying body" and "I am less myself, a young self who has lots of robust living to do." As Améry puts it, an elder is "closer to herself, with all her weariness and intimate familiarity, than ever before [her body undeniably reveals her age and dire circumstances, but it is "her" body], and that in front of her mirror image, now a stranger to her [as she feels young and wants to live well, but "her" body won't cooperate], she is condemned to become more and more oppressively herself" (ibid., p. 31). That is, she experiences again and again the stark awareness that she is undeniably an "old woman" forever excluded from certain pleasures and joys associated with youth.

With all of these ambiguous and ambivalent emotions evoked when looking into the mirror, it is no wonder that this entwined self-alienation and heightened sense of self, this disconnection between the "reality" of what one is (old) and the "fantasy" of what one would like to be (young), can easily turn into a depressive moment, or worse. As Améry claims, a "narcissistic melancholy" is the "fundamental experience" of all aging people (1994, p. 32). Without being able to maintain much, or any narcissistic satisfaction associated with one's earlier life as a young person, says a sarcastic Améry, the elder is left trying to revive one's youthful and enlivened sense of self by reaching for the photograph album. Indeed, the photograph album gives an objective perspective to the fact that one was once young, beautiful and full of enthusiasm for living. For a few moments one can feel transported into a glorious, if not self-transcending, past.

In light of Freud's well-known statement, "The ego is first and foremost a bodily ego," stressing the fact that the earliest sense of ego and self is rooted in bodily sensations (1961b, p. 26), it is not surprising that most elders, at least episodically, have a heightened narcissistic relationship with their obviously aging and aged bodies, including along the lines of Améry's dark characterization. Indeed, as French phenomenological philosopher Maurice Merleau-Ponty noted, we are first and foremost "body-subjects," that is, all of human consciousness must be comprehended via our bodies, their way of relating to other bodies, and the world they create and inhabit. Emotions are crucial to this sense of "embodiment," as emotions like the self-loathing that an aging de Beauvoir felt while gazing into the mirror are primary elements of our existence that always work through our bodies (Langdridge, 2015, p. 105). For example, our relation to our body is, in part, a reflection of the unconscious internalization of sociocultural norms about what constitutes the ideal body image and beauty, and this can have dire consequences for the deteriorating elder when gazing into the mirror and beyond. In other contexts, as Sartre noted in his play *Nausea*:

> People who live in society have learnt how to see themselves, in mirrors, as they appear to their friends. I have no friends: is that why my flesh is so naked? You might say – yes you might say, nature without humanity.
>
> (1964, p. 18)

Sartre is emphasizing that our experience of our body and the world, in this case, our relationship to other bodies, are inevitably connected. We view our body the way we fantasize others see us, which can be a psychologically rough moment when the fantasy is accusative. In the case of the typical elder whose friendship circles are shrinking due to bodily illness and death, the deteriorating elder is left gazing into the mirror feeling horridly vulnerable, "naked" and, even worse, as "nature without humanity," as Sartre starkly put it.

And yet, there are some who are able to take some of the "sting" out of looking into the mirror. Some even experience it as an uplifting moment. I am thinking of those who are animated by the Axial ethical spirit and are able to maintain a high degree of autonomy, integration and humanity when they see the harsh reality of their aging visage. For them, looking into the mirror can point toward the transcendent, to something "more," "higher" and "better" because they "see the unseen." One's "flesh" will appear less atrophied, maybe even beautifully sanctified, when we think of all the good that we have brought to others through putting our literal body in the service of the other's best interests, especially before our own. Whether our body is used to give our significant other sexual joy or tend to her illness, or it is used to feed, bathe, comfort and protect our child, assist a fellow colleague or friend with a challenging task, or simply offer a helping hand to a stranger, it is through these concrete bodily actions that our mere "dying" flesh becomes a monument to the "living" because it has been dedicated to Goodness. It is through Goodness that one abstracts oneself from one's inordinately narcissistically cathected bodily subjectivity, from dwelling in the realm of the mere senses and the selfish perspective that it implies, toward something better (Hadot, 2009, p. 88).

When an elder can activate his capacity for metaphorical attunement and re-description and can skillfully implement such imaginative renderings into other-directed, other-regarding and other-serving behavior, he can experience his inordinately narcissistically animated, literal mirror visage with a degree of self-detachment, as a reflection of what Marcus Aurelius called the "daimon," an "inner divinity" (ibid., pp. 86, 67). While the ancient Greek thought the "daimon" was generally a divine power, fate or god, for Aurelius it was equated with "the absolute value of moral intent and the love of moral good" (Hadot, 1998, p. 124). In an instant, the elder's inordinately narcissistically driven despair over his lack of "outer" beauty gives way to the joy of his "inner" beauty. As Ann Cheng pointed out in her history of Chinese thought, the Axial sages emphasized in their discussion of the Tao that it is just such a transformation of self-perception that is correlated with actualizing the "good life": "Every form of spirituality begins by a 'letting go,' a renunciation of the limited and limiting self" (Hadot, 2009, p. 86).

### The alienation of physical aches and pains and chronic illness

Saint Augustine might have slightly overstated the matter when he said, "The greatest evil is physical pain," but he was not far from the mark, as any very sick person will tell you (Leonard, 2015, p. 22). However, for the reasonably healthy elder, it is less the pain associated with feared "big ticket" illnesses like cancer, a heart attack or dementia that uncomfortably impinges on the everyday sense of self; rather, it is the ordinary aches and pains and non-life-threatening illnesses that unnerve and undermine ontological security. In staying with this chapter's theme, it is the jarring "ambiguity of alienation from, and familiarity with, ourselves" (Améry, 1994, p. 38) evoked by these "stalking" physical aches and pains that rupture one's will and ability to positively "lean in" to the future, on which I comment.

Aches, pains and chronic illness make an elder all too aware of his existential condition as a rapidly aging, old and dying organism. He is simultaneously "inside" and "outside" of himself, for his aches and pains feel at once deeply personal (think of arthritic pain), and from the outside, as if they are foreign invaders that have to be defended against. This awareness is *not* how one usually felt when young, when we took for granted feeling like an integrated, whole and wholesome embodied being.[10] As Améry graphically notes about being old, "We cannot keep from seeing" in the mirror, and at other times:

> our hands on which our veins protrude, the stomach that is getting flabby and foldy, the feet whose toenails have become thick and cracked. We cannot run away from our body, even if blind; we cannot get out of our skin, no matter how much we would like to.
>
> (1994, p. 35)

The body that once effectively mediated our relationship between us and the world now becomes the body that alienates us from the world and space. Through the body's undeniably downwardly modified functionality and appearance, it can become our metaphorical "concentration camp" (ibid.). What Améry calls the "essence of aging" is the fact that the elder's significantly diminished bodily subjectivity fosters the sense that the world has become a mean-spirited adversary. Such a bellicose relation highlights all the things the elder cannot do, at least not "like he used to," like walking, climbing and running, as well as all the pleasures that are forever denied him, like rigorous sex: "Miserable leg, wayward heart, rebellious stomach, [flaccid penis, dry vagina]: you hurt me, you're my adversaries" (ibid., p. 40). At its worst, this leads to the narrowing and constricting of one's life-world that is typical of elders, the sense that one cannot prevail against the adversarial world, so the best thing to do is to disengage from it, a kind of "dissociation of the ego" (ibid., p. 39). In its extreme, such a response to the perceived hostile world calls to mind R.D. Laing's description of "petrification," a protective response to the upsurge of ontological insecurity (a lack of trust in one's physical existence and continuity of the world) associated with schizophrenia, such that the elder switches off and disconnects himself from the everyday world, as if a rock, and thus feels safely depersonalized (Langdridge, 2015, p. 48).

On the other hand, the elderly religious/spiritually inspired aspirant views his predicament not as a "concentration camp" from which he cannot escape, but rather as a "last shelter" (ibid., p. 35), one that involves a life-affirming, if not transcendent, self-detachment. That is, by undoing himself from his narcissistically animated bodily subjectivity, from the partiality of his personal and impassioned self, he can reside in what the ancient Greeks called "the universality of the rational self," roughly meaning "a cosmic and oceanic sentiment," what Hadot evocatively called "the look from above" (2009, p. 137). As Plato viewed it in the *Phaedo*, one has the will and ability to "detach the soul from the body," to unhitch oneself from the earthly passions and sensible knowledge and enter into the higher and purer intellectual and immaterial realm (ibid., p. 105). The loss of the infantile body ego becomes the mature ego's gain. In psychoanalytic language, as Hans Loewald explains, the "mature individual" is "able to reach back into his deep origins and roots of being [his "soul"], find[ing] in himself the oneness from where he stems [the ultimate "ground" of his being], and understand[ing] this in his freedom as his bond of love with God," with the non-corporeal "whole," cosmic consciousness, ethicality. Loewald's "god talk" is his way of describing the cosmic vision and oceanic sentiment and its associated ethical outlook and the analytic goal of helping analysands to become "spiritual beings" as he called them, to achieve the "highest form of awareness ... the freedom for faith and love" (1953, pp. 13, 14, 15).[11]

The "dissociation of the ego" is especially manifest when a typical elder has to contend with chronic illness: "If only this damned cadaver would leave one in peace." When one has to surmount a chronic illness one distressingly relates to one's body as an unavoidable and extreme "materialization and substantiation," that is, he is "thrown" into a mode of self-relating that experiences the body as "*more* mass and *less* energy" (Améry, 1994, p. 39).[12] This "heaviness of being" can feel as if one were strapped to a dying beast. This is in contrast to one's former mode of self-relating, the "lightness of being" associated with youth and health. The elder is again caught in the paradox of becoming a stranger to himself through his chronic illness while also becoming more himself as an embodied being. As Améry aptly puts it, "I [the elder] am myself *through* my body and *against* it" (as it is an adversary), while in earlier life, "I was myself when I was young *without* my body and *with* it" (ibid., p. 40). In other words, the elder's body is simultaneously experienced in terms of its gradual reduction of energy and self-efficacy and its gradual enlargement as a mere material entity and site of inadequacy, horridly signifying that he is an organism getting ready to rest.

Indeed, it is a huge challenge not to be subverted as a person, to lose much of one's sense of autonomy, integration and humanity, when one has to contend with chronic illness. And yet, there are some people who are able to transcend their condition to the extent that it does not taint their life-affirming outlook and behavior. Playing off the metaphor of "heaviness of being" associated with being demoralized by chronic illness, the great Austrian-German poet Rainer Maria Rilke suggested one of the paradoxical valuative attachments, often best practiced by the elderly religious/spiritual aspirant, that is correlated with better managing chronic illness. Such a valuative attachment has been described as "a falling upward and onward into a broader and deeper world" (Rohr, 2011, p. 153), beyond one's chronic illness, toward self-transcendence. Rilke wrote:

> How surely gravity's law, strong as an ocean current, takes hold of even the smallest thing and pulls it toward the heart of the world…This is what the things [chronic illness] can teach us: to fall, patiently to trust our heaviness.
>
> (Rohr, 2011, p. 153)

This calls to mind the aspirational words of Loewald mentioned earlier. As all great Axial religiously inspired sages have affirmed, at its best, the way down can be the way up, the experience of the suffering body can be the place of spiritual vision and psychological uplift.[13]

### The waning of sexuality

Améry called the waning of the elder's capacity for sexuality on the rigorously sexual level as the "calamity of conjugal pleasure," such that the bedroom becomes "a grim place of mockery" (1994, p. 41). Indeed, Améry's dismal characterization of the elder's sexual life mirrors how Freud described it, as "being in [the] process of involution [atrophy] as a function" (1961a, p. 105). Moreover, this characterization has become common knowledge among ordinary people, ever the butt of jokes. Yet for many elders, the waning of sexuality is no laughing matter, for once again the feeling of alienation from one's own self, the ambiguous and ambivalent blend of self-weariness and self-seeking through physical demise, in this case of the sexual function, is put into painful focus (Améry, 1994, p. 38). The "revolt of the flesh," said Camus, "is absurd" (1955, p. 14).

While Améry is describing a grim aspect of the facticity of elderly existence, a "given" that cannot be significantly modified, he is leaving out the fact that for many elders there is an "avenue of flight" from this biological inevitability, a way of transcending the worst aspects of this sexual down spiraling that points to something "more," "higher" and "better." In a word, I am talking about the transformative role of the imagination – "the faculty or action of forming new ideas, or images or concepts of external objects not present to the senses."[14] Without a cultivated imagination, the elder is unable have the sensibility to adequately appreciate what is beautiful and pleasing in the world, which includes one's sexual partner. Such a "disordered imagination" of being unable to properly visualize and generate imagery, including mentally stimulating purposeful action in a context-sensitive manner, such as occurs in autism and schizophrenia, is disastrous in the bedroom. What is needed is an "aesthetic attitude," a specific way of experiencing or focusing on people and objects, one that is characterized by a heightened receptiveness, a sharpened reactivity to what is going on inside and outside oneself (Marcus, with Marcus, 2011, p. 213).[15]

While the subject of the imagination is a philosophically and psychologically complex one, I want to briefly discuss it by mainly drawing from the insights of the great theatrical acting teachers, actors and actresses who universally regard the use of the imagination as the "royal road" to delivering a masterful stage performance. Indeed, as far-fetched as it sounds, there is a helpful, if not compelling, analogy between the imaginative techniques that a skilled actor uses to put forth a great performance on the stage and the elder's "great performance" in the bedroom (Marcus, with Marcus, 2011). The immortal Russian theatre practitioner and character actor Constantin Stanislavski has noted the seminal role of the imagination in great acting, which has been repeated and elaborated by all of his followers, like Lee Strasberg, Stella Adler, Sanford Meisner and Viola Spolin (the "high priestess" of improvisation), to name a few (ibid.). But what do these great acting teachers mean by the imagination, and how does it decisively contribute to a beautifully believable stage performance that moves the audience (and the performer) to the heights of aesthetic pleasure, similar to what the elder lover wants to experience in the bedroom? As Donald Winnicott argued, the goal of psychoanalysis is to transform "the patient from a state of not being able to play into a state of being able to play ... It is in playing and only in playing that the individual child or adult is able to be creative and to use the whole personality, and it is only in being creative that the individual discovers the self" (1971, p. 10). Moreover, "it is the creative apperception more than anything else that makes the individual feel that life is worth living" (ibid., p. 65). Indeed, there is an important moral truth embedded in Winnicott's psychological observations, that "man defines himself by his make-believe as well as by his sincere impulses" (Camus, 1955, p. 11). It is precisely by tapping the elder's capacity to creatively/imaginatively "play," similar to how a great stage actor "plays" to his fellow thespians and audience, that the conditions of possibility for an erotically charged, emotionally satisfying experience between elder partners in the bedroom are created.

### The enlivened and enlivening imagination

While detailing the role of the imagination in acting theory and technique, let alone how it can animate sexual behavior, is beyond the scope of this chapter, I do want to lay the groundwork for its potential. It was Stella Adler, acting teacher of Marlon Brando, Anthony Quinn and Robert De Niro, to name a few, who best discussed the role of the imagination in acting technique. The "imagination consists of your ability to imagine things you have never thought"; on the stage, "every circumstance you find yourself in will be an imaginary one."[16] Moreover, says Adler, "an enormous wealth of material exists in the mind of the actor, never to be tapped except in plays" (1988, p. 17). This self-awareness and self-knowledge can be used in one's real life, including in the elder's bedroom. Joanna Rotté, one of Adler's students and colleagues, wrote that for Adler, accessing the imagination involves drawing from the unconscious, a domain that Adler described as "the life within." The imagination, said Adler, includes "everything that you know consciously, and at least ten billion times more that you know unconsciously" (Rotté, 2000, p. 59). In other words, the actor must be able to use his conscious awareness to evoke unconscious processes that constitute and superbly feed his imagination that, ideally, also strongly animates his performance both on the stage and in the bedroom.

For Adler, the main function of the imagination is that it "can alert the actor toward immediate reaction. He can see fast, think fast and imagine fast" (1988, p. 18). Adler describes what it means to be "seeing imaginatively"; for example, in one exercise she asks her students to imagine a scene in which "snow has fallen" or they are "looking into a pot." Most importantly, "imagination refers to the actor's ability to accept new situations of life and believe in them." (ibid, p. 20).

Adler also notes that the actor must develop his capacity for "seeing and describing." The gist of this skill is to "take in a specific image carefully," say "an apple tree" or "a wooden fence" (or one's partner's body). The actor must be able to visualize the images vividly, intensely and exactingly prior to him being able to describe what he has seen. It is only after the actor does this that he can convince the audience (and his sexual partner) that he has seen what he has seen. According to Adler, the finely tuned capacity of taking "an image in and giving it back" is "what makes you an artist" both on stage and in the bedroom (ibid., pp. 20, 21). Put differently, one has to "feel things vividly and deeply," said French Catholic philosopher Jacques Maritain (Hadot, 2009, p. 18).

Adler further notes that there are many ways that an actor sees. For example, an actor must be able to see specifically and rapidly. He must also be able to mindfully see what grabs his attention, as well as see "everyday activities in life and place them in circumstances." Finally, the actor must be able "to see the simple, eternal scenes of human behavior in its historical setting" (Rotté, 2000, p. 24). What Adler is getting at is the need for the actor to greatly sharpen his observational skills, skills that have important bearing for the non-actor, including the elder lover: "you must be continually aware of the ongoing changes in your social world." In particular, continues Adler, "go to things that are forever, like a particular tree or a particular flower" (ibid.). The idea here is that to the extent that you can view things as vividly unique (and take nothing for granted that you observe), then the apt feeling is likely to be evoked that can be conveyed in a believable and truthful manner: "the feeling evoked by the description is more important than the description itself" (ibid., p. 25). Adler is being extremely literal when she insists that the actor perfect his observational skills.

Adler indicates that there are many resistances in the actor (and the non-actor) to imaginatively and vividly engage the world via one's observational modality, especially if the situation being imagined requires a strong response (or, analogous to the bedroom, engaging in acts that are out of one's comfort zone but one's partner likes). Holding back, that is, defending oneself against the experience of what one is imagining, leads to an inhibited and muted performance, and in real life to a blunted self-presentation. The actor must be able to be mindful of what he is experiencing in the moment, with the fullness of his whole being, that is, in a free, flowing and unrestrained manner. Anxiety about revealing oneself, of being vulnerable, of looking stupid or unskilled, for example, is quite common. Adler's straight-talking advice is: "I say to you, do not push, but be able to let go." Most importantly, to live imaginatively, the actor must make choices that will make the actor strongly react (including in the bedroom, erotically tinged fantasies). These choices are crucial to a great performance: "in your choice is your talent." Living imaginatively, according to Adler, thus requires seeing and acting in imaginative circumstances, emotionally and intellectually embracing everything one imagines as believable and truthful.

Adler's discussion of the imagination has tremendous bearing on how one creatively lives one's everyday life, which, I have claimed, includes in the elder's bedroom. As Adler has suggested and Axial-inspired Irish poet, philosopher and Catholic scholar John O'Donohue has elaborated (2004, pp. 144–149), the imagination brings "wonderful gifts" to those who mindfully nurture and use it, including accessing the beauty, truth and goodness in the world and in one's sexual partner.[17] O'Donohue said that the imagination is "like a lantern" that illuminates new "inner landscapes" and "regions of the mind" that help create an openness to the transcendent which allows one to glimpse what is *not* said in words but is critically important and meaningful in an experience. For the person with a rich imagination, the mind is not dulled and the heart is not blunted; in psychoanalytic language, such a person is not trapped in the endless thicket of neurosis, rigidly relating only to surface reality. Rather, he "engages the world visually in an imaginative way," and thus he notices that new things around him have a vibrant "life," a deeper "reality" to them. Adler insinuated this enhanced consciousness when she wrote about using props on the stage, saying "you cannot use a prop unless you give it dignity and unless you have a liking for it" (1988, p. 59). The application of these "techniques" of the imagination in the elder's bedroom is obvious.

A robust imagination, as Adler describes it, also requires what O'Donohue calls "grace of innocence." This refers to the notion that the imagination does not easily give way to the blast of facts, detached analysis and explanations that constitute the received wisdom about a particular thing or experience (such as the claim that elders lack summoning, let alone "high octane" sexual desires). It is not persuaded by that which is considered settled, finished, fixed or framed by authoritative knowledge and authoritative figures. As Adler said to her students:

> Write this down. "My aim is to be independent from Miss Adler or anybody else [or expert-driven 'normalizing' assumptions about elders]. I know this as well as you do, and in the sense that I know it as well as you do, I don't need you."
>
> (1988, p. 13)

In other words, the imagination believes that there is "more" than what meets the eye; there are "secret worlds" and "hidden treasures" – similar to what Levinas calls "otherness" – concealed in the simplest and clearest things, if only, as the Buddhists say, one mindfully engages the world, develops the practical mental skill of attentiveness and emotional openness to one's moment-to-moment awareness of what one is experiencing. For the robust imaginer, reality is not closed, but continuously offers new possibilities and hope, especially for self-transformation and self-transcendence. According to O'Donohue, "the imagination is the faculty that bridges, co-presents, and co-articulates the visible and invisible"; it "creates and constructs your depth experience" (1997, pp. 51, 95). Put differently, the imagination is the organ of fresh perception for discerning manifestations of the "more" and the "beyond" that we associate with the transcendent (or with God), both on and off the theatrical stage.

For O'Donohue, a related aspect of the imagination is that it has a "passion for freedom." The nature of the imagination is to press ahead beyond the usual frontiers. It wants to roam freely beyond the well-traveled borders without using the usual maps of experience and understanding to make sense of things. In his essay "Fate," Ralph Waldo Emerson says that "the revelation of thought [i.e., the imagination] takes man out of servitude into freedom. We rightly say of ourselves, we were born and afterward we were born again, and many times" (Geldard, 2001, p. 114). The imagination paradoxically waits to be surprised, for it knows that there is something about the unforeseen and unanticipated that powerfully touches us, just as it provides insights into what really matters. Thus, the robust imaginers, both non-actor and actor, have much in common. Both want to engage the world with a "dishabituated eye," "defamiliarizing the familiar," in order to better apprehend the wonders of ordinary life (Abrams, 1971, pp. 384–379). It is, in part, this inner readiness to be intrigued, surprised and "disrupted" by the otherness and strangeness of people and things (e.g., fellow actors, the circumstances, the props, the script) that is a distinguishing feature of the robust imaginer, including the elder making love with his partner.

The robust use of the imagination also provides us with a renewed sense of youthfulness, especially playfulness of spirit. One is enlivened through one's playful, imaginative use of mind and heart and, by doing so, one reclaims the depth and intensity of experience, as well as the "urgency, restlessness and passion," "the wildness of heart," most frequently associated with youth. Winnicott famously located this imaginative capacity in a magical realm he called "transitional space," the psychic place where a young child uses a "transitional object," like a loved doll or piece of cloth, as a way of being midway between himself and his mother in the service of separating from her and further individuating, yet still being connected to her: "it is within the space between inner and outer world, which is also the space between people – the transitional space – that intimate relationships and creativity occur" (Winnicott, 1971, p. 82).

Art (and religion and philosophy) represents an adult form of this imaginative dwelling in this transitional space, and this includes "acting" on the stage or in the bedroom. Such a creative use of the imagination allows one to relate to others and the world as sources of deepening personal growth and development, enlivening (including erotically) and interconnectedness to people, things and animals. Adler implicitly acknowledged this point when she taught her students "animal movement." The purpose was to eliminate the social mask of the actor and to free him of his anxieties and inhibitions. For the elder in the bedroom this "unmasking" is crucial to potentiate erotic upurging.

Finally, the robust imaginer, similar to the God-seeker, is open to "revelation." By revelation I do not only mean the showing of divine will or truth, as the religious usually characterize it. I also mean the disclosure, especially of a surprising nature, of something previously hidden or secret, often in one's everyday life, which is judged as extremely valuable and good. As theologian Paul Tillich noted, life-altering existential questions, especially in the theological context, are asked on the basis of "ultimate concern," and they are best answered through revelation. The imagination is the psychic vehicle for receiving such revelations (e.g., the so-called "x factor" in performance that distinguishes the great actor, or the "chemistry" in the bedroom), and it usually does not do so in a flash, says O'Donohue, as popular culture would have it. Rather, he says, the imagination gently coaxes us into new situations, questions and possibilities that are analogous to how one looks at a beautiful painting rather than a dramatic unfolding, though that too can be part of revelation. As we look at the painting (or our naked partner), as we gradually engage its otherness, its loveliness and splendor emerge.[18] The same gradual process often characterizes the love relation, whether to a person or to God. As we gradually engage the other, her summoning nature, her mysterious layering and deep presence moves us, just as her beauty of spirit, mind and body captivates us. The imagination, as Adler and O'Donohue suggest, thus often operates according to a principle of suggestiveness and insinuation, even seduction. As Rotté wrote, Adler's "spiritual standard was to extend oneself outward to the maximum degree ... she was advising us to open ourselves up to the experience of love" (2000, p. 37).

There is more to say about the role of the imagination in acting theory and technique, including how it can be skillfully exploited by those attempting to fashion the "good life," such as in counteracting the elder's sexual waning (Marcus, with Marcus, 2011). In his *Varieties of Religious Experience*, the 66-year-old William James, who died two years later, probably had this vital issue in mind when he asked the following question: "How can the moribund old man reason back to himself the romance, the mystery, the imminence of great things with which our old earth tingled for him in the days when he was young and well?" (1908, p. 151). The short answer to James would be something like this: "Bill, while it is true that the elderly lover does not have the powerful, unprompted sexual drive associated with youth at his disposal, he still can learn to do great 'improv' in the bedroom that is terrific erotically tinged fun, and more." Camus has paraphrased Nietzsche, saying, "What matters, is not eternal life but eternal vivacity" (Camus, 1955, p. 82). Through the skillful application of his imagination, there can be an upsurge of greater sensory, physical and emotional expressiveness in the bedroom that can point to experiential transcendence. This is not simply "storytelling" to oneself and one's partner, but rather "storymaking." Like in improv, this entails the ability to creatively produce and co-produce new realities. These are mainly the result of spontaneous processes that in the imaginatively choreographed bedroom setting can become not only highly erotically charged, but can also offer a glimpse into something "more," "higher" and "better," namely, the ineffable, mystical and "sacred." As Viola Spolin put it, "a story is an epitaph: the ashes of the fire" (Marcus, with Marcus, 2011, p. 94).

## The verdict of others

Confucius has noted that old age is not pleasant, as the elderly are edged out of view and into the role of spectator (Ozdemir, 2013, n.p.). Most elders to varying degrees seriously struggle with the sense of "invisibility and insignificance" connected to one's social age. No longer young and vibrant, elders are left feeling "their quarantine" (Améry, 1994, pp. 54, 53). Frequently, elders don't simply benignly accept being "gently shouldered off the stage," as Confucius put it; but rather they feel the severe judgment of others, that they are "creatures without potential," without a sense "of what we could be," without a meaningful and productive future (ibid., p. 55). Often they spend inordinate amounts of time running from one doctor to another for one real or imagined condition or another, filling up their vacuous lives that become geared toward "survival at any price." If philosopher William Barrett is correct – "What you find in the mirror you will find in the reality it mirrors"(1979, p. 43) – then the elder discovers the difficult truth that what he is in reality correlates with what he believes others judge him as; and, in our society that idealizes youth and youthfulness, that means that the reality-conscious elder is judged as "played out," the rest of his irrelevant life destined to be lived out in "numbness and petrification" (Améry, 1994, p. 56).

One of the important reasons for this grim sense of being judged as "played out" is that the elder feels that in our highly technological world that values "having" much more than "being," he has no worthwhile "possessions" to give, certainly compared to the young and vibrant, the risk-taking innovators that society idealizes. As Erich Fromm (1976, pp. 100–111) described it, in the "having" mode of living, the primary focus is on possessing, and thus on competitive consumption of life's many resources. Such people are mainly "pleasure-seeking": driven by the powerful desire for peak experiences and gratification by tension-relief, while the "being" mode of living focuses on participation in life, on depth experience, and on being at one with life and attuned to others. These people are mainly "joy-seeking": becoming more fully what one is, aliveness, becoming, participating and experiencing (Monte, 1980, pp. 503–506). Indeed, in contemporary technological society, adults fashion their narrative of self-identity and their existential orientation in the realm of "possessions" in which the market value they represent tends to be lodged. This is a "world of being that is only given through having" (Améry, 1994, p. 60), and the elder is judged by both others and himself as having nothing of great value to offer. He feels it is best if he simply stays out of the way or recedes into oblivion. Quoting from the famous military barrack ballad in his farewell speech, General Douglas MacArthur put this point just right: "Old soldiers never die; they just fade away."[19]

The experience of being ignored and excluded, including when it is not deliberately punitive ostracism, can be a deeply distressing experience for the elder (Case & Williams, 2004). To have to endure "oblivious ostracism," to feel unworthy of attention, is a radical assault on one's social existence that cuts deeply into a person's sense of belonging, self-esteem, control and meaningful existence. Being subjected to pronounced, longstanding social ostracism can be evocatively conceptualized as a "mortality metaphor" because it involves "experiencing what life would be like if one was dead" (ibid., p. 338).[20]

For most people, being closed off from one's social network over an extended time, such as after a spouse or significant other dies, or being struck down with a "life-changing," incapacitating illness, can feel like one does not exist as a social being, a form of social death. However, there are some elders who do not respond to ostracism with the alienation, despair, depression and sense of worthlessness that is so typical of elders who have to contend with long-term ostracism (ibid., p. 341). Researchers have found that, in general, targets of everyday, short-term ostracism (such as in the workplace) engage in efforts to restore their threatened needs of belonging, self-esteem, control and meaningful existence, either by reconstituting connections with those who have ostracized them (colleagues or bosses), affiliating with others within the organization or even changing jobs. Prosocial responses to ostracism can include increasing conformity and efforts in cooperative tasks that are aimed at improving belonging and self-esteem, or even targeted aggression that is meant to reassert a sense of control (ibid., p. 343).

However, for the typical elder, his sense of social ostracism exists because of an ontological fact that he cannot change or remedy – namely, that he is biologically old and he is in the "final act" of his life. Like the Jew in Nazi Europe who was "unworthy of life" because of his very despicable existence, so the elder is unworthy of social life because he is despicably old. That is, there is no escaping this accusatory fact pattern: Biologically, the elder is a rapidly atrophying body, an organism getting ready to permanently rest. Socially, he has no future and is invisible and insignificant. Such awareness of the unbridgeable separation between the elder and everyone else evokes his primal existential fears of isolation and vulnerability. The much-praised (but less-practiced) Confucian virtue of "filial piety" – the adult offspring's central obligation of respect, obedience and care for one's parents, elderly family members and ancestors – only slightly helps take the sting out of the elder's ordeal.

What can the typical elder do to improve his radically diminished sense of belonging, self-esteem, control and meaningful existence in light of the fact that he has little or no social value in the eyes of most people (even perhaps his own), especially when he is feeling socially ostracized, excluded and rejected? How does one permanently break out of the social prison that one has been "thrown" into simply for being old? To age with dignity requires revolt without lamentation. As Camus has discussed, not to rebel is to assume guilt of having failed oneself and those one cares about (Santoni, 2003, p. 104).[21] Améry, however, has a troubled and troubling view of "revolt" as it applies to aging with dignity. He claims that those who attempt to live the truth of their condition as aging persons accept their social annihilation,

> knowing that in this acceptance they can only preserve themselves if they rise up in revolt against it, but that their revolt – and here the acceptance is an affirmation of something irrevocable – is condemned to failure. They say no to annihilation and at the same time yes to it, for only in this futile denial can one present oneself at all *as oneself* to the inevitable.
>
> (Améry, 1994, p. 76)

What Améry is getting at is this: the ostracized elder must be what society dictates, namely, socially dead:

> what they are, a nothing, and yet in the recognition of being nothing still something. They make their negation in the look of the others into something of their own and rise up against it. They embark on an enterprise that cannot be accomplished. That is their chance and is, perhaps the only possibility they have of truly aging with dignity.
>
> (ibid., p. 77)

Améry's "final solution" to the "aging with dignity problem" may strike some elders as reflecting his ambiguous, contradictory and cynically dark assumptions, both about what constitutes the typical aging person's experience in contemporary society and what is possible in terms of flourishing. Calling to mind Camus's *Myth of Sisyphus*, for Améry it is the intense awareness of the futility of old age, its absurdity, that constitutes personal triumph. "The struggle itself toward the heights [to create meaning in old age, despite one's limitations] is enough to fill a man's heart. One must imagine Sisyphus [the elder] happy," even though his efforts are doomed to failure (Camus, 1955, p. 123; Cooper, 2017, p. 33). What matters is residing in one's consciousness of one's destiny with strength and self-respect, such that the elder can go up the mountain in joy and sorrow. Such an outlook inevitably leads Améry to conclude that the only possibility of aging with dignity is to embrace the societally bestowed "peace of nothingness, by letting [the elder] be what they are and were." That is, society "no longer expects much from them, only that they replay what's departed from this life and been declared dead – a profound relief" (1994, p. 76). In short, for the paradoxical Améry, it is accepting and learning to live with one's social extinction that is the only viable life-affirming option for dignified aging. However, is such a "victory through defeat" really the only dignified option for the elder?

Elders animated by the Axial sensibility think otherwise. Listen to the very different emotional tone of the great Roman Stoic philosopher Seneca as he reflects on old age:

> Let us cherish and love old age; for it is full of pleasure if one knows how to use it. Fruits are most welcome when almost over; youth is most charming at its close; the last drink delights the toper, the glass which souses him and puts the finishing touch on his drunkenness. Each pleasure reserves to the end the greatest delights which it contains. Life is most delightful when it is on the downward slope, but has not yet reached the abrupt decline.
>
> (1917, Letter 12)

Despite Seneca's encouraging words about old age, there are surely aspects of Améry's forbidding formulations that resonate with the typical elder. In the spirit of resignation without despair, the elder must embrace his human frailty, his limitations and the fact that he imagines himself transcending what is not actually possible. However, Améry's dark characterization of the condition of aging is only one side of the dialectical tension that the typical elder resides in. That is, there are other less daunting "usable truths" that provide the Axial-inspired elder with the ability to fashion the "good life," to flourish in the twilight years. Indeed, the problem with Améry's formulations is that like most "sceptic-humanistic intellectuals," as he describes himself (1980, pp. 13–14), he is too tied to "reality" as he construes it. This is ironic because in his concentration camp memoir he distinguished the particular way the "believer" constructed reality from the secular intellectual, and in the context of the camps – and I will argue in old age – it was the "believer" who was better able to maintain his autonomy, integrity and humanity amidst the Nazi assault. The "believer" was "unshakeable, calm strong" because "whoever is, in the broadest sense, a believing person, whether his belief be metaphysical [e.g., Jehovah Witnesses, practicing Catholics, Orthodox Jews] or bound to concrete reality [e.g., militant Marxists], transcends himself. He is not the captive of his individuality; rather he is part of a spiritual continuity that is interrupted nowhere, not even in Auschwitz" (Améry, 1980, p. 14). Améry further elaborates the "believer's" way of experiencing reality, which resonates with the ordeal of old age:

> He is both estranged from reality and closer to it than the unbelieving comrade. Further from reality because in his Finalistic attitude he ignores the given contents of material phenomenon and fixes his sight on a nearer or more distant future; but he is also closer to reality because for just this reason he does not allow himself to be overwhelmed by the conditions around him and thus can strongly influence them. For the unbelieving person, reality, under adverse circumstances, is a force to which he

submits; under favorable ones it is material for analysis. For the believer,
reality is clay that molds, a problem that he solves.

(Améry, 1980, p. 14)

As Geertz (1973) points out, in contrast to the religious "believer," the secular
intellectual "questions the realities of everyday life out of an institutionalized
skepticism which dissolves the world's givenness into a swirl of probabilistic
hypotheses" (p. 112). However, the religious aspirant questions everyday reality in terms of a "wider, non-hypothetical" truth, as he construes it (ibid.).
"Detachment" and "analysis," the watchwords of the secular intellectual, are
replaced by "commitment" and "encounter," if you will, subjectivity. It is
"the imbuing of a certain specific complex of symbols – of the metaphysic
they formulate and the style of life they recommend – with a persuasive
authority which, from an analytic point of view, is the essence of religious
action" (ibid.). In the camps, this meant that religious inmates had the symbolic capacity to transform their reality, at least to some extent, into something other than dehumanizing reality. Through their faith, including the
rituals that they participated in, frequently in a communal context, they had
the ability to move beyond the realities of everyday life to more transcendent
realities that, says Geertz, corrected and completed the painful realities of the
camp (and of old age).

In contrast, secular intellectuals were lodged in a more common-sense
mode of experiencing the world. This involves "a simple acceptance of the
world, its objects, and its processes as being just what they seem to be" (ibid.),
even after they are coated with an intellectualized gloss, including a psychoanalytic one. Such a view, with its "pragmatic motive" – i.e., "the wish to act
upon the world so as to bend it to one's practical purposes, to master it, or
when that proves impossible, to adjust to it" – does not allow secular intellectuals to fuse together "the world as lived and the world as imagined" into
one world under "a single set of symbolic forms" (ibid., p. 111). The religious/
spiritual person does so by means of religious ritual, thus transforming their
consciousness into another mode of existence. Devout Jews, for example,
viewed Nazi brutality against the background of The Fall and other Jewish
calamities which, though it does not adequately explain the brutality, at least
places it in a moral, cognitive and affective context. The devout Jew's beliefs
tended to render their experience intelligible and within cognitive understanding. In short, whether a religious inmate in the camps or a "prisoner" in
old age as Améry described it (1994, p. 71), by anchoring their identity in a
cosmic reality, religious inmates were to some extent protected from the terror
associated with anticipating and facing death.[22] Such devout inmates were
better fortified against many of the dehumanizing Nazi realities (Marcus, 2008,
pp. 174, 175). Unlike religious inmates, the secular intellectuals did not have
this symbolic capacity to place the proximate acts in ultimate meaning-giving,
life-affirming contexts that would allow for alteration of the Nazi landscape.

With some creative extrapolation, recasting and elaboration drawn from the Axial vision, Améry's insights about the religious inmate in the camps can reasonably be applied to the ordeal of old age, whether one describes oneself as a religious or secular elder. In the mind and heart of the Axial-inspired elder, what Améry is leaving out of his discussion of dignified aging, especially his questionable claim that he must resign himself to the inescapability of "social extinction" (1994, p. 73), is that the elder has a choice whether to care about what others think, including the judgments of the young who shape the normative values, conduct and what is judged as "good/bad" and "desirable/undesirable." This is one of the key Stoic insights that has found its way into psychoanalysis.[23] As Long describes it, Epictetus claimed that the "essence of the self" is our decision-making, purposive and evaluative nature. Any assignation of unconditional value to external contingencies or possibilities is both a retraction of self-respect ("esteeming indifferent things above one's rationality and internal goodness," in Stoic language) and a sure formula for lack of personal integrity in one's way of behaving toward others. Moreover, in many ways, our emotions are judgments and functions of our volition (our will). They are, as Epictetus said, "up to us," and therefore not required by anything external (Long, 2002, pp. 220, 228, 250). To quote Sartre, "I don't align myself with anybody else's descriptions of me. People can think of me as a genius, a pornographer, Communist, a bourgeois, however they like. Myself, I think of other things" (Kappler, 1964, p. 88).

In psychoanalytic language, Sartre's assertion is an affirmation of one of Freud and his follower's core convictions – that the goal of a successful analysis is "the emergence of a relatively autonomous individual ... the culmination of human development" (Loewald, 1979, p. 771). Such a person is committed to actualizing his freedom, independence and individuation, to view himself as agentic and choice-making. However, as all Axial sages have stressed, this centrally includes a mindfulness that the most profound way to actualize one's own freedom is through the relational task of enabling the freedom of others (Cooper, 2015, p. 112). As it says in the *Bhagavad Gita*, "Strive constantly to serve the welfare of the world: by devotion to selfless work one attains the supreme goal of life" (Easwaran, 2007, p. 106). This quote refers to the deep self-understanding that "I" am not a distinct autonomous actor, but that "I" am in sync with divine reality, and my ultimate freedom emanates from fashioning my actions in agreement with that reality. Moreover, "Do your work with the welfare of others always in mind. It was by such work that [King] Janaka attained [inner] perfection; others too have followed this path" (Easwaran, 1985, p. 19). For the autonomous elder, this relational task of enabling the freedom of others is often expressed in facilitating the flourishing of the next generation, from one's own grandchildren to all children. Such "generativity," as Erikson called it, is rooted in a self-transcending desire to nurture and guide younger people and contribute to supporting the best interests of the next generation.

For example, in contrast to the elderly religious/spiritual aspirant's outlook, the aging skeptic-humanistic intellectual, Simone de Beauvoir, says that we should contrast life with old age instead of with death (1996, p. 539). Indeed, the religious aspirant tends to reside in a different dimension of the spirit than the secular intellectual. His "inner center of gravity" is rooted in his "spiritual" outlook that points to the intangible, ineffable, almost magical Infinite – conceived as something-outside-everything, God, or the Other. Such a transcendent sensibility, what amounts to "seeing" things never seen before, like when one turns a light on in a pitch-black room, has been beautifully evoked by Rumi in one of his stirring poems about non-attachment:

> Out beyond ideas of wrongdoing and rightdoing there is a field. I'll meet you there. When the soul lies down in that grass, the world is too full to talk about. Ideas, language, even the phrase "each other" doesn't make any sense.
>
> (Milosz, 1996, p. 276)

In other words, with an Axial-inspired religious/spiritual outlook, whether it is lodged in a traditional God formulated as the external author of the world or as a person's internal "divinity," or another theological meaning, the elderly religious aspirant views his existence radically differently than a typical secular intellectual. Briefly, despite the objective physical and psychological hardships of old age, the religious/spiritual aspirant is steeped in gratitude for reaching old age; he regards it as one of God's "blessings." Moreover, he is willing and able to accept that what is, and what will be, is part of God's plan for his life; and he is grateful for the "gifts" he is privileged to have every day, even amidst the difficulties of old age. Most importantly, he embraces an outlook that is geared toward the future, both this- and other-worldly (e.g., heaven). Such a feeling of cosmic transcendence, of being attuned to the universe, ironically, informs his present sense of the bountifulness of the world, as he becomes more skillfully responsive to its Beauty, Truth and Goodness. Such a religious/spiritual elder has at last properly intuited how to engage and fully participate in the "infinite sea of being underlying the waves of our finite selves" (Smith, 1991, p. 33). He calls such self-awareness "grace," a reflection of God's love. The elderly secularist typically describes such an epiphanic self-consciousness as the "joy of existing" or "the richness of the universe." When old age is lived through creative theological poetics, the starkness of this final phase of life, at least as we know it, takes on an enhanced, sheltering and comforting "feel." As one becomes more receptive, responsive and responsible to the animate and inanimate otherness of everyday life, to its mysteriousness, amazement and fleeting eternity, there grows a soulful transcendence and plentitude of being that is coterminous with being deeply enmeshed with the highest dimensions of Beauty, Truth, Goodness and Justice. "It takes a long time to become young," said Picasso (Fonda, 2011, p. 3).

## Not understanding the world anymore

Our youth-obsessed culture, which stresses health/fitness, longevity and happiness, fosters novelty notions and challenges to our everyday way of being-in-the-world, including rapid technological changes and new forms of both knowledge (e.g., "the age of information") and activities (e.g., the "age of virtuality").[24] Thus, it is not surprising that Améry focuses on cultural aging as one of the central problematics of the ordeal of aging with dignity. Cultural aging refers "to the loss of the ability to understand new developments in the arts and in a changing society's values and the feeling of becoming useless and out of touch with the world" (Marinova, 2013, p. 2). The opposite of cultural aging is the robust capacity to be open, flexible and creatively adaptive in the current social system in the later years. Améry emphasizes that cultural alienation is a common experience in old age – feeling as if one is an obsolete person, estranged from any meaningful involvement in the rapidly changing social conditions. Erich Fromm aptly described this sense of self-alienation that is evoked when one is lodged in an alienating social system, which is how the elder typically perceives his relation to society:

> By alienation is meant a mode of experience in which the person experiences himself as an alien. He has become, one might say, estranged from himself. He does not experience himself as the center of his world, as the creator of his own acts – but his acts and their consequences have become his masters, whom he obeys, or whom he may even worship. The alienated person is out of touch with himself as he is out of touch with any other person. He, like the others, is experienced as things are experienced; with the senses and with common sense, but at the same time without being related to oneself and to the world outside positively.
>
> (Fromm, 1956, p. 120)

Indeed, the elder can feel like an "alien" in modernity, especially in terms of its befuddling technomania and the associated pervasive mindset and social practices that animate everyday life. Often, his response is to disengage from the modern world and retreat into the protective cocoon of the past, of former "tried and true" cultural attitudes. To some extent, all elders are mindful of the fact that they no longer have a clear, vivid perception of their everyday social world (Marinova, 2013), and that there is a degree of social alienation at play such that they feel they don't exactly "get" what is going on and are being left behind. I am reminded of the time when my wife and I went for dinner at an Italian restaurant with another couple in their early 70s. I noticed that a group of about ten young women was celebrating a friend's 21st birthday (I had inquired in passing). At one point, I noticed that literally all of the women were eating their main courses while operating their iPhones, and not a word of talking transpired among them for about fifteen minutes. This was in stark contrast to the lively conversation we were having while dining. As Améry noted, "Getting culturally old in the widest sense – usually becomes clear in a rather slow, undramatic process of successive insights. At first there is often only a numb feeling of aversion against ... the 'cultural jargon' of his epoch" (e.g., the young women's bewildering cultural ideas used to regulate social interaction at the restaurant) (Améry, 1994, p. 76).[25] In the restaurant context, there was a "cultural lag," a strangely off-putting disconnect between the cultural ideas we elders used to regulate our social lives (i.e., that one engages in energetic conversation during a dinner with friends, undistracted by electronics) compared to the young adults' solitary, silent focus on their phones.

When one multiplies these incidental, repellent experiences as one gets older, eventually, says Améry, the elder feels unable to effectively "manage," let alone flourish, in the social world they live in, leaving them little choice but to retreat into past ways of thinking and acting, feeling like strangers to the new era. Over time, an elder may not only be unable to effectively navigate the rapidly changing social world; not only does he feel obsolete, useless and unproductive in a capitalistic society that highly values the business of production and acquiring possessions (De Beauvoir, 1996), but he may also become consciously unwilling to try to stay relevant and up to date. That is, he tends to resist accepting and understanding the new cultural forms with which he has to contend. This is the near-lethal psychological moment when he decides to become a "spectator" to the workings of the everyday youth-centered world and folds into himself. This is a form of extreme social alienation that can lead to an insidious reduction in self-esteem and self-efficacy, increased isolation, and what ultimately can be the fertile psychological breeding ground for the development of depression and other such debilitating "states of the soul." Resignation with despair rules the day.

What is the elder's "way out" of this "soul-destroying" feeling of cultural alienation? De Beauvoir explains her antidote to feeling like the diminished, depreciated "other" as she called it (1996, p. 288): "Retirement ... may be looked upon either as a prolonged holiday or as a rejection, a being thrown on to the scrap-heap" (ibid., p. 263). In other words, the way to avoid the worst aspects of cultural alienation associated with old age is to engage in meaning-giving, affect-integrating and action-guiding projects and activities that bolster one's sense of self-esteem, self-continuity and self-coherence. Such a recommendation is entirely in sync with conventional gerontological wisdom. As psychologist Dennis Kravetz (2013) summarized it, typically an elder is encouraged to fashion a "positive" mental attitude and outlook, to not act his chronological age, to oppose mobility aides until he absolutely requires them, to continue working in some form in retirement, and to generate reachable future goals. This is sound advice; as are the many suggestions, often research-based, that can be accessed from "self-help" literature and elsewhere to make twilight years more "positive."

However, as gerontological researchers have reported, this practical wisdom is extremely hard to implement because as people get older they become more conservative in outlook – that is, their values, beliefs, attitudes and normative notions become highly resistant to modification and, therefore, it is very difficult to change behavior, which is what is critical to not feeling "played out." As Kierkegaard noted, what matters most in any kind of existential decision-making is the impact the decision has on how one lives their concrete, everyday life: "Truth is for the particular individual only as he himself produces it in action" (1980, p. 138). For the elder who desires not to feel nor be treated by society as if he were "an outdated past, an outsider, as less competent and as one who no longer belongs to the newly formed ideas and cultural value of the present day" (Marinova, 2013, p. 11), the antidote is to embrace an attitude of "revolt," as discussed earlier in this chapter.

Like the skeptic-humanistic intellectual, the religious/spiritual aspirant tries to stay current and skillful with "managing" the rapidly changing cultural forms of knowledge and activities, for he, too, wants to be able to effectively function in his everyday life and enjoy the benefits of technological innovation and other novelties. However, where the skeptic-humanistic intellectual derives his self-value and dignity mainly from his functional effectiveness, his "success" in the everyday world as described above, enjoying the ego-enhancement that it provides in terms of fame, fortune and power, the religious/spiritual aspirant mainly resides in a different dimension of being. He sees the world similarly to how Emerson, who was greatly influenced by the Axial outlooks of Plato and the *Bhagavad Gita*, saw the world – as "a metaphor of the Spirit" (Geldard, 2001, pp. 14–15). For Emerson, spirit-seeking meant participating in a life that was a mindful and radical interplay with exquisitely subtle forces (i.e., unseen but intuited) and principles of actions and meaning. This included a mindful pursuit of a transcendent reality (i.e., universal law, Divine Thought, "masterpieces of God") that was behind and beyond the surface appearances of the manifest world.

This is a very different way of seeing and being compared to the skeptic-humanistic intellectual lodged in a conventional scientific outlook (ibid., pp. 21, 109). Thus, when the "props" on which the skeptic-humanistic intellectual's self-esteem and sense of identity are dependent – such as feeling competent in metabolizing new cultural forms of knowledge and activities (what Barthes calls the "bastard form of mass culture")[26] – are taken away, or are in other ways inaccessible, he becomes like a deflated balloon. Such a moment of disruption in self-esteem and identity is experienced as humiliation, being unable to adequately integrate events that are occurring into an ongoing, coherent story about the self. In contrast, the religious/spiritual aspirant mainly derives his self-value and dignity in terms of doing "God's work" as it were, in being willfully engaged in the interminable task of actualizing the transcendentals of Beauty, Truth and, especially, Goodness in the world. When one's self-esteem, self-continuity and self-coherence are ultimately linked to something "more," "higher" and "better," at least as one construes these matters, then one is not as vulnerable to spiraling self-esteem and identity-diffusion associated with the cultural alienation that Améry claims is inevitable in old age. Put differently, when one's existential roots are in "heaven," one is not as deeply affected by "earthly" erosion.

Thus, the religious/spiritual aspirant's response to the problem of "not understanding the world anymore," as Améry called it, is to affirm that this is not a huge problem because it has never been one. The "world" that ultimately matters to him is a radically different one. It is infused with the intuited hints and traces of the eternal, infinite and transcendent, where one's self-value is judged as praiseworthy to the extent that he is willing and able to actualize Beauty, Truth, Goodness and Justice, in what he sees as a weeping world desperately in need of redemption. When one's self-definition and self-fashioning are not intimately linked to the "broken world" of the mass society (which is now global) – with its technomania, its atomization, collectivization, pervasive anonymous bureaucracy, over-reliance on so-called experts, its totalitarian potential and, even worse, its nuclear self-destructive possibility – but rather, it is lodged in the eternal, infinite and transcendent, one is immune from feeling the cultural alienation that Améry claimed was a "given." The Axial-inspired elderly religious/spiritual aspirant's "revolt" is not mainly about accepting the "broken world" with or without despair, and/or detaching from it, or "succeeding" or in other ways prevailing in it; but rather, it passionately involves transforming it, "protesting against the world that is ['broken,' fragmented, at war], in the name of the world that ought to be" ("repaired," whole, at peace) (Sacks, 2017, p. 2).

## Living with dying

The Buddha evocatively described old age in the most widely read Buddhist scripture, *The Dhammapada* (a collection of sayings): "Look at this beautified body: A mass of sores popped up, Full of illness, [the object] of many plans, With nothing stable or lasting" (Fronsdale, 2005, p. 39). Given Buddha's rather gloomy depiction of old age, you would think that most elders would be depressed. And yet, researchers have found "that, overall, clinical depression is not more, and probably is less prevalent in older than younger adults." Moreover, "there is evidence that elders cope more effectively with stressful life events than do younger ones" (Williamson & Christie, 2009, p. 167). Researchers have also reported that those elders who are happiest are acutely mindful that they are in the final part of their lives, but they are not demoralized or immobilized by this self-awareness. Rather, they live as if "time is of the essence"; they "live as though life is short – because it is." Such elders are not "depressed by this knowledge"; instead they "act on it, making sure to do important things *now*" (Pillemer, 2011, p. 244). Indeed, research has demonstrated that an increased mindfulness of death facilitates a person becoming more concentrated on individuated goals and values and less focused on living according to societally conditioned standards and sanctioned ways of behaving. Death awareness can also increase empathy and sympathy, giving a person a feeling of solidarity with other human beings who are going through the same experience (Cooper, 2017, p. 102).

What the above researchers have found is a reaffirmation of Stoic and Epicurean practical wisdom (Hadot, 2009, pp. 166, 173). Stoics and Epicureans advocated a complete modification in a person's relationship to time: to live in the only moment we actually live – the here-and-now (i.e., the vitally immediate present); to live as if it were the final day, the final moment of one's life, in relation to both ourselves and others. Above all, this means seeing the world as if one were like a toddler having a "love affair with the world," as Margaret Mahler described it (Mahler et al., 1985, p. 74). In this way, one would experience the world as if for the first time, with all the freshness, magnificence and joy that typically eludes most unimaginative and jaded adults – i.e., "spirits in deeper prisons" as Emerson called them (Geldard, 2001, p. 86).

Psychoanalysts have weighed in on the issue of "living with dying," in terms of the inordinate "fear of death" that some patients manifest. Such "spirits in deeper prisons" are similar to the anguished elderly that Améry has in mind. These people are excessively afraid of dying because they have unresolved, unconscious, infantile fears about castration, of separation and the loss of the needed object, of one's strong masochistic wishes, and of retaliatory punishment by the super-ego for having death wishes toward others. Following Freud, psychoanalysis recognizes that there is a psychological inclination toward death or non-humanness that is especially strong in those who have undergone early childhood loss of a significant other (e.g., Améry's father died when he was age 4), which is, in part, an expression of their wish to fuse with the beloved lost object (Akhtar, 2009, pp. 107–108). "The fear of death," said the Axial-inspired historian/philosopher Will Durant, "is strangely mingled with the longing for repose" (2014, p. 28).

Being the rather brooding skeptic-humanistic intellectual he was, Améry raises some important issues that the thoughtful elder has to reckon with, consciously or unconsciously, in order to embrace the life-affirming outlook described above. "Dying is also *living*, just as living is a permanent dying," said Améry (1994, p. 105).

Améry provides a sweeping characterization of what it feels like to the elder "to live with dying," a self-awareness that he characterizes by using such disquieting words as "terror," "*horror* and *angor* [constriction], horror and anguish," "fear," "pain," "suffocating" and "pure negativity" (ibid., pp. 116–118). At the end of his chapter on aging, Améry pulls together all of his earlier themes, those around which I have organized this chapter, as he summarizes his troubled and troubling view of the elder's struggle with "living with dying":

Aging, through which the Not and the "un" of our existence makes themselves known and become evident to us, is a desolate region of life, lacking any reasonable consolation; one should not fool oneself. In aging we become the worldless inner sense of pure time. As aging people we become alien to our bodies and at the same time closer to their sluggish mass than ever before. When we have passed beyond the prime of life, society forbids us to continue to project into the future, and culture becomes a burdensome culture that we no longer understand, that gives us to understand that, as scrap iron of the mind, we belong to the waste heaps of the epoch. In aging, finally, we have to live with dying, a scandalous imposition, a humiliation without compare, that we put up with, not in humility, but as the humiliated.

(Améry, 1994, pp. 127–128)

Améry is surely accurately identifying some of the distressing aspects of the typical, secular elder's struggle "to live with dying"; but while his "desire to tell the truth" is sincere and praiseworthy (ibid., p. 128), it is open to criticism, or at least an alternative "telling." Améry provides only one version of "the truth" of the elder's "living with dying" in that his characterization and conclusions are strictly lodged in his skeptic-humanistic intellectual assumptions about "the human condition," "reality" and what is imaginatively possible. In his admitted secular outlook, aging is inevitably "lacking any reasonable consolation."

This outlook is to be contrasted with the religious/spiritual aspirant's very different way of seeing and being, one that is lodged in an Axial sensibility. For example, briefly consider the Stoic view on dying as well as some of those outlooks rooted in ancient religious wisdom and spirituality. The Stoics often quoted Plato's famous assertion that "to philosophize is an exercise in dying." Hadot interprets this statement in an interestingly paradoxical way: "to exercise at being dead to one's individuality, to one's passions, to see things from the perspective universality and objectivity." In other words, while honoring the body was important to the Stoics, one must become aware that one is a "minuscule object," and there are matters that are much more significant than one's physical existence and survival, namely, transcendent values that are "absolute" (Hadot, 2009, p. 149).

Such "absolute" values originate in the Divine, what Epictetus called Zeus, God, Nature or the gods (Long, 2002, p. 143). Thus, in the Stoic view, ideally one's death was not deeply distressing because, like Socrates, who was fortified with sincere and complete transcendent moral virtue at his trial, "No harm can come to the good man in life or in death, and his circumstances are not ignored by the gods" (ibid., p. 68). Epictetus paraphrased this Socratic insight by drawing on the words of Socrates as he spoke to his Athenian prosecutors: "Anytus and Leletus can kill me, but they cannot harm me" (ibid., p. 69). Such an outlook may seem strange to modern ears, but, drawing from the Socratic tradition, with its transcendent sensibility and "God talk," it strengthened and comforted the typical Stoic's confrontation with death and "living with dying."

The great ancient religious and spiritual wisdom traditions had their powerful reflections on the elder's ordeal of "living with dying" that not only strengthened and comforted the "believer" but also potentiated his passionate commitment to living the "good life," one that was dedicated to actualizing Beauty, Truth and Goodness in the everyday world until his last breath. What these "believers" have is an "all-embracing," coherent "fabric of meaning" "that comprehends him and all of his experiences," and by its very nature involves "a transcendence of individuality" (Berger, 1967, p. 54). Such an ideologically informed, over-arching universe of "higher" meaning, including emotionally infused, flexibly applied, transcendent guiding beliefs, is believed by the individual to be absolute. The "believer" is thus able to make sense of and endure, with grace, the disquieting existential facts of "living with dying." Améry himself wrote on his concentration camp experiences that for the "believer":

> the grip of the horror reality [read: "living with dying"] was weaker where from the start reality had been placed in the framework of an unalterable idea. Hunger was not hunger as such, but the necessary consequence of atheism ... A beating or death in the gas chamber was the renewed sufferings of the Lord.
>
> (1980, p. 13)

With his powerful symbolic and practical resources, the religious/spiritual aspirant is able to transcend the worst aspects of "living with dying" and can project himself into a future that not only potentiates his dedication with the fullness of his whole being – to Beauty, Truth and Goodness in this world – but his hallowed actions also have redemptive significance in an eternal cosmic reality. While the Axial-inspired religious/spiritual aspirant wants to continue to live a flourishing life like anyone else, he views his existence as a "gift," a "borrowed" one from his beloved Heavenly Creator; and when he is finally called "home," he wholeheartedly submits to the will of his God.

## Final comment

I end this long chapter by mentioning what is one of my favorite passages in the Axial *oeuvre*, from the Hebrew Bible. This is the death of Moses (Deuteronomy 34), when God tells the very old Moses to ascend to the top of Mt. Nebo to view the Promised Land: "This is the land which I swore unto Abraham, unto Isaac, and unto Jacob, saying: I will give it unto thy seed; I have caused thee to see it with thine eyes but thou shalt not go over thither" (shall not enter) (Hertz, 1960, p. 916). Exactly why God thought it reasonable that the greatest prophet of Israel, the leader/liberator of His Chosen People, should be barred from entering the Promised Land has been debated by Jewish sages from time immemorial.[27] While Moses had committed some relatively small sins, that he was only allowed to view the Promised Land but not enter it is a painful and poignant irony.

The late Chief Rabbi of the United Kingdom, Joseph H. Hertz, in his commentary on this troubling passage, cites a scholar who aptly explicates the passage, which I find to be a fitting end to this chapter. It beautifully suggests how a "believer" and non-believer can best reckon with the ordeal of aging, "living with dying," and death if only he embraces without reserve the following insight and valuative attachment: Like with "blessed" Moses, "To labour and not to see the end of our labours; to sow and not to reap; to be removed from the earthly scene before our work has been appreciated, and when it will be carried on not by ourselves but by others" (Hertz, 1960, p. 916), reflects the "highest" development of character, of autonomy, integration and humanity. Most importantly, perhaps, God was teaching us that, like Moses – who led his deeply flawed but loved Israelites to freedom in the Promised Land – to be other-directed, other-regarding and other-serving toward those we love ultimately requires that we "back away," even "stay behind," so that the "other" can potentiate their growth, development and individuation. Such sacrifice of one's narcissistic gratification, whether it is rooted in the need or desire for self-aggrandizement or control, or some other self-centric motivation, is not only the main thrust of "good enough" parenting, but in its "being for the other" before himself, epitomizes the elder's internalization of the best of the Axial ethical spirit.

## Notes

1  An Israeli study reported that elderly Israeli Holocaust survivors were three times more likely to attempt suicide compared to other patients in the same phase of life (Traubmann, 2005).
2  www.poets.org/poetsorg/poem/rabbi-ben-ezra, retrieved 7/11/17.
3  Translation from www.chabad.org, Chassidic Thought: Insights & Readings by Yanki Tauber.
4  Used with permission. Details have been changed to protect patient privacy.
5  https://en.oxforddictionaries.com/definition/nostalgia, retrieved 4/3/17.
6  http://monumenttotransformation.org/atlas-of-transformation/html/n/nostalgia/nostalgia-svetlana-boym.html, retrieved 4/6/17.
7  Ibid.
8  There is no "real" or "actual" past, in that how the past is remembered, or at least narrated, is always consciously and unconsciously mediated by one's current and future outlook. In psychoanalysis, this problematic is discussed in terms of narrative versus historical truth.
9  One is reminded of Sartre's statement, "The body is what consciousness is, it is not even anything except body. The rest is nothingness and silence" (Van Deurzen, 2009, p. 88).
10  Kafka, who was 41 when he died, was an exception to this observation. He wrote in his *Diaries*, "I was afraid of mirrors, because they showed an inescapable ugliness" (Veale & Neziroglu, 2010, p. 37).

11  Jung had a similar view: "I have treated many hundreds of patients. Among those in the second half of life – that is to say, over 35 – there has not been one whose problem in the last resort was not that of finding a religious outlook on life" (Jones-Smith, 2016, p. 65).

12  "Thrownness" is a catchy term Heidegger used to describe the fact that we come into a world that predates us – a specific place, time and culture that gives us the means to manage our lives but also truncates our understanding (Langdridge, 2015). The ability to creatively respond to the "thrownness" of existence is the art of living the "good life."

13  In terms of translating these lofty insights into practical wisdom, one cannot help but call to mind the famous words of the great Axial-inspired St. Francis of Assisi: "Start by doing what's necessary; then do what's possible; and suddenly you are doing the impossible" (Sorenson, 2016, p. 115).

14  https://en.oxforddictionaries.com/definition/imagination, retrieved 5/16/17.

15  The so-called "sapiosexuals" have rediscovered the long-known truth, as the *New York Times* titled its article, "the hottest body part is the brain" (North, 2017, p. A18).

16  According to Stanislavski, imagination and fantasy are different: "Imagination creates things that can be or can happen, whereas fantasy invests things that are not in existence, which have been or will be" (Marcus, with Marcus, 2011, p. 211).

17  I have liberally drawn from O'Donohue's writings (1997, 1998, 2004) and lectures in our discussion of the imagination.

18  This appreciating of otherness, loveliness and splendor can include calling upon "perverse" fantasies and mutually consented to "perverse" behavior, in sync with Freud's notion of "polymorphous perversity." This is the idea that the infant's sexual wishes (the pre-genital, pre-Oedipal ones) are not channeled in any single direction and therefore, the various erotogenic zones are substitutable (Rycroft, 1995, p. 135). For the elder this can mean accessing the "perverse" tendencies of infantile sexuality, the "component" or "partial instincts" such as sucking, biting and smelling, not only during foreplay, which is common, but in other less conventional ways. The French essayist and memoirist Anaïs Nin put this just right: "I will not be just a tourist in the world of images, just watching images passing by which I cannot live in, make love to, possess as permanent sources of joy and ecstasy" (1975, p. 262).

19  www.americanrhetoric.com/speeches/douglasmacarthurfarewelladdress.htm, retrieved 5/22/17.

20  This sense of forsakenness was powerfully captured by Kierkegaard: "Deep within every human being there still lives the anxiety over the possibility of being alone in the world, forgotten by God, overlooked by the millions and millions in the enormous household" (Van Deurzen, 2009, p. 28).

21  For Camus, "revolt" in the face of the absurdity of existence is what "gives life its value." The three consequences of confronting the absurdity of existence are "my revolt, my freedom, my passion." Also worth mentioning is that for Camus, revolt is not conceived as a judgment or speech; rather, it always involves an act (Heffernan, 2017, pp. 5, 15).

22  One thinks of Thoreau the day before he died. He was visited by a longstanding friend who noted that he had heard robins singing on his way to visit. In a whisper, Thoreau responded, "this is a beautiful world, but soon I shall see one that is fairer. I have so loved nature" (Montaigne, 2017, p. 17).

23  Long, for example, mentions that Foucault praised Epictetus's pioneering techniques of self-examination that culminated in Freud. Likewise, it was Epictetus who first linked integrity with healthy consciousness, a connection that is part of the received wisdom of psychoanalytic theory and practice (Long, 2002, p. 274).

24  Van Deurzen, an existential psychologist, believes that the age of information has replaced the age of knowledge, which had itself replaced the age of wisdom (2009, p. 17).

25  Durant has argued that old age is made easier "by an apathy of sense and will," this reduced vitality being part of the process of the organism getting ready for its final rest. "*Jam satis vixi* – 'I have already lived enough,'" said Caesar (Durant, 2014, pp. 28, 39).

26  Barthes is worth quoting in full: "The bastard form of mass culture is humiliated repetition: content, ideological schema, the blurring of contradictions – these are repeated, but the superficial forms are viewed, always new books, new programs, new films, new items, but always the same meaning" (Hugssen, 1986, p. 211).

27  Indeed, Moses died on Mt. Nebo as God ordained it, but the story does not end there. The *Midrash* presents a fascinating description of the death of Moses. After entering a cave where a rock bed has been prepared, God tells Moses to lie down, close his eyes and prepare to die. Immediately, Moshe's soul begins arguing with God. It says, "If you take me from Moshe, who will lead the Jewish people or who will sing your praises or who will teach your Torah anywhere near the capability, influence or spiritual dedication of Moses?" At this point, all the heavenly hosts are descended to watch this debate between Moses' soul and God. God answers, "For leadership there is Joshua. For praise singing there will be a King David, and for Torah teaching there will be a Rabbi Akiva." In other words, there will always be someone to take a leadership role in all the areas of Jewish life. Finally, the soul asks, "If you take me from Moshe what other body in the universe is pure enough to receive me?" To this, God answers that the soul's statement is correct, and God then bends down, kisses Moses and he dies.

   The obvious question is that if the soul was correct, that there is no other body as pure as Moses' within which she can be placed, why does God kill Moses? One interpretation goes like this: When one makes a kissing sound, one automatically sucks in the air. Thus, when God kissed Moses, He sucked the soul back into Himself, which would be the only place pure enough for the soul to reside. We also now have a marvelous completion of the Torah. At the beginning of the Torah, God animates man with life by "blowing into his nostrils the breath of life (the soul)." At the end of the Torah, God sucks that life (the soul) out of man (Moses), completing the cycle (Rabbi Dr. Stuart Grant, Personal communication, 6/20/17). More generally, this *Midrash* is suggesting that, like Moses, when one has lived a life dedicated to and animated by the "highest" ethicality, by Truth, Justice, Goodness and spiritual beauty, when one has embraced and transfigured suffering, one's death can be a wonderfully creative event opening you up to the invisible embrace of the divine. In the spiritual imagination, such a passionate kinship with the divine is nothing short of a homecoming (O'Donohue, 1997, pp. 217, 234, 227).

## References

Abrams, M.H. (1971). *Natural Supernaturalism: Tradition and Revolution in Romantic Literature*. New York: Norton.

Adeyemo, W.L. (2004). Sigmund Freud: Smoking Habit, Oral Cancer and Euthanasia. *Nigerian Journal of Medicine*, 13(2), 189–195.

Adler, S. (1988). *The Technique of Acting*. New York: Bantam.

Akhtar, S. (2009). *Comprehensive Dictionary of Psychoanalysis*. London: Karnac.

Améry, J. (1980). *At the Mind's Limits: Contemplations by a Survivor of Auschwitz and Its Realities.* S. Rosenfeld and S.P. Rosenfeld (Trans.). Bloomington: Indiana University Press (Original work published 1964)

Améry, J. (1994). *On Aging: Revolt and Resignation.* J.D. Barlow (Trans.). Bloomington: Indiana University Press. (Original work published 1968)

Baldwin, M., & Landau, M.J. (2014). Exploring Nostalgia's Influence on Psychological Growth. *Self and Identity,* 13(2), 162–167.

Barlow, J. (1994). Translator's Introduction. In J. Améry, *On Aging: Revolt and Resignation* (pp. x–xviii). Bloomington: Indiana University Press.

Barrett, W. (1958). *Irrational Man: A Study of Existential Philosophy.* New York: Random House.

Barrett, W. (1979). *The Illusion of Technique: A Search for Meaning in a Technological Civilization.* New York: Anchor.

Batcho, K. (2011, 21 Dec.). Are Some People More Prone to Nostalgia Than Others? *Science and Religion Today.* Retrieved 4/4/17 from www.scienceandreligiontoday. com/2011/12/21/are-some-people-more-prone-to-nostalgia-than-others.

Batcho, K.I. (2013). Nostalgia: Retreat or Support in Difficult Times. *American Journal of Psychology,* 126(3), 355–367.

Berger, P. (1967). *The Sacred Canopy.* New York: Anchor.

Boym, S. (2001). *The Future of Nostalgia.* New York: Basic Books.

Camus, A. (1955). *The Myth of Sisyphus and Other Essays.* New York: Knopf.

Case, T.I., & Williams, K.D. (2004). Ostracisms: A Metaphor for Death. In J. Greenberg, S. I. Koole & T. Pyszczynski (Eds.), *Handbook of Experimental Existential Psychology* (pp. 336–351). New York: Guilford.

Cooper, M. (2015). *Existential Psychotherapy and Counseling: Contributions to a Pluralistic Practice.* Los Angeles: Sage.

Cooper, M. (2017). *Existential Therapies* (2nd ed.). Los Angeles: Sage.

Davenhill, R. (2007). *Looking into Later Life: A Psychoanalytic Approach to Depression and Dementia in Old Age.* London: Karnac.

De Beauvoir, S. (1965). *Force of Circumstances.* R. Howard (Trans.). New York: Putnam.

De Beauvoir, S. (1996). *The Coming of Age.* P. O'Brian (Trans.). New York: Norton.

Durant, W. (2014). *Fallen Leaves: Last Words on Life, Love War, and God.* New York: Simon & Schuster.

Easwaran, E. (Ed. & Trans.). (1985). *The Bhagavad Gita.* New York: Vintage.

Easwaran, E. (Ed. & Trans.). (2007). *The Bhagavad Gita* (2nd ed.). Tomales, CA: Nilgiri.

Erikson, E.H. (1950). *Childhood and Society.* New York: Norton.

Fenichel, O. (1945). *The Psychoanalytic Theory of Neurosis.* New York: Norton.

Fonda, J. (2011). *Prime Time.* New York: Random House.

Freud, S. (1961a). Civilization and Its Discontents. In J. Strachey (Ed. & Trans.), *The Standard Edition of the Complete Psychological Works of Sigmund Freud* (Vol. 21, pp. 57–146). London: Hogarth Press. (Original work published 1930)

Freud, S. (1961b). The Ego and the Id. In J. Strachey (Ed. & Trans.), *The Standard Edition of the Complete Psychological Works of Sigmund Freud* (Vol. 19, pp. 3–66). London: Hogarth Press. (Original work published 1923)

Fromm, E. (1956). *The Sane Society.* Abingdon, UK: Routledge.

Fromm, E. (1976). *To Have or To Be.* New York: Harper & Row.

Fronsdale, G. (2005). *The Dhammapada.* Boston: Shambhala.

Frost, R. (1916). *Mountain Interval*. New York: Holt.

Geertz, C. (1973). *The Interpretation of Cultures*. New York: Basic Books.

Geldard, R. (2001). *The Spiritual Teachings of Ralph Waldo Emerson* (2nd ed.). Herndon, VA: Lindisfarne.

Greenberg, T.M. (2016). *Psychodynamic Perspectives on Aging and Illness* (2nd ed.). San Francisco: Springer.

Greenson, R. (1958). On Screen Defenses, Screen Hunger and Screen Identity. *Journal of the American Psychoanalytic Association*, 6, 242–262.

Heffernan, G. (2017). The Meaningless Life Is Not Worth Living: Critical Reflections on Marcel's Critique of Camus. *Marcel Studies*, 2, 1–22.

Hadot, P. (1998). *The Inner Citadel: The Meditations of Marcus Aurelius*. M. Chase (Trans.). Cambridge, MA: Harvard University Press.

Hadot, P. (2009). *The Present Alone Is Our Happiness: Conversations with Jeannie Carlier and Arnold I. Davidson*. M. Djaballah (Trans.). Stanford, CA: Stanford University Press.

Hertz, J.H. (1960). *The Pentateuch and Haftorahs: Hebrew Text English Translation and Commentary* (2nd ed.). New York: Soncino.

Hoare, C.H. (2002). *Erikson on Development in Adulthood*. Oxford, UK: Oxford University Press.

Hockley, L. (2001). *Cinematic Projections: The Analytical Psychology of C.G. Jung and Film Theory*. Luton, UK: University of Luton Press.

Hugssen, A. (1986). *After the Great Divide: Modernism, Mass Culture, and Postmodernism*. Bloomington: Indiana University Press.

Hupfeld, H. (1897). *Encyclopedia of Wit and Wisdom: A Collection of Over Nine Thousand Anecdotes, Illustrations of Life, Character, Humor and Pathos in One Hundred Classifications*. Philadelphia: David McKay.

James, W. (1908). *The Varieties of Religious Experience: A Study in Human Nature*. London: Longmans, Greene & Co.

Jones-Smith, E. (2016). *Theories of Counseling and Psychotherapy: An Integrative Approach* (2nd ed.). Los Angeles: Sage.

Kappler, F. (1964). Sartre and Existentialism: A Spurned Nobel Prize Calls the World's Attention. Existentialism. *Life Magazine*, 11/6/64, 86–112.

Kierkegaard, S. (1980). *The Concept of Anxiety: A Simple Psychologically Orienting Deliberation on the Dogmatic Issue of Hereditary Sin*. R. Thomte & A.B. Anderson (Eds. & Trans.). Princeton, NJ: Princeton University Press. (Original work published 1844)

Kravetz, D. (2013). 8 Ways to Stay Young as You Age. *Huffington Post*, 7/23/13. Retrieved 6/8/17 from www.huffingtonpost.com/dennis-kravetz/aging-gracefully_b_3280506.html.

Kundera, M. (2009). *The Unbearable Lightness of Being: A Novel*. M.H. Heim (Trans.). New York: Harper Perennial.

Landman, J. (1993). *Regret: The Persistence of the Possible*. Oxford, UK: Oxford University Press.

Langdridge, D. (2015). *Existential Counseling and Psychotherapy*. London: Sage.

Lax, R. (2007). Psychoanalysis and Psychotherapy with the Aging and the Aged. *Issues in Psychoanalytic Psychology*, 29, 79–86.

Leonard, B.E. (2015). Pain, Depression and Inflammation: Are Interconnected Causative Factors Involved? In D.P. Finn & B.E. Lenoard (Eds.), *Pain in Psychiatric Disorders* (pp. 22–35). Basel, Switzerland: Karger.

Loewald, H. (1953). Psychoanalysis and Modern Views on Human Existence and Religious Experience. *Journal of Pastoral Care*, 7(1), 1–15.

Loewald, H. (1979). The Waning of the Oedipus Complex. *Journal of the American Psychoanalytic Association*, 37, 751–775.

Loewald, H.W. (2000). *The Essential Loewald: Collected Papers and Monographs.* Haggerstown, MD: University Publishing Group.

Long, A.A. (2002). *Epictetus: A Stoic and Socratic Guide to Life.* Oxford, UK: Oxford University Press.

Mahler, M.S., Pine, F., & Bergman, A. (1985). *The Psychological Birth of the Infant. Symbiosis and Individuation.* London: Karnac. (Original work published 1975)

Marcus, P. (1999). *Autonomy in the Extreme Situation: Bruno Bettelheim, the Nazi Concentration Camps and the Mass Society.* Westport, CT: Praeger.

Marcus, P. (2003). *Ancient Religious Wisdom, Spirituality, and Psychoanalysis.* Westport, CT: Praeger.

Marcus, P. (2008). *Being for the Other: Emmanuel Levinas, Ethical Living and Psychoanalysis.* Milwaukee, WI: Marquette University Press.

Marcus, P. (2017). *The Psychoanalysis of Career Choice, Job Performance, and Satisfaction: How to Flourish in the Workplace.* London: Routledge.

Marcus, P., & Rosenberg, A. (1998). Introduction. In P. Marcus & A. Rosenberg (Eds.), *Psychoanalytic Versions of the Human Condition: Philosophies of Life and their Impact on Practice* (pp. 1–11). New York: New York University Press.

Marcus, P., with Marcus, G. (2011). *Theatre as Life: Practical Wisdom Drawn from Great Acting Teachers, Actors and Actresses.* Milwaukee: WI: Marquette University Press.

Marinova, D. (2013). Cultural Alienation in the Ageing Person. *Psychological Thought, 6*(2). doi:10.5964/psycht.v612.63

Milosz, C. (1996). *A Book of Luminous Things: An International Anthology of Poetry.* Orlando, FL: Harcourt.

Montaigne, F. (2017). American Surveyor. *New York Times Book Review*, 7/23/17, p. 17.

Monte, C.F. (1980). *Beneath the Mask: An Introduction to Theories of Personality* (2nd ed.). New York: Holt, Rinehart and Winston.

Nin, A. (1975). *The Diary of Anaïs Nin* (Vol. 5, 1947–1955). G. Stuhlmann (Ed.). San Diego, CA: Harcourt Brace Jovanovich.

North, A. (2017). The Hottest Body Part? For a Sapiosexual, It's the Brain. *New York Times*, 6/3/17, p. A18.

O'Donohue, J. (1997). *Anam Cara: A Book of Celtic Wisdom.* New York: Harper Perennial.

O'Donohue, J. (1998). *Eternal Echoes: Exploring Our Huger to Belong.* London: Bantam.

O'Donohue, J. (2004). *Beauty: The Invisible Embrace.* New York: Perennial.

Ozdemir, I. (2013). *Rumi and Confucius: Messages for a New Century.* Clifton, NJ: Tughra.

Pillemer, K. (2011). *30 Lessons for Living: Tried and True Advice from the Wisest Americans.* New York: Plume.

Pillemer, K. (2016). Living a Life without (Major) Regrets. *Huffington Post*, 11/10/16. Retrieved 3/30/17 from www.huffingtonpost.com/karl-a-pillemer-phd/living-life-without-regrets_b_8459396.html.

Plato. (1871). *The Dialogues of Plato* (Vol. 2). B. Jowett (Trans.). London: Macmillan.

Rohr, R. (2011). *Falling Upward: A Spirituality for the Two Halves of Life*. San Francisco, CA: Jossey-Bass.

Rosen, I. (1993). Relational Masochism: The Search for a 'Bad-Enough' Object. *Transactions of the Topeka Psychoanalytic Society*, Summer, p. 399.

Rosenblum, R. (2009). Postponing Trauma: The Dangers of Telling. *International Journal of Psychoanalysis*, 90, 1319–1340.

Roth, P. (2006). *Everyman*. New York: Houghton Mifflin.

Rotte, J. (2000). *Acting with Adler*. New York: Limelight.

Rycroft, C. (1995). *A Critical Dictionary of Psychoanalysis* (2nd ed.). New York: Penguin.

Sacks, J. (2017). Beha'aloteha. *Shabbat Announcements*, 6/10/17, pp. 1–2.

Santoni, R.E. (2003). *Sartre on Violence: Curiously Ambivalent*. University Park: Pennsylvania State University.

Sartre, J.-P. (1964). *Nausea*. L. Alexander (Trans.). New York: New Directions.

Schur, M. (1972). *Freud Living and Dying*. London: Hogarth Press.

Sedikides, C., Wildschut, T., & Baden, D. (2004). Nostalgia: Conceptual Issues and Existential Functions. In J. Greenberg, S.I. Koole, & T. Pyszczynski (Eds.), *Handbook of Experimental Existential Psychology* (pp. 200–214). New York: Guilford.

Seneca. (1917). *Moral Letters to Lucilius* (Vol. 1). Cambridge, MA: Harvard University Press.

Smith, H. (1991). *The World's Religions*. San Francisco: Harper.

Sorenson, R. (2016). *A Cabinet of Philosophical Curiosities: A Collection of Puzzles, Oddities, Riddles and Dilemmas*. Oxford, UK: Oxford University Press.

Spinelli, E. (2015). *Practising Existential Therapy: The Relational World* (2nd ed.). Los Angeles, CA: Sage.

Sterba, E. (1940). Homesickness and the Mother's Breast. *Psychiatric Quarterly*, 14, 701–707.

Traubmann, T. (2005). Study: Holocaust Survivors 3 Times More Likely to Attempt Suicide. *Haaretz*. Retrieved 3/28/17 from www.haaretz.com/news/study-holocaust-survivors-3-times-more-likely-to-attempt-suicide-1.166386.

Van Deurzen, E. (2009). *Psychotherapy and the Quest for Happiness*. London: Sage.

Vandiver, E. (1999). *The Odyssey of Homer* (Course Guidebook). Chantilly, VA: The Teaching Company.

Veale, D., & Neziroglu, F. (2010). *Body Dysmorphic Disorder*. New York: Wiley.

Vess, M., Arndt, J., Routledge, C., Sedikides, C., & Widsschut, T. (2012). Nostalgia as a Resource for the Self. *Self and Identity*, 11(3), 273–284.

Vohs, K.D., & Baumeister, R.F. (2004). Ego Depletion, Self-Control and Choice. In J. Greenberg, S.I. Koole, & T. Pyszczynski (Eds.), *Handbook of Experimental Existential Psychology* (pp. 398–410). New York: Guilford.

Williamson, G.M., & Christie, J. (2009). Aging Well in the 21st Century: Challenges and Opportunities. In S.J. Lopez & C.R. Snyder (Eds.), *Oxford Handbooks of Positive Psychology* (pp. 165–169). Oxford, UK: Oxford University Press.

Winnicott, D. (1971). *Playing and Reality*. London: Tavistock.

Wittgenstein, L. (1999). *Tractatus Logico-Philosphicus*. Mineola, NY: Dover.

Zhou, X., Wildschut, T., Sedikides, C., Chen, X., & Vingerhoets, A.J. (2012). Heart-warming Memories: Nostalgia Maintains Physiological Comfort. *Emotion*, 12(4), 678–684.

# Chapter 6

# The suffering of work

Freud said that "to love and work" were the central therapeutic goals of psychoanalysis, these being the twin pillars of a sound mind and for living the "good life" (Erikson, 1959, p. 96).[1] Indeed, Freud regarded his work as his *raison d'être*: "I could not contemplate with any sort of comfort a life without work. Creative imagination and work go together with me; I take no delight in anything else" (1963, p. 35).[2] Freud's self-observation is in sync with his insistence that when choosing a career, one should ultimately listen to "the deep inner needs of our nature," the unconscious (Reik, 1983, p. 7). Such practical wisdom is also entirely in sync with the Axial vision, including those inspired by its humanistic/spiritual impulse: the great thirteenth-century Persian poet and Sufi mystic, Rumi, noted, "Everyone has been made for some particular work, and the desire for that work has been put in every heart. Let yourself be silently drawn by the stronger pull of what you really love."[3] Despite this wise counsel, researchers Heath and Heath have pointed out that career choices in contemporary western society are frequently "abandoned or regretted" (2013, p. 3). For example, an American Bar Association survey indicated "that 44% of lawyers would recommend that a young person not pursue a career in law" (ibid.). An investigation "of 20,000 executive searches found that 40% of senior-level hires 'are pushed out, fail or quit within 18 months'" (ibid.). Even more troubling, over 50 percent "of teachers quit their jobs within four years" (ibid.). Finally, Gallup's 2012 survey statistics about job satisfaction in the United States found that only 30 percent of those employed report feeling engaged and inspired at work, 52 percent have a chronic case of the Monday blues – they're present, but not excited about their job – while the remaining 18 percent are actively disengaged (Saad, 2012).

Such findings are not surprising when one considers that twenty-first century organizations are significantly different than those of previous eras, generating new challenges, and sometimes "suffering," for individual vocational identity (having a lucid and stable notion of one's goals, interests and abilities), career development and small group functioning. Today's "information age" with global organizations must be effective at negotiating a complex situation typified more by change than stability; organized around networks

rather than rigid hierarchical arrangements; fashioned on fluctuating part-
nerships and shifting alliances rather than self-sufficiency; and built on
technological savvy instead of "bricks and mortar" (Cascio, 2010, p. 22).

The prominent sociologist Zygmunt Bauman noted that we live "in a world
that no longer offers reliable career tracks and stable jobs" (2003, p. 42).
These considerations, among other destabilizing social changes, expose people
"to an uncharacteristically high level of risk and a prolific source of anxiety
and fear" (ibid.). For example, the pervasive use of automation software like
Kensho, "real-time statistical computing systems and scalable analytics
architectures," has led to many in the financial services being made redundant. Anthony Jenkins, the former chief executive of Barclays, a British mul-
tinational banking and financial services company, recently predicted "that
the number of branches and people employed in the financial sector may
decline by as much as 50 percent" (Popper, 2016, p. 59). About half of futur-
ologists and technologists surveyed believe that machines are taking over the
workplace and that jobs will "continue disappearing at a faster rate than they
are created" (ibid., p. 62).

This chapter was inspired by the evocative statement made by Camus that
life is rotten without work, but life becomes stifled and dead if that work is
soulless. Camus's astute observation resonates with people who seriously
reflect on the problem of fashioning a work life that is joyful (or at least
satisfying) over a sustained period of time.[4] To loathe one's work, or to
experience it as barely tolerable, is a kind of personal horror, a form of "suffering" that calls to mind a bad marriage or failed relationship in which one
feels utterly trapped. Regrettably, in western society this feeling of disen-
chantment with one's work life is fairly common; phrases like "I am burned
out," "I am only working for the pay check," "I can't stand my job" puncture
ordinary conversations with adults. In my activities as a psychoanalyst and
psychologist I have been struck by how so many patients are deeply troubled
for one reason or another by their work life, the subject getting more talking
time than their love lives. Indeed, it is a blessed soul who can affirm what
Thomas A. Edison said: "I never did a day's work in my life. It was all fun"
(Wahl, 2017, p. 72).[5]

I have organized this chapter under three headings that typically reflect the
extreme distress or "suffering" of employees: (1) the irrational boss; (2) the
irrational work group; (3) the irrational organization. For each context I
provide suggestions about how the Axial-inspired employee can best
"manage" and prevail over his ordeal.[6] These categories are based on Sartre's
famous line from his one-act masterpiece *No Exit* – "Hell is other people" –
which I will discuss in more detail below (1976, p. 45). While Sartre was not
describing everyday existence in the workplace, he could have been if you
consider the above-mentioned dismal Gallup statistics about job satisfaction.
Similar survey findings were reported in the United Kingdom in 2015:
"60 percent of UK workers are not happy in their jobs."[7]

While problems related to job design (e.g., boredom) and poor extrinsic rewards (e.g., low salary) contribute to employee unhappiness, explicitly interpersonal factors related to organizational health (e.g., job stress) and managerial quality (e.g., overbearing supervision) are also key factors. Interestingly, after salary, workplace culture – the personality of an organization with its unique values, traditions, beliefs, interactions, behaviors and attitudes – was the most cited reason for job satisfaction. The better the "fit" between the employee and workplace culture, the happier an employee tends to be (Grant, 3013; Miller, 2016, p. 36).

Indeed, just about every workplace setting requires near continuous social interaction, whether it is with colleagues, supervisors, managers or leaders (and of course, with the public, such as customers, clients, patients, etc.). A supervisor (and, relatedly, any employee) must be able to: provide constructive feedback, effectively manage emotional eruptions and complaints, mediate disputes, appropriately respond to criticism, make and deny requests, and assist staff to generate sensible solutions to work-related interpersonal difficulties. A supervisor must also be capable of wisely delegating responsibility, holding fast in the face of resistance to change, convincing others to do things differently, building consensus, presiding over effective meetings, foreseeing and eliminating impediments to communication, dealing with troublesome people and providing unambiguous instructions. In the context of small groups or teams, a range of social skills for effective collaboration are required, such as providing helpful criticism and positive suggestions and giving encouragement for creative and innovative ideas (Gambrill, 2004, p. 243). Thus, given the extent of social interaction at a typical workplace, it is not surprising that distressing interpersonal conflicts are a common experience. For example, there are conflicts regarding the perception of unfair treatment such as not receiving a promotion, raise or bonus; poor "fit" problems between the employee and the tasks of a job; dysfunctional team or group dynamics that exclude employees; and poor "fit" between the employee and the organizational culture (Frew, 2004, p. 299). For these and other reasons, many workers complain "this job is driving me crazy," a colloquial way of expressing their "suffering."

## The irrational boss

"And I particularly like the whole thing of being boss," quipped Golden Globe-winning English actor and producer Hugh Grant: "Boss and employee … It's the slave quality that I find very alluring" (FeatsPress, n.d.). Grant is putting into sharp focus one of the important conscious and/or unconscious motivations that propels a person to passionately want to be a boss, manager or leader; namely, the crude or subtle sadistic pleasure in being a person in charge.[8] Simply put, a person's private need to dominate is gratified in the public setting of the workplace. To some degree such a perverse motivation is probably always operative, depending on the instinctual make-up, defenses, childhood history and other psychological factors of the person. While power is a constituent aspect of human experience and is the "lifeblood of organizational life," it also has its "darker" side that workers have to contend with if they are to survive, let alone flourish, in the job (Kets de Vries, 1991, pp. 123, 121). This is an old story. If you have to endure a "crazy" boss, your work life can become an utter misery. Understanding the psychodynamics can be helpful in better coping with the person, unless the situation becomes so intolerable that finding a new job is the only realistic solution.

There are many different types of "crazy" bosses that emerge in the psychological space on the interface of the person and organization. Researchers have suggested that in general, the most difficult personality types to work with have "high needs for control, perfection, approval and attention" (Aamodt, 2007, p. 501). The most troubling personality/organizational "type" is the extreme narcissist, especially the regressive, destructive processes that animate their behavior. I focus on the more malignant type of narcissistic boss to highlight the pathological features that are operative in the less pathological bosses that are more frequently encountered in the workplace.[9] I will describe these psychodynamics from both sides of the pathological relationship: from the mode of the narcissistic boss and from that of the employee who is ill-fated to be a "satellite in his orbit," as they are in dynamic interplay within the context of an organization that often facilitates and perpetuates such dysfunctional leader/follower relations. Intrapsychic and social conflicts always potentiate and strengthen each other (Kernberg, 1998, p. 13). All work organizations "select and mold character," and they can bring out psychopathology in their employees that was not necessarily there in the first place (Maccoby, 1984, p. 99). Thus, psychopathology is best phenomenologically conveyed and deconstructed in terms of individual psychology that is indissolubly context-dependent and setting-specific.

Otto Kernberg, one of the great psychoanalytic theoreticians on the narcissistic personality, has described this kind of character structure, which includes manifestation in leaders in the workplace:

> [Such person's] interpersonal relations are characterized by excessive self-reference and self-centeredness; whose grandiosity and overvaluation of themselves exist together with feelings of inferiority; who are over-dependent on external admiration, emotionally shallow, intensely envious, and both depreciatory and exploitive in their relations with others.
>
> (Kernberg, 1979, p. 33)[10]

By way of giving an everyday work context to this clinical definition, in the world of popular culture much of Kernberg's description calls to mind the comedy-drama film based on the novel about a demanding, unempathic fashion magazine editor, Miranda Priestly (played by Meryl Streep), in *The*

*Devil Wears Prada* (2006); or, in a much more troubling manner, the Italian-American Mafia "boss" Tony Soprano (played by James Gandolfini) in the TV drama series *The Sopranos* (1999–2007). In both of these characters we sense a fragile and feeble sense of self beneath their outward façade of self-confidence and effectiveness. Indeed, such narcissistic bosses, managers and leaders are prone to extreme anger, if not rage, when their self-esteem and self-worth are threatened. In this context, rage is best understood as "love outraged," that is, their fury is a response to what they intensely experience as narcissistic wounding. Such bosses unconsciously construe threats to their self-esteem and self-worth as a violent attack on their delusional feeling that they are totally lovable and perfect. Their rage and power strivings are magical solutions to their profound sense of vulnerability and helplessness (Labier, 1984, p. 15). An unpacking of some of the other salient characteristics of a narcissist boss is provided below.

While the typical narcissistic boss is both extremely self-centered and grandiose, he is also powerfully resentful of others' success, qualities, possessions and luck. Such envy, as Melanie Klein noted, is rooted in the wish to appropriate what is perceived as "good" in the other. The psychological basis of envy is the infant's experience with his mother's gratifying "good breast," the "part-object" symbol of abundant nurturance and unshakeable stability, and his wish to be the ultimate source of such "goodness." Under conditions of frustration, especially of a lack of attunement to and understanding of the infant's painful affects by the mother, the infant's envious wishes of the "good breast" become more extreme and morph into a wish to completely exhaust the "good breast," not simply to possess all of its "goodness" but, in addition, to intentionally deplete it so that it no longer contains any contents that will evoke envy. While certain forms of envy can spark reasonable ambition, when it is pathological, it can lead to intense anguish and paralysis of will (Akhtar, 2009, p. 96), though in the case of the narcissist, most often it turns into hatred. While in the adult, envy is perhaps a more psychologically passive dislike of the other, hatred is its active expression.[11] As Victor Hugo noted, "The wicked envy and hate; it is their [perverse] way of admiring" (1907, p. 359).

Precisely what the envious person hates in the other varies; however, almost always it has to do with some aspect of the other's capacity for loving, for joyfully being other-directed, other-regarding and other-serving in comportment. Kernberg makes this point rather well, saying, "Envious of what they could not themselves enjoy, they had to 'spoil, depreciate and degrade' the capacity others had to find emotional gratification in love" (Lunbeck, 2014, p. 109). As Freud remarked, the envy-driven narcissist lives in a loveless hell because the very act of loving requires an "unselving" or "transelving" that is out of his reach: "A person in love is humble [unlike the puffed-up narcissist]. A person who loves has, so to speak, forfeited a part of his narcissism, and it can only be replaced by his being loved" (1956, p. 98). Freud's remark is in sync with the Axial sages who emphasized that self-divesting or self-emptying of one's selfish desires and infantile "neediness" was the precondition for giving love, especially in its "higher" forms.

Within the context of the workplace, the envious boss will find anyone as threatening and highly suspect who displays prosocial behavior and attitudes such as altruism, trust and reflexivity (Richardson & West, 2010, p. 236), or courteousness – being a good sport, willing to go above and beyond the call of duty for the sake of the greater good (Judge et al., 2006, p. 765). The narcissistic boss sees the bad in what others do, in part due to his competitive nature that cannot tolerate another appearing to be better than him, including in the ethical realm, when derivative behavior related to love is at play, as it is when helping a colleague with no expectation of reward. What the narcissistic boss finds so horrifying about "for the other" behavior of a subordinate is that such a person can "lose himself" in others by assisting them to effectively manage the same challenges he may have had to manage himself, which avoids the hazard of becoming inordinately narcissistic like his boss (Kets de Vries, 1991, p. 133). This is one of the important reasons why narcissists can easily work themselves up into a fine lather of moral indignation over something that they believe a subordinate has done wrong (but actually right in the eyes of most others) according to their warped perception. As Erich Fromm aptly pointed out, "There is perhaps no phenomenon which contains so much destructive feeling as moral indignation, which permits envy or hatred to be acted out under the guise of virtue" (1947, p. 235). Such a person has the perverse gratification associated with feeling contemptuous of someone they perceived as threatening and altogether "bad."

When the meaning, direction and purpose of work is only self-glorification, competition and conflict (Huntley, 1997, p. 128), it is not surprising that narcissists are typically unwilling and unable to evaluate their own motives and behavior in detail and depth (e.g., they rely on social clichés and trivialities; Kernberg, 1998, p. 28). As a result they are not able to make reasonable judgments about what is "good" or "bad" about themselves or others, or implement ethically animated self-corrections. Thus, narcissists typically have truncated ties to empathy; they are not able to "feel" their way into another person, to engage deeper needs and wishes while maintaining a sense of themselves in the process. Since identification and attunement with another person's emotional life is beyond their interest and reach, they focus on superficial markers of a person like status and political expediency as their evaluative touchstones (Rycroft, 1995, p. 47). This is not surprising when we consider what is psychologically entailed in empathic listening. According to Daniel Stern, empathy has four interrelated, interdependent and interactive aspects to it:

- First, one must be mindful of feeling the other's "inner" state, such as hurt or anger (i.e., the other's feeling must emotionally resonate).

- Second, one must have the intellectual acumen to cognitively conceptualize the hurt or anger as, in fact, hurt or anger – that is, to abstract this empathically-derived knowledge from the other's experienced feelings.
- Third, one must be able to use the empathically derived knowledge as the basis for an empathic response to, and for, the other.
- And last, one must be capable of a fleeting role identification, of putting one's feet in the other's shoes (Akhtar, 2009, p. 93).

Thus, without the well-developed capacity to understand and appreciate the other qua other – that is, firstly for his sake rather than with a self-serving agenda – the narcissist who is a boss, manager or leader will not be able to compassionately and effectively interact with subordinates.[12] In short, he has the mindset of any close-minded fundamentalist who is "stuck in one truth," that he is the only one who matters (Friedman, 2015, p. A23).

To make matters even more challenging and unpleasant for subordinates, when narcissistic bosses have been frustrated in actualizing wishes for power and prestige, they may not become briefly depressed or feel a sense of personal failure as with ordinary reasonable people, but rather assume a more paranoid way of being, which can make organizational life that much more dysfunctional and unbearable for subordinates. Not only do narcissistic leaders ignore and disregard their realistic functions as leader and administrator in an organization, including being properly responsive to the human needs, wishes and values of those they are leading, but they are also entirely unaware that they are doing so; and most often they are unconscious of having created a constellation of pathological relationships of people, tactics and ideas that negatively ripple throughout the organizational culture and create a highly toxic emotional environment (Kernberg, 1979, p. 33; Zaleznik, 1984, p. 309).

This observation should not be surprising given the fact that empirical researchers like Penney and Spector (2002, p. 126) found that narcissism was positively correlated with deviant or counterproductive work behaviors (CWBs). CWBs are actions intended to harm the organization or its members, such as stealing, sabotage, relational aggression, work slowdowns, wasting time and/or materials and disseminating rumors. Narcissists are also more at ease with ethically dubious sales practices because they feel less obligated to organizational rules, guidelines and property (Judge et al., 2006, p. 76). Destructive narcissists express their narcissistic rage via deviance and CWBs (Penney & Spector, 2002, p. 133). This "emotional contagion," as social psychologists call this tendency to feel and express emotions similar to and influenced by those of others, when animated by the perverse needs, wishes and behavior of a narcissistic boss, is near lethal in terms of its negative impact on the subordinates' moods, motivations and productivity.

Ironically, not only do narcissistic managers and leaders demand the psychological subjugation of their subordinates, they paradoxically also want to be loved and admired by them. Thus, those who interact with them recognize that the only way for them to stay out of the "line of fire," as it were, to feel relatively psychologically safe as an employee, is to approach the boss in a submissive manner that makes him feel thoroughly adulated. Subordinates learn quickly to "lay it on like a trowel," that "flattery will get you every-where" when it comes to interacting with a narcissistic superior. Indeed, like the ancient Greeks who viewed flattery as a base form of companionship, the Axial-inspired Spinoza recognized its tactical advantage in certain challenging interpersonal situations: "None are more taken in by flattery than the proud who wish to be the first and are not."[13]

As a result of this self-aggrandizing outlook, the narcissist only promotes the careers of junior staff and administration to the extent that it is self-serving; and when the juniors want to become more professionally independent and autonomous, or they appear to be edging close to the narcissistic boss's level of success, he can become ruthless in his efforts to put the juniors down and undermine their successful career trajectory. For example, a narcissistic manager who envies a more qualified coworker may seriously overstate and broadcast the coworker's inconsequential failings while simultaneously greatly playing down important accomplishments. Even more pathetic, while the narcissist may envy the junior colleagues for their deep inner convictions and professional and human values (his envy being partially a consequence of the above-mentioned superficial moral outlook), his resentment undermines any fragments of those convictions and values that he himself may have (Kern-berg, 1979, pp. 34, 35), leaving him feeling even more empty, enraged and retaliatory. An anonymous saying highlights this point: "Resentment is like drinking poison and waiting for the other person to die."

As a consequence of the narcissist's need for continuous ego "stroking" and to feel safe and secure within the organization, the narcissist tends to sur-round himself with a staff of weak people who always agree with him. This is because the narcissistic boss tends to envelop himself with people he uncon-sciously regards as reflected images of himself drawn from infantile experi-ences (Zaleznik, 1984, p. 236). Such sycophants have learned to "play" their boss in a way that satisfies his narcissistic needs while also subtly promoting the manipulative underlings' personal "agenda" for advancement. In a sense, the narcissist surrounds himself with other narcissists operating on a lower register, with people who can happily dwell in such a noxious emotional cli-mate as they share similar psychological characteristics, which can ironically include a self-promoting propensity for betrayal. As the great Taoist philoso-pher Chuang Tzu noted, "I have heard that those who are fond of praising men to their faces are also fond of damning them behind their backs."[14]

As a result of surrounding himself with those who agree with him, staff members and administrators who would provide more truthful, constructively critical and helpful feedback to enhance the organization are relegated to the margins and can become a disenfranchised "fifth column" that, in a variety of unconscious ways, tends to undermine the healthy and wholesome aspects of the organizational culture. Usually, the narcissistic boss senses there are rebellious forces at work in the organization, which can bring out paranoid tendencies and mean-spirited behavior that further create a poisonous emotional environment. Thus, the narcissistic boss may fall into a dire state of mind, as he cannot discern constructive criticism from often imagined menacing rumblings. As the Axial-influenced Emerson noted in his journal, "Let me never fall into the vulgar mistake of dreaming that I am persecuted whenever I am contradicted" (1984, p. 206). Paradoxically, the resentment that the narcissist boss feels when criticized is experienced unconsciously as proof that he deserved the criticism, further fueling his hurt and outrage. Needless to say, having to work with and for such an obsessively anxious, unreasonably suspicious boss is nothing short of nightmarish.

Kernberg makes the important point that the more the administrative structure of an organization becomes corrupted by the narcissist's perverse leadership needs and typical defenses, such as his use of splitting, primitive dissociation of the ego and projective identification,[15] "the more compensating mechanisms may develop in the form of breakdown of boundary control and boundary negotiations so that the institutional functions may actually go 'underground'" (1979, p. 35). In other words, the organization begins to unconsciously re-make itself in the image of narcissistic leaders' "crazy" internal object worlds, and their accumulated perceptions get disseminated such that the separation between self and other becomes very fuzzy (Kets de Vries & Miller, 1985, p. 590).

Narcissists mainly relate to others as extensions of themselves, so what they want and expect from others must be satisfied; if not, the other does not exist. Reasonable boundaries and limits that define us from others and foster a modicum of personal integrity and wholesome organizational culture tend to give way to warped emotions and reactions, distorted perceptions, questionable moral values, dubious goals and concerns, and alienating and destructive social roles. As it says in the great fourth-century Taoist text of practical living, the *Lieh Tzu*, you must abandon the acquisition of wealth if you want integrity, and if you are unwilling to do so, you must accept that you will have given up your integrity in the pursuit of wealth. Gone is the sense of psychological safety that is correlated with having a relatively clear self-definition.[16] Social order within the organization tends to become eroded, which causes confusion about one's relationships to others, and that all-important sense of empowerment that we derive from reasonable boundaries regarding how we will be treated by others becomes seriously compromised.[17] In such an amorphously "sick" emotional environment where behavior that causes individual and collective harm is commonplace, it is nearly impossible for an individual or organization to function properly, especially when most of what emotionally and practically "really matters" to the individual and organization is clandestine.

Take, for example, the narcissistic boss's use of defensive splitting, defined as "the separating of positive feelings and perceptions, either toward the self or toward others, from negative feelings and perceptions so that the self and object is seen as either 'all good' or 'all bad'" (Person et al., 2005, p. 560). While there are many subtleties to the various formulations of the confusing concept of splitting in the psychoanalytic literature, Kernberg notes:

> [The] defensive division of the ego, in which what was at first [in the infantile ego] a simple defect in integration [of distinguishing the pleasurable and unpleasurable] is then used actively for other purposes [like managing anxiety and maintaining self-esteem], is in essence the mechanism of splitting.
>
> (Akhtar, 2009, p. 270)

Consider how horrible it would be to have to work with a boss where the defensive use of splitting is a common occurrence: the narcissistic boss has an inability to relate to you with any ambivalence or ambiguity; he cannot reside in the "gray zone," the psychic space of half-tints where most of us as fallible and flawed humans live the majority of the time. Rather, you are judged as either "all good," such as supportive and kind, or "all bad," such as rejecting and mean-spirited.

The narcissist runs his interpersonal world demanding loyalty and devotion: "Are you with me, or against me?" is his mantra, as winning is all that matters. Such a boss has major fluctuations in his confidence; his self-esteem and self-respect are insecurely anchored in any robust narrative of self-identity and dearly held beliefs and values. Narcissistic bosses are prone to intense expression of feelings, both negative and positive, which are hard for subordinates to metabolize and reasonably manage. Narcissistic bosses tend to make decisions without adequate consequential thinking because their sense of omnipotence leads them to believe that they will always get it right. Rather than focusing on working through the details of a work project, they are only interested in the grand scheme that prevents projects from coming to fruition (Lubit, 2002, p. 130). Moreover, their lack of impulse control in relations with others does not register as something problematic, let alone guilt-inducing vis-à-vis the other when they get things wrong (ibid.). To make matters worse, most of the time narcissists are unconscious of how they use splitting in a myriad of destructively self-regulative ways. They do not realize that their self-referential perceptions are gross distortions of social reality, which leaves the subordinate with no reasonable person with whom concerns may be expressed or conflicts resolved. In such a context, for the sake of self-preservation, the underling tends to frequently behave fraudulently, if not becoming something of an imposter in his overall way of relating to his boss, coworkers and, worst of all, to himself, eroding his sense of self-respect and personal dignity.

The narcissistic boss's use of projective identification makes organizational life feel even more "crazy" for the subordinate than his use of splitting.

Similar to splitting, projective identification is a confusing and complex notion in the psychoanalytic literature, though a serviceable definition for our purposes is "a fantasy in which one inserts oneself, or part of oneself, into an instinctual object [i.e., a person invested with powerful emotional significance] in order to posses it, control it, or harm it" (Colman, 2009, p. 607). Most importantly perhaps, projective identification always commences with the denial and rejection of troubling emotions lodged in a person's unconscious fantasy of a situation (Krantz & Gilmore, 1991, p. 309). Projective identification can have its positive role in child and adult development (e.g., it can be a mode of communication and the basis of empathy). It also has important defensive functions. Projective identification shields the projector from an unpleasant feature of his own self-experience, including fusing with an external object (i.e., a real person, place or thing that he has invested with psychic energy and suffused with emotional significance) in order to avoid painful separation; control of the destructive "bad object" (i.e., the split-off, frustrating and hated part of the self that has been projected onto the object, the other). This "bad object" is experienced as a menacing, persecutory threat to the person's survival. The safeguarding of "good," gratifying and loved aspects of the self are split off and projectively deposited and identified in the sheltering other for "safe keeping" (Moore & Fine, 1990, p. 109).

The most troubling relational aspect of projective identification for the target is that powerful feelings are evoked, giving him the unsettling sense that he has been inhabited by the projective element, which most often in the narcissist's case is a "bad" feeling that needs to be jettisoned, like envy or hatred. It is as if the target has been taken over by something like a "dybbuk," which in Jewish folklore is a malevolent spirit of a dead person, a demon believed capable of taking over a living person's body and controlling his behavior unless exorcised by a religious ceremony. As I have indicated, in projective identification the projector identifies with the target person, and thus can control the target while also unconsciously pressuring the target to play out the designated role to gratify the projector's infantile wishes and/or sinister needs. For example, a dependent boss may insinuate that he needs assistance, even though he does not actually require it, and the target complies with his subtle demand, thus manipulated by the control of the "dependent" boss. An angry or depressed boss may accuse the target of being angry or depressed to such a degree that he actually becomes angry or depressed. A boss who feels "crazy" may relentlessly accuse the target of being "crazy" (he projects his "crazy" thoughts and feelings into the other), with the aim of making the target believe that he is in fact "crazy." Such manipulation of a person by psychological tactics into doubting their own sanity is called "gaslighting." Likewise, the narcissist's lack of moral scruples and impressive "street smarts," the shrewd ability to survive hostile situations, allow him to engage in various forms of scapegoat behavior (Lubit, 2002, p. 129). Finally, Kets de Vries cites another good example of projective identification involving a high-level group of business executives in a department. First, they deny or reject (and thus downwardly modify) a painful experience to their self-concept and self-esteem by fantasizing that it belongs to another group of executives. The other group, the recipients of the projection, are then drawn into the situation and induced by subtle pressure from the first group to feel, think and act in accordance with the received projection (2011, p. 38).

It is worth noting that one of the appealingly seductive qualities of the narcissist, at least initially, is that he often exudes great powers of charm and influence. While the digital revolution has undeniably "sped up, flattened out and depersonalized communication," and the capacity for charm, the power or quality of giving delight or arousing admiration, has for the most part "become a lost language and forgotten skill," the narcissist has honed his ability "to entrance/allure/captivate" someone else in order to manipulatively win them over (Doonan, 2015, p. 10). Such charisma can have a short-term positive impact on subordinates and organizations since the heightened personal expansiveness, if not grandiosity, of the narcissist can stimulate excitement and prompt an upsurge of fleeting productivity in employees and organizations. However, such temporary individual and collective enhancement gives way to the pathological aspects of the narcissist's way of being with others, a mode of comportment that demands dependency, compliance and agreement.

In such a subjugating emotional environment, there is little motivation or opportunity for worker creativity, innovation or other kinds of autonomously driven change. Due to the prevalence of the narcissist's powerful conscious and unconscious envy, tendency to diminish and denigrate others, lack of "deep" moral values and his insatiable need for novelty and high-octane excitement that is a defense against affective self-awareness, he is not able to satisfy the reasonable dependency needs of those around him, such as for compassionate listening, responsibly helping workers with their realistic problems and concerns, and affirming the subordinates' wishes for approval and warm relations. Moreover, from the organizational point of view, when employees feel unsupported, the collective tends to split into two groups, "the submissive and dependent ingroup and the depressed and angry outgroup" (Kernberg, 1979, p. 36). When there is an ingroup – a cohesive, closed, social unit that fosters preferential treatment for its members and emphasizes loyalty among them and to their narcissistic boss – and an outgroup – one that is different from one's own that is most often an object of hostility or abhorrence – something resembling a psychological "war zone" has been co-produced, and the integrity, functionality and creativity of an organization becomes seriously compromised.

Before I discuss the difficult problem of how one can individually "manage" and organizationally "contain" a destructive narcissistic boss, manager or leader (Lubit, 2002), I want to round out my portrait of a narcissist by mentioning some of these different narcissistic "subtypes." While there are many similarities to how a "destructive narcissist" (ibid.) behaves, there are some subtle differences in their way of being that are worth distinguishing.

Kets de Vries and Miller and Lapierre characterize the unconscious fantasies that animate three types of narcissistic leaders, each with a different experience of their early parenting: The most severe kind and the most difficult leader to work with is the "reactive narcissist." He fantasizes, "I was let down and I deserve to be compensated; I have special rights" (Kets de Vries & Miller, 1985, pp. 591). Such a leader comes into being mainly as a result of parenting that consistently lacked attunement, meaning his parental caregivers were emotionally unresponsive and rejecting. The "self-deceptive" narcissist fantasizes, "I was so favored that I must be (or I am) perfect" (ibid., p. 592). This sort of person was encouraged by their delusional parents to believe this, regardless of their contrary behavior and lack of supportive evidence of their child's alleged god-like state. The "constructive narcissist" that is equated with "normal" or "healthy" narcissism has the fantasy, "I have special talents that allow me to make an impression on the world, but I have to deal with my personal limitations and those imposed by external reality" (ibid., p. 593; Lapierre, 1991, p. 73). Such a person is blessed with a "good-enough mother" (that is, an effective parental caregiver). As Winnicott described it, such a mother calls to mind a master gardener: "The good-enough mother ... starts off with an almost complete adaptation to her infant's needs, and as time proceeds she adapts less and less completely, gradually, according to the infant's growing ability to deal with her failure" (Winnicott, 1953, p. 94). Moreover, "this active adaptation demands an easy and unresented preoccupation with the one infant; in fact, success in infant-care depends on the fact of devotion, not on cleverness or intellectual enlightenment" (ibid.). As a result of such parental attunement, understanding and support, the child develops a robust sense of self-esteem and self-confidence (ibid.). The "structural cohesiveness, temporal stability, and positive affective coloring of the self-representation" are the hallmarks of the "constructive narcissist" (Stolorow, 1975, p. 198).

### *"Strategic" tips for coping with the narcissistic boss, manager or leader*

A narcissistic boss is very challenging to effectively manage, especially for a subordinate. The greatest military strategist of all times, who lived during the Axial Age, Sun Tzu, advised in his famous *Art of War* the following: "Anciently the skillful warriors first made themselves invincible [they put themselves beyond the possibility of defeat] and awaited the enemy's moment of vulnerability" (Tzu, 1963, p. 85). Indeed, such advice is entirely compatible with the recommendations of contemporary organizational psychologists – that is, the best way of containing the narcissistic boss is to keep your distance. Lubit advises that "moving to another position within the company in order to avoid the destructive narcissist manager is generally the best long-term strategy" (2002, p. 137). However, once a subordinate has moved out of the psychologically uninhabitable position, the competent subordinate is more threatening to the narcissistic manager and is someone he wants to undercut or retaliate against. As Sun Tzu explained, "It is a doctrine of war not to assume the enemy will not come, but rather to rely on one's readiness to meet him; not to presume that he will not attack, but rather to make's one's self invincible" (1963, p. 114). Thus, the subordinate should report to his new superiors verbally and in writing how he and coworkers have been poorly treated (preferably with coworkers since there is strength and protection in numbers; Lubit, 2002, p. 137).

Savvy subordinates have learned the triggers of a narcissistic boss and do their best to stay away from them. Self-protection becomes his touchstone and his "victory" in the larger "war." "Thus," said Sun Tzu, "those skilled in war subdue the enemy's army without battle" (1963, p. 114). For example, subordinates have learned that gossiping or casual conversations that are not carefully thought through can later go wrong in unanticipated ways for the subordinate. Borrowing something from a narcissistic boss, or lending him something, is likely to put the subordinate in harm's way. It is best to get written directives from the boss rather than rely on verbal ones since narcissists are prone to self-servingly interpret ambiguous information at the expense of the subordinate. Getting important information in writing reduces the uncertainty and chance that a complaint will be lodged against the subordinate. It is important for the subordinate to carefully document his work to protect himself from possible allegation of failings or wrongdoings on the job.

This documentation can be very useful when you have to defend yourself to higher-ups who, in most cases, are psychologically and organizationally allied with superiors rather than subordinates (Lubit, 2002, p. 137). As Sun Tzu emphasized, "All warfare is based on deception," and therefore, the subordinate must be "Subtle and insubstantial, the expert leaves no trace; divinely mysterious, he is inaudible. Thus he is master of his enemy's fate" (1963, pp. 66, 92). Advised Sun Tzu, "He who knows when he can fight and when he cannot will be victorious" (ibid, p. 82). Indeed, a narcissistic boss is not willing and able to have a reasonable give-and-take discussion about something that is troubling a subordinate. This is in part because they are markedly intolerant of hearing, let alone effectively metabolizing, constructive criticism and taking self-corrective action.

Similarly, with their truncated ties to empathy, the narcissistic boss is prone to say nasty things to a subordinate who wants to raise an interpersonal or other problem that implicates the boss. Taking to heart what a narcissistic boss says to or about a subordinate can be psychologically lethal in terms of maintaining emotional equipoise, just as is getting into a quarrel or lively discussion with them can be futile, if not dangerous, in terms of the narcissist's tendency to engage in punitive retaliation like making the subordinate look bad to others. "Pretend inferiority and encourage his arrogance," said Sun Tzu (ibid., p. 67). Such a strategy will not only keep the subordinate out of harm's way, but it is also the condition of psychological possibility for the narcissistic boss to make mistakes on which the subordinate can capitalize.

"Invincibility [defense] depends on one's self; the enemy's vulnerability on him," observed Sun Tzu (ibid., p. 85). Thus, the opportunity to protect ourselves against the narcissistic boss lies in our own hands, but the opportunity of vanquishing him is provided by the narcissist himself. Sensible advice on how to best manage a narcissistic coworker (and, with some nuancing, a boss) includes setting clear and consistent boundaries with them. For example, a narcissist coworker who enters your office and borrows things without your consent needs to be firmly but skillfully held accountable. Likewise, such destructive narcissists frequently expect favors but almost never do them in return, and this should not be taken personally. Coworkers who are prone to give instructions as if they were in fact your superiors need to be effectively challenged. Narcissistic coworkers are also willing and able to steal your good ideas, so put ideas in writing to superiors before sharing them with coworkers. Finally, if a coworker tells you that the boss wants you to do something, first request clarification about what your tasks and responsibilities are from your boss, for such coworkers are known "to play fast and loose" with the truth (Lubit, 2002, p. 137). While "invincibility lies in the defence," said Sun Tzu, "the possibility of victory is in the attack" (1963, p. 85). Moreover, "When the strike of a hawk breaks the body of its prey, it is because of timing" (ibid., p. 92). Forcefully confronting the coworker when he least expects it about his taking liberties with your belongings, stealing your ideas or self-servingly lying about what your boss said will usually deter such future acts of aggression.

Most importantly, when dealing with the hostile and degrading words and actions of a destructive narcissistic boss or coworker, one should keep in mind the self-protective insight embedded in Sartre's explanation of his often misinterpreted statement from *No Exit* mentioned earlier in this chapter, "hell is other people." Namely, there are dangers to comprehending oneself through one's own comprehension of the perception that others may have of them. The "take home" point of Sartre's insight is that when dealing with a narcissist, the overarching goal is to do the best you can to never align yourself with anyone else's description of yourself. If you relinquish responsibility for your own self-definition and behavior, you will lose your "inner center of gravity" and will be left to the mercy of others' judgments and opinions. In the case of the narcissistic boss, this leads to an orgy of disorder and interpersonal hell. Indeed, Sun Tzu had a similar view, but added a point that personifies the best of the Axial outlook – namely, that by living by "higher" values, those that are other-directed, other-regarding and other-serving, you not only insulate yourself against personal assault but, paradoxically, you are often affirmed by others:

And therefore the general who is advancing does not seek personal fame, and in withdrawing is not concerned with avoiding punishment [fearing disgrace], but whose only purpose is to protect the people and promote the best interests of the sovereign, is the precious jewel of the state.

(Tzu, 1963, p. 128)

## The irrational work group

"In individuals, insanity is rare," said Nietzsche in *Beyond Good and Evil*, "but in groups, parties, nations, and epochs, it is the rule" (Christian, 2012, p. 494). While less pithy in his formulation, Freud made a similar point:

Some of [a group's] features – the weakness of intellectual ability, the lack of emotional restraint, the incapacity for moderation and delay, the inclination to exceed every limit in the expression of emotion and to work it off completely in the form of actions – these and similar features ... show an unmistakable picture of a regression of mental activity to an earlier stage such as we are not surprised to find among savages or children.

(1955, p. 117)

Indeed, given the emotional environment of the work world today with its cutthroat rivalries and competition, the more limited nature of important resources and the amplified financial accountability (Youssef & Luthans, 2010, p. 285), it is not surprising that there has been an upsurge of the use of team-based working in organizations (a 2001 survey indicated that 72 percent of Fortune 1000 companies use teams; Aamodt, 2007, p. 490). Compared to individuals working in isolation, "teams can integrate and link to produce synergies that individuals cannot," often leading to "outstanding productivity and innovation" (Richardson & West, 2010, pp. 235, 236). However, while teams can help streamline inefficient processes, expand and deepen employee participation, improve quality and create a positive sense of a shared accountability in which employees are both individually responsible but share in rewards and losses (Twenge & Campbell, 2010, p. 30), teams also frequently get "off track," sometimes pathologically, and it is this aspect of team functioning and its negative impact, if not "suffering," of the individual trying to flourish, to create the "good life" in the workplace, on which I will focus.[18]

The psychology of work literature has empirically demonstrated what tends to bring about optimal team or small group functioning in the workplace. As summarized by researchers Richardson and West (2010, p. 246):

1   Teams have an inspiring task and clear objectives.

2    Team members are clear about their roles and those of their team colleagues.
3    Teams have an autonomy and authority to decide the means of accomplishing their objectives.
4    Teams regularly review their performance and how it can be improved.
5    Teams have an excellent team leader who has the skills to develop effective team processes.

These practical guidelines are helpful for the successful implementation of team-based working, including increasing group cohesion, the building of positive relationships, and the accelerated expansion and deepening of creativity and personal growth (Sole, 2006, p. 805). When one gets down to the "nuts and bolts" of implementing these five guidelines, one realizes that it is much easier said than done. Individuals working as part of a team or other kind of small group have tremendous resistance to rationally approaching their tasks and collaboratively implementing sensible and realistic procedures to accomplish their goals. There are mostly unconscious, irrational forces at work that tend to undermine, if not obliterate, that wonderful human capacity for combined action of a group that is effective and efficient. High levels of intra-team conflict, such as frequent and intense disagreements, tensions and personal frustrations, can characterize teams that get "off track." In fact, according to an organizational psychology researcher, "The scientific literature suggests that teams are seldom more effective than individuals" (Aamodt, 2007, p. 495).

Before reviewing the details of some of these destructive processes that impede successful teamwork, I want to summarize what is probably the single most important psychoanalytic theoretical contribution to understanding small group processes, namely, the work of Wilfred R. Bion. Bion's descriptions in *Experiences in Groups* (1959) of the primitive defenses, object relations and anxieties that can implode a group's high-level functioning have become "classic" in the psychology of group processes (Kernberg, 1998, pp. 92–93). Moreover, his work on groups is regarded as "a cornerstone of the study of organizational dynamics" (Kets de Vries, 2011, p. 32). This is especially noteworthy as his observations and formulations relate to a sub-specialty of psychotherapy – group psychotherapy, a field that has greatly contributed to the psychoanalytic understanding of both small and large group processes, dynamics and psychopathology. Ironically, group psychotherapy is a field that is currently characterized by "theoretical confusion and contradiction in both theory and practice ... [and is] bewildering in its diversity" (Nitsun, 2015, p. 63).

### Bion's view of small group behavior

Bion defines his famous basic group assumptions as "the capacity of the individual for instantaneous combination with other individuals in an established pattern of behavior" (1959, p. 160). In other words, basic assumptions are the unconscious group dynamics, the "common, agreed upon, and anonymous obedience prevalent in a group at a given time" (Akhtar, 2009, p. 33). When a group is lodged in a basic assumption, its capacity to work efficiently and effectively is seriously compromised, often leading to more primitive, archaic and infantile modes of behavior that make the realistic business of the team nearly impossible to reasonably engage in. Bion describes three types of basic assumption – dependency, fight-flight and pairing – though others have formulated fourth, fifth and sixth assumptions: namely, "oneness" (Turquet, 1975), further elaborated as "incohesion: aggregation/massification" (Hopper, 2003); "Me-ness" (Lawrence et al., 1996); and "violent destructive aggression" mainly expressed in large groups (Roth, 2013, p. 527). These latter three assumptions have not "caught on" in small group theory the way Bion's three assumptions have, and Nitsun raises the criticism that any conceptualization of basic assumptions tends to create "confusion and overlap ... between different versions of assumptions" as well as arbitrary "fixed polarities" that do not do justice to the real-life complexity and fluidity of group process (2015, p. 243).

The first of Bion's assumptions, dependency, "is that the group is met in order to be sustained by a leader on whom it depends for nourishment, material and spiritual, and protection" (1959, p. 132). This basic assumption thus postulates a "collective belief in a protective deity, leader, or organization that will always provide security for the group" (Akhtar, 2009, p. 33). For example, the group leader may ask a thought-provoking question, only to be received by the members with passive silence, as if he had not spoken at all. The leader may be idealized into something of an omnipotent and omniscient god who can perfectly look after his docile children, a role that certain types of zealous leaders may be prone to assuming. However, resentment at being dependent on the god-like leader may gradually stimulate in the group members the wish to depose the leader, and then look for a new leader, only to repeat the destructive process.[19]

As Kets de Vries points out, groups that are under the sway of the dependency assumption seek out a charismatic leader because, like small children, they feel helpless, inadequate and needy, and are afraid of the external world. In such groups, one frequently hears statements like "What do you want me/us to do?" or "I can't take this kind of decision; you'll have to talk to my boss." Moreover, while group cohesiveness and goal directedness may be keen in such groups, for the most part the group is not capable of autonomy, criticality or creativity. Even when the leader has left the group and they can, in principle, independently grow and develop, they tend to reside in a retrospective consciousness, fantasizing about what the long-lost leader/parent would have done in a decision-making situation if he still was the leader of the group. In such instances, the group may fall back on bureaucratic inactivity and apathy and, thus, function without a trace of initiative or innovation (Kets de Vries, 2011, p. 33).

The fight-flight group assumption "is that the group has met to fight something or to run away from it. It is prepared to do either indifferently" (Bion, 1959, p. 138). In other words, the group believes in "the existence of an external enemy who one must vanquish or avoid" (Akhtar, 2009, p. 33). An important characteristic of this group culture is that it puts into sharp focus the individual with "paranoid trends," causing the work world to be divided into those who are loved friends and hated enemies, an "us-versus-them" outlook (Bion, 1959, p. 63; Kets de Vries, 2011, p. 33). As Kets de Vries notes, fight responses are expressed in aggressive behavior against the colleagues, bosses or the self. "Envy, jealousy, competition, elimination, boycotting, sibling rivalry, fighting for a position in the groups and privileged relationships with authority figures" are typical reactions in this group culture (2011, p. 33). Flight reactions may include avoidance of colleagues, managers and bosses, absenteeism and an overall comportment of having given up caring. Common remarks of such groups are "Let's not give those updated figures to the contracts department; they'll just try to take all the credit" and "This company would be in good shape if it weren't for the so-and-sos who run the place." In addition, there is a lack of embracing of individual responsibility in such groups; rather, there is a marked tendency to project and externalize, blaming others for one's mistakes or for the team's lack of success. In such groups there is an inevitable strengthening of group cohesion and identity and increased dependence on a strong, charismatic leader who self-righteously fosters this "you are either with us, or against us" way of thinking, and further "fires up" group members to adhere to their irrational group mentality (ibid.).

Finally, we come to the pairing group assumption, "the opposite pole to feelings of hatred, destructiveness, and despair" that may exist in fight-flight group cultures, what Bion describes as "the air of the hopeful expectation." The function of the pairing group "is to provide an outlet for feelings centered on ideas of breeding and birth, that is to say for Messianic hope … a precursor to sexual desire," and "without ever arousing the fear that such feelings will give rise to an event that will demand development" (1959, pp. 136, 143). Thus, the pairing basic assumption expresses "the Messianic hope that someone from the future generations will solve the problems of the group" (Akhtar, 2009, p. 33). As Kets de Vries notes, the pairing assumption is a way for an individual group member to connect to a perceived powerful other, a colleague, manager or boss, and assist him in effectively managing his "anxiety, alienation and loneliness." Not only does such a tactic provide a modicum of safety and security, it also satisfies the fantasy that by connecting with a powerful other, individual and collective creativity will magically upsurge.

This being said, when there is pairing, there is a loss of group integrity in that sub-groups emerge via the splitting up process and create both intra- and inter-group disagreements, including ganging up against, even bullying, the designated aggressor, whether they are a colleague, manager or boss. In high-tech companies, for example, where there is a tendency toward individuals maintaining grandiose notions, the paring assumption leads to an under-playing of feasibility and profitability in favor of co-produced fantasies of creative breakthroughs and innovation. In pairing assumption teams, one typically hears statements like "Leave it to the two of us, we can solve this problem" or "If only the CEO and COO had a better relationship our company would be in really good shape" (Kets de Vries, 2011, pp.33, p. 34).

The main thrust of Bion's contribution to the psychology of small group process, including team-based working, is that when the group is under the sway of one of the basic assumptions, it cannot reasonably think, so it becomes "psychotic, albeit temporarily," engaging in "patterns of psychotic behavior" (Lawrence et al., 1996, p. 119; Bion, 1959, p. 165). For example, there are severe impairments in representing, mentalizing, remembering and acknowledging, mainly because the group's tendencies for direct hallucinatory gratification of early developmental wishes for safety and security have a strong interpretive grip on the group process (Roth, 2013, pp. 535, 527). That is, Bion's brilliant two-tier psychology of the small group shows how the internal mental state of the group, the "group culture," together resonates with particular primordial unconscious anxieties and fantasies that greatly hinder and obstruct the efficient and effective "surface" work of productivity of any type of rationally conceived group function (ibid., p. 526). Bion calls the standard, normative group structures that promote adaptation to reality, that are instantiated by the accomplishment of realistic group goals and gratify the members' reasonable needs, the "work group culture." As I have suggested, the "work group culture," specifically within a team context, is vulnerable to assault from many perspectives. It is to this subject that I now briefly turn.

### Common problems in team-based working

Trust – that firm belief in the reliability, truth, ability and/or strength of one's coworkers and leader – is perhaps most important for a team to function efficiently, effectively and happily. (In teams there is the designated team leader, the facilitator, but in actuality, psychologically speaking, there are often many leaders depending on the issue, the group process and other contextual factors.) Trust – and its sister interpersonal quality, mutual respect – fosters a sense of group psychological safety, an important precondition for good teamwork. This emotional and social need for trust is rooted in the human propensity for positive attachments in relationships and a sense of belonging. Without trust between and among team members not much productive work can get accomplished, for mutual trust brings about a team's willingness and ability to venture out of their comfort zone and engage in risk-taking behavior, consider novel venues and implement helpful interventions that both maintain team cohesion and integrity and advance performance. Trust, especially of those who are different in background and knowledge, is especially relevant in fostering team performance excellence in decision-making. Research has demonstrated that a demographically varied team, one that values diverse perspectives and experiences, is "more creative in their decision-making" (Richardson & West, 2010, pp. 236, 243, 238).[20] Without intra-group trust and mutual respect, the twin pillars of group safety and security, members are quite likely to "suffer" through their team experience.

One of the main causes of the absence of trust in a team is the lack of clear communication. Clear communication has been niftily formulated in terms of "the 7 Cs" – clear, concise, concrete, correct, coherent, complete and courteous.[21] Not only is clear communication a precondition for developing trust, but it also promotes a more far-reaching rapport, that all-important emotional bond and friendly relation between people lodged in trust, mutual liking and a sense that they understand and share each other's concerns. Extrapolating from Erikson's first stage of psychosocial development, when the team leader(s), the symbolic parental presence, does not provide adequate "maternal" care – that is, he operates in a way that is emotionally and practically unreliable, unclear or frustrating – he induces in the group the unconscious proclivity toward pessimism, withdrawal, lack of faith and paranoia (Akhtar, 2009, p. 35).

"If you want to build a ship," said Antoine de Saint-Exupéry, the author of the wonderful novella *The Little Prince* (1943), "don't drum up people together to collect wood and don't assign them tasks and work, but rather teach them to long for the endless immensity of the sea" (qtd. in Von Stamm & Trifilova, 2009, p. 17). Indeed, another major problem in teams is that there is no inspiring task, one that puts forth a noble and ennobling vision that group members can cognitively and emotionally identity with and justify working hard to actualize. As Richardson and West succinctly note, regardless of the particular goals, it is vital that the tasks through which they are accomplished offer "challenge, opportunities for growth, and a sense of self-efficacy" (2010, p. 238). Self-efficacy is an individual's belief in his capacity to implement behaviors required to generate specific performance attainments. High levels of self-efficacy indicate a person's confidence in his capacity to control his own motivation, behavior and social context. Thus, boring and deadening team tasks are lethal to a high-level team performance. Tasks that provide an opportunity for "personal growth, achievement, and recognition" promote performance excellence (ibid.). Unless a team member feels that the work they are engaged in is meaningful and purposeful in terms of their deeply held values, they are unlikely to generate the motivation to work efficiently, effectively and creatively. Research has shown that team members who are "intrinsically motivated," who are propelled by internal rewards, show "more interest, persistence, creativity, and enhanced performance" (ibid., p. 238).

One of the major obstacles in efficient and effective team functioning is lack of clarity about individual roles, responsibilities and goals as the team's work progresses. As the team is a developing group process, one that is context-dependent and setting-specific, each team member must have their role, responsibilities and goals frequently updated and fine-tuned depending on what is needed and wanted by the group and personally doable. Moreover, this updating must always be guided by principles of fairness, equality and respect for individual autonomy. The more skillful this critical negotiation of the individual's changing role is, and the more the role is tailored to foster personal growth and development, the more likely that the team member will be motivated to work hard and well. When this is happening, the group synergy leads to greater team efficiency and effectiveness, mainly because team members are happier with what they are doing (ibid., p. 239). As Aristotle noted, "Pleasure in the job puts perfection in the work" (qtd. in Schmelzer, 2006, p. 447).

While the above point appears rather obvious, at least theoretically speaking, the fact is that it is enormously difficult to consistently implement a reasonable group process of updating and fine-tuning the individual's role. Team members are often derailed from focusing on realistic and important issues related to increased individual productivity because unresolved conflicts between and among them, both before the team has been established and during meetings, are at play. In this context, unresolved issues of power, status, prestige and competition, and other neurotic individual needs and wishes, get in the way of making timely and sensible decisions and engaging in a "work group culture" (Kets de Vries, 2011, p. 49).

In "power hoarding," the team is controlled by a few individuals such that those in power are more focused on "winning" than in effective problem-solving, while those who are on the losing end or are outside of the power grab become apathetic and/or function in the group as docile bystanders, often keeping their "real" opinions and feelings about important issues private. As a result of this dysfunctional group configuration, premature, ill-conceived and ill-fated decisions may be made. This includes disgruntled team members undermining decisions and their implementation in a variety of overt and covert, conscious and unconscious ways (ibid., p. 50).

In a similar way, status differences in teams may erode group functioning effectiveness. If, for instance, one member is a specialist compared to the other members, his deference-conferred role in decision-making about a particular issue will be less inclined toward inclusive group process. Lower-status team members may begin to question their ability to thoughtfully contribute to the group. They tend to inordinately monitor, limit and censor their input in the constructive group process, often leading to premature, poorly thought through agreement among the team members. In addition, sometimes hidden agendas may be enacted among the team, with lower-status members being more focused on "looking good" to a senior team member than with engaging in realistic problem-solving and task completion (ibid.).

### Groupthink and group polarization

Irving Janis, the brilliant originator of the social psychological phenomenon known as "groupthink," began his investigation as part of the American Soldier Project. In his 1972 book *Victims of Groupthink: A Psychological Study of Foreign-Policy Decisions and Fiascoes*, Janis defined groupthink as "A mode of thinking that people engage in when they are deeply involved in a cohesive in-group, when the members' strivings for unanimity override their motivation to realistically appraise alternative courses of action" (pp. 8–9). Groupthink thus involves "a deterioration of mental efficiency, reality testing, and moral judgment." It is rooted in group pressures for conformity, compliance and the avoidance of anxiety and conflict.[22] Groupthink thus shuns opposing perspectives from being articulated and critically assessed, and it rejects non-traditional or innovative ideas. As a result of groupthink, premature, ill-conceived and ill-fated decisions are made. For example, Janis describes how groupthink led to disastrous foreign policy decisions such as the failure to expect and foresee the Japanese attack on Pearl Harbor, Hitler's decision to invade the Soviet Union, the Bay of Pigs invasion debacle and President Lyndon B. Johnson's ruinous prosecution of the Vietnam War. What makes groupthink a form of "suffering" is not only having to live with the horrendous consequences of bad decision-making; in addition, as with toxic radiation exposure, you don't feel it damaging you until it is too late.

While scholars have challenged some of Janis's formulations, and his theory has been further developed, many of his insights have stood the test of time. They deserve to be mentioned, for they highlight the dangers of how the average person makes "bad" decisions within the small group context that ultimately cause suffering. Janis outlines three conditions of possibility that tend to bring about groupthink: (1) a cohesive, like-minded and isolated group is sanctioned and authorized to make decisions; (2) independent and impartial leadership is missing inside or outside the group; and (3) there is pronounced stress on the group decision-making process to satisfy specific goals and objectives. He further described six symptoms of groupthink:

1 "closed-mindedness," where group members are averse to considering alternative points of view;
2 "rationalization," where group members make a great effort to defend and justify both the method and the result of the decision-making process, often twisting reality in the service of convincing others;
3 "squelching of dissent" – those who express contradictory viewpoints are disregarded, criticized or sometimes ostracized;
4 formation of a group "mindguard," where one self-appointed group member becomes the enforcer of the group's norms and ensures that others are compliant;

5   "feeling invulnerable," whereby the group members fantasize that they
    must be correct in what they are deciding given how smart they all are
    and the information to which they have access;
6   "feeling unanimous," where the group members have the conviction that
    the whole group has the same opinion.

As a result of these six group processes, there is a biased processing and evaluation of information alternatives. Moreover, risks are inadequately and insufficiently considered, as are contingency plans, leading to faulty decision-making.

Janis and others have suggested some practical counter-measures to
groupthink, such as the group leader fostering and encouraging a diversity of
viewpoints, constructive debate and criticism, and the leader withholding his
preferred view in the beginning. A group can also seek input from impartial,
independent others who are outside of the group and do not have a vested
interest in the result. A group can also divide itself into smaller sub-groups to
consider other options.

All of these tactics work against groupthink. As one of the devoted readers
of Sun Tzu and Axial military classics, General George S. Patton said, "If
everyone is thinking alike, someone isn't thinking" (Martin, 2006, p. 34).
There are other techniques that are used in group decision-making that,
depending on the task characteristics, can work against groupthink and other
negative group influences on decision-making, like production blocking and
evaluation apprehension. In general, these techniques encourage the generation of alternatives, debate and criticality: brainstorming, nominal group
technique, the Delphi technique and devil's advocacy, and dialectical inquiry
(Nelson & Quick, 2008, pp. 240–241).

Another form of "suffering" in a collective context is called "group polarization." This refers to the fact that within decision-making groups there is a
tendency, after interaction and discussion, for the group and individuals to
take more extreme positions, both in terms of risk-taking and cautiousness.
Moreover, research has shown that after discussion, group members who at
first opposed a subject become more radically against it, and members who
were in support of the subject become more aggressively supportive. In the
context of war and other comparably dangerous decision-making contexts,
this can be catastrophic. For example, if group members are inclined to make
riskier decisions in a dangerous context, they are more likely to be supportive
of doing so after interacting with other group members (Nelson & Quick,
2008, p. 239).[23] When, for example, soldiers with the same opinion about an
enemy spend most of their time interacting with each other, their opinions
tend to become considerably stronger and more extreme. Such a polarization
effect can have obvious detrimental effects on collective decision-making that,
like groupthink, can generate much suffering.

Organizational psychologists have recommended regular team meetings
that promote free, open and constructive critical discussion about realistic

issues, though these discussions must also be mindful of the irrational unconscious group processes that may be at play.[24] In addition, the encouragement of "positive, warm experiences and relationships in teams" can help its members to not be capsized by intra-group conflict (Richardson & West, 2010, p. 240). Needless to say, as Bion and his followers have so aptly pointed out, this is a lot easier said than done in light of the powerful hold that the irrational anxieties and archaic wishes have on all small groups. The extent to which team members are self-aware, self-critical, psychologically minded and emotionally committed to the group's flourishing has an impact on the likelihood that group processes will not become wayward for long periods of time. Perhaps most importantly, as the American author and international management consultant Ken Blanchard noted, "the productivity of a work group seems to depend on how the group members see their own goals in relation to the goals of the organization."[25] It is to this subject, the psychopathology of organizational life, that I now turn.

## The irrational organization

"An organization's ability to learn and translate that learning into action rapidly," said Jack Welch, former chairman and CEO of General Electric (GE), "is the ultimate competitive advantage" (Slater, 1988, p. 12). While Welch is putting his finger on one of the key elements that make for a successful organization – indeed, during his CEO tenure between 1981 and 2001 GE's value increased 4,000 percent – a psychoanalytic gloss on his observation suggests that this is a lot harder to accomplish than it sounds. For, as Bion noted, individuals have a conscious and unconscious "hatred of learning by experience," what amounts to "a hatred of a process of development" (1959, pp. 75, 77). One of the important reasons for this is that "experience" is the name we give to our mistakes, and mistakes are hugely narcissistically wounding. Learning by "experience" also requires the will and ability to venture into unfamiliar and challenging situations that generate anxiety about one's self-efficacy, another important aspect for maintaining a modicum of narcissistic equilibrium. As is abundantly clear from individual psychoanalytic treatment, most people "do not have much belief in their capacity for learning by experience," that is, neurotic attitudes and behavior are extremely hard to decisively and lastingly modify, and most neurotics sense this. To put emphasis on this point, Bion comments, "what we learn from history is that we do not learn from history" (ibid., p. 75).

The Axial sages were well aware of Bion's point, which is why they stressed the transformational significance of certain kinds of learning. For example, Confucius noted in the *Analects*, "Learning without thought is labor lost; thought without learning is perilous" (II.15). Confucius is distinguishing learning, that is, mental processes that involve the attainment of knowledge and the storage of information, from thought. Thought is reasoning, deliberating and reflecting about what has been learned. The danger of thought without knowledge is that it can become utterly impractical, if not fantasy (Taylor, 2011). Most importantly, for the Axial sages, the best learning brings understanding, and with understanding comes freedom to do otherwise. Such learning includes calmly learning to be wrong, patiently unlearning what is not true and not unlearning what is most essential to make things better.

While there is scholarly and popular literature on what promotes organizational success, I will describe some of the manifestations of "suffering," the anxiety, hostility and other negative emotions toward the organization that can chip away at its constructive, collaborative and creative potential – what Nitsun has called the "anti-group" phenomenon. Such disruptive and disintegrative processes can not only severely compromise an organization's adaptation and survival; it also leaves the individual employee feeling demoralized, if not traumatized (Nitsun, 2015, pp. 2, 3). I will briefly comment on two interrelated, interdependent and interactive elements, best viewed as processes that, when "off track," can contribute to an individual employee feeling he is working in a "crazy" organization: one with bad leadership and bad organizational culture, especially lack of support during times of adversity.

### Bad leadership

"A fish first rots from the head down," the popular proverb goes. When an organization fails, the ultimate cause is the leadership.[26] I have earlier commented on the tremendous practical psychological difficulties for the employee having to cope with an inordinately narcissistic boss, but there are many other aspects of bad leadership that can make a worker feel horrid or unhinged. Leaders have a central role in fostering a "healthy" and flourishing group and organization, one that goes beyond establishing clear and well-formulated goals and evaluating the progress of a team. Leaders "become the emotional center" of an organization, and they "are in the best position to deal with anxieties that develop" (Swogger, 1993, p. 112). "Regard your soldiers as your children," said Sun Tzu, "and they will follow you into the deepest valleys; look on them as your own beloved sons, and they will stand by you even unto death (1910, p. 79).[27]

While the main qualities of a great leader in the business context are well researched (e.g., honesty, communication skills, a sense of humor, confidence, commitment, a positive attitude, creativity, intuition and an ability to inspire[28]) the fact is that great leaders are hard to come by. For example, a Harvard Business School study found that "half of employees" (20,000 studied from around the world) "don't feel respected by their bosses" (Porath, 2014). This leader behavior had the biggest effect on employees compared to all other outcomes that were measured. That is, "being treated with respect was more important to employees than recognition and appreciation, communicating an inspiring vision, providing useful feedback – even oppor-tunities for learning, growth, and development" (ibid.). This is a dismal research finding, for one would think that a boss giving an employee respect would be axiomatic. This and other disheartening findings, such as the 2013 Gallup finding that many employees "complained of 'bosses from hell' who ignored talent and didn't cultivate growth," put into sharp focus what a boss, manager or leader does or doesn't do that can seriously negatively impact job satisfaction (Stebner, 2013). While literature on leadership describes an almost infinite number of ways leaders can be lousy – psychologists have cited "that 50% of executives fail and that 60–75% of US managers are incompetent" – I want to mention a few of the more common types of "bosses from hell" that can make employees feel like they are being driven "out of their minds" (Riggio, 2009).

"Nothing is more difficult, and therefore more precious, than to be able to decide," said Napoleon Bonaparte (Marcus, 2014, p. 199). Indeed, the "lais-sez-faire leader," as Ronald E. Riggio, a professor of leadership and organi-zational psychology, calls him, is one that renounces his main leadership responsibility – to make decisions – especially tough ones (Riggio, 2009). From the perspective of the subordinate, a leader who will not make deci-sions, or not make timely ones, is putting the subordinate in a position ana-logous to a child waiting for gratification from his parent, in this instance, of direction that never comes, or comes too late. Conversely, such enforced pas-sivity makes the subordinate feel similar frustration to the parent trying to get the toddler to make a "pooh" in the toilet. Indeed, while there are many psychodynamic reasons why a boss may not make decisions, from the per-spective of the subordinate who is waiting, it feels like one is up against an anal-retentive character. To be anal-retentive is to need to be in control of all aspects of one's surroundings; in short, such a person "won't let go of his shit," his symbolic "gift" to his parents. He does this to both keep his prized "gift" all for himself while at the same time irritatingly defying his parent's socially sanctioned requests. Needless to say, such a procrastinating boss angers and demoralizes subordinates, fostering a feeling within the organiza-tion that it is without a leader. Over time workers simply give up caring. Iro-nically, in one variation such controlling bosses can be prone to over-manage instead of lead. As the "Great One," hockey icon Wayne Gretzky noted, "Procrastination is one of the most common and deadliest of diseases and its toll on success and happiness is heavy."[29]

Another category of leaders who are likely to upset employees are the "incompetent leaders," a group that includes a wide range of behaviors and personality types that demonstrate seriously defective managerial and leader-ship skills. For example, such leaders can be markedly rigid, habitually applying the same strategy and tactics regardless of the circumstances, often with unsuccessful outcomes. As Einstein allegedly said, "insanity is doing the same thing over and over again and expecting different results" (White, 2004,

p. 36). In other instances, incompetent leaders can display very low levels of motivation that lead them to make ill-conceived and ill-fated decisions, in part because they have not put adequate time into studying the details of the problem or doing what is necessary to make a smart decision. Moreover, they do not actually care about the negative impact of a bad decision as long as they are not seriously implicated in the consequences. In another variation, such leaders may also over-delegate making important decisions with little oversight of their subordinates, often creating troubling imbalances in work-loads such as over- or under-utilization of individuals or groups. Such bosses mainly do this to avoid taking responsibility for failure that could be attributed to them (Riggio, 2009; Hamel, 2011).

The fact that there are so many incompetent leaders should not be sur-prising when we consider the famous managerial "law," the Peter Principle. This is "the observation that in a hierarchy people tend to rise to 'their level of incompetence.' Thus, as people are promoted they become progressively less effective because good performance in one job does not guarantee similar performance in another."[30] According to the Peter Principle, there are two types of managers: those who move up the leadership hierarchy, and those who have gone as far as their competence allows them to move. Moreover, once a person enters a job in which they are not competent they tend to stay there for many years or until retirement. In this context, it is inevitable that such poorly qualified leaders will make a high percentage of bad decisions that negatively impact the organization and particular individuals (Ovans, 2014).

The main negative impact on the individual who has an incompetent leader is analogous to a child who has an incompetent parent or teacher, namely, a profound loss of trust that fosters high levels of anxiety. A competent parental caregiver is the "psychological parent," the one who most symbolizes nur-turance and stability. If a "good-enough mother," as Winnicott famously called the imperfect though competent parent, is devoted to the child, the incompetent boss leaves the subordinate feeling largely adrift, if not aban-doned; if the "good-enough mother" tries to identify with and understand the child's thoughts and feelings, the incompetent boss is unwilling and unable to do so toward his employees, for he often lacks the listening and communica-tion skills and the patience and empathy. If the "good-enough mother" is able to contain the child's assaults and help him psychologically metabolize them, the incompetent boss experiences criticism as an attack that deserves retalia-tion; if the "good-enough mother" almost never fails in meeting the child's developmentally appropriate ego needs for encouragement and support, while at the same time frustrating his inordinate id wishes, the incompetent leader hardly cares about being helpful to his underlings and is overly frustrated by the employee's work-related playful and creative desires, such as "playing" with new ideas or taking risks. Finally, while the "good-enough mother" is willing and able to give the child his space to explore the world at his own pace and in his own way, the incompetent boss makes little or no effort to give underlings autonomy of thought, feeling and perhaps most importantly, of action (Akhtar, 2009, p. 124).

Riggio describes "toxic leaders," or extreme narcissists, and "evil leaders," though there are many variations on such leaders who engage in destructive behavior and display markedly dysfunctional personality characteristics that foster a poisonous work environment. For example, such leaders tend to give yes or no or black and white answers to complex questions, for they are unwilling and unable to think deeply about a problem or consider very far into the future, as they are moving from one crisis to another in which damage control is their only concern. As a result, workers feel unheard, not understood and disrespected. Such leaders often selfishly let their personal lives and self-seeking needs and wishes intrude into their work, and are not able to properly attend to important matters of underlings who feel ignored and disregarded. These leaders don't graciously tolerate mistakes or use them for learning purposes like a master teacher; in fact, they are prone to humiliate others in a group setting when underlings are found to have erred. In short, such self-centered and egotistical leaders most often leave their organization "worse off than how they found it." Enron executives Andrew Fastow and Jeffrey Skilling are excellent examples of toxic business leaders. Evil business leaders would certainly include Bernard Madoff, the former stockbroker and mastermind of the "swindle of the century" who was convicted of fraud. Madoff drastically hurt, if not destroyed, many organizations and individual lives because of his pathological obsession to dishonestly accumulate vast sums of money and power (Riggio, 2009).

Exactly why so many people tolerate remaining in devaluing and debasing positions with "bosses from hell" is a complex and important question, one that deserves a study of its own. Pragmatically speaking, most reasonable people would probably claim that having a hated job is still better than being unemployed, especially if one has a family to support, given the current challenging job market and harsh economic climate. There are two other psychologically based considerations that no doubt have considerable applicability to many employees staying put when they have to endure a "boss from hell": so-called "commitment effects" and "reflected glory" (Pfeffer & Fong, 2005, p. 377).

Within the context of the individual employee's escalation of cognitive and emotional commitment to a position that one has consciously chosen, there is a pronounced tendency to reconstruct and rationalize their circumstances as being better than they really are. Social psychologist Leon Festinger (1957) famously calls this "cognitive dissonance theory," that is, in circumstances that involve conflicting attitudes, beliefs or behaviors, the feelings of discomfort bring about a modification in one of the attitudes, beliefs or behaviors to diminish the discomfort and reinstate psychic equilibrium. Moreover, this compelling motivation to uphold cognitive consistency can foster irrational and highly maladaptive behavior.[31] Research in organizational psychology has demonstrated that people often prefer to continue in their chosen course of action, like staying in a job with an abusive boss, even though it is very disagreeable. Even more strikingly, they persist in an unpleasant course of action when they no longer realistically have to. Such findings are best understood in terms of "self-enhancement" theory, "the desire, or observed reality of seeing oneself and by extension one's actions, traits, and attitudes in the most positive light" (Pfeffer & Fong, 2005, pp. 377, 374).

Similarly, individuals may also tolerate horrible bosses because they wish to feel favorably about themselves, that is, they want to increase their self-esteem and enhance their self-concept by associating with "winners." In this scenario, many subordinates are willing and able to sustain a fair amount of mistreatment, even abuse, to "bask" in the "reflected glory" of high-status superiors, which includes self-subjugating, to varying degrees, aspects of their own best interests and painful feelings, at least for significant periods of time. Moreover, if the successful boss is willing to symbolically share some of his success with his subordinates, this can intensify the latter's attachment to the abusive boss (ibid., pp. 377, 378).

There is probably a complex interaction between these and other psychological factors in understanding why employees allow themselves to be subjugated by their bosses. For example, voluntary subjugation to a boss can be simply viewed as a reflection of low self-esteem and a poor self-concept that is typical among those who feel personally and organizationally powerless. Abuse is conceived as self-verifying, including being unconsciously deserved in a way that can easily fuse with an individual's masochistic proclivities. However, such employees may in certain contexts and settings also calculate that short-term mistreatment is worth imagined long-term benefits (ibid., p. 378).

### Organizational culture

The American industrialist who revolutionized the automotive industry, Henry Ford, famously described organizational culture at its best: "Coming together is the beginning, keeping together is progress. Working together is success."[32] Indeed, it is near impossible to have a lasting successful organization without a flourishing organizational culture. An organizational culture has been aptly defined as "the values and behaviors that contribute to the unique social and psychological environment of an organization." Specifically:

> Organizational culture includes an organization's expectations, experiences, philosophy, and values that hold it together, and is expressed in its self-image, inner workings, interactions with the outside world, and future expectations. It is based on shared attitudes, beliefs, customs, and written and unwritten rules that have been developed over time and are considered valid.[33]

Given the broad nature of this definition, there are many aspects of organizational culture that can promote in the employee a strong sense that he inhabits a workplace that is very disagreeable, if not maddening. Moreover, since the nature of organizational culture is heavily influenced from above, and leadership style is rooted in personality dynamics in complex interaction with the environment, it is not surprising that there are nearly an infinite number of ways that an organizational culture can turn nasty for an employee, causing much personal suffering.

Kets de Vries aptly describes "organizational archetypes," each with its strengths and weaknesses: the "dramatic/cyclothymic, suspicious, compulsive, detached and depressive" (2006, pp. 323–327). Each one of these archetypes creates a set of potentially obnoxious psychological and practical problems for employees that I here briefly describe.

The "dramatic/cyclothymic" leaders are mainly motivated by their inordinate narcissistic need for affirmation from outsiders. They desire to win people over with "flow" or "in the zone" experiences; they are prone to superficial thinking and interacting; they tend to be emotionally labile, moving from extremes of elation and depression; they are over-reactive to minor matters; and they have an over-reliance upon intuition, so-called "gut feelings," in their decision-making style that often leads to ill-conceived and ill-fated audaciousness, risk-taking and unpleasant showiness. Moreover, such leaders are too confident that they are the masters of their fate, not properly reckoning with the fact that they have much less control of their lives, and the organizations they lead, than they imagine. In short, says Kets de Vries, dramatic/cyclothymic leaders' decision-making can be summed up like, "We want to get attention from and impress the people who count in the world." English billionaire investor Richard Branson's Virgin Group is an example of a dramatic/cyclothymic organization. Such a CEO wants to be noticed and applauded; he longs for high-octane excitement, and seeks out situations that are characterized by flamboyance and drama (ibid., p. 323).

"Suspicious organizations" are mainly built on what Melanie Klein called paranoid anxiety, a foreboding of being assaulted by "bad objects," which are either "internal, projected internal, or external." Most often, at least according to Klein, this anxiety is projected onto objects (that is, to people) and, in another variation, "into" objects in the case of projective identification, as a primitive defense against one's own disavowed destructive impulses, and ultimately, denied self-destructive wishes (Rycroft, 1995, p. 125). Such organizations are characterized by hyper-vigilance against often imagined "enemies." A profound feeling of mistrust and doubt pervades such an organization, especially when something wrong may have happened that has not been adequately explained or dealt with. In light of such organizational suspiciousness, there is a centralization of power and a consolidation of influence, one that uses a conservative business strategy combined with unadventurous tactics. As a result, autonomy is discouraged and initiative muted, and unsuitable and unbending responses from superiors become the norm. The FBI under J. Edgar Hoover, with its secret abuses of government powers, illegal ways of evidence collection, and intimidation of governmental leaders and others who were afraid of retaliations, is a good example of such an organization (Kets de Vries, 2006, p. 323).

This being said, it is worth mentioning that the upsurge of workplace spying has for good reason increased paranoia among workers. A survey from the American Management Association (AMA) reported that no less than 66 percent of U.S. companies monitor their employees' internet use, while 43 percent track employee emails. Office workers are not the only people in the grip of "Big Brother": in Amazon's warehouses, workers are mandated to carry tablets that record their speed and efficiency as they retrieve merchandise for shoppers; in hospitals, nurses have to wear badges that record how frequently they wash their hands. Within the context of our surveillance society, where "privacy in today's workplace is largely illusory," paranoid thought process and behavior is being potentiated.[34]

Similar to the mode of being-in-the-world of an obsessive-compulsive neurotic, a "compulsive organization" can be best understood when we juxtapose it with its opposite way of being – namely, spontaneous, voluntary, free and ego-syntonic (Rycroft, 1995, p. 24). These maladjusted organizations are characterized by an exaggerated concern about unimportant matters; they tend to be inflexible and structure-bound, excessively exacting about rules, and they apply complicated information systems and highly formalized, painstaking evaluation procedures that are both slow and overbearing. They tend to squash any unprompted and improvisational tendencies. Thus, in a "compulsive organization," the business strategy is overly calculated and focused, motivated by a reliance on one entrenched, deeply rooted concern, such as cost-cutting or quality, without adequately reflecting on any other important considerations at play. Moreover, such organizations tend to use a conventional management-hierarchical bureaucratic model such that an employee's standing, rank and position emanates from their place in the power "pecking order" rather than from more important qualitative, performance-based considerations. As a result, instead of emphasizing social connection and collaboration in the workplace, an approach that is lodged in an interactive and dynamic premise about what matters most to workers (as in self-organizing teams), relationships are largely governed by control and submission. Compulsive organizations are characterized by high levels of anxiety in which employees are frequently asking themselves, "Will we do it right?," "Will they do it right?," "Can we let them do it?" and "How will it threaten us?" A "compulsive organization" that failed miserably was IBM under the leadership of John Akers (Kets de Vries, 2006, p. 324), who was described by CNBC as one of "the worst American CEOs of all time."[35] Not only did Akers not know his product, as he was trapped in an antiquated way of thinking about computers that emphasized mainframe when personal computing was beckoning, but he was also a terrible procrastinator about making important decisions.

"There is no detachment where there is no pain," said French philosopher Simone Weil, and the same applies to an organization (Martusewicz, 2001, p. 35). A "detached organization" is similar to the one earlier described as run by a "laissez-faire" leader and calls to mind the schizoid personality, characterized by a marked unresponsiveness to social relationships and a truncated range of emotional expressiveness (i.e., flat affect) and experience. Psychoanalytically speaking, while such pained people are "overtly detached, self-sufficient, absentminded, uninteresting, asexual and idiosyncratically moral" – for example, the stereotypical "loner" who exudes an attitude of "leave me the fuck alone" – covertly, they are "exquisitely sensitive, emotionally needy, acutely vigilant, creative, often perverse, and vulnerable to corruption" (Akhtar, 2009, p. 252). Thus, in such an organization, the emotional environment is characterized by a palpable chilliness, a lack of engagement both within and outside the organization, and a leadership that avoids any hands-on involvement with the everyday life of the organization. As a result, a power vacuum is generated that leads to an upsurge in the use of aggressive or dubious tactics among the leadership, such as psychological intimidation to gain an advantage over one's colleagues while still technically observing the organization's rules. Such gamesmanship, especially among mid- and lower-level executives, permits strategies and tactics that are markedly erratic and wavering. Moreover, since the leadership is generally not responsive to the healthy dependency needs of subordinates, such as for positive connection rooted in acknowledgment of the need for others and letting others need you, leaders at all levels tend to fashion their own spheres of influence and control, their little kingdoms, including generating obstacles to the lifeblood of any successful organization, namely, the free and uninterrupted flow of information. The reclusive American business tycoon who probably suffered from obsessive-compulsive disorder (OCD), Howard Hughes, is a good example of a detached leader (Kets de Vries, 2006, pp. 324–325).

The influential existential psychologist Rollo May noted that the main problem in clinical depression "is the inability to construct a future."[36] Likewise, a "depressive organization" is characterized by its lack of confidence, where employees collectively feel a lack of trust and faith in themselves and their abilities to put things right, or at least make them significantly better. As a result, "depressive organizations" are typically dull, sluggish and stagnant. They discourage new ideas, are unwilling and unable to change, especially drastically, and they tend to be markedly inward-looking. They are often lodged in a retrospective consciousness which makes effective decision-making nearly impossible; they avoid adventure, they are locked into shrinking and outdated markets, and their leadership is characterized by indifference. Many governmental organizations are depressive in character, and, not surprisingly, so was the Walt Disney Company after the death of its charismatic founder (Kets de Vries, 2006, p. 325).[37]

To be a subordinate in any of these neurotic organizations can be markedly destructive to one's vocational identity. Perhaps the best one can say is that by being knowledgeable of the limitations, strengths and dynamics of these fundamentally flawed organizations, one can protect oneself from their worst aspects. To be forewarned was to be forearmed was precisely Sun Tzu's point in his discussion on "employment of secret agents" (1963, p. 145). For example, a greater mindfulness of the limitations of each type of organizational culture can help one better understand some of the more troubling aspects of the behavior of its leaders and colleagues in both individual and group contexts, which is more likely to foster adaptive responses to them. Moreover, such knowledge and awareness helps the subordinate craft psychological "safe zones" where one can function more creatively and productively while staying out of harm's way. If one is a leader in such an organization, greater awareness and knowledge of the dynamics of the neurotic aspects of one's organization is the first critical step in changing the organizational culture for the better. Such a "positive culture," as it is often described, is one in which "professionalism, high achievement and team-building is concentrated" such that employees will be more likely to happily work at a higher level.[38]

## Final reflections

The prominent Canadian psychoanalyst and organizational psychologist Elliott Jaques noted that "The system [i.e., the current organizational structure] we have now is much more crushing to the individual."[39] Indeed, what I have tried to suggest in this chapter is that there are many irrational, deleterious individual, group and organizational processes operative in a typical workplace that, when not individually and collectively properly addressed, tend to undermine an average worker's sense of autonomy, integration and humanity, causing much personal suffering. To again quote Jaques, one of the key cohesive elements that binds "individuals into institutionalized human association is that of defense against psychotic anxiety" (1974, p. 279). While it would be incorrect to say that an institution or organization is inevitably, generally speaking, "psychotic," as I have suggested, there are group relationships that show psychotic aspects such as "unreality, splitting, hostility, suspicion" and other expressions of seriously "maladaptive" and maladjusted behavior (ibid.). If one is on the "receiving end" of these group relationships one is quite likely to greatly suffer.

Indeed, there is considerable research-based evidence that in today's workplaces there are many risk factors for significant mental health problems. For example, a landmark Johns Hopkins study from 1990 summarized in the *New York Times* reported that lawyers were "3.6 times as likely as non-lawyers to suffer from depression, putting them at greater risk than people in any other occupation" (Zimmerman, 2017, n.p.). A 2014 Yale Law School study found that "70 percent of its students were affected by mental health issues," suggesting that lawyers may be more susceptible to mental health problems for a variety of complex reasons related to the nature of their everyday work and practice (Quenqua, 2015, n.p.). Likewise, "Of all occupations and professions, the medical profession consistently hovers near the top of occupations with the highest risk of death by suicide."[40] In England, "The suicide rate among primary school teachers ... is nearly two times higher than the national average" (Bulman, 2017, n.p.).

More generally, as industrial and organizational psychologist Jay C. Thomas noted,[41] "modern organization design, with its flat hierarchies, team emphasis, goal setting, fast pace, accountability, the need for flexibility and continual change, and high-stress conditions" puts severe demands on the interpersonal skills, coping techniques and initiative of an employee, too often prompting one to declare, "This job is driving me crazy" (2004, pp. 5, 6). Researchers have found a number of risk factors that tend to foster troubling mental health problems in the workplace, factors that have been clustered into nine categories that, conceptually and practically, co-mingle with many of the psychoanalytically oriented formulations described throughout this chapter (Stewart et al., 2004, p. 333).

Examples of risk factors in "organizational function and culture" are inadequate problem-solving environment, inadequate communication and an unsupportive culture, which negatively impact the mental health of employees. In the category of "role in the organization," risk factors included role ambiguity, role conflict and high responsibility for others. In "career development," career uncertainty, career plateau, inadequate salary and fear of job loss were correlated with compromised mental health. In "decision latitude/control," the paucity of decision-making and the paucity of control over work negatively impacted psychological adjustment. Likewise, in the category of "interpersonal relationships at work," the degree of social or physical isolation; troubled relationships with bosses, managers and leaders; relational conflict in all of its varieties or violence; and lack of social support, especially during challenging times, were significant risk factors. Risk factors in the category of "home/work interface," which connotes the disparate and contradictory demands of work and home, inadequate social or practical encouragement and support at home, and dual career difficulties all negatively impacted on mental health. "Task design," which refers to problems around poorly defined work, uncertainty of work, lack of variety or abbreviated work cycles and over-exposure to demanding people, clients or customers, were also important risk factors. "Workload" (whether too much or too little), lack of control over the pacing and speed of work, and time pressure or unreasonable deadlines also compromised mental health. The final category of factors that aggravate the maintenance of psychological equipoise was "work schedule," with risk factors such as shift work and working long, unsociable hours (ibid.).

In light of the above, it is a near "miracle" that anyone is able to psycho-logically survive at work;[42] and yet, despite some previously cited dismal sta-tistics about the lack of job satisfaction in the United States and England (and other parts of the western world), there are some people who flourish on the job. While I have, in an earlier publication (Marcus, 2017), provided a plausible account for the job satisfaction of this group of resourceful and inventive people, one that emphasizes "work as the created birthplace of the transcendent," I want to emphasize that the capacity to flourish on the job as an individual depends on one's emotional self-mastery, especially "emotional creativity." The robust attunement to one's self-identity, including a watchful mindfulness about one's feelings, thoughts and actions, expresses the best of the Axial outlook. While working in an organization that is animated by "strengths-based" and "positive" organizational psychology principles is most likely to bring out the best in workers and lead to higher levels of job satis-faction, what probably matters most on the personal level is "emotional crea-tivity." By this I mean the vigorous capacity for "novel, effective and authentic" receptiveness, responsiveness and responsibility; an openness, curiosity and imagination that promotes what Nietzsche called "spiritualization of the pas-sions," a process of greater "self-realization and expansion" and increased "vitality, connectedness and meaningfulness" (Averill, 2009, p. 255).

To the extent that one can conceive of one's work in broadly aesthetic terms, analogous to fashioning a work of art or an imaginative undertaking that draws from personality qualities like "playfulness, creativity, sense of humor, ego-strength, and self-actualization" (APGICO, 2011) while simulta-neously shielding oneself from the destructive aspects of one's job (and the suffering it produces), the more likely that one has mastered the art of living the "good life" in the workplace. One should never forget that from the point of view of individual freedom, a worker, like anyone else, is capable of psy-chologically nurturing something in one's fantasy and imagination, a creative visualization, which one has to live without in objective reality. Such "life longings," as they have been called in the Axial-inspired psychology of wisdom literature, may serve as the best defense against situations character-ized by unattainability, failure and loss (Scheibe et al., 2009, p. 179). As the Axial sages believed and Paul Tillich reaffirmed, "In the encounter with the universe, man is able to transcend any imaginable limit" (1954, p. 78).

## Notes

1　Gedo believed that Freud was "excessively careerist" in his viewpoint. Gedo claims that Freud would have been less tied to his bourgeois socioeconomic values and more psychologically right if he simply put forth the notion that mental health required the "freedom from any incapacity" to love and work. Indeed, there are normative circumstances where it is not unhealthy not to work, such as in retire-ment (1997, pp. 134, 133). Also worth noting is a troubling report from the National Bureau of Economic Research (NBER) that found that the hours worked by men between ages 21 and 30 have decreased about 12 percent, in part, because about a third of these men prefer to immerse themselves in the addictive "world of gaming." Most important, 89 percent of these "basement-dwelling video-gamers" who usually live with relatives claim to be "very happy" or "pretty happy." These workforce dropouts have defied conventional psychological wisdom, that unemployment makes people feel miserable (Young Men: Video Games Instead of Jobs, *The Week*, July 28, 2017, p. 17).

2 And again, "A man like me cannot live without a hobby-horse, without a consuming passion, without – in Schiller's words – a tyrant. I have found one ['working well, writing well']. In its service I know no limits" (Freud, 1895 [1985], p. 129).

3 https://rockwoodleadership.org/rwl/wp-content/uploads/.../PWB-II-Supplemental. pdf, retrieved 10/3/17.

4 I am aware that the claim that work should be self-fulfilling reflects a set of possibly elitist and ethnocentric values, especially since "the majority of people in contemporary societies do not do the kinds of work that could be a source of self-fulfillment" (Rosso et al., 2010, p. 117).

5 Edison's incredible confession may be rooted in the fact that he had an enviably healthy attitude toward failure as an inventor: "I have not failed. I've just found 10,000 ways that won't work" (Farrington, 2014, p. 75).

6 This chapter draws from my book on how to flourish in the workplace (Marcus, 2017).

7 www.investorsinpeople.com/press/60-cent-uk-workers-not-happy-their-jobs, retrieved 9/2/17.

8 Depending on how you define and conceptualize the murky terms of boss, manager and leader, there are differences and similarities. For example, managers tend to focus on process while leaders focus more on generating imaginative ideas (Zaleznik, 1991, p. 109). As the late leadership scholar Ralph Stogdill noted, "there are almost as many definitions of leadership as there are persons who have attempted to define the concept" (Kets de Vries & Miller, 1985, p. 584). In this chapter I treat all of these organizational roles as roughly equivalent in terms of those who have authority over employees, and when this authority becomes hard-going or abusive, it presents serious adaptational difficulties for subordinates to flourish on the job.

9 Narcissism as a personality trait is conceptualized along a continuum in psychoanalytic theory, for example, from normal or healthy narcissism to the narcissistic personality disorder. The latter is a rare character disorder that affects less than 1 percent of the general population (Campbell et al., 2005, p. 1359). Psychoanalysis has described different types of narcissism, such as the "antisocial," the "malignant" and the "destructive" (Silver, 2017, p. 398).

10 In my discussion of narcissism in the workplace I am liberally drawing from Kernberg (1979, 1998).

11 I am paraphrasing Goethe, who made this very point: "Hatred is active, and envy passive dislike; there is but one step from envy to hate" (www.whale.to/a/goethe_q. html, retrieved 6/1/15).

12 Research has indicated that those people in "high-powered roles," even temporarily, tend to show "brain activity consistent with lower empathy." This may be due to the fact that "they have less incentive to interact with others." In other words, narcissists (and psychopaths) are able to feel empathy, but they choose not to (Cameron et al., 2015, p. 12). Other research indicates that among low-skilled workers on a professional path, it is not the traditional markers of success – such as education, industry experience and employer recommendations – that most matter, but rather "optimism and empathy" (Davidson, 2016, p. 43).

13  www.unitedearth.com.au/spinoza.html, retrieved 3/20/15.

14  www.reformtaoism.org/Zhuangzi_Translations/watson_26-30.php, retrieved 3/23/15.

15  Dissociation and splitting are hard to distinguish; in the clinical psychoanalytic literature most analysts have not bothered to do so, though some have described dissociation more in terms of impacting "processes" while splitting impacts "structures" (Zaleznik, 1991, p. 102). For the most part, such complex notions are used interchangeably in the psychoanalytic literature.

16  In a well-publicized quest for the "perfect team" ("Project Aristotle"), Google researchers have rediscovered what capable managers and psychoanalysts have known for many years; namely, that the best-performing teams and groups are composed of members who empathically listen to one another and show responsiveness to feelings and needs within a secure and trusting context (Duhigg, 2016, p. 75).

17  www.glassmanpsyd.com/the-importance-of-boundaries, retrieved 3/26/15.

18  Teams, called "quality circles" in the 1970s, have been conceptualized as somewhat different from "groups" and "committees." While there is some confusion in the literature about what constitutes a "work team," one serviceable definition is "a collection of three or more individuals who interact intensively to provide an organizational product, plan, decision, or service." To make matters even more complicated, there are "work teams," "parallel teams," "project teams," "management teams," "crews" and "virtual teams," each somewhat different in their characteristics and dynamics (Aamodt, 2007, pp. 491, 493, 494).

19  http://achakra.com/2013/11/30/wilfred-bion-group-dynamics-the-basic-assump tions-from-wikipedia/, retrieved 4/27/15.

20  This section liberally draws from Richardson and West's (2010) excellent review article.

21  www.mindtools.com/pages/article/newCS_85.htm, retrieved 4/29/15.

22  A revised edition of this book came out in 1982; see pp. 174–175 in particular.

23  There are two main theoretical explanations for group polarization, one based on social comparison theory (Moscovici & Zavalloni, 1969) and the other on a persuasive arguments theory (also known as informational influence theory; Van Swol, 2009).

24  Research has shown that many employees dislike most meetings, finding them boring and useless. One study calculated that over $37 billion is wasted in the US in "unproductive meetings" (Heffernan, 2016, pp. 29, 30).

25  www.leadersbeacon.com, retrieved 9/12/17.

26  Well-intentioned bosses, supervisors and leaders have their own set of anxieties, fears and challenges to becoming the best they can become in their critical roles. However, understanding in detail what personality and other factors impair their effectiveness is beyond the scope of this book. One psychoanalytically informed investigation of organizational leadership is Kets de Vries (2006).

27  Here I have drawn from a different, highly regarded translation of Sun Tzu than used throughout this chapter, as the translation is more suitable to my point.

28  www.forbes.com/sites/tanyaprive/2012/12/19/top-10-qualities-that-make-a-great-lea der/#28bccc3f7754, retrieved 5/8/15.

29  http://izquotes.com/quote/75728, retrieved 5/12/15.

30  www.businessdictionary.com/definition/Peter-principle.html, retrieved 5/13/15.

31  www.simplypsychology.org, "Social Psychology: Attitudes," retrieved 5/15/15.

32  www.usdreams.com/FordW19.html, retrieved 5/19/15. In today's workplace there is a lack of "collaborative, innovative social space," indicated by the fact that about 62 percent of professionals surveyed say they typically eat lunch at their desks, called "desktop dining." Eating alone allows one to answer emails and catch up on

to-do lists or use Facebook rather than bond with colleagues. About a quarter of millennial wage earners preferred to eat alone so they could multitask more effectively. However, work performance and satisfaction tends to be correlated with eating with colleagues, which is typical in, for example, firehouses, where there is a strong sense of fellowship (Wollan, 2016, pp. 54, 50).

33  www.businessdictionary.com/definition/organizational-culture.html, retrieved 5/14/15.
34  The Rise of Workplace Spying, *The Week*, July 5, 2015, p. 11. Slack, the hugely popular office collaboration app, has over 2.3 million daily active users. Companies as diverse as Salesforce, eBay and HBO use this platform to assist widespread teams with communicating more quickly and efficiently through group chat and instant messages rather than email or conference calls. However, "Slack workplaces are environments of total surveillance," said one technical expert. That is, the software keeps all conversations, including private messages, forever, unless they are deleted. If a company is sued, an employee's messages can be used, and they are subject to government subpoena (Apps. How Slack is Changing Work, *The Week*, March 25, 2016, p. 20).
35  www.cnbc.com/id/30502091/page/12, retrieved 6/19/15.
36  www.scientificamerican.com/section/mind-matters/, retrieved 5/22/15.
37  Kets de Vries points out that each of these organizational archetypes has its advantages. For example, a "dramatic/cyclothymic" organizational culture tends to generate "entrepreneurial initiative"; a "suspicious organization" can spot unreasonable risks to proposed business ventures; "compulsive organizations" can be efficient, strategically focused and have precise internal organizational controls; a "detached organization" is able to exploit the points of view of a wide range of contributors from different levels in the hierarchy as they fashion business strategy; and the "depressive organization" is characterized by a marked "consistency of internal processes" (2006, p. 326). As is almost always the case when discussing organizational processes, they have both enabling and constraining elements.
38  www.yourbusiness.azcentral.com/poor-company-culture-affect-employees-4410, retrieved 5/25/15.
39  www.nytimes.com/2003/03/17/obituaries/17JAQU.html, retrieved 5/26/15.
40  www.emedicine.medscape.com/article/806779-overview, retrieved 9/12/17.
41  Thomas is paraphrasing from the research of Miller (1998).
42  In France, "between 300 and 400 employees each year commit suicide, the cause of which is attributed to working conditions." This is quite likely an underestimation of the problem (Amado, 2013, p. 13).

## References

Aamodt, M. G. (2007). *Industrial/Organizational Psychology: An Applied Approach* (6th ed.). Belmont, CA: Wadsworth.

Akhtar, S. (2009). *Comprehensive Dictionary of Psychoanalysis*. London: Karnac.

Amado, G. (2013). Psychic Imprisonment and Its Release within Organizations and Working Relationships. In L. Vanisina (Ed.), *Humanness in Organizations: A Psychodynamic Contribution* (pp. 7–28). London: Karnac.

APGICO. (2011). *ECCI XII Proceedings: The Ultimate Experience in Collaboration*. Faro: Portuguese Association of Creativity and Innovation. Retrieved 5/29/15 from http://studylib.net/doc/8317907/the-ultimate-experience-in-collaboration

Averill, J.R. (2009). Emotional Creativity: Toward "Spiritualizing the Passions." In C.R. Snyder & S. J. Lopez (Eds.), *Oxford Handbook of Positive Psychology* (pp. 249–257). Oxford, UK: Oxford University Press.

Lawrence, W.G., Bain, A., & Gould, L.J. (1996). The Fifth Basic Assumption. *Free Associations*, 6, Part 1, 37, 1–20.

Bauman, Z. (2003). *Liquid Love.* Cambridge, UK: Polity.

Bion, W.R. (1959). *Experiences in Groups.* New York: Ballantine.

Bulman, M. (2017, March 17). Primary School Teachers' Suicide Rate Nearly Double National Average, Figures Reveal. *Independent.* Retrieved from www.independent.co.uk/news/uk/home-news/primary-school-teachers-suicide-rate-double-national-a verage-uk-figures-a7635846.html

Cameron, D., Inzlicht, M., & Cunningham, W.A. (2015). Empathy Is Actually a Choice. *New York Times*, 7/12/15, p. 12.

Campbell, W.K., Bush, C.P., Brunell, A.B., & Shelton, J. (2005). Understanding the Social Costs of Narcissism: The Case of the Tragedy of the Commons. *Personality and Social Psychology Bulletin*, 31, 1358–1368.

Cascio, W.F. (2010). The Changing World of Work. In P.A. Linley, S. Harrington, & N. Garcea (Eds.), *Oxford Handbook of Positive Psychology and Work* (pp. 13–23). Oxford, UK: Oxford University Press.

Christian, J. (2012). *Philosophy: An Introduction to the Art of Wondering.* Boston, MA: Wadsworth.

Colman, A.M. (2009). *Oxford Dictionary of Psychology.* Oxford, UK: Oxford University Press.

Davidson, A. (2016). Cleaning Up. *New York Times Magazine*, 2/28/16, p. 43.

Doonan, S. (2015). Viewpoint. *The Week*, 4/3/15, p. 10.

Duhigg, C. (2016). Group Study. *New York Times Magazine*, 2/28/16, p. 75.

Emerson, R.W. (1984). *Emerson in His Journals.* J. Porte (Ed.). Cambridge, MA: Belknap Press.

Erikson, E.H. (1959). *Identity and the Life Cycle: Selected Papers.* New York: International Universities Press.

Farrington, C. (2014). *Failing at School: Lessons for Redesigning Urban High Schools.* New York: Teacher's College Press.

FeatsPress. (n.d.). *Bridget Jones's Diary: Interview with Hugh Grant.* Cinema.com. Retrieved from http://cinema.com/articles/332/bridget-joness-diary-interview-with-hugh-grant.phtml

Festinger, L. (1957). *A Theory of Cognitive Dissonance.* Redwood City, CA: Stanford University Press.

Freud, S. (1955). Group Psychology and the Analysis of the Ego. In J. Strachey (Ed. & Trans.), *The Standard Edition of the Complete Psychological Works of Sigmund Freud* (Vol. 18, pp. 65–143). London: Hogarth Press. (Original work published 1921)

Freud, S. (1956). On Narcissism: An Introduction. In J. Strachey (Ed. & Trans.), *The Standard Edition of the Complete Psychological Works of Sigmund Freud* (Vol. 14, pp. 67–102). London: Hogarth Press. (Original work published 1914)

Freud, S. (1963). *Psychoanalysis and Faith: The Letters of Sigmund Freud and Oskar Pfister.* H. Meng & E.L. Feder (Eds.), E. Mosbacher (Trans.). London: Hogarth Press. (Original work published 1910)

Freud, S. (1985). *The Complete Letters of Sigmund Freud to Wilhelm Fliess 1887–1904.* J. M. Masson (Trans.). Cambridge, MA: Belknap Press. (Original work published 1958)

Frew, J. (2004). Motivating and Leading Dysfunctional Employees. In J.C. Thomas & M. Hersen (Eds.), *Psychopathology in the Workplace: Recognition and Adaptation* (pp. 293–311). New York: Brunner-Routledge.

Friedman, T. (2015). Contain and Amplify. *New York Times*, 5/27/15, p. A23.

Fromm, E. (1947). *Man for Himself: An Inquiry into the Psychology of Ethics*. Oxford, UK: Routledge.

Gambrill, E. (2004). Social Skills Deficits. In J.C. Thomas & M. Hersen (Eds.), *Psychopathology in the Workplace: Recognition and Adaptation* (pp. 243–257). New York: Brunner-Routledge.

Gedo, J.E. (1997). In Praise of Leisure. In C.W. Socarides & S. Kramer (Eds.), *Work and Its Inhibitions: Psychoanalytic Essays* (pp. 133–141). Madison, CT: International Universities Press.

Grant, K.B. (2013). Americans Hate their Jobs, Even with Perks. *USA Today*, 6/30/13. Retrieved 3/13/15 from www.usatoday.com/story/money/business/2013/06/30/americans-hate-jobs-office-perks/2457089/

Hamel, G. (2011). First, Let's Fire All the Managers. *Harvard Business Review*, December 1. Retrieved 4/27/15 from https://hbr.org/2011/12/first-lets-fire-all-the-managers

Heath, C., & Heath, D. (2013). *Decisive: How to Make Better Choices in Life and Work*. New York: Crown Business.

Heffernan, V. (2016). Meet Is Murder. *New York Times Magazine*, 2/28/16, pp. 29–30.

Hopper, E. (2003). *Traumatic Experience in the Unconscious Life of Groups: The Fourth Basic Assumption: Incohesion: Aggregation/Massification or (ba) I:A/M*. London: Jessica Kingsley.

Hugo, V. (1907). *Intellectual Autobiography (Postscriptum)*. L. O'Rourke (Trans.). New York: Funk & Wagnalls. (Original work published 1901)

Huntley, H.L. (1997). How Does "God-Talk" Speak to the Workplace? An Essay on the Theology of Work. In D.P. Bloch & L.J. Richmond (Eds.), *Connections Between Spirit and Work in Career Development: New Approaches and Practical Perspectives* (pp. 115–136). Palo Alto, CA: Davies-Black.

Janis, I. (1972). *Victims of Groupthink: A Psychological Study of Foreign-Policy Decisions and Fiascoes*. Boston, MA: Houghton Mifflin.

Janis, I. (1982). *Groupthink: Psychological Studies of Policy Decisions and Fiascoes* (2nd ed.). New York: Houghton Mifflin.

Jaques, E. (1974). Social Systems as Defense against Persecutory and Depressive Anxiety. In G.S. Gabbard, J.J. Hartmann, & R.D. Mann (Eds.), *Analysis of Groups* (pp. 277–299). San Francisco, CA: Jossey-Bass.

Judge, T.A., LePine, J.A., & Rich, B.L. (2006). Loving Yourself Abundantly: Relationship of the Narcissistic Personality to Self- and Other Perceptions of Workplace Deviance, Leadership, and Task and Contextual Performance. *Journal of Applied Psychology*, 91(4), 762–776.

Kernberg, O.F. (1979). Regression in Organizational Leadership. *Psychiatry*, 42, 24–39.

Kernberg, O.F. (1998). *Ideology, Conflict, and Leadership in Groups and Organizations*. New Haven, CT: Yale University Press.

Kets de Vries, M.F.R. (1991). On Becoming a CEO: Transference and the Addictiveness of Power. In M.F.R. Kets de Vries et al. (Eds.), *Organizations on the Couch: Clinical Perspectives on Organizational Behavior and Change* (pp. 120–139). San Francisco: Jossey-Bass.

Kets de Vries, M.F.R. (2006). *The Leader on the Couch: A Clinical Approach to Changing People and Organizations*. San Francisco: Jossey-Bass.

Kets de Vries, M.F.R. (2011). *Reflections on Groups and Organizations*. San Francisco: Jossey Bass.

Kets de Vries, M.F.R., & Miller, D. (1985). Narcissism and Leadership: An Object Relations Perspective. *Human Relations*, 38(6), 583–601.

Krantz, J., & Gilmore, T.N. (1991). Understanding the Dynamics between Consulting Teams and Client Systems. In M.F.R. Kets de Vries et al. (Eds.), *Organizations on the Couch: Clinical Perspectives on Organizational Behavior and Change* (pp. 307–330). San Francisco: Jossey-Bass.

Labier, D. (1984). Irrational Behavior in Bureaucracy. In M.F.R. Kets de Vries (Ed.), *The Irrational Executive: Psychoanalytic Explorations in Management* (pp. 3–37). New York: International Universities Press.

Lapierre, L. (1991). Exploring the Dynamics of Leadership. In M.F.R. Kets de Vries et al. (Eds.), *Organizations on the Couch: Clinical Perspectives on Organizational Behavior and Change* (pp. 69–93). San Francisco: Jossey-Bass.

Lubit, R. (2002). The Long-Term Organizational Impact of Destructively Narcissistic Managers. *Academy of Management Executive*, 16(1), 127–138.

Lunbeck, E. (2014). *The Americanization of Narcissism*. Cambridge, MA: Harvard University Press.

Maccoby, M. (1984). The Corporate Climber Has to Find His Heart. In M.F.R. Kets de Vries (Ed.), *The Irrational Executive: Psychoanalytic Explorations in Management* (pp. 96–111). New York: International Universities Press.

Marcus, P. (2014). *They Shall Beat Their Swords Into Plowshares: Military Strategy, Psychoanalysis and The Art of Living*. Milwaukee, WI: Marquette University Press.

Marcus, P. (2017). *The Psychoanalysis of Career Choice, Job Performance and Satisfaction: How to Flourish in the Workplace*. New York: Routledge.

Martin, S.W. (2006). *Heavy Hitter Sales Wisdom*. Hoboken, NJ: Wiley.

Martusewicz, R.A. (2001). *Seeking Passage: Post-Structuralism, Pedagogy, Ethics*. New York: Teachers College Press.

Miller, C.C. (2016). About Face. *New York Times Book Magazine*, 2/28/16, p. 35.

Miller, D. (1998). Workplaces. In R. Jenkins & T.B. Ustun (Eds.), *Preventing Mental Illness: Mental Health Promotion in Primary Care* (pp. 343–351). Chichester, UK: Wiley.

Moore, B.E., & Fine, B.D. (Eds.). (1990). *Psychoanalytic Terns & Concepts*. New Haven, CT: American Psychoanalytic Association and Yale University Press.

Moscovici, S., & Zavalloni, M. (1969). The Group as a Polarizer of Attitudes. *Journal of Personality and Social Psychology*, 12, 125–135.

Nelson, D.L., & Quick, J.C. (2008). *Understanding Organizational Behavior* (3rd ed.). Mason, OH: South Western Cengage Learning.

Nitsun, M. (2015). *Beyond the Anti-Group: Survival and Transformation*. Hove, UK: Routledge.

Ovans, A. (2014). Overcoming the Peter Principle. *Harvard Business Review*, December 22. Retrieved 10/5/17 from https://hbr.org/2014/12/overcoming-the-peter-principle

Penney, L.M., & Spector, P.E. (2002). Narcissism and Counterproductive Work Behavior: Do Bigger Egos Mean Bigger Problems? *International Journal of Selection and Assessment, 10*(1/2), 126–134.

Person, E.S., Cooper, A.M. & Gabbard, G.O. (Eds.). (2005). *Textbook of Psychoanalysis*. Washington, DC: American Psychiatric Association.

Pfeffer, J., & Fong, C.T. (2005). Building Organization Theory from First Principles: The Self-Enhancement Motive and Understanding Power and Influence. *Organization Science*, 16(4), 372–388.

Popper, N. (2016). Stocks and Bots. *New York Times Magazine*, 2/28/16, pp. 59, 62.

Porath, C. (2014). Half of Employees Don't Feel Respected by their Bosses. *Harvard Business Review*, November 19. Retrieved 10/5/17from https://hbr.org/2014/11/half-of-employees-dont-feel-respected-by-their-bosses

Quenqua, D. (2015). Lawyers with Lowest Pay Report More Happiness. *New York Times*, 5/12/15. Retrieved 5/28/15 from http://well.blogs.nytimes.com/2015/05/12/lawyers-with-lowest-pay-report-more-happiness/?_r=0.

Reik, T. (1983). *Listening with the Third Ear*. New York: Farrar, Straus and Giroux.

Richardson, J., & West, M.A. (2010). Dream Teams: A Positive Psychology of Team Working. In P.A. Linley, S. Harrington, & N. Garcea (Eds.), *Oxford Handbook of Positive Psychology and Work* (pp. 235–249). Oxford: Oxford University Press.

Riggio, R.E. (2009). Bosses from Hell: A Typology of Bad Leaders. *Psychology Today*, April 6. Retrieved 5/12/15 from www.psychologytoday.com/blog/cutting-edge-leadership/200904/bosses-hell-typology-bad-leaders

Rosso, B.D., Dekas, K.H., & Wrzesniewski, A. (2010). On the Meaning of Work: A Theoretical Integration and Review. *Research in Organizational Behavior*, 30, 91–127.

Roth, B. (2013). Bion, Basic Assumptions, and Violence: A Corrective Reappraisal. *International Journal of Group Psychotherapy*, 63, 525–543.

Rycroft, C. (1995). *A Critical Dictionary of Psychoanalysis* (2nd ed.). London: Penguin.

Saad, L. (2012). U.S. Workers Least Happy with their Work Stress and Pay. Gallup, 11/12/12. Retrieved 10/3/17 from http://news.gallup.com/poll/158723/workers-least-happy-work-stress-pay.aspx

Sartre, J.-P. (1976). *No Exit and Other Plays*. S. Gilbert (Trans.). New York: Vintage.

Scheibe, S., Kunzmann, U., & Baltes, P.B. (2009). New Territories of Positive Life-Span Development: Wisdom and Life Longings. In S.L. Lopez & C.R. Snyder (Eds.), *Oxford Handbook of Positive Psychology* (pp. 171–183). Oxford: Oxford University Press.

Schmelzer, J.W.P. (2006). *Nucleation Theory and Applications*. New York: Wiley.

Silver, C.B. (2017). Erich Fromm and the Making and Unmaking of the Sociocultural. *Psychoanalytic Review*, 104, 388–414.

Slater, R. (1998). *Jack Welch and the G.E. Way: Management Insights and Leadership*. New York: McGraw-Hill.

Sole, K. (2006). Eight Suggestions from the Small-Group Conflict Trenches. In M. Deutsch, P.T. Coleman, & E.C. Marcus (Eds.), *The Handbook of Conflict Resolution: Theory and Practice* (pp. 805–821). San Francisco: Jossey-Bass.

Stebner, B. (2013). Workplace Morale Heads Down: 70% of Americans Negative about their Jobs, Gallup Study Shows. *New York Daily News*, 6/24/13. Retrieved 5/9/15 from www.nydailynews.com/news/national/70-u-s-workers-hate-job-poll-article-1.1381297

Stewart, C., Ward, T., & Purvis, M. (2004). Promoting Mental Health in the Workplace. In J. C. Thomas & M. Hersen (Eds.), *Psychopathology in the Workplace: Recognition and Adaptation* (pp. 329–343). New York: Brunner-Routledge.

Stolorow, R. (1975). Toward a Functional Definition of Narcissism. In A.P. Morrison (Ed.), *Essential Papers on Narcissism* (pp. 97–209). New York: New York University Press.

Swogger, G., Jr. (1993). Group Self-Esteem and Group Performance. In L. Hirschhorn & C. K. Barnett (Eds.), *The Psychodynamics of Organizations* (pp. 99–116). Philadelphia: Temple University Press.

Taylor, R.L. (2011). Who Was Confucius and Why Does It Matter? *Huffington Post*, 5/18/11. Retrieved 9/17/17 from huffingtonpost.com/rodney-l-taylor-phd/who-is-confucius-and-why-_b_863122.html.

Thomas, J.C. (2004). Introduction. In J.C. Thomas & M. Hersen (Eds.), *Psychopathology in the Workplace: Recognition and Adaptation* (pp. 3–8). New York: Bruner-Routledge.

Tillich, P. (1954). *Love, Power and Justice*. Oxford, UK: Oxford University Press.

Turquet, P. (1975). Threats to Identity in the Large Group. In L. Kreeger (Ed.), *The Large Group: Dynamics and Therapy* (pp. 57–86). London: Constable.

Twenge, J.M., & Campbell, S.M. (2010). Generation Me and the Changing World of Work. In P.A. Linley, S. Harrington, & N. Garcea (Eds.), *Oxford Handbook of Positive Psychology and Work* (pp. 25–35). Oxford, UK: Oxford University Press.

Tzu, S. (1910). *The Art of War*. L. Giles (Trans.). London: British Museum.

Tzu, S. (1963). *The Art of War*. S.B. Griffith (Trans.). Oxford: Oxford University Press.

Van Swol, L.M. (2009). Extreme Members and Group Polarization. *Social Influence*, 4 (3), 185–199.

Von Stamm, B., & Trifilova, A. (Eds.). (2009). *The Future of Innovation*. Burlington, VT: Gower.

Wahl, E. (2017). *The Spark and Grind: Ignite the Power of Disciplined Creativity*. New York: Portfolio/Penguin.

White, R. (2004). *Living and Extraordinary Life: Unlocking Your Potential for Success, Joy and Fulfillment*. Denver, CO: Balance Point International.

Winnicott, D. (1953). Transitional Objects and Transitional Phenomena. *International Journal of Psychoanalysis*, 34, 89–97.

Wollan, M. (2016). Failure to Lunch: The Lamentable Rise of Desktop Dining. *New York Times Magazine*, 2/28/18, pp. 54, 50.

Youssef, C.M., & Luthans, F. (2010). An Integrated Model of Psychological Capital in the Workplace. In P.A. Linley, S. Harrington, & N. Garcea (Eds.), *Oxford Handbook of Positive Psychology and Work* (pp. 277–288). Oxford: Oxford University Press.

Zaleznik, A. (1984). Management and Disappointment. In M.F.R. Kets de Vries (Ed.), *The Irrational Executive: Psychoanalytic Explorations in Management* (pp. 224–246). New York: International Universities Press.

Zaleznik, A. (1991). Leading and Managing: Understanding the Difference. In M.F.R. Kets de Vries et al. (Eds.), *Organizations on the Couch: Clinical Perspectives on Organizational Behavior and Change* (pp. 97–119). San Francisco: Jossey-Bass.

Zimmerman, E. (2017). The Lawyer, the Addict. *New York Times*, 7/15/17. Retrieved from www.nytimes.com/2017/07/15/business/lawyers-addiction-mental-health.html?mcubz=1

# Chapter 7

# The suffering of the psychoanalyst

In *Analysis Terminable and Interminable*, written two years before he died, Freud expressed his "sincere sympathy" for the psychoanalyst who is engaged in one of the "'impossible' professions." Along with education and governing, the analyst "can be sure beforehand of achieving unsatisfying results" (Freud, 1937, p. 248).[1] Freud was alluding to the tremendous unconscious resistance patients have to making personal change, even when they are in great psychic pain and are paying an analyst to help them alleviate their suffering.[2] Indeed, Freud put his finger on the troubling fact that despite his best efforts, the chances of the analyst co-producing a "good enough" outcome with most patients is fairly slim, if not "impossible." As if the endless and unavailing Sisyphean task of doing analysis wasn't bad enough, Freud also noted that the analyst will likely be psychologically harmed in the process of trying to help patients: "No one who, like me, conjures up the most evil of those half-tamed demons that inhabit the human beast, and seeks to wrestle with them, can expect to come through the struggle unscathed" (Freud, 1905, p. 109).[3] It is in part for this reason that Freud implied that the practicing analyst must have a bit of unanalyzed "masochism" in his personality,[4] otherwise, why spend his whole work life engaging in a likely futile activity, one that "cuts" so deeply into the analyst's life-giving, form-molding force, in a word, his "soul" (Durant, 2014, p. 38)?

In this chapter I describe some underappreciated ways the analyst gets "scathed," that is, "suffers," as he does his emotionally daunting and humbling work, and what he can internally do to make things better for himself, and ultimately, his patients.[5] For an analyst who has not preserved his being will be unwilling and unable to fully engage his patients, significantly contributing to the trajectory of their doomed treatment. Thus, throughout my discussion of the analyst's "suffering," I have tried to be mindful of what I regard as the uncanny duality of structure that constitutes the contextual psychological background of the psychoanalytic encounter. On the one hand, the analyst must be willing and able to fashion a way of being that is receptive, responsive and responsible to the patient's suffering presence; in short, he must be "loving," like a parent or teacher at their best (Marcus, 2008). On the other hand, he must be willing and able to engage in "hand-to-hand combat," like a great military strategist/tactician (Marcus, 2014), with an unconsciously impervious, refractory, irresponsible adversary that wants to "defeat" the analyst every step of the way. As Freud famously said, neurotics "complain of their illness, but they make the most of it, and when it comes to taking it away from them they will defend it like a lioness her young" (1926a, p. 222).

As I have elsewhere discussed (Marcus, 2014, pp. 77–78), similar to Epictetus' teachings in *The Enchiridon*, a handbook "for a stoic field commander in the campaign of life" (Ambrosio, 2009, p. 23),[6] Freud's *oeuvre* is partially animated by a "militaristic" way of understanding social existence and psychoanalytic treatment (e.g., life is a conflict between culture and desire, the "war" between Eros and Thanatos, defense and resistance). Drawing from the strategic board game that most simulates war – chess (Marcus, 2015, p. 88) – Freud noted:

> For it is really too sad that in life it should be as it is in chess, where one false move may force us to resign the game, but with the difference that we can start no second game, no return-match.
>
> (1915, p. 291)

Freud described the therapeutic goal as including the "demolition" of the authoritarian super-ego, an obsolete and infantilizing internalized parental/societal authority functioning "like a garrison in an occupied city" (Carveth, 2017, p. 491). Thus, as Freud implied, for the analyst to prevail in the bellicose activity of psychoanalysis requires a little bit of masochism, courage to sustain psychological assaults from the patient, and the ability to fearlessly metabolize the wide range of distressing emotions stirred up in him that appear to be intrinsic to the analytic process. Drawing again from a military practical wisdom, as Mao Zedong noted in his famous *The Little Red Book*, "He who is not afraid of death by a thousand cuts dares to unhorse the emperor" (i.e., vanquish the patient's resistance to positive personal change) (2017, p. 132).

## When love is not enough

Freud noted in a letter to Carl Jung that psychoanalysis "is actually a cure by love," love being the dynamic/creative moving power of life (McGuire, 1974, pp. 12–13). While unpacking this evocative notion is beyond the scope of this chapter, what does need to be highlighted is the fact that Freud believed that, for "sure," the practitioner of the "impossible profession" is destined to "achiev[e] unsatisfying results." Despite his best efforts, the analyst's "love is not enough" to help facilitate the patient's capacity to love deeply and widely and to work creatively and productively, the bedrock of a "successful" analysis and the "good life" as I have described it. Indeed, if the great Axial philosopher Epicurus was right – "Empty is the argument of the philosopher [or the psychoanalyst] which does not relieve any human suffering" (LeBon, 2001, p. 10) – then the analyst may be left feeling that his loving efforts have been in vain. Such a felt lack of self-efficacy can undermine the analyst's self-esteem and self-concept as being a skillful practitioner of his identify-defining and life-enhancing "healing art." Perhaps even worse, it can make him vulnerable to troubling and lingering conscious and/or unconscious guilt that he has "failed" the suffering patient. After all, so this line of internal reasoning goes, like in all forms of psychotherapy, the analytic relationship is not a symmetrical one in terms of responsibility, for it is the analyst who is by far the more accountable party. The trained analyst is the one who is empowered to help the suffering patient. He is the "provider," the "giver" of a desired service, while the patient is the "beneficiary," the "receiver," of his skillful care that is meant to assist him in reducing, if not eliminating, his suffering. As my straight-talking, hard-hitting Freudian supervisor told me many years ago when I was in psychoanalytic training, "Marcus, never forget, that when an analysis or psychotherapy fails, it is always *your* fault, *always*, never the patient's."[7]

### The suicided patient

It is, of course, true, as all analysts know, that every adult patient is ultimately responsible for living his life the way he chooses, including how he engages and fashions the analytic process. The patient alone has to bear the full brunt of the intended and unintended consequences of his decisions and actions, especially the ill-conceived and ill-fated ones. As Freud noted, "Analysis does not set out to make pathological reactions impossible, but to give the patient's ego *freedom* to decide one way or another" (1923, p. 50). However, the ironic fact is that for many analysts, certainly those who are animated by the Axial ethical spirit, they strongly feel that they are their "brother's keeper." Recall the biblical story in which, subsequent to Cain murdering his brother Abel, God asked him where his brother was. Cain responded, "I know not; am I my brother's keeper?" Cain's words have come to personify a person's refusal to accept responsibility for the welfare of their "brothers," in the extended meaning of the term. A further complication for the Axial-inspired analyst is that, while he may intellectually "know" his patient is ultimately responsible for how he fashions his life, and the analyst has done just about everything he could do to help reduce the patient's suffering and facilitate his living the "good life," nevertheless, the analyst "feels" irrationally guilty: "I could have done more, I should have done better." Indeed, it is the analyst's critical self-reflection and judgment, his felt sense of moral failure, that I want to further comment on, not only because it depicts the heart of his "suffering" but also because it provides the basis for his "redemption."

The sense of moral failure, irrational guilt and the yearning for "redemption" came into extremely sharp focus many years ago when I was treating a depressed young man twice a week in psychoanalytic psychotherapy for about a year. He committed suicide, on my watch. The patient was employed in IT, made a decent living, and was married with a one-year-old child. He described his work and marriage as "ok," except when he was episodically depressed, which he said happened too often, causing his wife to get upset and angry with him as he folded into himself. He felt bonded to his son, though not hugely so; and his wife, who was not working, was the main, hands-on parental caregiver. She resented my patient's lack of parental engagement when he was depressed. He was on antidepressants while seeing me. He had been into serious illegal drugs about ten years earlier, including heroin, but had been "clean" for over a decade, though he smoked marijuana from time to time to calm his agitated depression. While my patient came from a "typical crazy" Irish Catholic background, as he described it, his fireman father had an aggressive side to him when he drank too much and was otherwise usually emotionally remote, and his mother was self-occupied and a "drama queen," though a dutiful mother. He told me that his childhood was overall "not too bad." He had a couple of siblings whom he had cool relations with, and from his descriptions of them they sounded rather dysfunctional. My patient was very smart, street savvy, funny in a tragicomic sort of way and had a sweet side to him. He knew that I liked him a lot, as he did me, and while I saw him very late at night, I always looked forward to speaking with him and I was never bored or in other ways not emotionally present.

What was so troubling to me about this young man is that throughout the year of treatment, we could not adequately grasp why he felt such terrible psychic pain, given the fact that he described his childhood as neither abusive, neglectful, nor characterized by trauma. While he had unresolved issues related to his parents and siblings, nothing sounded so bad that would reasonably account for the depth of despair he would fall into, often provoked by small mishaps in his life which he agreed did not warrant the depressive tailspin into which he would go. His psychiatrist told me that this man was psychopharmacologically perplexing, and it was unclear why the medications he prescribed him were not more effectively stabilizing his periodic depression. Nevertheless, I found it very disconcerting that I could not convincingly fathom why my patient was suffering so much, let alone how to help him alleviate his condition. During the treatment I often recalled to myself Paul Tillich's advice that the "first task" of love is "to listen" (1954, p. 84); and so I listened, including with "the third ear," as attentively as I could to my patient's relentlessly pained and painful "tellings." And yet, after many self-critical ponderings, including supervisory discussions with an experienced colleague, I was not able to successfully navigate him out of the "minefield" of his incendiary mind.

It was in this context, amidst a depressive episode that lasted about a month, that my patient told me that he could not "take it" anymore and planned on killing himself. He said that nothing felt worth living for and he had lost the will and ability to press on. Moreover, he felt there was "no exit" from his horrid condition, the psychotherapy and medications were not significantly helping him, and "checking out" was the only option to end his excruciating ordeal. Indeed, there was a striking irony at play with my patient: while he was willing and able to take the risk to terminate his life ("perchance to dream," said Hamlet), he was not willing and able to risk living it. Despite my best efforts to discourage him from killing himself, which included giving all of the usual psychoanalytic interpretations, appealing to his guilt in terms of abandoning his wife, son, and extended family, and my alerting his wife and parents of his dire state, he overdosed on heroin in a hotel room on the weekend he said he would. I went to the wake and funeral, and was treated with great respect and gratitude by his wife, parents (both of whom I spoke to during the year's treatment, with my patient's permission) and his extended family for the "extra mile" efforts I made to help this young man find his way out of his self-imposed psychological "concentration camp." Still, I felt terrible about this suicide, and, 35 years later, I still do, when I let myself think about it.

Thank God, to date this was my only patient who killed himself, but the painful impact of this young man's death on me has been played out time and again to a much lesser degree, in terms of my sense of guilt for failing my other patients. In a variety of ways and psychological contexts I was not able to help my patients significantly reduce their suffering, or fashion an existence that approximated the "good life." The fact is that, despite my best conscious efforts, there are many occasions where I do not do my analytic work at the highest level of which I am capable because of some personal limitation that I later realize was operative. This can manifest itself in, for example, truncated empathy, a lack of presence, sarcasm and other self-centric acts of omission and commission that reflect my many personal flaws. In psychoanalytic terms, this is usually discussed in terms of counter-transference "dead spots," collusions, counterenactments and unwarranted indulgences or unwanted deprivations that are deleterious to the patient (Akhtar, 2009, p. 61). If you agree, as I do, with the Axial-inspired philosopher Emmanuel Levinas that "the very node of the subjective is knotted in ethics understood as responsibility," and the other's suffering "face"[8] inescapably "orders and ordains me ... to serve him," in my case, to successfully help "heal" my patient's psychic wounds, then my guilty sense of having inadequately served my patients makes perfect sense (Levinas, 1985, pp. 95, 97). A guilty feeling can be amplified when the analyst remembers that throughout the treatment, he deliberately inflicted some pain on the patient, "having to pick away at the scab that the patient tries to form between himself and the analyst to cover over his wounds. The analyst keeps the surface raw, so that the wound will heal properly" (Malcolm, 1982, p. 113). Within the context of a botched treatment, this self-awareness can easily destructively boomerang into the analyst.

Thus, a degree of existential guilt is inevitable for feeling I have not lived up to my possibilities, potentialities and professional standards in terms of being skillfully other-directed, other-regarding and other-serving to my patients enough to prevent the young man from killing himself, or, with other patients, not effectively enough to help them get their lives "on track." Extreme as this criterion of self-judgment may seem to some, it leaves the analyst feeling sorely morally wounded. While all wounds eventually heal or, as the saying goes, they simply stop bleeding, they leave their psychological scar tissue. What is true about the buildup of physical scar tissue for the patient who has had a musculoskeletal injury is also true for the morally wounded analyst – at first, it causes some irritation and inflammation, but ultimately it causes long-term pain, reduced range of motion and flexibility, and imbalances. For the analyst, such psychological/spiritual scar tissue has a profound negative impact on his "emotional muscles," his capacity to be receptive, responsive and responsible to his patients. Without a robust capacity for such love and understanding (Marcus, 2013), the five essential elements of psychotherapeutic support – presence, holding, caring, challenging and confirming – are hardly possible (Heery & Bugental, 2005, p. 287). Moreover, if the psychotherapy outcome research is correct that the primary element that determines effectiveness is therapist–patient "alliance," or the degree to which the patient feels bonded, trusting and part of a collaborative partnership (Ardito & Rabellino, 2011), but the analyst lacks the "emotional muscle" and compassion to evoke such an attachment, the chance of the treatment flourishing is nearly zero.

### The absconded patient

Most analysts have had the terribly upsetting experience of treating a patient who leaves treatment without notice and refuses to discuss the matter or respond to the analyst's outreach. The patient just "vanishes," leaving the analyst feeling utterly bewildered at the patient's behavior. Some patients declare they are leaving treatment for a flimsy, far-fetched or frivolous reason without adequate discussion. No matter what the analyst says, the patient's mind is made up and they leave treatment, sometimes having worked themselves up into a fine lather of moral indignation, thinking that the analyst does not agree with their decision and that the analyst is possibly motivated by self-centric ulterior motives, such as financial enhancement. In psychoanalytic theory, these types of patients are usually discussed in terms of "resistance," the variety of conscious and unconscious ways that patients "defend" against facing something powerfully threatening to their taken-for-granted way of being-in-the-world. As Shakespeare wrote in *Macbeth* (4.2), "All is the fear, and nothing is the love, as little is the wisdom, where the flight so runs against all reason." Freud brilliantly described the different types of patient resistance the analyst must reckon with: repression resistance, transference resistance, id resistance, super-ego resistance and epinosic resistance (not wanting to give up symptoms that afford significant primary and secondary gratification) (1926b, p. 160). Regardless of the type of resistance, the patient's unconscious "end-game" is to avoid self-awareness and self-knowledge of his painful infantile wishes, fantasies and impulses.

When a patient "vanishes" without any prior notification, it initially leaves the analyst feeling like anyone who has been suddenly, massively and decisively "thrown over" within the context of a longstanding love relationship: it "rocks his universe." The analyst feels shocked, unintelligibly abandoned; he feels the loss of a deep connection with a person he cared for, a loss that inevitably evokes self-questioning: "Why was I not good enough to stay with?" The analyst's sense of "lovability," of being appreciated for his clinical effectiveness, is challenged in a way that feels profoundly troubling. Along with self-doubt, the analyst can feel "castrated." In one fell swoop the patient has rendered him utterly impotent in terms of his *raison d'être*, being a skillful practitioner of his healing art. Indeed, the analyst feels that, in conjunction with the "vanishing" patient's motivation, to leave the analyst in the "shocking" way he did was a sadistic impulse. For when a longstanding patient leaves treatment without warning, the intention is, in part, to violently assault the analyst, to humiliate him by rendering him permanently mute. Taking away the analyst's capacity to speak the truth is, at least in the mind and heart of the analyst, a kind of "soul murder." Soul murder, as Henrik Ibsen and August Strindberg first formulated the notion, is the obliteration of the love of life of another person (Marcus, 2013, p. 145). The analyst who is violently condemned to silence by his "vanishing" patient is to have his love of psychoanalytic healing temporarily sucked out of him. Whether it is the suffering of "abandonment" and/or "castration," in these "circumstances of radical disjuncture of an unpredictable kind" (Giddens, 1984, p. 60), the analyst's normative sense of his desirability and agency, two important aspects for maintaining a coherent narrative of self-identity, has been seriously challenged, if not undermined.

### The untimely departed patient

When a patient prematurely leaves treatment with some perfunctory discussion, the analyst's "suffering" tends to be experienced somewhat differently. In these scenarios, the analyst feels intense irritation, if not anger. Like in the work context when one feels unreasonably fired or for some other unconvincing reason laid off or made redundant (Marcus, 2017), the analyst feels as if the patient is not only acting incredibly "stupidly," but he is also utterly disregarding the analyst's compelling rationale (at least according to the analyst) for why the patient's decision to leave treatment is ill-conceived and likely ill-fated. While the analyst believes that the patient's decision to leave treatment is a form of resistance/defense, and he tries very hard to point this out and exploit this understanding to convince the patient to remain in treatment, the fact is that, like with the "vanishing" patient, he feels as if he is being forced into a unwarranted and unwanted grief. This grieving process can operate on the conscious and/or unconscious levels. In fact, in many ways, this process calls to mind Elisabeth Kübler-Ross's (1969, 2005) path-breaking work on "death and dying," particularly on people who have lost or are about to lose a loved one.

In the "denial" stage, the person left behind, the analyst, is unwilling and unable to admit to himself that the therapeutic relationship is over. The analyst may continue to seek the former patient's attention by reaching out to convince him that his decision to leave the treatment relationship was radically ill-conceived and ill-fated. Sometimes this "denial" phase is undergone mainly on the fantasy level, depending on the real and/or imagined circumstances of the patient's departure.

In the "anger" stage, the analyst may blame the departing patient (e.g., he is "acting out") or himself (e.g., I "screwed up" the treatment). His anger is at the loss of the patient, someone he was very connected to, and the unfairness of how he was treated. This stage is when the analyst's sense of "abandonment" is felt most acutely.

In the "bargaining" stage, the analyst may "plead" with a patient that the stimulus that motivated the departure will not occur again. The analyst may say to the patient in reality or fantasy, "I can change what you hated. Please give me another chance." Sometimes, the analyst may try to renegotiate the rules of engagement, that is, the terms of the therapeutic relationship, in effect saying, "I promise greatly improved behavior if you come back to treatment."

In the "depression" stage, the analyst usually feels disheartened that their bargaining plea did not convince the patient to remain in treatment. Once it becomes apparent that anger and bargaining will not reverse the loss of the patient, he may then sink into a depressive mood, where he faces the irreversibility of his loss and his helplessness to change the outcome. During this period the grieving analyst may subtly internally withdraw from other therapeutic relationships while he processes the loss he has withstood. Frequently, this involves blaming himself for having caused or contributed to the patient's departure, regardless of whether this self-judgment is justified.

Finally, in the "acceptance" stage the analyst gives up all real and fantasized efforts toward renewal of the therapeutic relationship. He has processed his initial feelings and is willing and able to accept that the loss has happened and cannot be reversed. He now fully re-engages in his daily therapeutic life, while "promising" to himself that he will never again make the mistakes he made in the botched treatment. For, as I have said, to the Axial-inspired analyst, a bungled treatment is always his fault.

As Kübler-Ross pointed out, the above-described stage theory is not a linear and predictable progression. In fact, not all phases are experienced by everyone, or at all. Moreover, as Kübler-Ross's critics have pointed out, there are other forms of grief that she does not describe (Shermer, 2008; Konigsberg, 2011). This being said, my sense is that most analysts who have endured the different types of "absconding" patient to some degree experience aspects of the grieving process along the lines of Kübler-Ross's findings. Moreover, a modified grieving process occurs when a patient appropriately leaves treatment. In these contexts the analyst may feel a bittersweet sadness that someone he was deeply connected to, like a good friend, has taken leave and will not likely be heard from again. These feelings are not sentimental outbreaks, something that most analysts are not prone to, but rather reflect the fact that he takes relationships very seriously and is therefore prone to the same painful feelings as most emotionally attuned people are in the context of "endings."

In the mind of the Axial-inspired analyst, the most important question emanating from the analyst's grieving process over his "failed" treatments or daily instantiations of his personal limitations in his analytic work is: what can he internally do to generate the will and ability to carry on at a "higher" level of autonomy, integration and humanity as he continues to practice his healing art, the "impossible" profession that he mysteriously loves? For unless the analyst can minimize the amount of his psychological scar tissue and callus, he is unlikely to be willing and able to function effectively as an analyst or consistently enjoy his therapeutic work. As with other "helping professionals," analysts are vulnerable to becoming "burned out." Burnout is the emotional and physical exhaustion produced by protracted experiences of stress and frustration in the workplace that leads to the analyst or psychotherapist's loss of strength and motivation (Mayo Clinic, 2015).

In a variation on burnout, what was once experienced as a "calling" now feels like a mere "career" or "job." In vocational terms, a "career" is a way to advance oneself in terms of accomplishment, status and prestige, while a "job" is geared toward earning a living for oneself and one's family to prosper and maximize leisure time. In contrast, a "calling" is a work orientation in which work is viewed as a central part of one's identity, as deeply satisfying and socially beneficial (Marcus, 2017, p. 49). In addition to burnout, the analyst is vulnerable to other forms of dehumanization, such as the loss or compromise of his dignity and integrity, sometimes without noticing it. Thus, the analyst needs to continuously engage in internal efforts to minimize and mitigate the buildup of psychological/spiritual calcifications, the conditions of possibility for being dehumanized.

While there is "self-help" literature on coping with burnout and other forms of dehumanization in the work context (ibid.), for illustrative purposes I want to end this section by making three points about how the Axial-inspired analyst tends to transform his moral wounding into moral insight. That is, within the context of his analytic work, I demonstrate what can be heeded from therapeutic "failures" and an everyday awareness of personal limitations and flaws that can enhance the analyst's autonomy, integration and humanity.

In *Antigone*, the Axial-inspired Sophocles notes that although all people make mistakes, those good people admit their mistake and fix it. In other words, the analyst who accepts with the fullness of his being that he "failed" his patients because of his personal limitations and flaws, usually because of some form of self-centrism, is affirming that he has not been the true bearer of his being. That is, if you agree with Levinas's ethical account of human existence, then by shirking responsibility for and to the patient, the analyst is unequivocally affirming that he is inescapably and inexcusably guilty. "Genuine guilt," as I call it, reflects the awareness that one has let down, if not radically betrayed or abandoned, the vulnerable and weak patient. The only compelling response to this self-accusation of moral failure of responsibility to the "absconded" patient's "distress call" and to the distress of current patients is a reaffirmation of the Axial ethical spirit of self-sacrifice, a kind of visceral ethics that demands skillfully "giving until it hurts." Guilt that does not evoke a greater commitment to responsibility for and to the other before oneself is pseudo-guilt or neurotic guilt, for it does not lead to a change of moral consciousness and behavior – to the upsurge of the analyst's will and ability to be skillfully other-directed, other-regarding and other-serving to his suffering patients. As Confucius has said, glory comes from rising after we fail, not from never failing at all (Kothari, 2010, p. xix).

Transforming the analyst's moral wounding into moral insight also requires him to embrace an outlook on his clinical work that accepts not only his therapeutic "failures" and the daily destructive acts of omission and commission he perpetrates on his patients, but also the sobering fact that even the small victories do not come easily. Drawing from the poetic wit of the great Axial-inspired Arabic scholar Al Hariri, Freud noted in the last sentence of *Beyond the Pleasure Principle*, "What we cannot reach flying we must reach limping ... The Book tells us it is no sin to limp" (1920, p. 64). The analyst must cultivate a profound humility in the face of his well-intentioned efforts to reduce his patient's suffering, efforts that quite likely will only lead to a moderately satisfying outcome from the analyst's perspective. Indeed, doing analytic work, or for that matter any kind of in-depth psychotherapy, requires that the analyst come to terms with the absurdity of his endeavor. By absurdity I mean, following Camus (1991), the fact that for the secular intellectual, as opposed to the religious believer, human existence is perceived to be unjust and unintelligible. If absurdity emanates from disparity (Zaretsky, 2013, p. 28), a perceived radical incongruence between our expectations and fate, between our wishes and reality, especially about meaningful matters like a marriage (as in the case of Camus's imploding marriage), or practicing our vocational "calling" (as in the case of the analyst), then indeed, in many ways the analytic encounter is an absurd one. The patient consciously claims that he wants help with his problems but unconsciously fights "tooth and nail" to maintain the integrity of his painful neurosis. The analyst's chances of a satisfactory therapeutic outcome are minimal, according to Freud, and yet he is willing and able to fight against all odds to prevail against his patient's neurotic need/wish to suffer ad infinitum.

Even more absurd is that verbal communication is the main medium through which that patient and analyst relate to each other, and yet the way they communicate reflects their radically different outlooks on life. If Wittgenstein is correct, "The limits of language (of the language which alone I understand) mean the limits of my world" (Schroeder, 2006, p. 95), and Derrida is correct that all "communication is always miscommunication" (Van Deurzen, 2009, p. 127), then the analytic couple are thrown into what feels like an endless thicket of communicative misunderstandings, misrepresentations and misinterpretations, often eliciting further obfuscated emotional storms. As Derrida noted:

> No one [including a patient] gets angry at a mathematician or a physicist whom he or she doesn't understand at all, or at someone who speaks a foreign language, but rather at someone [like an analyst] who tampers with your own language, with this "relation," precisely, which is yours.
>
> (1995, p. 115)

Within this communicative maelstrom of misattunements, the analyst passionately tries to be a "truth-teller" to a patient who passionately wants to unconsciously "lie" to himself. As Freud noted, "the analytic relationship is based on a love of truth – that is, on a recognition of reality – and that it precludes any kind of sham or deceit" (1937, p. 248). For the analyst to earnestly believe that within this bizarre, agonistic relational context he will be able to therapeutically prevail, to help co-produce a modulating bridge of understanding and insight between him and his patient, can be judged as farfetched and, at worst, contrary to reason. Such a belief personifies Camus's "essential concept and the first truth," the absurd. As Camus noted:

> The gods had condemned Sisyphus to ceaselessly rolling a rock to the top of the mountain, whence the stone would fall back of its own weight. They had thought with some reasons that there is no more dreadful punishment than futile and hopeless labor.
>
> (1991, p. 119)

I doubt there is one analyst in the world who has not felt, at least once, that he was engaged in an endless repetition of a meaningless task. Who has not felt the sickening sense that daily analytic work is ultimately inconsequential (Zaretsky, 2013, pp. 38, 49)?

Similar to Freud, Camus felt that the only effective way to respond to absurdity is lucidity: "The misery and greatness of this world: it offers no truths, but only objects for love. Absurdity is king, but love saves us from it" (ibid., p. 58). Indeed, the analyst steeped in the Axial ethical spirit lives his professional and personal life according to two interrelated principles. The first is a "negative" one that Camus, the secular intellectual, put just right. One must continuously ask oneself, "Have I done nothing to degrade my life or another's" (ibid., p. 123)? By critically reflecting on one's way of being with one's patients using this moral criterion, the analyst remains ethically centered, compassionately human and continuously geared to self-correction. The second principle is a "positive" one that has a religious/spiritual resonance to it, and which was beautifully stated by the Axial-influenced Rabbi Tarfon, a third-generation Mishnah scholar: "It is not our responsibility to finish the work [of perfecting the world], but neither are you free to abstain from it" (author's translation). That is, the Axial-inspired analyst understands that what matters most is his effort to grow and nurture the patient's capacity for Goodness (which is co-mingled with the valuative attachments of Justice, Truth and Beauty that are instantiated in "real-life"). While he may not achieve this satisfying therapeutic result, he must keep trying to do better, which is a kind of desperate heroism, as Camus conceptualized it (Zaretsky, 2013, p. 6).

However, the Axial outlook allows the analyst to go even further in his moral reflection, and here lies the "redemptive" moment when he thinks about his practice of his "impossible" profession, including its often "unsatisfying results" as Freud described it. That is, every analyst has had some clinical success in his work, even a few very good outcomes, and the memory of having made a huge positive difference in a person's life is a transformative moral experience that allows him to carry on working, always with the hope that his help with each patient will be as significant. This moral insight has been stated in nearly all Axial religious/spiritual traditions, most clearly perhaps in the Talmud (Sanhedrin 37a), where Camus's "negative" assertion and the Axial-inspired "positive" one is joined: "Whoever destroys a soul, it is considered as if he destroyed an entire world. And whoever saves a life, it is considered as if he saved an entire world" (Hosseini, 2015, p. 157).

The upshot of this moral outlook is that it allows the Axial analyst to give the daily grind of his therapeutic work a cosmic significance, one that gives him the strength and motivation to skillfully "give until it hurts" in service to his patients. Camus, who regarded himself as one of the "stubborn sons of Greece," noted that such a transcendent outlook works against the "darkest nihilism." This is a faith-driven transcendence that emanates "from an instinctive fidelity to a light which I was born, and in which for thousands of years men have learned to welcome life even in suffering" (Zaretsky, 2013, p. 8). For the "suffering" analyst who against all odds can kindle a little bit of light in the being of his "suffering" patient can feel that his existence has been justified.

## Suffering the other's suffering

R.D. Laing put it just right when he described what it is like for the "suffering" analyst to therapeutically encounter the much more profoundly "suffering" patient: "We are bemused and crazed creatures, strangers to our true selves, to one another, and to the spiritual and material world – mad, even, from an ideal standpoint we can glimpse but not adopt" (1983, p. 13). Indeed, when one is face to face with a suffering patient, one has to be willing and able to skillfully engage all the aspects of his alienation and trauma, always from *his* wounded perspective, and always with an eye to helping reduce his suffering and to live better. While discussing how this is technically accomplished with the range of "types" of patient – depressives, anxiety-ridden, narcissistic, borderline, psychotic and the like – is beyond the scope of this chapter, I briefly comment on the specific types of "suffering" that depressive, anxious and psychotic patients tend to engender in the analyst in terms of his efforts to maintain his "center of gravity" or autonomy, integration and humanity while also trying to help his patient.[9]

This existential challenge of being immersed in the patient's deeply troubled and troubling "world" can be perilous for the analyst, especially if he is mindful that the psychological difference between the "suffering" patient and the "suffering" analyst is minimal. As Freud noted, "Every normal person, in fact, is only normal on the average. His ego approximates to that of the psychotic in some part or other and to a greater or lesser extent" (1937, p. 235). Put more starkly, one should recall what the great American mythologist Joseph Campbell wrote, "The psychotic drowns in the same waters in which the mystic swims with delight," as there is a fine line between what is judged as crazy versus spiritual (Grof, 2000, p. 136).[10] The Axial-inspired analyst recognizes that the difference between the patient and analyst, at least in terms of the painful imagery in his mind, is one of degree, less of kind. As Theodor Reik noted, the most important difference between the analyst and the patient (the latter of whom may be more intelligent and/or creative) is a pragmatic moral one: the analyst has "faced" himself, honestly and courageously confronting his personal flaws, limitations, failures and "demons," while the patient has not.[11] Likewise, the analyst recognizes that in a world that often feels soaked in pure contingency, it is to a large extent by happenstance that his fate has been better than that of his alienated, traumatized and wounded patients. Such ironic awareness almost always induces an upsurge of humility and gratitude in the analyst, who cannot help but say to himself the thankful words attributed to the twentieth-century English evangelical clergyman Edward Bickersteth: "There but for the grace of God go I."

In this section I take my organizational lead from a statement that Levinas made: "The other [e.g., the patient] is ... the first rational teaching, the condition of all teaching" (1969, p. 203). Moreover, what this "first teaching teaches ... [is] transcendence itself ... the ethical," that is, goodness, conceived as responsibility for the other without reciprocity (ibid., p. 173). Patients, regardless of their "type" of psychopathology, teach the analyst something about himself, about his moral limitations, if not failures, and what he should strive to do better. Indeed, Kohut made this point rather well:

If there is one lesson that I have learned during my life as an analyst, it is the lesson that what my patients tell me is likely to be true – that many times when I believed that I was right and my patients were wrong, it turned out, though often only after a prolonged search, that *my* rightness was superficial whereas *their* rightness was profound.

(Orange, 2016, pp. 181–182)

While the issue of the analyst's moral limitations and failures is a huge subject, it deserves at least some comment in this chapter, for it is a major contributing factor to the analyst's "suffering" and "redemption."

### The depressed patient

Working with chronically depressed patients, who are notoriously self-centric, is enormously challenging for the analyst because it situates him in the patient's unrelentingly closed, suffocating world of radical hopelessness and helplessness. I have always thought of the chronically depressed as like "a drop of wine in a cake of ice." Most chronically depressed patients are nearly impossible to consistently motivate to actively participate in the complex practices of self-fashioning their thoughts, desires and emotions toward the reduction of suffering and to the actualization of the "good life." For a variety of psychodynamic, contextual and, perhaps biochemical reasons, they refuse to "think differently" about their painful condition, let alone act differently in their concrete lives, the two conditions of possibility that can help the depressed patient feel better. Indeed, when it comes to treating chronically depressed patients, often the movement of the therapy works like certain Axial religions and philosophies were said to operate on the spiritual aspirant's "soul." As one rabbinic scholar in the Middle Ages wrote, "the heart [i.e., the emotions] will follow the action" [i.e., the behavior]. Likewise, the Hellenistic medical conception of the philosopher as the compassionate doctor/healer of the soul emphasized a "commitment to action" along with critical thought (i.e., self-examination and self-discovery), as a necessary valuative attachment for a pupil to be better able to pursue the Good (Nussbaum, 1994, p. 33).

Part of Axial practical wisdom is that in some contexts it is the "doing" before the motivation, before the "thinking" and "feeling," that makes the difference between defeat (e.g., remaining depressed) and victory (e.g., feeling better) in life. Analysts are used to working from the patient's "inside" world (e.g., examining motives, beliefs, wishes and fantasies) to the "outside" world (changing the patient's behavior in "real life"). Helping the chronically depressed to be willing and able to engage in "doings" before he "thinks" and "feels" allows him to better viscerally understand the significance of what he did, and to see the positive impact of his "doings" on his mood and how others respond to him (the latter of which further positively impacts his mood). With repetition and some luck, this interrelated, interdependent and interactive dialectical scrutiny of action/thought/feeling can be the beginning of life-enhancing change.

The chronic depressive suffering of the patient, combined with his emotional "battering" of the analyst who must metabolize the patient's persistent hopelessness and other negative emotions, can evoke a similarly depressive sentiment in the vulnerable analyst. What feels true for the patient begins to feel true for the analyst, which can have dire consequences for the analyst's outlook and behavior. As Camus (1991) noted, anyone who knows he lacks hope is no longer a part of the future. Even worse, the analyst's psychoanalytic "wisdom" does not always significantly diminish the patient's chronically depressive condition, which adds to the analyst's lack of self-efficacy that can undermine his sense of professional competence, identity and sense of purpose. Like his chronically depressed patient, the analyst can begin to wonder whether his work life is meaningful and not merely a "tale told by an idiot." This can especially be the case if other patients are also floundering or "stuck." This reaction can be made even more complicated in terms of the analyst's negative self-judgment if he recalls what Freud wrote in a letter to the French author and psychoanalyst, Princess Marie Bonaparte:

> The moment a man questions the meaning and value of life, he is sick, since objectively neither has any existence; by asking this question one is merely admitting to a store of unsatisfied libido to which something else must have happened, a kind of fermentation leading to sadness and depression.
>
> (Razinsky, 2013, p. 248)

While Freud may have rhetorically magnified his claim in this letter, the typical analyst unsuccessfully treating a chronically depressed patient often struggles with his own sense of hopelessness, helplessness and the subversion of his meaning-structures, especially in terms of his vocational identity and career trajectory (Marcus, 2017). What the chronically depressed patient strikingly "teaches" the analyst takes place in the ethical domain, namely, the critical need to cultivate a powerful patience alongside his humility and fortitude. As Lao Tzu said, "Trying to understand is like straining through muddy water. Have the patience to wait! Be still and allow the mud to settle" (Freke, 1999, p. 77).

Likewise, the idea that "patience is the companion of wisdom," as St. Augustine put it (Akers, 2014, p. 280), has been reaffirmed by analysts time and again: Freud noted that "He who knows how to wait need make no concessions" (Grinstein, 1990, p. 334), while Bion wrote "'Patience' should be retained without 'irritable reaching after fact and reason' until a pattern evolves" (Sosnik, 2012, p. 133). Erikson concurred with his wife in a joint newspaper interview at age 86, saying, "The more you know yourself, the more patience you have for what you see in others."[12] Finally, psychoanalyst Kets de Vries quoted Jung, saying, "Even a happy life cannot be without a measure of darkness, and the word happy would lose its meaning if it were not balanced by sadness. It is far better to take things as they come along with patience and equanimity" (2007, p. 8).

The fact is that analysts who work with chronically depressed patients are prone to feeling a wide range of emotions that run counter to patience, such as frustration and anger. Analysts, like those who live with a chronically depressed family member, sometimes feel utterly "fed up" with their depressed patients, as if their complex condition was their fault, something they should be willing and able to quickly overcome, to "snap out of." Even Freud was not immune to such episodic cynical feelings in his analytic work, having written to Sándor Ferenczi, "'patients are rabble' ... patients only serve to provide us with a livelihood and material to learn from. We certainly cannot help them" (Orange, 2011, p. 88).[13] These reflexively pessimistic reactions are often rooted in the analyst's sense of helplessness and fear that he can't potentiate "putting things right," mixed in with the sense of guilt and sadness for possibly having "made things worse" by stimulating the patient's false hopes, and to "add insult to injury" to the patient by charging him a fee in the process. To add to the analyst's "suffering" is the fact that while he deliberately summons his patience as a counterpoint to the frustration and anger the chronically depressed patient evokes in him, he intuits that in his own unconscious mind his patience is actually a cover-up for a darker and more ironically troubling emotion. As the great Ambrose Bierce noted, "Patience is a minor form of despair, disguised as a virtue" (2000, p. 129).

Indeed, the Axial-inspired analyst must exert a fair amount of willpower to generate the necessary patience and caring watchfulness to not give in to his despair about having the unenviable responsibility to slog through the well-fortified stronghold that the chronically depressed patient is "holding out" in. Above all, the analyst needs patient trust that if he does not prematurely break off his methodical compassionate and skillful engagement with his chronically depressed patient, eventually he will prevail in "thawing" his patient's mind. The philosopher/Jesuit priest Pierre Teilhard de Chardin put this point just right: "Above all, trust in the slow work of God."[14] Indeed, when patient trust is supported by firmness and strength of mind, that is, the fortitude (i.e., the ego strength) that analysts value so dearly, along with the attentiveness that is the core of humility (and analytic listening), the chances of the analyst being willing and able to help suffering patients free themselves from their oppressive way of being are greatly increased.

### The anxious patient

"Nothing in the affairs of men is worthy of great anxiety," said Plato (Price & Budzynski, 2009, p. 453). While the iconic Axial philosopher was surely right from the aspirational point of view, he was surely wrong when it comes to how most people live their everyday lives in contemporary society. W.H. Auden called the twentieth century the "Age of Anxiety" in his poetic masterpiece (2011). Indeed, by the time the chronically anxious person comes to an analyst for help, his anxiety has become an almost permanent condition of mental tension, a world that is nearly unbearable to inhabit, and which also evokes distress in the analyst who has to enter deeply into his patient's nightmarish way of being-in-the-world. Such people display more than the "monkey mind," as Buddha metaphorically called the unsettled, restless, uncontrollable nature of human consciousness (our mind is analogous to drunken monkeys, jumping about, shrieking, babbling, carrying on endlessly). In addition, the chronically anxious person is often fending off something much direr, at least beneath the surface experience of his mind. As Heidegger noted, "If I take death into my life, acknowledge it, and face it squarely, I will free myself from the anxiety of death and the pettiness of life – and only then will I be free to become myself" (Stolorow, 2014, p. 184).[15] If Heidegger is right, the chronically anxious person feels radical unsafety and insecurity in the face of his mortality. If Levinas is right, that he also feels radical guilt and shame about avoiding/ignoring his responsibilities to others, especially those he cares most deeply about, then the chronically anxious patient is trapped in a maze of grotesque happenings. These considerations often underlie the so-called "flight/fight/freeze" system that is associated with highly anxious patients and stress-related conditions.

The above-described moral anguish of the chronically anxious patient can make the analyst feel befuddled in terms of how to help his patient achieve a reasonable and calm perspective on his overdetermined, if not neurotic, anxiety. This is especially challenging for the analyst since his main tools, his words that rely on logic and reasoning as much as emotional attunement, do not continuously work in relieving his patient's suffering. The Stoic philosopher Epictetus's famous maxim that is meant to bestow a modicum of autonomy and serenity to how a patient relates to his distressing thoughts – "Men are disturbed not by the things which happen, but by the opinions about the things" – means almost nothing to a chronically anxious person (2009, p. 3).[16]

As with the chronically depressed patient, the "suffering" analyst may feel an upsurge of helplessness when facing a chronically anxious patient. Moreover, he may feel a sense of endangerment that calls to mind the chronically anxious patient's sense of unsafety and insecurity. This is mainly because the patient's panicky neediness and desperate clinging greatly impede the analyst in his willingness and ability to wholeheartedly give his compassionate therapeutic skillfulness, his "love," to his "drowning" patient. The analyst's underwhelming response leaves him feeling guilty, and in other ways deeply troubled for his minimalist, if not failed, response. Indeed, Anaïs Nin aptly described how the analyst feels: "Anxiety is love's greatest killer. It makes others feel as you might when a drowning man holds on to you. You want to save him, but you know he will strangle you with his panic" (1971, p. 185). Indeed, for these and other reasons pertinent to the phenomenology of the chronically anxious patient, the analyst may keep himself "at arm's length" from his patient, an indication that he is failing in his "holding" and "caring" function. Figuratively speaking, the analyst unconsciously maintains an ill-conceived and ill-fated distance from his patient that affords him a level of safety that excludes intimacy, contributing to the patient's anxious suffering.

The Axial sages gave wise counsel to the analyst who shies away from his moral responsibility to do everything he can to "save" his anxious patient. As Socrates said, "He is a man of courage who does not run away, but remains at his post and fights against the enemy; of that you may be very certain" (Plato, 1871, p. 83). What often prevents the analyst from behaving courageously is that he is self-occupied rather than other-directed, other-regarding and other-serving. That is, his own needs and desires for safety and security take precedence over those of his patient's, which boils down to a preponderance of selfishness and failure of nerve. Indeed, at these self-centric moments the analyst is relinquishing his role as "good-enough mother," leaving the "drowning-in-anxiety" patient to fend for himself, with dire consequences to the patient. As Anna Freud has pointed out, "It is only when parental feelings are ineffective or too ambivalent or when the mother's emotions are temporarily engaged elsewhere that children feel lost, but, in fact, get lost" (Geissmann & Geissmann, 1998, p. 66). Thus, what the Axial-inspired analyst knows in his mind and heart is that it is his duty to be willing and able to be self-forgetting, self-emptying, to be "a radically non-self-centered self" as he engages in extended empathic immersion and practical clinical skillfulness for the sake of the other (Orange, 2016, p. 75). This is the analyst's way of throwing a life-saving "rope" to the "drowning" patient. As Confucius said, "Faced with what is right, to leave it undone shows a lack of courage," which is the basis for the upsurge of shame for being so wrapped up in oneself (1979, p. 24).

### The psychotic patient

If psychoanalytically treating the chronically depressed patient is like trying to extract a drop of wine from a cake of ice, and if treating the chronically anxious patient is like trying to rescue a drowning swimmer, then treating a psychotic patient is like trying to "batten down the hatches" on a boat amidst a raging tempest. Indeed, the treatment of a psychotic patient requires the analyst to enter in their world of extreme internal and external chaos. While Buddha noted, "Chaos is inherent in all compounded things. Strive on with diligence," I doubt he had in mind a psychotic patient whose life feels to him, and presents to the analyst at first encounter, like a "chaotic dump."[17] Indeed, helping the psychotic out of his extreme confusion, frenzy and darkness to find an inner center of gravity and reinvent himself is nearly impossible, even with the assistance of anti-psychotic medications. And yet it is the analyst's responsibility to attempt just that, even though it often feels like trying to find a black cat in a pitch-black cabin on a ship twisting and contorting during a terrible storm: "In all chaos there is a cosmos," said Jung, "in all disorder a secret order, in all caprice a fixed law, for everything that works is grounded on its opposite" (1969, p. 32). In other words, the analyst has to use his clinical skills to help potentiate some clarity and existential grounding in being and meaning to the psychotic patient's everyday life of radical disarray. Rather than being a centered, decision-making, free and responsible self (Tillich, 1954, p. 114), he assumes a jumbled mode of self-relating that protects him from an awareness of his profound despair, including about his estrangement and grossly under-actualized social identity, among other compelling vulnerabilities and deficits that are apparent to him in the "real world." Freud made this point clear when he noted:

> the most important genetic difference between neurosis and psychosis: neurosis is the result of a conflict between the ego and the id, whereas psychosis is the analogous outcome of a similar disturbance in the relations between the ego and the external world.
>
> (1924, p. 149)

For the analyst to be amidst the "orgy of disorder"[18] that the psychotic patient exudes is no easy thing to live with over an extended period of time, for the obvious reasons. Most importantly, it makes one feel out of control, if not helpless, and it tends to drain one's *élan vital*, that impulse of life, especially its creative aspect that Henri Bergson so aptly described. The seventeenth-century English philosopher, poet, playwright and essayist Margaret Lucas Cavendish succinctly described the downside of being around too much disorder for too long: "For disorder obstructs: besides, it doth disgust life, distract the appetites, and yield no true relish to the senses" (1872, p. 35). Indeed, the psychotic's way of being often requires that the analyst metabolize and counterforce many of the noxious qualities associated with "toxic" individuals, those tainted by unconscious malevolence who are prone to be devaluing if not abusive in their behavior.

For example, similar to "toxic" people, psychotic patients are prone to be "deaf" to what you meaningfully say, even more than most other types of "resisting," "less sick" patients. Their only concern is that you listen to the point they are putting forth; they are prone to monologues, not dialogues, a tendency that works against the dialectical interchange and scrutiny that is the bailiwick of psychoanalytic process and illumination. Every inch of the way, the psychotic patient consciously and unconsciously aggressively fights the analyst's reality-oriented insights, more than neurotic patients. Unlike the great Stoic teachers that applied narrative and example to help induce the qualitative shift in their highly motivated pupil's perception of reality, the analyst strives to bring about soul-transforming change in his aggressively "resisting" psychotic patient, often feeling as if he has "one hand tied behind his back" (Vlastos, 1991, pp. 98, 99). The psychotic's use of primitive defense mechanisms, such as denial, fantasy and regression, makes getting them to be willing and able to "listen" to what the analyst is saying especially challenging.

Like with "toxic" people, in his word and deed the psychotic exudes an arrogantly superior and disdainful attitude that is geared to make the analyst feel that he is incompetent and insufficient, this being one of the ways that the psychotic boosts his own self-esteem and distances himself from the analyst. When confronted about this defensive way of being, the psychotic tends to blame the analyst and/or play the victim rather than critically reflect on his behavior and take responsibility for it. Needless to say, this can be a very hard-going moment for the analyst.

The psychotic's "toxicity" extends to his being consciously and/or unconsciously manipulative. This can take the form of inducing ill-conceived guilt for things the analyst did not actually say or do. The psychotic's goal here is to make the analyst feel like the "bad guy," the one who did something wrong or stupid. This can be done so craftily that the analyst can begin to question the veracity of his own perception of reality, as if he is the delusional one, the one who is "mad." As the Axial-inspired Catholic theologian/mystic Thomas Merton noted:

> The devil is no fool. He can get people feeling about heaven the way they ought to feel about hell. He can make them fear the means of grace the way they do not fear sin. And he does so, not by light but by obscurity, not by realities but by shadows; not by clarity and substance, but by dreams and the creatures of psychosis.
>
> (Merton, 1948, pp. 29–30)

When the analyst begins to feel he is on an extended "crazy ride" with his patient, he may well wonder to himself, "is it me or the patient who is 'crazy'"?

Similar to other "toxic" people, another source of great frustration for the analyst treating the psychotic patient is that he tends to be impervious to critical reason and argumentation once his mind is made up. This is mainly because he lacks accurate empathy and does not concern himself with where the analyst, or anyone else, is coming from. A "frontal assault" on the psychotic's delusional system and other steadfastly held beliefs only makes things worse. Instead, one has to be willing and able to engage in a philosophy of very gradual change that involves patient and skillful attunement and deep and abiding compassion as one enters into the psychotic's extremely troubled, troubling and rigidly maintained mode of being-in-the-world. Only after trust exists between the analyst and the psychotic will he be willing and able to open the gates to his psychotic center. While such considerations are operative with all patients, what is in sharper focus with the psychotic is that their inner experience appears to be nearly hermetically sealed from the critical "give and take" interpersonal compromises and concessions that "less sick" patients are able to make – and the analyst is better equipped and comfortable to engage in.

Like other "toxic" people, the psychotic is typically highly narcissistic in that he drastically lacks adequate self-esteem and his self-concept is greatly impoverished. As a result of being so insecurely grounded as a person he compensates by becoming overly self-occupied, self-referential and selfish in outlook and behavior. Not only does he demand that others, including the analyst, be satellites in his orbit, he also rarely easily defers to the needs and wishes of the other, even urgent or important ones. This can include not taking in, let alone graciously, the "gifts" of insight and support that the analyst offers that are meant to help him better orient himself to reality. Indeed, for a variety of complex psychodynamic, existential and contextual reasons the psychotic has the wish to not be comprehended alongside its opposite. As Kahlil Gibran ironically noted, there can be a freedom and safety in madness (2002, p. 8). For the analyst, the psychotic's "closedness" – his narcissistically driven, self-protective wish to remain distant, unrelated and inaccessible – can be very off-putting, especially to analysts who feel they are effective caregivers.

To wield against the psychotic's disorder and "toxicity," an experience that can "suck the life" out of the analyst if he is not resilient enough, the analyst has very little in his armamentarium that can help the patient get some control over the destructive power of his condition. However, helping the patient to derive some awareness of what is going on inside him can be the beginning of "refinding" himself and providing a small measure of hope for the patient and analyst that "this, too, shall pass." In some cases, "reinventing" himself is possible. Understanding one's madness, that is, having some kind of reasoned, meaningful framework to make sense out of it, especially when lodged in a loving relationship between patient and analyst, can have a gradually far-reaching, positively transformative impact on the patient's life. Sartre has skillfully made this point. It is worth quoting in full as the coda to this section:

> A lucid view of the darkest situation is already, in itself, an act of optimism. Indeed, it implies that the situation is thinkable; that is to say, we have not lost our way in it as though in a dark forest, and we can on the contrary detach ourselves from it, at least in mind, and keep it under observation; we can therefore go beyond it and resolve what to do against it, even if our decisions are desperate.
>
> (Van Deurzen, 2009, p. 99)

### A word about child and adolescent patients

Most analysts would agree that in general, treating children (especially "under fives") and adolescents is much more clinically challenging compared to adults. Indeed, for a variety of psychodynamic, developmental and contextual reasons, trying to help children and adolescents get their lives on track developmentally is intellectually complicated and emotionally demanding. Treating such patients puts into sharp focus a particular "suffering," or at least distress, that the analyst may feel; namely, he is engaged in a coercive relationship with the child/adolescent. That is, most children and adolescents do not willingly come to treatment; they are usually "forced" to go by their parents, school or court, which means the analyst is a co-conspirator in a process that feels to their young patient like "bullying." While the child/adolescent's parents and analyst believe they are "forcing" their offspring to go into treatment for their own good (or "best interests" if it is a court referral), the fact is the young patient is being given an offer he can't refuse. This heavy-handed aspect of the treatment context can make the analyst feel like a kind of brute rather than a loving caregiver who is honoring his patient's autonomy and freedom, two of the valuative attachments intrinsic to the psychoanalytic outlook and practice.

The only way the analyst can nullify his sense of being a coercive, bullying brute is to intensify his efforts to engage his young patient in a respectful manner, to understand his predicament from his perspective on its own terms, to ally with him as being someone he can trust, and to always be willing and able to advocate for him. Moreover, by emphasizing that it is through deferential understanding, through the "give and take" of psychoanalytic dialectical interplay and scrutiny, that the patient hopefully begins to feel that while the original basis of the treatment was coercive, the actual experience of the treatment is its opposite or "for the other."

A second distressing consideration that is unique to treating children and adolescents is the fact that typically the analyst is not the primary psychological figure in their lives, the one who most symbolizes nurturance and stability, as this is the parental role. As a result of this contextual consideration, the analyst must defer to the judgment of the parents about a number of important everyday issues pertinent to treatment, including about whether treatment continues. The analyst can begin to feel a degree of helplessness vis-à-vis his young patient because he does not ultimately have reasonable control, or even influence, over the course of treatment the way he does with a consenting adult. In other words, in a variety of ways related to the everyday life of the child and adolescent, it is the parent's "call" and not the analyst's that matters most. This can be a huge source of frustration for the analyst, especially when the parent does not follow the analyst's suggestions and/or prematurely takes the child out of treatment. Indeed, compared to being an adult analyst, the child analyst must "know his place" – he must not allow any residual infantile omnipotent and controlling wishes to dominate his reactions to the trajectory of treatment. In short, he must be willing and able to humble himself in the face of parent-controlled reality.

## Conclusion

Being a psychoanalyst is not for "wimps." Any residual childhood-based timidity or cowardliness must have no role in the analyst's self-relation and in how he comports himself with his patients. As I have tried to show throughout this chapter, those who choose the "impossible" profession as a career must be willing and able to "suffer" with, and for, patients in a variety of distressing ways, ever mindful that what is true for patients is also true for the analyst. As Jung wrote:

> There is no coming to consciousness without pain. People will do anything, no matter how absurd, in order to avoid facing their own soul. One does not become enlightened by imagining figures of light, but by making the darkness conscious.
>
> (Hessed, 2017, p. 151)

An Axial-inspired analyst understands that, against all odds, he must approach the suffering and challenges intrinsic to his clinical work with great practical wisdom, wisdom that takes at least two forms, both suggested or at least implied by Freud. One metaphorically draws from a militaristic spirit, and the other an ethical one. "I am actually not at all a man of science, not an observer, not an experimenter, not a thinker," wrote Freud to Wilhelm Fliess: "I am by temperament nothing but a conquistador – an adventurer, if you want it translated – with all the curiosity, daring, and tenacity characteristic of a man of this sort" (Freud, 1985, p. 398). While in this quote Freud played down the literal meaning of the word "conquistador," the term can be reasonably interpreted as including the soldiering aspect of its meaning, as one who embodies the best of the moral values and strategic and tactical skillfulness associated with a great military leader.[19] As Sun Tzu, the greatest military strategist of all times, who also lived during the Axial period, noted: "The general encompasses wisdom [sincerity], benevolence [humanity], courage, and strictness [discipline]" (1993, p. 157); "Know the enemy [e.g., the patient's defense/resistances] and of yourself [e.g., your counter-transferences]; in a hundred battles you will never be in peril" (1963, p. 84);[20] "Thus, what is of supreme importance in war [in psychoanalysis] is to attack the enemy's strategy" (e.g., the patient's unconscious plan of action meant to accomplish his long-term and overall goal of not changing) (ibid., p. 77).[21]

My point is that one of the underappreciated ways the analyst can minimize his and his patient's unnecessary "suffering" is to be smart and skillful in how he does treatment. This requires not only drawing from the insights of the great psychoanalytic clinicians but also drawing from the practical wisdom of the great military strategists of the Axial Age and beyond. They have brilliantly defeated conventional armies, insurgencies and terrorists, which are helpful analogues for how the analyst can prevail in his battle with the patient's defenses/resistances and self-fortifications, and, most importantly, his destructive tendencies (Marcus, 2014).

Whether it is the analyst's suffering, the patient's suffering or the suffering that the analyst and patient cause each other, the most effective way to make such suffering "sufferable," at least generally speaking, is to view it as an ethical dilemma, one that demands an other-directed, other-regarding and other-serving response. Indeed, as mentioned earlier, Freud felt similarly when he wrote that psychoanalysis is "a cure by love" (McGuire, 1974, pp. 12–13). As Levinas pointed out, practically speaking, "this goodness, the nonindifference to the death of the other, this kindness, is precisely the very perfection of love" (Robbins, 2001, p. 58). I want to end this chapter with a short Freud vignette that shows that it was precisely this kind of ethical spirit and behavior that Freud clinically advocated when he was face to face with a suffering patient, and that no doubt also strengthens the analyst's sense of humanity:

> In the fall of 1904, Bruno Goetz, a young poet and a student at the University of Vienna, consulted Freud because of persistent headaches. Freud took a brief history – Goetz was spending what little money he had on books – then engaged the young man in a long discussion of contemporary writers. At the end of the hour Freud announced that he was writing a prescription for the headaches and after sealing it in an envelope sent Goetz on his way, with the warning that psychoanalysis might not be good for poetry. When Goetz reached the street, he opened the envelope and found both Freud's assessment and his remedy. The headaches were caused not by neurosis but by hunger, and Freud enclosed money for Goetz to buy a few good meals.
>
> (Kerr, 1994, pp. 82–83)

## Notes

1 Freud was speaking from the point of view of the analyst, not the patient. The latter may feel otherwise, as is common knowledge among analysts. A recent a comprehensive review of outcome studies and meta-analyses of effectiveness studies of psychodynamic therapy for the major categories of mental disorders indicated that such therapies are effective for depression, some anxiety disorders, eating disorders and somatic disorders. Also, long-term psychodynamic treatment of some personality disorders, particularly borderline personality disorder, has shown to be effective (Fonagy, 2015).

2 I have used the term "patient" rather than "analysand" or "client" because I believe, following the magnificent Hellenistic philosophical schools in Greece and Rome, the Epicureans, Skeptics and Stoics, that the psychoanalyst should practice his craft "as a compassionate physician whose arts could heal many pervasive types of suffering" (Nussbaum, 1994, p. 3). A similar sentiment was articulated by Chuang Tzu, the great Axial Taoist philosopher: "Through the simple art of gentle

conversation the Wise charm away people's sufferings and help them accept their lives" (Freke, 1999, p. 114).

3  Freud was an admirer of ancient Greek thought and may have been influenced in his view of the human condition by Plato's statement in the *Republic*, one which also anticipated Freud's theory of dream-interpretation: "In all of us, even in good men, there is a lawless wild beast nature which peers out in sleep" (Kramer, 1993, p. 155).

4  Freud allegedly said, "A certain degree of neurosis is of inestimable value as a drive, especially to a psychologist" (Wortis, 1954, p. 153).

5  Of course, practicing psychoanalysis can be very enjoyable: it can be intimate, funny, surprising, intellectually stimulating and poignant. This mainly depends on the individual personality and outlook of the analyst, including whether he judges the "pleasure/pain" ratio of clinical work as acceptable.

6  It is worth mentioning the little-known fact that the wisest of ancient Greek philosophers, Socrates, personified the best of military values. He was a decorated military hero and was regarded as an exemplary model of courage and self-discipline (Robertson, 2013, p. 7).

7  The subject of treatment failures, including its impact on the psychotherapist's mental health, has been discussed in the psychotherapy literature. In psychoanalysis, the issue has been less addressed, especially in terms of how it "cuts" into the analyst, the focus of this chapter. See for example, Reppen & Schulman (2002) and Goldberg (2012).

8  For Levinas, the "face" is not to be taken literally as physicality, but rather it is his term for that which disrupts, destabilizes and defamiliarizes thought and its tendency toward totality and sameness; it is "disincarnate presence of the Other" as Levinas scholar Edith Wyschogrod called it. The "face" of the other summons me to be responsible for his welfare before my own. However, this responsibility for the other must be expressed in "real-life" compassion, care and self-sacrifice (Marcus, 2008, p. 26).

9  Listening to the testimonials of patients who have undergone terrible experiences leaves an unforgettable trace of woundedness in the listener. I have listened to Holocaust survivors, victims of political torture, physically and sexually abused adults and children, survivors of natural disasters, and terminally ill patients describe their horrific experiences, and I have never been the same as a result. My reaction may be typical, for no feeling and thinking human being can remain impartial to hearing the testimonials from these "witnesses" to extreme suffering. See, for example, Felman and Laub (1992).

10  In his masterpiece *The Varieties of Religious Experience*, William James suggests why there is a fine line between "crazy" and "spiritual": "The lunatic's visions of horror are all drawn from the material of daily fact" (Capps, 2016, p. 88).

11  This statement was told to me by my late analyst, Philip M. Stone, who was in supervision with Reik during his training at the National Psychological Association for Psychoanalysis. Allegedly, Reik was conveying to Dr. Stone an observation that Freud had made to him in a conversation in Vienna.

12  www.nytimes.com/books/99/08/22/specials/erikson-old.html, retrieved 7/24/17.

13  To be fair to Freud, his cynical view of patients was in sync with his generally pessimistic appraisal of most humans: "The unworthiness of human beings, including the analyst, always impressed me deeply" (Hale, 1971, pp. 163–164). Many other such quotes can be cited.

14  www.ignatianspirituality.com, Ignatian Prayer, retrieved 7/21/17.

15  Long before Heidegger and the advent of existentialism, the Roman poet and Epicurean philosopher Lucretius (*On the Nature of Things*) discussed with great perceptiveness the negative impact of the fear of death on how one lives one's life.

16 Cognitive-behavioral therapists have made this Stoic maxim the bedrock of their theorizing and practice. For example, in Albert Ellis's Rational Emotive Behavior Therapy clients were literally taught this maxim. Stoic thought and practice has influenced Aaron T. Beck's "cognitive distancing" strategies and D. Meichenbaum's "stress inoculation training," as well as some of the "self-monitoring and postponement" and meditation techniques used by later therapists (Robertson, 2013).
17 www.buddhist-tourism.com/buddhism/buddha-quotes.html, retrieved 8/1/17.
18 This evocative phrase is from General George C. Patton's description of battle (Marcus, 2014, pp. 17–18).
19 A conquistador was a soldier residing during the sixteenth and seventeenth centuries who vanquished people in the Americas and their territories for Spain.
20 I have quoted from two different translations of *The Art of War* because their different wordings more aptly convey my points.
21 Another way to think of "attacking" the patient's strategy is to focus on what William James and, later, Erich Fromm described as the patient's philosophy of life; that is, those values, beliefs and meanings that matter to the patient and animate his behavior which are frequently different from his consciously stated ones. For Fromm, the greater the patient's inconsistency between his unconscious and conscious philosophy of life, the more disturbed he is. Both the therapeutic goal and the art of living the "good life" is to consciously fashion a philosophy of life that animates his lived existence (Maccoby, 2017, p. 527). Put differently, as Ibsen noted, "What's man's first duty? The answer is brief: to be himself" (Van Deurzen & Arnold-Baker, 2005, p. 160). .

## References

Akers, M.J. (2014). *Morning and Evening Meditations from the Word of God: Education, Challenges, Inspirations and Encouragement.* Bloomington, IN: Westbow.
Akhtar, S. (2009). *Comprehensive Dictionary of Psychoanalysis.* London: Karnac.
Ambrosio, F.J. (2009). *Philosophy, Religion, and the Meaning of Life* (Course Guidebook). Chantilly, VA: The Teaching Company.
Ardito, R.B., & Rabellino, D. (2011). Therapeutic Alliance and Outcome of Psychotherapy: Historical Excursus, Measurements, and Prospects Of Research. *Frontiers of Psychology*, 2, 270. doi:10.3389/fpsyg.2011.00270
Auden, W.H. (2011). *The Age of Anxiety: A Baroque Eclogue.* Princeton, NJ: Princeton University Press.
Bierce, A. (2000). *The Unabridged Devil's Dictionary.* D.E. Schultz & S.J. Joshi (Eds.). Athens: University of Georgia Press.
Camus, A. (1991). *The Myth of Sisyphus and Other Essays.* New York: Vintage International.
Capps, D. (2016). *The Religious Life: The Insights of William James.* Cambridge, UK: Lutterworth.
Carveth, D.L. (2017). Beyond Nature and Culture. *Psychoanalytic Review*, 104(4), 485–501.
Cavendish, M. (1872). *The Cavalier and His Lady: Selections from the Works of the First Duke and Duchess of Newcastle.* E. Chenkins (Ed.). London: Macmillan.
Confucius. (1979). *The Analects.* D.C. Lau (Trans.). London: Penguin.
Derrida, J. (1995). *Points: Interview, 1974–1994.* E. Weber (Ed.). Stanford, CA: Stanford University Press.

Durant, W. (2014). *Fallen Leaves: Last Words on Life, Love, War, and God.* New York: Simon & Schuster.

Epictetus. (2009). *The Enchiridion.* E. Carter (Trans.). The Internet Classics Archive. Retrieved 12/18/17 from http://classics.mit.edu/Epictetus/epicench.html

Felman, S., & Laub, D. (Eds.). (1992). *Testimony: Crisis of Witnessing in Literature, Psychoanalysis and History.* New York: Routledge.

Fonagy, P. (2015). The Effectiveness of Psychodynamic Psychotherapies: An Update. *World Psychiatry,* 14(2), 137–150.

Freke, T. (1999). *Taoist Wisdom: Daily Teachings from the Taoist Master.* New York: Sterling.

Freud, S. (1905). Fragment of an Analysis of a Case of Hysteria. In J. Strachey (Ed. & Trans.), *The Standard Edition of the Complete Psychological Works of Sigmund Freud* (Vol. 7, pp. 3–122). London: Hogarth Press.

Freud, S. (1915). Thoughts for The Time of War and Death. In J. Strachey (Ed. & Trans.), *The Standard Edition of the Complete Psychological Works of Sigmund Freud* (Vol. 14, pp. 273–300). London: Hogarth Press.

Freud, S. (1920). Beyond the Pleasure Principle. In J. Strachey (Ed. & Trans.), *The Standard Edition of the Complete Psychological Works of Sigmund Freud* (Vol. 18, pp. 1–64). London: Hogarth Press.

Freud, S. (1923). The Ego and the Id. In J. Strachey (Ed. & Trans.), *The Standard Edition of the Complete Psychological Works of Sigmund Freud* (Vol. 19, pp. 3–66). London: Hogarth Press.

Freud, S. (1924). Neurosis and Psychosis. In J. Strachey (Ed. & Trans.), *The Standard Edition of the Complete Psychological Works of Sigmund Freud* (Vol. 19, pp. 149–156). London: Hogarth Press.

Freud, S. (1926a). The Question of Lay Analysis. In J. Strachey (Ed. & Trans.), *The Standard Edition of the Complete Psychological Works of Sigmund Freud* (Vol. 20, pp. 179–249). London: Hogarth Press.

Freud, S. (1926b). Inhibitions, Symptoms and Anxiety. In J. Strachey (Ed. & Trans.), *The Standard Edition of the Complete Psychological Works of Sigmund Freud* (Vol. 20, pp. 77–174). London: Hogarth Press.

Freud, S. (1937). Analysis Terminable and Interminable. In J. Strachey (Ed. & Trans.), *The Standard Edition of the Complete Psychological Works of Sigmund Freud* (Vol. 23, pp. 209–254). London: Hogarth Press.

Freud, S. (1985). *The Complete Letters of Sigmund Freud to Wilhelm Fliess 1887–1904.* J.M. Masson (Trans.). Cambridge, MA: Belknap Press.

Geissmann, C., & Geissmann, P. (1998). *A History of Child Psychoanalysis.* London: Routledge.

Gibran, K. (2002). *The Madman: His Parables and Poems.* Mineola, NY: Dover.

Giddens, A. (1984). *The Constitution of Society.* Berkeley: University of California Press.

Goldberg, A. (2012). *The Analysis of Failure: An Investigation of Failed Cases in Psychoanalysis and Psychotherapy.* New York: Routledge.

Grinstein, A. (1990). *Freud at the Crossroads.* Madison, CT: International Universities Press.

Grof, S. (2000). *Psychology of the Future: Lessons from Modern Consciousness Research.* Albany: State University of New York Press.

Hale, N.G. (Ed.). (1971). *James Jackson Putnam and Psychoanalysis.* J.B. Heller (Trans.). Cambridge, MA: Harvard University Press.

Heery, M., & Bugental, J.F.T. (2005). Meaning and Transformation. In E.V. Deurzen & C. Arnold-Baker (Eds.), *Existential Perspectives on Human Issues* (pp. 253–264). Basingstoke, UK: Palgrave Macmillan.

Hessed, C. (2017). *The Freedom Trap: Reclaiming Liberty and Wellbeing.* Chatswood, Australia: Exisle.

Hosseini, R. (2015). *Wittgenstein and Meaning in Life: In Search of the Human Voice.* New York: Palgrave Macmillan.

Jung, C.G. (1969). *The Archetypes and the Collective Unconscious.* Princeton, NJ: Princeton University Press.

Kerr, J. (1994). *A Most Dangerous Method: The Story of Jung, Freud, and Sabina Spielrein.* New York: Vintage.

Kets de Vries, M.F.R. (2007). *The Happiness Equation: Meditations on Happiness and Success.* New York: iUuniverse.

Konigsberg, R.D. (2011). New Ways to Think about Grief. *Time.* Retrieved from http://content.time.com/time/printout/0,8816,2042372,00.html

Kothari, V.B. (2010). *Executive Greed: Examining Business Failure that Contributed to the Economic Crisis.* New York: Palgrave Macmillan.

Kramer, K.P. (1993). *Death Dreams: Unveiling Mysteries of the Unconscious Mind.* Mahwah, NJ: Paulist Press.

Kübler-Ross, E. (1969). *On Death and Dying.* New York: Routledge.

Kübler-Ross, E. (2005). *On Grief and Grieving: Finding the Meaning of Grief through the Five Stages of Loss.* New York: Simon & Schuster.

Laing, R.D. (1983). *The Politics of Experience.* New York: Pantheon.

LeBon, T. (2001). *Wise Therapy.* Los Angeles: Sage.

Levinas, E. (1969). *Totality and Infinity: An Essay on Exteriority.* Pittsburgh, PA: Duquesne University Press.

Levinas, E. (1985). *Ethics and Infinity: Conversations with Philippe Nemo.* R.A. Cohen (Trans.). Pittsburgh, PA: Duquesne University Press.

Maccoby, M. (2017). Learning and Doing: Working with Fromm and Applying What I Learned. *Psychoanalytic Review*, 104(4), 523–537.

Malcolm, J. (1982). *Psychoanalysis: The Impossible Profession.* New York: Vintage.

Marcus, P. (2008). *Being for the Other: Emmanuel Levinas, Ethical Living and Psychoanalysis.* Milwaukee, WI: Marquette University Press.

Marcus, P. (2013). *In Search of the Spiritual: Gabriel Marcel, Psychoanalysis, and the Sacred.* London: Karnac.

Marcus, P. (2014). *They Shall Beat Their Swords Into Plowshares: Military Strategy, Psychoanalysis and the Art of Living.* Milwaukee, WI: Marquette University Press.

Marcus, P. (2015). *Sports as Soul-Craft: How Playing and Watching Sports Enhances Life.* Milwaukee, WI: Marquette University Press.

Marcus, P. (2017). *The Psychoanalysis of Career Choice, Job Performance and Satisfaction: How to Flourish in the Workplace.* New York: Routledge.

Mayo Clinic. (2015). Job Burnout: How To Spot It and Take Action. Retrieved 9/3/17 from www.mayoclinic.org/healthy-lifestyle/adult-health/in-depth/burnout/art-20046642.

McGuire, W. (Ed.). (1974). *The Freud/Jung Letters.* Princeton, NJ: Princeton University Press.

Merton, T. (1948). *The Seven Storey Mountain: An Autobiography of Faith.* Orlando, FL: Harvest/Harcourt.

Nin, A. (1971). *The Diary of Anaïs Nin: 1944–1947* (Vol. 4). G. Stahlman (Ed.). New York: Harvest/HBJ.

Nussbaum, M.C. (1994). *The Therapy of Desire: Theory and Practice in Hellenistic Ethics.* Princeton, NJ: Princeton University Press.

Orange, D.M. (2011). *The Suffering Stranger: Hermeneutics for Everyday Clinical Practice.* New York: Routledge.

Orange, D.M. (2016). *Nourishing the Inner Life of Clinicians and Humanitarians: The Ethical Turn in Psychoanalysis.* London: Routledge.

Plato. (1871). *The Dialogues of Plato.* B. Jowett (Trans.). New York: Scribner.

Price, J., & Budzynski, T. (2009). Anxiety, EEG Patterns and Neurofeedback. In T.H. Budzynski, H.K. Budzynski, J.R. Evans, & A. Abarbanel (Eds.), *Introduction to Quantitative EEG and Neurofeedback: Advanced Theory and Applications* (pp. 453–470). Burlington, MA: Academic Press.

Razinsky, L. (2013). *Freud, Psychoanalysis and Death.* Cambridge, UK: Cambridge University Press.

Reppen, J., & Schulman, M.A. (Eds.) (2002). *Failures in Analytic Treatment.* Madison, CT: International Universities Press.

Robbins, J. (Ed.). (2001). *Is It Righteous to Be? Interviews with Emmanuel Levinas.* Stanford, CA: Stanford University Press.

Robertson, D. (2013). *Stoicism and the Art of Happiness.* New York: McGraw-Hill.

Schroeder, S. (2006). *Wittgenstein: The Way Out of the Fly Bottle.* Cambridge, UK: Polity.

Shermer, M. (2008). Five Fallacies of Grief: Debunking Psychological Stages. *Scientific American.* Retrieved from www.scientificamerian.com/article/five-fallacies-0of-grief/-fallacies-0of-grief/

Sosnik, R. (2012). The Work That Leads to Interpretation. In C. Seulin & G. Saragnano (Eds.), *On Freud's "On Beginning Treatment"* (pp. 120–136). London: Karnac.

Stolorow, R.D. (2014). Intersubjective, Existential, Phenomenological Psychoanalysis. In D.T. Kerry (Ed.), *From ID to Intersubjectivity: Talking about the Talking Cure with Master Clinicians* (pp. 179–212). London: Karnac.

Tillich, P. (1954). *Love, Power and Justice.* Oxford, UK: Oxford University Press.

Tzu, S. (1963). *The Art of War.* S.B. Griffith (Trans.). Oxford, UK: Oxford University Press.

Tzu, S. (1993). The Art of War. In R.D. Sawyer (Trans.), *The Seven Military Classics of Ancient China.* New York: Basic Books.

Van Deurzen, E. (2009). *Psychotherapy and the Quest for Happiness.* Los Angeles: Sage.

Van Deurzen, E., & Arnold-Baker, C. (2005). The Self. In E.V. Deurzen & C. Arnold-Baker (Eds.), *Existential Perspectives on Human Issues: A Handbook for Therapeutic Practice* (pp. 160–170). New York: Palgrave Macmillan.

Vlastos, G. (1991). *Socrates: Ironist and Moral Philosopher.* Ithaca, NY: Cornell University Press.

Wortis, J. (1954). *Fragments of an Analysis with Freud.* New York: Simon & Schuster.

Zaretsky, R. (2013). *A Life Worth Living: Albert Camus and the Quest for Meaning.* Cambridge, MA: Harvard University Press.

Zedong, M. (2017). *Quotations from Chairman Mao Tse-tung (The Little Red Book) & Other Works.* [Morrisville, NC]: Lulu.com.

# Postface

There is certainly some troubling truth to the words of the great Stoic philosopher, Marcus Aurelius, that "life is warfare and a sojourn in a foreign land." That is, that amidst the "violence and injuries" and the "harmful pains or pleasures" one needs to preserve one's "inner genius or divine spark" – that inner center of gravity – to have the will and ability to press on, and if fate or God will have it, to prevail amidst life's outrageousness (*Meditations*, 2:15, quoted in Robertson, 2013, p. 2). In psychoanalytic language, Aurelius is emphasizing the need to vigorously maintain one's autonomy, integration and humanity amidst the painful challenges, if not "suffering," that to the reflective person feel intrinsic to the human condition. The art of living the "good life" requires just such a skillful capacity, what is called a "heart of wisdom" in the Psalms (90:12) (*Holy Scriptures*, 1964, p. 842).

I will conclude my study with some of my favorite "go to" quotations, taking my lead from Epictetus, who at the end of *The Enchiridion*,[1] a handbook "for the stoic field commander in the campaign of life" (Ambrosio, 2009, p. 23), provided quotations from authors that he believed conveyed both the "spirit" of his outlook and practical wisdom to prevail as a "veritable warrior of the mind" in the face of life's suffering (Robertson, 2013, p. 5). These "ready-at-hand" Axial or Axial-inspired quotations help me to be emotionally resilient amidst life's painful challenges; in short, they make my "suffering sufferable."[2] I offer these quotations in no particular order and without explanation, as to elaborate them would be to denude them of their summoning power.

## Rabbi Yannai

It is not in our power to explain either the peace of the wicked or the suffering of the righteous.

(*Ethics of the Fathers*, in Sacks, 2009, p. 664)

## Chuang Tzu

Chuang Tzu's wife died. When Hui Tzu went to convey his condolences, he found Chuang Tzu sitting with his legs sprawled out, pounding on a tub and singing. "You lived with her, she brought up your children and grew old," said Hui Tzu. "It should be enough simply not to weep at her death. But pounding on a tub and singing – this is going too far, isn't it?"

Chuang Tzu said, "You're wrong. When she first died, do you think I didn't grieve like anyone else? But I look back to her beginning and the time before she was born. Not only the time before she was born, but the time before she had a body. Not only the time before she had a body but the time before she had a spirit. In the midst of the jumble of wonder and mystery a change took place and she had a spirit. Another change and she had a body. Another change and she was born. Now there's been another change and she's dead. It's just like the progression of the four seasons, spring, summer, fall, winter. Now she's going to lie down peacefully in a vast room. If I were to follow after her bawling and sobbing, it would show that I don't understand anything about fate. So I stopped."

(Watson, 1968, p. 212)

## Confucius

The mind of man is more perilous than mountains or rivers, harder to understand than Heaven.

(ibid., p. 358)

## Kahlil Gibran

You can chain my hands, you may shackle my feet; you may even throw me into a dark prison; but you shall not enslave my thinking, because it is free.

(Sheban, 1966, n.p.)

Keep me away from the wisdom which does not cry, the philosophy which does not laugh and the greatness which does not bow before children.

(Sheban, 1966, n.p.)

## Epictetus

Keep before your eyes day by day death and exile, and everything that seems catastrophic but most of all death; and then you will never have any abject thought, nor will you crave anything excessively.

(Epictetus, 1995, p. 21)

## Socrates

Crito, I owe the sacrifice of a rooster to Asklepios; will you pay that debt and not neglect to do so?

(Socrates' last words before drinking the hemlock; quoted in Nagy, 2015)

## Sophocles

Let no mortal be called happy until the final fated day.

(Sophocles, 2009, p. 171)

## Aeschylus

We must suffer, suffer into truth.

(Aeschylus, 1975, p. 109)

## The Upanishads

[He] who sees all beings in his own Self [the *Atman*, the "eternal" or "higher" self], and his own Self in all beings, loses all fear. When a sage sees this great Unity and his Self has become all beings, what delusion and what sorrow can ever be near him?

(*The Upanishads*, 1965 p. 49)

## Buddha

Virtuous people always let go. They don't prattle about pleasures and desires. Touched by happiness and then by suffering, the sage shows no sign of being elated or depressed.

(Buddha, 2006, p. 21)

## Shalom Aleichem

This is an ugly and mean world, and only to spite it we mustn't weep. If you want to know, this is the constant source of my good sprit, of my humor. Not to cry, out of spite, only to laugh out of spite, only to laugh.

(Marcus, 2013, p. vi)

## Bruno Bettelheim

But most of all, as I have intimated all along, autonomy, self-respect, inner integration, a rich inner life, and the ability to relate to others in meaningful ways were the psychological conditions which, more than any others, permitted one to survive in the camps as much a whole human being as overall conditions and chances would permit.

(Bettelheim, 1979, p. 109)

## Sigmund Freud

A strong egoism is a protection against falling ill, but in the last resort we must begin to love in order not to fall ill, and we are bound to fall ill if, in consequence of frustration, we are unable to love.

(Freud, 1956, p. 85)

I have found little that is "good" about human beings on the whole. In my experience most of them are trash, no matter whether they publicly subscribe to this or that ethical doctrine or to none at all. That is something that you cannot say aloud, or perhaps even think.

(Freud, 1963, p. 61)

Anyone who gives more than they have is a rogue.

(Freud & Zweig, 1970, p. 119)[3]

## Emmanuel Levinas

To be human is to suffer for the other, and even within one's own suffering, to suffer for the suffering my suffering imposes upon the other.

(Levinas, 1990, p. 188)

## Notes

1 Hadot (2009) ended his book with a postface that was inspired by Epictetus.
2 As with Epictetus, these quotations are helpful in jolting me out of my complacency when life bears down on me (Long, 2002, p. 194).
3 This quotation is an amalgamation of two sentences that Freud wrote to Zweig in Haifa, in a letter dated 1/20/36.

## References

Ambrosio, F.J. (2009). *Philosophy, Religion, and the Meaning of Life* (Course Guidebook). Chantilly, VA: The Teaching Company.

Aeschylus. (1975). *The Oresteia*. R. Fagles (Trans.). New York: Penguin.

Bettelheim, B. (1979). *Surviving and Other Essays*. New York: Knopf.

Buddha. (2006). *The Dhammapada*. G. Fromsdale (Trans.). Boston, MA: Shambhala.

Epictetus. (1995). *The Discourses, The Handbook, Fragments*. R. Hard (Trans.). London: Everyman.

Freud, S. (1956). On Narcissism: An Introduction. In J. Strachey (Ed. & Trans.), *The Standard Edition of the Complete Psychological Works of Sigmund Freud* (Vol. 14, pp. 67–102). London: Hogarth Press. (Original work published 1914)

Freud, S. (1963). *Psychoanalysis and Faith: The Letters of Sigmund Freud and Oskar Pfister*. H. Meng & E.L. Feder (Eds.), E. Mosbacher (Trans.). London: Hogarth Press. (Original work published 1910)

Freud, S., & Zweig, A. (1970). *The Letters of Sigmund Freud and Arnold Zweig*. E.L. Freud (Ed.), E. Robson-Scott & W. Robson-Scott (Trans.). New York: Harcourt, Brace & World.

Hadot, P. (2009). *The Present Alone Is Our Happiness: Conversations with Jeannie Carlier and Arnold I. Davidson*. M. Djaballah (Trans.). Stanford, CA: Stanford University Press.

*Holy Scriptures, The: A New Translation*. (1964). Philadelphia, PA: Jewish Publication Society of America.

Levinas, E. (1990). *Nine Talmudic Readings.* A. Aronowicz (Trans.). Bloomington: Indiana University Press.

Long, A.A. (2002). *Epictetus: A Stoic and Socratic Guide to Life.* Oxford, UK: Oxford University Press.

Marcus, P. (2013). *How To Laugh Your Way Through Life: A Psychoanalyst's Advice.* London: Karnac.

Nagy, G. (2015, March 27). The Last Words of Socrates at the Place Where He Died. *Classical Inquiries: Studies on the Ancient World from CHS.* Retrieved 12/18/17 from http://classical-inquiries.chs.harvard.edu/the-last-words-of-socrates-at-the-place-where-he-died/

Robertson, D. (2013). *Stoicism and the Art of Happiness.* New York: McGraw-Hill.

Sacks, J. (Trans.). (2009). *The Koren Siddur.* Jerusalem: Koren.

Sheban, J. (Ed.). (1966). *The Wisdom of Gibran: Aphorisms and Maxims.* New York: Philosophical Library.

Sophocles. (2009). *Oedipus the King, Electra.* E. Hall (Ed.), H.D.F. Jitto (Trans.). Oxford, UK: Oxford University Press.

*The Upanishads.* (1965). J. Mascaro (Trans.). London: Penguin.

Watson, B. (1968). *The Complete Works of Chuang Tzu.* New York: Columbia University Press.

# Index

Aamodt, M.G. 201
abandonment anxiety 20, 179n20
Abraham, Karl 122, 123
Abrahamite religions 73
absurdity 67, 76, 101, 120, 131n23;
  psychoanalyst and 238–9
abused/neglected child 66–7, 69
abusive relationships 23–4, 26–7
acting, imagination and 159–62
Adam and Eve 35
Adler, Stella 159–62
Adorno, Theodor 27
Aeschylus 1, 260
*Agamemnon* (Aeschylus) 1
aggression 38–9
Akers, John 216–17
Al Hariri 238
Aleichem, Shalom 260
Alexander, Franz 114
Alford, C.F. 100–1, 108
alien systems 118
Allen, Woody 16
altruism 113
Améry, Jean 121, 123–4, 141–3, 153,
  155–8, 167–9, 172, 175–6
*Analects* (Confucius) 27, 209
anal-retentive 211
*Analysis Terminable and Interminable*
  (Freud) 229
analysts 90; narcissism 56
anger: depression and 123; irrational
  boss 189; rage responses 26, 65
anthropodicy 70
*Antigone* (Sophocles) 94
anxiety 89; abandonment 20, 179n20; as
  breakdown or breakthrough 95–7;
  castration 97, 235; control of life 94–5;
  death anxiety 61, 81, 88, 103, 253n15;

as dizziness of freedom 91–2;
  Heideggerian 103–4; horror and 94–6,
  100–1; living as "real" or "fake" self
  92–3; moral challenge of 91–5;
  otherwise than being 109–10; paranoid
  215; primary and signal 97;
  psychoanalyst and 244–6; psychotic
  218; realistic 95; "there is" 95–110;
  two dimensions 95. *See also* mental
  anguish
Apollonian outlook 119
apology 29–30
Appelfeld, Aharon 113
Arendt, Hannah 71–2
Aristotle 18, 206
Armstrong, Karen 4, 12n10
Aron, A. 46n10
Aron, E.N. 46n10
art of living 2, 5, 8, 12, 12n13
*Art of War* (Sun Tzu) 197–200
Asch, Solomon 113
asymmetrical and symmetrical
  relationships 25–30; revisited 31–3
atheistic self 110, 111
atonement 144–5
attachment theory 52
Atterton, P. 32–3
attribution theory 118
Auden, W.H. 245
Augustine, Saint 18–19, 37, 71, 78, 155,
  243; *Confessions* 89; on mental
  anguish 88; original sin, concept of
  55–6
Aurelius, Marcus 155, 258
authentic/inauthentic distinction 93, 100,
  102, 107, 110, 119, 130n10
Axial Age and outlook 1–7, 17, 27, 30,
  45; Beauty, Truth and Goodness

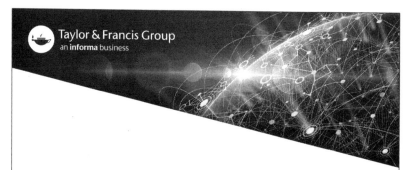